SOUND OBJECTS

SOUND OBJECTS

EDITORS | James A. Steintrager and Rey Chow

DUKE UNIVERSITY PRESS

Durham and London

2019

Printed and bound by CPI Group (UK)
Ltd, Croydon, CR0 4YY
Designed by Matthew Tauch
Typeset in Scala Pro and Scala Sans Pro
by Westchester Publishing Services

Library of Congress Cataloging-in-Publication Data
Names: Steintrager, James A., [date] editor. | Chow, Rey,
[date] editor.
Title: Sound objects / James A. Steintrager and Rey Chow, editors.
Description: Durham : Duke University Press, 2018. | Includes
bibliographical references and index.
Identifiers: LCCN 2018021935 (print)
LCCN 2018030091 (ebook)
ISBN 9781478002536 (ebook)
ISBN 9781478001096 (hardcover : alk. paper)
ISBN 9781478001454 (pbk. : alk. paper)
Subjects: LCSH: Sound—Social aspects. | Auditory percep-
tion. | Sound (Philosophy)
Classification: LCC QC225.7 (ebook) | LCC QC225.7 .S68 2018
(print) | DDC 534.01—dc23
LC record available at https://lccn.loc.gov/2018021935

Cover art: Paul Klee, *Fuge in Rot* [*Fugue in Red*], 1921,
69. Watercolor and pencil on paper on cardboard,
24.4 cm×31.5 cm. Private collection, Switzerland, on
extended loan to the Zentrum Paul Klee, Bern.

Contents

Acknowledgments

This volume is the third installment of an ongoing project and intellectual collaboration that began with a special double issue of *differences: A Journal of Feminist Cultural Studies* that appeared in 2011 and that we titled "The Sense of Sound." We started more with a sense of curiosity and interest than expertise and certainly without realizing that sound studies was rapidly congealing into a field—if, thankfully, not quite a discipline. Several of the contributors to that initial foray return here: Michel Chion, Veit Erlmann, John Mowitt, and Jonathan Sterne. We thank them for sticking with us and continuing in multifarious and creative ways to deepen our explorations of the sonic field. The second installment was James A. Steintrager's translation of and critical introduction to Michel Chion's *Sound: An Acoulogical Treatise*, which appeared in 2016 with Duke University Press. The author's profound engagement with the legacy of Pierre Schaeffer and his notion of the "sound object" helped shape the path we have chosen for this collection.

Along the way, we have benefited enormously from conversations, criticism, and debates, both in and out of academic settings. Special thanks go to Julie Napolin, Dominic Pettman, and Pooja Rangan for organizing and bringing us to the Sonic Shadows symposium at the Eugene Lang College of the New School in the spring of 2015 (JS and RC); to Luis Carcamo-Huechante for the Future of Sound Studies symposium at the National Humanities Center in the spring of 2014 (RC); to Jacqueline Waeber for the Study Day: Voices and Noises workshop at the Franklin Humanities Center, Duke University, held in the spring of 2015 (RC); to Frances Ferguson for the invitation to deliver the Frederic Ives Carpenter Lectures ("Acousmatic Sound and the Writing Voice in Cinema: A Preliminary Discussion") at the University of Chicago in the fall of 2015 (RC); to Louise Meintjes for the Remapping Sound Studies: A Turn to the Global South symposium at Duke University in the spring of 2016 (RC); to Nina Sun Eidsheim and Annette Schlicter for convening and guiding the Keys to Voice Studies: Terminology, Methodology, and Questions across Disciplines Multicampus Research Group at the University of California from 2012 to 2014 (JS); and to J. D. Connor, Ben Glaser, and Brian Kane for the Techniques of the Listener conference-cum-workshop at the Whitney Humanities Center at Yale University in the spring of 2016 (JS). We also thank individuals whose scholarship and friendship over the years inform these pages: Giorgio Biancorosso and Andy Hamilton (JS); Mladen Dolar, Mark Hansen, Brian Kane, and Alenka Zupančič (RC).

Duke University Press has been with us for the entire trajectory, and our gratitude and debt to Courtney Berger, senior editor and editorial department manager, and to Sandra Korn, editorial associate, only grows. Thanks, as well, to Christopher Catanese, our project editor, and to Susan Deeks, for her thoughtful and thorough copyediting. The comments and criticisms of the generous anonymous reviewers helped make this a better book than it would have been without them. Sophie Smith and Blake Beaver of the Program in Literature at Duke helped coax the manuscript into shape at different stages, and to both we are grateful. To Blake, in particular, we owe the meticulously compiled, indispensable bibliography.

Above all, we thank each and every one of the contributors to this volume for putting in the hard work and putting up with our editorial interventions, and for gamely and profoundly thinking along with us.

—JS AND RC

JAMES A. STEINTRAGER, WITH REY CHOW

Sound Objects

An Introduction

The collective thrust of this volume is to make a multifaceted case for thinking the topic of sound objects theoretically. By "theoretically" we do not intend the establishment or application of a pristine set of methodological assumptions or conceptual givens. On the contrary, whatever the real need for abstraction and high-order conceptualization, we think that theory must always also entail something akin to what Michel Foucault has taught us to call the analysis of a *discourse*. Such analysis requires unpacking the ample historical and institutional baggage that (often silently) accompanies a particular topic, and its task is to situate the topic in question epistemologically and practically through multiple connections that hitherto have failed to be articulated. Let us right away add that "theory" itself is such a discourse and cannot be naïvely summoned or applied. We might begin, then, by schematically evoking the moment that the academic discourse of "theory" emerged in the 1960s in contrast to the then mainstream philosophical currents of existentialism and, more particularly for our purposes, phenomenology and contemplate the place of sound therein.

Although other senses certainly came under discussion, the phenomenological approaches of Edmund Husserl, Martin

Heidegger, and Maurice Merleau-Ponty largely tended to the visual: appearances and images in relation to an intending consciousness *qua* observer. In their collective rebellion against phenomenology, structuralist and poststructuralist thinkers from Roland Barthes to Paul de Man countered with symbolic or semiotic systems and with an insistence on the text: the immediacy of the image became remediated through the (written) word; language and figuration inscribed the heart of the visual. As far as sound was concerned, it was primarily the human voice that attracted interest and here, too, as subject to critique. Thus, for Jacques Derrida the phenomenological voice was like the image: yet another attempt to capture presence that the inherent textuality of language—regardless of medium—always already thwarted.[1] This crucial postwar philosophical encounter between phenomenology and its critics came to define "theory" in the North American academy, where the emphasis on textuality understandably appealed to literary scholars and where the *distinction* of engaging with certain varieties of European philosophy inflated, if only for a while, their cultural capital.[2]

As rapid technological innovations pressed theory to keep up and to incorporate a broader array of media into its machinery, the shift from analog to digital often appeared as a mere extension of the textual: now recast as "code," this digital text was once again shown to underlie, if not undermine, a thoroughly constructed visual realm. Consider, for example, the interest in identity formation in virtual worlds and in the ontological status of computer-generated images that characterized much premillennial theorizing. The most infamous intellectual in this regard certainly indulged in prophetic rhetoric but is not uncharacteristic: Jean Baudrillard, who declared traditional notions such as "aesthetic illusion" and "representation" to be in general "cancelled out by technical perfection." He writes, "As hologram or virtual reality or three-dimensional picture, the image is merely the emanation of the digital code which generates it."[3] The recent return to aesthetics, affects, and the senses has likewise oscillated between image and text, showing scant interest in the topic of sound as such.

Take the work of Jacques Rancière, a vital link to what we might call classical French theory, however critical he may be of it. Rancière has joined investigation into the effects of new technologies with multifarious meditations on aesthetics and has questioned media-deterministic notions that the shift to the digital is responsible for sundering the image from reality.[4] He has argued instead that aesthetic programs in cinema had long since engineered such a change by drawing on operations that were first worked out in the modern novel. Elaborating how "aesthetic experience" transforms "the cartography of the perceptible, the thinkable, and the feasible" by introducing "a multiplicity of folds and gaps in the fabric of common experience," Rancière, with few exceptions, has almost entirely limited his examples to photography and painting, to literature, and to cinema.[5] He tends to conceive cinema, moreover, not so much as an audiovisual medium as a narrative-cum-visual one. This tendency to emphasize the visual and textual is evident even when Rancière is critically following the trail of Gilles Deleuze and Félix Guattari's discussion of art in *What Is Philosophy?*, a work that argues that, as exemplars of "all art," music and painting "similarly extract new harmonies, new plastic or melodic landscapes, and new rhythmic characters that raise them to the height of the earth's song and the cry of humanity" from "colors and sounds."[6] Yet if Rancière's tendency to revert to the visual and textual as default modes gives us pause, so, too, should Deleuze and Guattari's blithe blurring of the visual and aural, which threatens to obliterate particularity.

In sum, both historical and ongoing theoretical inquiry and media studies in anxious, celebratory, or critical mode has generally condensed around visuality, and much less studied has been the position and role of aurality. We might situate this relative neglect as a reverberation of the emergence of aesthetics as a branch of philosophical enquiry in the late eighteenth century and particularly of the ongoing resonance of Kantian philosophy. Indeed, Kant, who set up the paradigm for doing "critique," was deeply revered by the poststructuralists even as they sought to undermine "the subject" he placed at the center of his philosophical project. Take the Kantian sublime, for example, wherein the faculty of the *imagination* is blocked and its powers of representation meet their limit. Is not the *failure of representation* the poststructuralist and particularly deconstructionist theme *par excellence*? As for the beautiful, Kant wed a rather anodyne account of harmony as the essence of sonic beauty to a basic distrust of music. In his hierarchy of artistic modes, Kant placed poetry at the top, painting in the middle, and music at the bottom (along with what he called "material for laughter"). As an example of merely formal purposiveness and not an obvious carrier of representational content, music—even so-called programmatic music—should have seemingly come out on top. Nonetheless, Kant determines that, while arising from a "play with aesthetic ideas or even representations," music is an art by which "in the end nothing is thought" and that provides only a revivifying "movement of the viscera."[7] Certainly, positions such as this also provoked strongly dissenting philosophical reactions. Arthur Schopenhauer elevated music to the highest of arts, and

Friedrich Nietzsche, at least initially, lionized Wagner as the composer who, in melding Apollonian structure to Dionysian ecstasy, achieved the modern apotheosis of the tragic spirit. Yet, as we shall subsequently argue, perhaps such dissent served only to condemn sound to forever playing the role of disruptor of the hegemonic visual within philosophy—to only ever being "noise," some inchoate beyond of representation.

Trompes l'Oreille?—or, The Trouble with Theorizing Sound

Kant's lasting impact notwithstanding, we might also consider the place of visuality in the longue durée of Western philosophy, where the visual frequently enough has been treated as both the sovereign mode of perception *and* a source of illusion and error. We do not need to rehearse Plato's simultaneous distrust of the visual and reliance on visual metaphors in his conception of knowledge. We might recall, however, that "theory" itself is derived from the Greek word for viewing. For instance, while he downplayed the role of spectacle (*opsis*) in tragedy in favor of plot and character, Aristotle drew in his ethical philosophy on the visual figure of *theoria* to define intellectual contemplation as the highest end of human existence.[8] Let us take this derivation as a suggestion. That is, while we are putting forward the need for theory, maybe theory (as seeing) is also what we must disentangle ourselves from if we are to give our subject its due. Thus, while a whole host of questions having to do with truth and deception has traditionally accompanied sight, giving rise to what, in his study of contemporary French philosophy, Martin Jay has called "iconophobia," sound does not seem to operate in the same manner.[9] Needless to say, sounds, too, can be used to deceive. Let us cite Kant again, at a rare moment in which he does consider sound. In this case, he imagines the effect on listeners who, thinking they are enjoying the "bewitchingly beautiful song of the nightingale," discover that the source is a "mischievous lad" hiding in the bushes and imitating the bird with a pipe or reed.[10] According to Kant's logic, the natural sound would fulfill the criterion of disinterested interest necessary for the beautiful: a birdsong serves no end for us, but we find its play pleasing nonetheless—or rather, it grounds the harmonious play of our faculties of imagination and understanding. Once exposed as artificial rather than natural, however, the sound is no longer of interest in and of itself; our attention instead shifts to the landlord's aim to enchant us.

As the listener discovers a (profit) motive behind the source, sonic charm turns into disgust. But let us be clear about something crucial: while the sound sources (nightingale and pipe) are quite different, the sounds, for all practical purposes, are identical. In other words, the deception relates to the sources, not to the sounds in themselves.

If our ears are in a manner tricked (or trickable), Kant's example does not exactly provide the aural equivalent of a trompe l'oeil. And what might be the analogue of the trompe l'oeil, in which two-dimensional images produce an effect of three-dimensionality? Can sounds deceive in a manner analogous to vision at all? Perhaps we should not be so quick, however, to argue that Kant's example is not a *trompe l'oreille.*[11] One way to think about this odd category is precisely in terms of how vastly different sound sources can create sound events that we perceive as similar or even identical, thus thwarting our usual ability to accurately infer causes, as well as location, from sounds in our environment. In his argument that we need a better understanding of "everyday listening" and the ways in which we operate in a sonic ecology, William Gaver notes that we rarely confuse sounds made by "vibrating solids" with those made by water, although there are exceptions, such as "rain sticks," made by inserting rows of pegs within a tube: "When the tube is turned over, small beads and shells run down its length, striking these pegs and producing a sound remarkably like that of running water." Gaver adds that such is "an example of an illusion in everyday listening of the sort exploited by Foley artists creating sound-effects."[12] Along these lines, in his analyses of audiovisuality, Michel Chion has spent considerable time examining the specific ways that sounds in cinema "render" events and objects rather than representing them.[13] In fact, a sound that is not strictly mimetic might be more effective—more effectively deceptive—than the real thing. A snapped stalk of celery may better render a broken bone when matched to an appropriate visual than the sound of actual bone being broken.

If we are to think about trompes l'oreille, therefore, we should focus on their specific differences from illusionary visual effects as well as on interactions between the visual and aural. But we should also ask: What do they matter? Are there critical and ultimately practical implications? To take up ideology, for example, if sounds can be reified and fetishized—as Theodor Adorno certainly claimed for popular music—do they obey the same laws as commodities presented in image form? Marx's notion of commodity fetishism, after all, is based on a visual metaphor: the fetish captures our gaze and asserts its facticity, thereby occulting the actual relations of production.

Why is there so much talk about the society of the spectacle and not that of the . . . sonic what? We seem to lack an equivalent term. Or to shift the topic from Marxism to poststructuralism: Was there any aural analogue of the tellingly named Panopticon, Jeremy Bentham's prison project that Foucault generalized to modern disciplinary regimes, their tactics of surveillance, and the formation of the subject through the internalization of observation? Did or does sound play a role in modern modes of subjectivation? Interestingly, Bentham considered a prisoner's ability to make "noise" as the sole weakness of his system: resistance as sonic externalization rather than visual internalization (although he also thought that the mere threat of a gag would likely be sufficient to enforce silence).[14] These questions and comparisons seem to demand for sound an order of conceptualization that is distinct from the visually oriented, an order that, to be specific, runs counter to the concreteness and the alluring—indeed, *blinding*—obviousness of the visual. Calling for a theory (or, more pluralistically, theories) of the sonic ought to acknowledge the terminological misfit, at least in etymological terms: sound objects are not contemplated at all; they are apprehended in ways other than the visual. This suggests that the very framework and rhetorical resonances of "theory" are potentially misleading and inadequate—and that theory itself must also proceed otherwise, with sound.

Sound Objects: The Problematic

Why sound objects, then? What are they, anyway? We intend and believe it necessary to have these question marks hover over this undertaking. We do not assume that sounds are objects; nor are we providing the catalogue for a cabinet of sonic curiosities. To investigate and interrogate the very existence of such "things" and their interrelations instigated this project and was the directive given to our contributors. To be sure, we began with an awareness that the term "sound objects" has a genealogy. In the middle of the twentieth century, Pierre Schaeffer formulated a research program for what he initially termed *musique concrète*. Based primarily on recordings of noninstrumental sounds—including, famously, the hissing steam engines and metallic wheel clacks of trains—such music would be *concrete* in the sense of a drawing on the material qualities of these captured sounds rather than assuming an abstract (pitch-centered and notational) musical system and working from there. The dichotomy, however, never entirely held. By the middle of his essay *In Search of a Concrete Music* (*A la recherche d'une musique concrète*; 1952), Schaeffer himself admits that he could have just as easily described his endeavor as a quest for "abstract music."[15] With sufficient technological manipulation the concrete can readily be transformed into its opposite: deracinated sonic matter for composition, at most haunted by its real-world origins. Schaeffer would eventually abandon the label *musique concrète* in favor of the more open-ended *musique expérimentale*. Nonetheless, two key concepts that Schaeffer had developed during his exploratory forays carried over into his subsequent work and would become central to his summa on sonic thinking, the *Treatise on Musical Objects* (*Traité des objets musicaux*; 1966).[16] These concepts were acousmatic listening—that is, listening without visual access to a sound source—and *objets sonores*, or "sound objects."

Kant's hidden warbler who tricks his enraptured listeners is a good example of an acousmatic situation. Of course, there have always been sounds heard without visual accompaniment of their sources: bells in the distance, footsteps in the hallway, cicadas in the trees. Still, Kant's example pinpoints an uncommon occurrence insofar as the boy functions as a sort of human synthesizer who must be deliberately obscured so as not to ruin the effect. By contrast, such obscuring of sonic sources would come increasingly to *define* modern audial environments. In Schaeffer's day, acousmatic listening simply named a situation that had already become generalized through technological media of broadcast and of reproduction: radio transmission, magnetic tape, and phonography. Interestingly, what survived the transition to the new media is the old question of willful deception. We see in Adorno's mid-century excoriations of the culture industry's holding radio listeners in distracted thralldom and R. Murray Schafer's later diagnosis of listeners in the age of sound reproduction as suffering from "schizophonia."[17] Such misgivings notwithstanding, by separating listeners from the sight of the original *sounding objects*, the technologies of broadcast and of reproduction brought about a fundamental conceptual shift to—and promised the material possibility of—what Schaeffer, calling on Husserlian phenomenological terminology and applying the move of *epochē* (phenomenological bracketing), would label reduced listening: attending to sounds in themselves, and analyzing sounds strictly in terms of their formal attributes rather than in relation to cause, context, or semantic information.

For Schaeffer, acousmatic listening and its conceptual derivative, reduced listening, were in many ways means to an end: they underwrote a research program that aimed to develop a descriptive morphology and typology of sounds regarded as self-standing *sound objects*. Schaeffer, in other words, approached sounds as discrete and multifaceted phenomena rather than as carriers of meaning or as effects bound to sources and causes. For all of the insistence on concreteness in Schaeffer's earlier writings, there is something idealist about this phenomenological approach. This idealism is nicely captured in Brian Kane's characterization of Schaefferian sound objects as phantasmagoric.[18] At the same time, Schaeffer's attempt to provide formal schemata—annexing arbitrary markers such as x′ for sound objects that are impulses with complex pitch and fixed mass, y″ for objects with somewhat variable mass and iterative, and so forth—pushed his program further into abstraction, revealing deep structuralist affinities in his thinking alongside his phenomenological tendencies. There is, as well, a more general scientific trend at work here. Schaeffer's attempts to render sound objects in graphic terms are a telltale example of the turn toward to "structural objectivity" (which focused on invariant structures and eschewed forms of presentation that suggested subjectivity) that, in their magisterial historical study *Objectivity*, Lorraine Daston and Peter Galison locate as emerging in the late nineteenth century and early twentieth century and that is still very much part of scientific discourse today.[19]

That said, we would insist that the genealogy of the "sound object" in Schaeffer's conceptual apparatus is inseparable from the technological media of reproduction at his disposal. The sound object arose, conceptually, from the ability to record and to create loops of magnetic tape and closed grooves on phonograph records. For sound to become object—since it could not be observed like a static visual object—required a chartable consistency enabled only by repetition: something to master or, at least, temper its temporal flux and ephemerality. This was accomplished by fixing and isolating a sound with a looped magnetic tape or a locked groove on a record.[20] This process not only wrenches a sound from its source and context; as the loop or groove repeats a sonic event, the sound *becomes* an object for the listener. The sound object was thus neither found nor captured. It was in part machine-made; in part, a construct of iterative perception. Described in this way, the emergence of the sound object in Schaefferian terms recalls Deleuze's account of *difference and repetition* in the work bearing that name in 1968.[21] According to Deleuze, for identity to arise there must be repetition; repetition always involves difference, and so difference needs to be placed at the heart of identity. Deleuze notwithstanding, we imagine that for anyone who came of academic age when poststructuralist French thought was a dominant force, our description of the construction of the Schaefferian object will chiefly bring to mind deconstruction. As we briefly noted earlier, Derrida's deconstruction took off from a specifically sonic version of this paradox of identity as difference: the critique, in *Voice and Phenomenon* [*La voix et le phénomène*], of the employment of *voice* as a transparent, self-present medium within Husserl's phenomenology. Derrida's essay was published in 1967 and formed part of a trio of works that he unleashed that year, along with *Of Grammatology* and *Writing and Difference*. In all three works, Derrida set out to show that voice—even the proverbial inner voice—is structured, and that structure itself entails difference and deferral, disrupting Husserl's quest to suspend ontological considerations and to simply describe and analyze phenomena as intentional correlates of consciousness. What Derrida did, in effect, was to weaponize structuralist linguistics in order to dismantle the phenomenological project.

At the same time, Schaeffer's attempt to categorize sound objects in morphological and typological terms recalls another crucial poststructuralist text: Michel Foucault's *The Order of Things* [*Les mots et les choses*], which appeared in 1966, the very same year as *Treatise on Musical Objects*. Although the former by no means concentrates on sound, Foucault does examine how what he called the classical *episteme* of representation and the subsequent epistemic regime of the nineteenth-century period handled the relation between sound and signification. In the classical episteme, "language arose when the noise produced by the mouth or the lips had become a letter," and this letter was linked to objects; language in the classical episteme is fundamentally centered on nouns and the indication of objects.[22] For nineteenth-century philologists, by contrast, language "exists when noise has been articulated and divided into a series of distinct sounds," and these sounds—ephemeral, vibratory—express poetic insights and actions; language has become fundamentally centered on verbs. We will not dwell on Foucault's assertions in this regard, except to say that they provide a fine instance of what we might call the historian's epochē: bracketing whatever constitutes the actual relations between sound and language (as they were used by speakers) to pinpoint a difference in how these relations were construed over time. Indeed, what we do want to underline is that at the very moment Schaeffer was attempting to classify "sound objects"—in a rather structural or schematic way, we might add—Foucault was attempting to historicize the structures underlying classificatory schemata of various sorts, structures that he would describe as the "unthought."

By contrast, others in the poststructuralist fold would call on sound as a figure of resistance to representation and to structure itself. Thus, Deleuze and Guattari would read instances of sound in Kafka's writings as a force of de-territorialization beyond the semantic and formal impositions. In the "warbling" that blurs Gregor's speech, the "cough of the ape," the "whistling of the mouse," and other embodiments of sonic disruption in Kafka's oeuvre, they find a force that draws "a line of abolition" across music and "a line of escape" that slices through language, liberating "a living and expressive material that speaks for itself and has no need of being put into a form."[23] We could locate many other examples of noise treated similarly, as a potentially emancipatory or ultimately constructive disruption of sense and a rent in the phenomenal fabric or texture of constructed reality. Let us mention a few crucial ones.

Conjoining Marxism and poststructuralism with a penchant for the Dionysian strand in Nietzsche's early writings, Jacques Attali celebrated the violent, revolutionary power of "noise" in the "rupture" of networks and "destruction of codes"—a power that simultaneously provided the material for new experiences, novel types of creativity, and emergent modes of communal organization.[24] To make his case, Attali drew further inspiration from Henri Atlan's cybernetic and biological notion of noise not only as entropy but also a source of order.[25] In a comparable fashion, Michel Serres would convert the aural parasites of information theory into powers of creation.[26] An echo of these constructions of noise is found in Friedrich Kittler, who provided the tightest link between poststructuralism and media studies in a McLuhanite vein. Arguing for the sundering of the sensorium and its reorganization by media technologies in the twentieth century, Kittler matched the typewriter to Lacan's Symbolic order; film, to the Imaginary; and phonography, to the Real. In Kittler's account, "The phonograph does not hear as do ears that have been trained to filter voices, words, and sounds out of noise"; rather, it "registers acoustic events as such [and] reproduces the unimaginable real."[27] Noise, then, is sound unmediated, prior but also posterior to language or music, and the phonograph captures what audition winnows and occludes: it is the technical apparatus that confronts us with the acoustic sublime. A more recent effort furthering Kittler's logic, one that places mathematical and machinic interventions at the center of sound capture and preservation, is found in the "media archaeology" work of Wolfgang Ernst.[28] For Ernst, sound—or what he prefers to call sonicity—needs to be liberated altogether from the conventional time domain that is still bound to the human sensorium, which tends to be partial and erratic. "The human auditory sense does not suffice for a proper archaeology of the acoustic in cultural memory," he writes, because the "real archaeologists in media archaeology are the media themselves—not mass media (the media of representation), but measuring media that are able to not only decipher physically real signals techno-analogically, but also represent those signals in graphic forms alternative to alphabetic writing."[29] Instead of the human ear, Ernst advocates the media-archaeological ear. Instead of acousmatic or reduced listening, he asks us to think of "diagrammatic listening": "if no algorithm is present to enact the transition of sound provenience to permanent storage, the collection remains idiosyncratic and random."[30]

This handful of quite different examples reminds us that, among other tasks and in a variety of ways, poststructuralist theory's signature contribution has been the unraveling of the object. The latter was simultaneously historicized as a construct and ontologically deconstructed. At the margins, the object was the enemy, and noise—the sonic abject—promised access to a deeper reality. There is no doubt that we could trace this unraveling farther back: through Kantian critique, Hegelian dialectics, and Nietzschean perspectivism, and beyond. While this is not the occasion for such an ambitious undertaking, what we intend with this volume is the more modest task of tracing and examining the effects of an interdisciplinary and intermedial encounter that never fully took place some fifty-odd years ago but that we think should have. In brief, we want to recuperate this lost opportunity and to entwine the genealogy of the sound object with the work of poststructuralist and related theory, to bring this encounter up to date, and, crucially, to open up paths of inquiry that both acknowledge and explore the limits of theory itself.

In his foundational account of "speculative realism," Quentin Meillassoux seeks a way out of the "paradoxical nature of correlational exteriority."[31] He concedes that whether "affective or perceptual, the sensible only exists as a *relation*" between "the world and the living creature I am," and yet he tries to find a path back to objects with properties "exempt from constraint of such a relation."[32] Object-oriented ontologists have followed a similar path. We are skeptical that these recent attempts to return us to objects and to realism truly provide routes out of the paradoxes of correlationism in its many guises, among which we would include phenomenology, constructivism, and deconstruction. At the same time, we acknowledge the frustration inherent in and urgency of these projects. To speak of sound without a listener, as object-oriented ontology or computer-centered media archaeology would suggest, seems to make little sense. Yet so, too, does speaking of sound as a construct that can be reduced to a listening subject. In recent philosophy, Casey O'Callaghan has offered an account of what he labels "sonic realism": sounds, while not objects per se, would be distal events, real occurrences outside of any perception.[33] Notwithstanding, in O'Callaghan's account the listener remains as a residuum, and a surreptitiously crucial one at that—what Derrida would have called a "supplement." On the other hand, Mark Grimshaw and Tom Garner, drawing on Deleuze and cognitive neuroscience, make a philosophical case for what they call "sonic virtuality": the notion that sound is an emergent phenomenon that encompasses both "endosonus" and "exosonus."[34] While Grimshaw and Garner ultimately revert to a conception of the sonic that privileges subjectivity and interiority, their thesis—or so we think—points in the right direction: that you cannot theorize sound without thinking the engagement of interior and exterior, of perceiver and environment. The temptation to avoid complications and paradoxes by explicitly or implicitly opting for one side or the other is great, but what truly calls for a theory of sound objects, we contend, is the ineluctable noncoincidence of emission and reception and the entanglement of subjectivity and objectivity. This noncoincidence and entanglement are what makes sound such an elusive and inexhaustible topic, and one that can be approached in various ways: as history, culture, discipline, fantasy, ideology, and much more.

A Lack within Sound Studies: The Work Ahead

Academic accounts that do focus on sound frequently assert that the subject has been overlooked, especially in relation to vision. Such assertions do not appear specific to any particular discipline and will be found in works of cultural studies, psychology, philosophy, and so forth. William Gaver, for instance, posits that research "on the psychology of everyday listening is valuable in its own right . . . balancing the typical bias towards studying vision in understanding how people perceive and act in the world."[35] Writing in the idiom of Anglo-American philosophy, Robert Pasnau argues that sound should be considered not a quality of a vibrating medium (gaseous, liquid, or solid) or as a perceptual construct (essentially mental) but, rather, as an actual quality of the sounding object. He considers the general tendency among his peers to misunderstand the nature of sound in large part as a function of neglect: they "have been too preoccupied with colour to give the case of sound much thought."[36] It is quite possible that the rhetoric of bias and neglect—of unfairness to sound—refers to real tendencies, and we have said as much ourselves about phenomenology at the outset. Yet phenomenology is not entirely lacking in considerations of sound, including *Listening and Voice,* Don Ihde's philosophical endeavor dedicated precisely to this topic.[37] As our own examples show, poststructuralist thinkers and media theorists, especially those interested in interactive media, have certainly had things to say about sound, too. Further, over the past decade or so, a loosely constituted, multidisciplinary correlate to visual studies has rapidly arisen: sound studies.[38] It may be useful to recall just how rapid this rise has been. In the introductory chapter to *The Audible Past: Cultural Origins of Sound Reproduction* (2003), Jonathan Sterne remarks that no "parallel construct" to a "conceptualization of *visual cultures*" exists for *"sound culture* or, simply *sound studies."*[39] Sterne's book, one of the key texts that helped bring that parallel construct into existence, is now canonical in the field. Even at the time, Sterne remarked that visual and textual bias at the expense of sound could be overstated: "As there was an Enlightenment, so too was there an 'Ensoniment.' . . . Between about 1750 and 1925, sound itself became an object and a domain of thought and practice."[40] And moving to the period on which he concentrates in *The Audible Past*: "There has always been a heady audacity to the claim that vision is the social chart of modernity. While I do not claim that listening is the social chart of modernity, it certainly charts a significant field of modern practice. There is always more than one map for a territory, and sound provides a particular path through history."[41]

Within sound studies broadly construed, it remains almost de rigueur to remark and often to bemoan that the object of interest has been overlooked. While we grant that sound may indeed have been overlooked, we think that ongoing pronouncements of the sort in sound studies appear increasingly less about balance than about the differentiation of research programs and the laying down of disciplinary boundaries. The same goes for "auditory cultures," the alternative rubric that carves out a space for aural practices within the larger domain of cultural studies. To be clear, then, we are interested not in re-litigating the case in defense of sound but in probing what we see as a lack *within* sound studies: a reluctance to think sound theoretically, and to do so not against history or culture—or without listeners, for that matter—but with them. Yet, as we have indicated, the work of theorizing sound, sound objects, and sound studies also entails locating and exploring the limits, paradoxes, and contradictions of applying a term anchored in contemplation to audition.

As sound studies has emerged as a discipline, so have origin myths, canonical references, pieties, and orthodoxies. Like much in the wake of Foucault—although certainly not Foucault alone—sound studies as a field has been deeply shaped by a now reflexive historicism. This is especially true of the histories of audio technology and the soundscapes of other eras and places. We cannot naively return to or assume objects after a history of objectivity such as Daston and Galison's. But we can and do want to resist the erasure of sound—as object? as event? as objective event?—that often accompanies such historicism. To be sure, any attempt to describe the discipline will inevitably produce narratives and counter-narratives, highlight certain contributions at the expense of others, and carve out of the multifarious past an all-too-coherent present. Our story is no different, although we would like to claim a degree of self-consciousness. Sound studies holds out as foundational a handful of figures. R. Murray Schafer's work on soundscapes in the 1970s is a frequent point of reference, albeit a point of reference often accompanied by oedipal remarks about Schafer's neo-Luddite dislike of new technologies of recording and transmission. We would note that another canonical work in sound studies—a work that has helped shape the historicist, culturalist, science-and-technology studies bent of a good portion of the field—has a title of openly Schaferian inspiration: Emily Thompson's *The Soundscape of Modernity*. Yet it is likely not Schafer but the oddly synonymic Schaeffer who holds the position of patriarch, not least because of the degree of mystery surrounding his work for non-Francophones, since his chief writings on sound were until recently untranslated. Filtering into academic discourse above all through the writings of Michel Chion, Schaeffer has nonetheless, as we argue, provided key terms and concepts to sound studies: *objets sonores* (sound objects)—the title of our volume, no less—and "acousmatic" listening. Then again, it is not exactly true that Schaeffer invented these notions, and origin stories, as usual, turn out to be complex, ramified, and even contradictory on close examination. With this observation, we can begin the overview of the chapters that constitute this volume.

We have organized *Sound Objects* by grouping essays that speak most clearly with one another, although each essay is heteroglossic, and resonances between and among chapters will be found throughout the volume. We begin with three contributions on "genealogies," and it is fitting that our opening chapter goes to Michel Chion, who reflects on his personal history with Pierre Schaeffer, puts the formulation "sound objects" and "reduced listening" into historical context, and considers their ongoing theoretical and practical significance. We then turn to John Dack, who, with a cotranslator, Christine North, has been instrumental in making Schaeffer's work available to a wider readership via English translations of *In Search of a Concrete Music* and the monumental *Treatise on Musical Objects*. Dack underscores, contra the emphasis on the acousmatic and attendant disembodiment and dematerialization of sounds, Schaeffer's deep interest in the *facture*, or making, of sounds and in the instrumental transformation of sounds; and Schaeffer's incipient formulation of the distinction between real and virtual sound production. Brian Kane, taking up the term *objets sonores*, considers the history of the term prior to and after Schaeffer and the vagaries of translation: how something that once signified "sounded objects" came to mean "an object's sound," and why attending to this transformation is important. For Kane, ontologies of sound do not so much give us access to or a final account of sound's being as they compel our recognition that sounds are ultimately a "sedimentation of historical and social forces."

Part II picks up this strand and offers what we might call an alternative or parallel history and theorization of sound as object. Focusing not on the Schaefferian genealogy but, rather, on commodification, reification, and fetishism, it opens with James Steintrager's chapter on Theodor Adorno's critique of music as commodity and how this critique rests on Adorno's more general claims about the congelation of objective social forces in sound and the fundamentally nonobjective nature of hearing and listening. Next, Jonathan Sterne returns us to sound sources: technologies, instruments, and other sound-making objects. He considers the trend of reissuing old analog recording hardware and the production of software meant to faithfully replicate the "sound" of such gear. Drawing on his own research on signal processing and on the "new organology"—the broad investigation of the agency and ends of instruments—Sterne sets up a critical engagement with Marxist theories of commodity fetishism, and in particular with Adorno's remarks on the fetishizing of musical instruments, to argue that for musicians, makers, and listeners instruments produce "spectral objectivity": not only timbres and other sonic characteristics that are associated with particular instruments and recording hardware, but also the trace of social and technical relations that are intangible to the senses.[42]

After exploring, unsettling, and offering alternative genealogies of sound as object, we turn in part III to two engagements with the topic of acousmatic listening, a key concept developed in the writings of both Schaeffer and Chion and, as such, one that has played an important role in the unfolding of sound studies as an emergent discipline. First, Rey Chow posits the mytheme of Pythagoras lecturing behind the curtain as a key addition to the tropes of modernism. She places the acousmatic situation, as told by Schaeffer and repeated in sound studies, alongside oedipal blindness, phenomenological epochē, Heideggerian erasure, and other figures of simultaneous repression and structuration. Given the ubiquity of technologies of sound reproduction and the sheer number of sounds that come to us separated from their original sources and as bits, bytes, and fragments, Chow argues that, much as Derrida contended that the supposed immediacy, interiority, and self-presence of the voice is structured by deferral, exteriority, and difference—what he called "arche-writing"—any approach to sound objects today must approach listening as *acousmatically* structured and trained. For Chow, acousmatic listening remains largely undertheorized despite its pivotal position in sound studies, and transdisciplinary borrowings from literary studies can help rectify this situation. Pooja Rangan takes up the notion of acousmatic listening as it has been applied to cinema to analyze racial discrimination—with an intentional play on words—and the ways in which voices and bodies are variously coupled and uncoupled on-screen and by viewers-cum-listeners. Acousmatic situations in cinema such as the classic documentary technique of voice-over narration become a site of critical engagement for filmmakers such as Mounira Al Solh—a site where the possibilities and limitations of realigning how voices are heard as subjects and objects unfold.

While the acousmatic situation has been imagined at times as ascetically attending to an incorporeal voice, the grouping of essays in part IV insists on the embodiment of sound and listening, and each essay explores in distinctive ways how sound relates to the boundaries of human and nonhuman. In the first, Veit Erlmann takes up Julia Kristeva's notion of "abjection"—the creation of the distinction between subject and object by the expulsion and repression of boundary-troubling *things*—in his analysis of how sound takes on an object status in law. Considering legal cases about free speech and the trial of the pop singer Simon Bikindi at the International Criminal Tribunal for Rwanda for incitement to genocide, Erlmann argues that juridical reason in objectifying sound for the purposes of legal discourse depends on expulsing or "abjecting" sound as "viscerally, vibrationally 'real.'" In the next chapter, Jairo Moreno and Gavin Steingo examine antenatal listening and what they call "vernacular phenomenology" in the Colombian Afro-Pacific and the Brazilian Amazon basin. Joining anthropological research to Kristeva's notion of "chora"—the inchoate, pre-linguistic stage of human development—Moreno and Steingo ultimately argue against sound as a relation and against the emphasis on the subjective contributions of the listener in favor of autonomous objecthood: sound as alluring, never graspable, and yet unmistakably *there*. Georgina Born then considers how nonhuman sounds—a rainstorm, the tonic buzz of a hospital bed—become entangled in social, affective human relations. In an analysis that is counterintuitively consonant with Moreno and Steingo's rejection of relationality, Born argues against the ontologization of sound and for sound's fundamental relationality. She does so in a moving mediation on her mother's final days that is joined to erudite analyses of the materialist revival, science and technology studies, the thought of Alfred North Whitehead, and recent philosophical approaches to sound in the writings of O'Callaghan, Grimshaw and Garner, and many others.

The final group of chapters, in part V, we have labeled "memory traces." In the first of these, John Mowitt takes up the work of Bernard Stiegler and his extension of the Deleuzian thesis that cinema *thinks*—not that it simply represents thought—to argue that sound should be considered "arche-cinema": a structuring that precedes the visual. Mowitt thus inverts the commonplace notion that sound is secondary to the medium and subverts the sound studies plaint that sound in cinema simply needs to be given its fair due. More profoundly, though, he speculates on how and why cinema as a sonic-cum-visual medium might serve as a model for memory and the unconscious. Next, Michael Bull considers the rise, demise, and odd after-life of air-raid sirens. These sounding devices responded to the "structural, political, and technological abolition and transformation of space" with the advent of modern warfare. As an attempt to instrumentalize sound for social purposes, however, the effects of air-raid sirens turned out to be various and unpredictable. Their diminishing but continued use today in a variety of contexts, moreover, haunts the present with psychic and somatic remembrances.

We close the volume with a contribution that might be described as more heretical than heterodox. David Toop has long been an innovative sound maker and an insightful interpreter of sonic experiences and cultures. In the final chapter, Toop takes off from the idea put forward in his *Sinister Resonance* that a painting could perhaps be a musical instrument to artfully blur the boundaries of the visual and the aural. If sound studies has frequently asserted its disciplinary bona fides by denouncing the supposed hegemony of the visual, Toop, eschewing academic protocols and border patrols, thoughtfully intermingles sight and sound in a series of reminiscences and meditations on—as well as illustrations of—the sounds of drawing, drawing as sounding, and the tenuous existence of what he calls "faint beings": sounds that are not quite objects at all.

Notes

1 See Derrida, *Voice and Phenomenon*.
2 "Distinction," that is, in the sense put forward by Pierre Bourdieu as a marker of accrued cultural capital: see Bourdieu, *Distinction*. For the classic if controversial account of the rise and fall of the capital of "theory" and particularly deconstruction, see Guillory, *Cultural Capital*.
3 Baudrillard, *The Perfect Crime*, 32.
4 See Rancière, "The Future of the Image."
5 Rancière, *The Emancipated Spectator*, 72.
6 Deleuze and Guattari, *What Is Philosophy?*, 76, cited in Rancière, *The Emancipated Spectator*, 55.
7 Kant, *Critique of the Power of Judgment*, 208.
8 On Aristotle's complex position on intellectual contemplation as key to the "good life," see Charles and Scott, "Aristotle on Well-Being and Intellectual Contemplation."
9 See Jay, *Downcast Eyes*.
10 Kant, *Critique of the Power of Judgment*, 182.
11 A coinage that Michel Chion invokes when discussing the rejection by nineteenth-century composers and later by the futurist "noise" musician Luigi Russolo of instruments designed to mimic sound sources: see Chion, *Sound*, 70.
12 Gaver, "What in the World Do We Hear?," 14.
13 See Chion, *Film, a Sound Art*, 237–45; Chion, *Sound*, 158–59.
14 Bentham, *The Panopticon Writings*, 49.
15 Schaeffer, *In Search of a Concrete Music*, 105.
16 See Schaeffer, *Treatise on Musical Objects*.
17 For Adorno's classic critique of popular music and the one to which we allude in our terminological choices, see Adorno, "On the Fetish-Character in Music and the Regression of Listening." On "schizophonia," see Schafer, *The Soundscape*, 90–91.
18 See Kane, *Sound Unseen*, 39–40, passim.
19 Daston and Galison, *Objectivity*, 253–307. Interestingly, while the authors highlight the work of Hermann von Helmholz in their account of the emergence and nature of "structural objectivity," they focus on his work on color sensation and not on his seminal research on sound. That Helmholz's research on sound would easily fit with their overarching thesis, however, is certain.

20 A particularly acute analysis of the "locked groove" in Schaeffer's conceptual apparatus is in Demers, *Listening through the Noise*, 26–31.

21 See Deleuze, *Difference and Repetition*.

22 Foucault, *The Order of Things*, 286.

23 Deleuze and Guattari, *Kafka*, 21. For a Lacanian twist on sound in Kafka, see Dolar, "The Burrow of Sound."

24 See Attali, *Noise*, 36.

25 See Atlan, "Noise as a Principle of Self-Organization (1972/1979)."

26 See Serres, *The Parasite*.

27 Kittler, *Gramophone, Film, Typewriter*, 22–23.

28 See Ernst, *Sonic Time Machines*.

29 Ernst, *Sonic Time Machines*, 114.

30 Ernst, *Sonic Time Machines*, 116.

31 Meillassoux, *After Finitude*, 7.

32 Meillassoux, *After Finitude*, 2–3.

33 See O'Callaghan, *Sounds*.

34 Grimshaw and Garner, *Sonic Virtuality*, 4, passim.

35 Gaver, "What in the World Do We Hear?," 27.

36 Pasnau, "What Is Sound?," 309.

37 See Ihde, *Listening and Voice*.

38 If anthologies and handbooks serve not so much to mark the birth of fields as to confirm them, we should note the following: Bull and Black, *The Auditory Culture Reader*; Pinch and Bijsterveld, *The Oxford Handbook of Sound Studies*; Novak and Sakakeeny, *Keywords in Sound*; Sterne, *The Sound Studies Reader*.

39 Sterne, *The Audible Past*, 3.

40 Sterne, *The Audible Past*, 2.

41 Sterne, *The Audible Past*, 3.

42 See Tresch and Dolan, "Toward a New Organology."

I | Genealogies

Reflections on the Sound Object
and Reduced Listening

The Schaefferian concept that I discuss in this chapter is formulated in French with the invented term *objet sonore* (noun followed by an adjective). This is usually translated into English
as "sound object," which is almost clearer. In France, it is both
one of the most frequently mentioned of Pierre Schaeffer's
concepts and one of the most misunderstood. Indeed, flipping
its meaning upside down, it is frequently made to designate
the source of a sound, notably when the latter is not a classical instrument. The source of a sound—which I have shown
in my essay *Sound* ought in most instances to be spoken of as
sources in the plural—Schaeffer labels *corps sonore* or "sounding body."[1] The sound object is something perceptual.

One of the many reasons for this lack of comprehension
is that the book in which this concept was developed bears
the title *Traité des objets musicaux* (*Treatise on Musical Objects*).[2]
Going by the title, it is not all sounds in general—which, notwithstanding, the greatest part of this large tome deals with—
that are at stake but sounds that will be selected, chosen,
elected to be *used in music of some sort*. For Schaeffer, in fact, the
sound object is only a transitional concept: it aims to describe
and classify sounds among themselves, with the goal of identifying those that are the most appropriate or, as he puts it,
the most *suitable* for music.[3] They will become musical thanks

to their employment, but they must be predisposed to this employment, albeit not necessarily by the usual criteria of traditional musical forms (often the presence of a recognizable note—of a "tonic mass," in Schaeffer's terminology—as well as an instrumental origin, referring to a sound source recognized as a musical instrument). Instead, they must be predisposed to this employment by novel criteria that are broader and more open than, and independent of, the sound's origin. Thus, a sound with complex mass—that is, without precise pitch—and not necessarily emanating from a recognizable musical source can be considered "suitable for music" and, consequently, as "musical" if it presents characteristics of "proper form" or brings out well a morphological criterion: grain, bearing, or unfolding intensity.

In spite of this, as I have mentioned, the greater part of Schaeffer's book is consecrated to the characteristics of sound objects—of all sounds in general. This is why in 1981 I decided to give my work dedicated to the *Traité des objets musicaux* the title *Guide des objets sonores* (*Guide to Sound Objects*).[4] This guide—and let me once more make this clear—is an introduction to a book concerning which I do not share all the hypotheses. To my mind, the title ought to have helped avoid one of the most common criticisms leveled at Schaeffer's book in France: that it does not discuss matters of form and of musical language. At the same time, while respecting and clarifying the *Traité*'s definitions, I committed a deliberate betrayal in choosing the title: I wanted to emphasize that the *Traité* does not speak only to musicians. I think, in fact, that the book might be of interest to anyone who is concerned with the perception of sounds and that Schaeffer's treatise would have been better understood if it had been given the title *Traité des objets sonores* (Treatise on Sound Objects).

For the sake of honesty, my work nonetheless includes as a subtitle "Schaeffer et la recherche musicale" (Schaeffer and Musical Research). "Musical research" is a concept that Schaeffer put forward at the end of the 1950s, at a different epoch and with a different meaning from that of *musique concrète*. We are no longer in 1948–50, the years that saw the birth of musique concrète. By that point, Schaeffer had long since stopped talking about musique concrète and turned instead to *musique expérimentale*, which set off in another direction entirely. Even if the locution did not enjoy the same success as musique concrète, it indicated a precise and different intention: a form of music that would experiment with associations of sounds of whatever origin, including but not limited to those of instrumental origin—why not?—to create a musical discourse that would build on the universal properties of listening. Certain composers, such as Ivo Malec, grasped this quite well. Malec wrote several pieces of "experimental music" with scores and for instruments, mainly for strings.

The classical stringed instrument in Western music is, in fact, well suited to producing different types of sound, depending on whether it is played *col arco* or *pizzicato*, played with or without vibrato, or whether special techniques such as *sul ponticello* are employed. Such techniques are already widely in use in the quartets of Béla Bartók, among others. For Schaeffer, however, this is not yet experimental music because it is organized primarily in terms of pitch and does not put other sonic criteria into scalar form.

In any case, the *Traité des objets musicaux* is in no way a treatise on musique concrète in the original sense—that is, a music based on recording media. It does not obligatorily presuppose a score and classical instruments. But, at the same time, it also does not obligatorily presuppose that a sound has to be recorded or—my stated terminological preference— "fixed" on a medium. In my view, Schaeffer made a major mistake when he decided to include in his massive work a few pages on studio techniques (the chapter in question is titled "The Laboratory"), which created a belief that the work had to do only with forms of music that at the time were labeled "electro-acoustic."

Already in the 1970s, when I was a young member of the Groupe de Recherches Musicales, from which I had to resign in 1976, I was skeptical about the notion of objects suitable for music and critical with regard to its normative character, and I expressed these criticisms during an exchange with Schaeffer that I produced for a radio broadcast in 1975. The dialogue was published in 1977 in the collection *La musique du futur a-t-elle un avenir?* (Does the music of the future have a future?).[5] Some of the exchanges show that Schaeffer was hoping at this time that notational symbols would be developed and clarified:

PIERRE SCHAEFFER. If, after having been a defender of the almost inexhaustible concrete character of sound and after having denounced deceptive "scores," I now tell you that I require a score, a solid schema, this is because after so many years of stammering, I think that what has undermined an almost non-existent research program—because everyone tried to produce works too quickly, without ever asking profound research questions—[is that] no one pursued, . . . no one pushed further that which I had tried to do with a music theory. This music theory proposed so many possible combinations that what was needed was to retain only a few. What was needed next was to try to find practical notations, and only afterward, beginning with that work on notation, which is a simplification based on a choice of criteria, would a certain combinatory—a certain architecture—become simultaneously more foreseeable and more intentional.

To be sure, there are different types of scores, between those that only contain instructions for execution and those that are the record of what is heard. Only the traditional score of Western musical forms provides a happy enough synthesis of doing and hearing. But why am I led to say that the existence of a score, in which I assume a suitable equilibrium between indications for carrying out the music and explanations aimed at listening, seems to me more important than the satisfaction of seeing music come alive, of seeing music made before my eyes? This is because I do not think that we will ever rediscover the equivalent of the traditional instrumental gesture.

MICHEL CHION. From your perspective, therefore, music has not stopped deteriorating from Bach up to today, because it has been less and less notatable, because it has more and more to do with orchestration, with timbres, with its concrete reality and less and less with abstract structures?

SCHAEFFER. Yes, music—the music in question—has not stopped deteriorating since Bach, I'm happy to think this is so. . . . But what must also be said is that there are other possible musics and that we can compare the value of these musics, albeit not on the aesthetic plane. The word "music" refers to several things . . . , but there could be other "musical domains" that would be worthy of better definition and not confused with that Western music that culminated with Bach.

CHION. I am nonetheless under the impression that, concerning these other musics, you are searching for a definition that corresponds to that of the music of Bach . . .

SCHAEFFER. Don't make me say something that I didn't. I simply said that they would have in common with that of Bach the tripod of these three reference points, in varying proportions: active execution, abstract notation, and sonic result. What is certain is that you will have a different modality in terms of execution, more or less active; that you will also have extremely different notational systems; and, finally, [you will have] sonic modalities—sonic relevancies—that are very different. But it's not because I refer to these three ways of defining music that the same thing is at stake. On the contrary.

CHION. Isn't there nonetheless in the *Traité des objets musicaux* something—pardon the expression—a bit suicidal, since you want to require of new music that it conform to a definition that it cannot satisfy, precisely because it is looking in a different direction? It is as if one were to demand of cinema, in order to become an "art," that it conform to definitions that refer to a non-technological art—to theater, for example.

SCHAEFFER. My answer to you is that there must be a common model among musics in order to appreciate their differences and that what is suicidal about current musical forms is that they want to be different but they don't want to accept their real difference from traditional music. At the same time, they say that they are the continuation of traditional music—that they're nearly the same, just as good, that it's progress. But they reject a frame of reference. You yourself show a bit of resistance in accepting that a given music has at least three fundamental points of reference in common with all music, about which I spoke a moment ago. These three criteria are so general—because I admit that there are enormous variations, different proportions—that it seems to me that they can encompass all music.[6]

As is evident from these sentiments, expressed in 1975, Schaeffer shifted positions with respect to *Traité des objets musicaux*, now insisting on the need for a score on which music is written (a notion that is absent from the *Traité*) and active execution (of the instrumental sort). Similarly, the *Traité* turned its back on the initial definition of musique concrète: on the one hand, it assumes that realistic sounds, which were very present in the initial works in the genre, have fallen by the wayside; on the other, it does not describe a form of music that requires a recording medium to exist.

Despite my reservations, the *Traité* seemed to me, and still seems to me, quite important, and I thought so very early on. I chose to follow the teaching of the Groupe de Recherches Musicales at the end of the 1960s because it struck me that, out of all of the speculative musical writings that appeared in France during the '60s, theirs was the only one not to avoid a crucial question that the others sidestepped—namely, can the auditor hear the effects and form that the composer has set up? At this time, the notable works at one's disposal were Pierre Boulez's *Penser la musique aujourd'hui* (translated as *On Music Today*), a collection of lectures given at Darmstadt; Iannis Xenakis's *Musiques formelles*; and, needless to say, René Leibowitz's writing on serial music.[7] The works of Boulez and Xenakis in particular revealed abstract speculations about the art of writing a musical score, but they did not deal with the perceptibility of the music when played. Published in the same decade but a bit later, the *Traité* did not waste time polemicizing against Boulez or Xenakis—who, for their part, were openly quite critical of Schaeffer, and even aggressively so—but proposed an entire series of concepts and experiments that allowed:

1   Opening music to all sounds produced from every possible source, based on truly rational foundations and building on listening. On the one hand, this means getting beyond the sound/noise distinction and thus avoiding conventional music as well, of which "bruitism" is nothing but the inverted reflection. On the other hand, it means not reducing music to sounds produced by instruments categorized as musical, whether or not "diverted," as in Cage's prepared piano.

2   Defining a common level where all sounds—whether they are figurative or not, instrumental or not—are put on the same plane. This level is that of reduced listening, which is interested in sound for itself, in the qualities that are proper to it, independent of its cause or of its meaning linked to a code. This type of perception has long existed for visual forms, since with regard to every visual object—no matter its kind, use, size, or "natural" or "manmade" character—we are capable of having an apprehension of its form. Whether we are talking about a ballpoint pen, the trunks of certain trees, the paws of certain animals, or cotton swabs for cleaning one's ears, we recognize in the objects a common form: that of being oblong and more or less regularly cylindrical. We will also recognize an object as spherical, or "spheroid," whether we are talking about a ping-pong ball, a planet, or certain types of fruit. In this manner, we unconsciously practice a sort of "reduced vision." The reduced listening defined by Schaeffer seeks to bring out that we have the same sort of perception in the case of sounds, but that it is lacking in words and is not culturally valorized.

3   Of speculating on the idea of a music that would be "experimental," meaning that this music aims to test sounds and combinations of sounds to discover a "musicality" that would be based not on a tradition, but on sonic properties in general and on the functioning of the ear. In this sense, what was at stake was the project of a universal music. (Recall that Schaeffer had worked in Africa. When I was attending his seminar in 1969–70, he invited ethnomusicologists such

as Simha Arom and Trần Văn Khê. Only later would he renounce this universalism.)

In parallel with my musical studies between 1963 and 1970, I had found Schaeffer's works in disarray, and it was only belatedly that I heard for the first time one of the oldest—and, in my view, best—works, composed with and co-signed by Pierre Henry: *Symphonie pour un homme seul*, dated 1950. Yet this symphony is the absolute antithesis of the music that Schaeffer would advocate twenty-five years later, for the following reasons:

- It was not solely addressed to reduced listening but brought in narrative sonic events: yells, sounds of footsteps and of hammering, groans, and even bits of sentences and words.
- It was unaware of the concept of sound object.
- It implied the recording medium as an indispensable condition—not as a passive means of storing and of reproducing recorded sounds, but as an active means with which one is in conversation. In the symphony there are interruptions; changes in scale; phenomena of enlargement, or distancing; and a very lively auditory montage. My music took direct inspiration from Schaeffer's symphony, and I am often told that it is quite "cinematographic," at which point I clarify that all I am doing is being logical with respect to the means employed and that I do not try to hide them. It is very odd that Schaeffer turned his back so quickly on the *Symphonie pour un homme seul,* the conception of which was his and the aesthetic of which he had defined, even if Henry composed it with him and contributed considerably to the creation of its constitutive sounds.

It is crucial to note that the Schaeffer who returned to France in 1957 after three or four years of absence (during which time he left the leadership of the Groupe de Musique Concrète to Henry and Philippe Arthuys), when he dedicated himself to working in Africa, no longer thought, said, or wrote the same things he had four years earlier.[8] First, as I mentioned earlier, he no longer spoke about concrete music; he spoke of experimental music. Second, the new music that he envisioned did not necessarily require a media platform; it could be carried out using instruments played before an audience. Third, this music rejected the figurative and picturesque effects—bizarrely characterized as surrealist—with which the *Symphonie pour un homme seul* teems. Nevertheless, I continued to find the research project of a universal music laid out in the *Traité* splendid. This project could be pursued only via collaborative work, and when Schaeffer left the steering of the Groupe de Recherches Musicales to François Bayle, it was set aside.

Some years later, circa 1979, when I had begun to study sound in film, I found a supplementary reason to advise reading the *Traité* and to finish my *Guide des objets sonores*. I had realized that reduced listening is a *practice*—I stress "practice," because texts have been published in France in which reduced listening is criticized in the abstract by people who have never practiced it—that this practice is interesting and instructive in domains other than music; and it should not be opposed to other manners of listening but, rather, articulated with them. I proposed and taught classes in reduced listening in diverse, often non-musical, contexts.

By applying reduced listening to sounds that feature in film sequences, I discovered that sonic characteristics allowed for better comprehension of the form of a cinematographic sequence. In my book *Sound*, I take as an example the famous opening of Sergio Leone's film *Once upon a Time in the West* (1968) and show that this sequence is a composition made up of sonic forms, whose sources should not be forgotten: the basis of its dramatic power, as well as of its aesthetic beauty, is not only the variety of sonic causes but also the variety of its sonic forms, which only reduced listening allows us to discern and understand.[9] The entrance of the sound of a fly is an event not only because it bothers the three bad guys who are waiting in the station for the arrival of the train carrying the nameless "Harmonica" (played by Charles Bronson), but also because this is the first time in the sequence, and thus in the film, that we hear a tonic and continuous sound (in the Schaefferian sense: a sound with a recognizable and set pitch, from the perspective of its "mass," and a sound unfolding without interruption or saccade for a certain length of time, from the perspective of its "sustainment"). In the same way, the drops of water that strike the head of the outlaw played by Woody Strode contrast formally with the other sounds in the sequence from the perspective of their mass (they are sounds of complex mass, without precise pitch, as opposed to tonic sounds) and of their sustainment (they are impulses—that is, sounds that are too brief to constitute a heard duration and that are perceived as points in time). A bit later, with the sound of a telegraph, enters that which Schaeffer calls a sound with iterative sustainment and complex mass. Thus, what we have is a composition of forms, like those produced in the natural world with vegetable forms and animal forms. Yet there is no need to forget that what we are hearing is a fly, a drop of water, and a telegraph. Reduced listening is superimposed on the type of listening known as causal (whence comes this sound?), but the formal beauty comes from the variety of sound forms, just like a natural or artificial object moves us because of its formal qualities and textural details. It was thus that I discovered that reduced listening does not forbid listening otherwise—that reduced listening overlaps with the others and enriches them.

Many students I educated in this practice believed at the outset that they were being asked to mentally repress any association of a sound to a cause, which is impossible. I answered, "Not at all. There is no need for you to forget; simply concentrate on the qualities peculiar to a sound." In the same manner, if I describe an object visible to me, I am not obligated to forget its concrete nature to identify and describe its form. As surprising as this might be, abstracting sonic forms beyond their natural or cultural aspect, their origin, and their scale had not been done before Schaeffer. To place reduced listening back in the arena of various manners of listening—without renouncing the latter—and to liberate it from the automatic association with the concept of the sound object are my proposals. But once again, an institution would be required to welcome this sort of collaborative work, and for the time being in France, where the contributions of Schaeffer are scorned and misunderstood (which is why I had to put on my website a work that the publisher no longer makes available), the opportunity has been lacking.

From this angle—that is, if we want to indicate a sound as an object of listening, and not merely of reduced listening but of *all listening modes* (causal, semantic, and so forth)—should the term "sound object" be retained? I am inclined to say no, since the term belongs to Schaeffer's thinking and to the research program set forth in the *Traité des objets musicaux*. In the *Traité*, moreover, the sound object is considered as a potential "musical object," as long as it fulfills certain conditions.

This is why I proposed in *Sound: An Acoulogical Treatise* that we speak instead of an *auditum* (Lat., "that which is heard"). The term would indicate that which is heard without presupposing the mode of listening of which it is the object and whether what is heard is musical—or "considered potentially musical"—or not. Using *auditum* would allow us to avoid certain kinds of confusion that the French word *son* and equivalents in several other languages (e.g., *sonido*, *suono*, sound, and so forth) entail, because the term simultaneously denotes both a vibratory physical phenomenon produced in a given medium (air, water, and so on) and the perception that this phenomenon causes in human beings (as well as in many other species, though this would merit a considerably longer discussion).

Auditum clearly denotes that which is heard, and this word, contrary to the Schaefferian notion of "sound object," does not presuppose an ideal duration, criteria of "proper form," or, again, a possible musical destiny. Finally, the word does not grant any general validity to the distinction between sound and noise. Yet the term "sound object" already did these things, and we must grant it, along with the major concept of reduced listening, the immense merit of having demonstrated that everything that is heard belongs to a common domain and is not hierarchized in advance.

Notes

This chapter was translated by James A. Steintrager.

1 See Chion, *Sound*, 101–20.
2 Appearing in French as Schaeffer, *Traité des objets musicaux*, and only recently published in English as *Treatise on Musical Objects*.
3 See Schaeffer, *Traité des objets musicaux*, 348.
4 Michel Chion, *Guide to Sound Objects*, trans. John Dack and Christine North, 2009, accessed March 1, 2017, http://ears.pierrecouprie.fr/spip.php?article3597
5 Michel Chion, *La musique du future a-t-elle un avenir?*. This collection is available for free download on my website, www.michelchion.com.
6 Michel Chion, *La musique du future a-t-elle un avenir?*, 94–97.
7 See, e.g., Leibowitz, *Schoenberg and His School*.
8 Between 1953 and 1957, Schaeffer was project leader of the Ministry of Overseas France's efforts to expand and administer a network of radio stations; this position led Schaeffer to spend considerable time in West Africa [trans.].
9 Chion, *Sound*, 83–91.

Pierre Schaeffer and the
(Recorded) Sound Source

In this chapter I argue that a reappropriation and elaboration of the sound source is an inevitable consequence of Pierre Schaeffer's theoretical framework as outlined in his Programme de la Recherche Musicale (Program of Musical Research). This program comprises the stages of typology, morphology, characterology, analysis, and synthesis. Since 1998, with my colleague Christine North, I have been engaged in translating key texts by Schaeffer and other French composer-theorists.[1] A major part of any translation is a detailed linguistic analysis of many common terms. "Sound source" is one such term. Sound source might seem either hopelessly vague or glaringly self-evident, and we might even ask whether this concept is worth revisiting at all. Despite such misgivings, my decision to emphasize its significance is deliberate. I believe that the sound source occupies a central but often unacknowledged position in Schaeffer's theories. After the stages of typology and morphology, sources assume increased importance at the stage of characterology, and this relationship needs to be teased out. A potential problem is that Schaeffer exhorts us to listen to a recorded sound "for itself," to direct our attention solely to the intrinsic qualities perceptible in the sound or, as he puts it, the "in-itself-ness of the sound."[2] But what precisely is meant by this "in-itself-ness"? What features are included or excluded in such an assessment? The acuity and analytical abilities of the ear and brain are capable of determining not just a sound's pitch, but also its spectral components and dynamic behavior. A process of pattern matching and source identification will be initiated whether a recorded sound originates from physical causality or lines of computer code. Some sounds will be perceived to have a distant or even nonexistent relationship with familiar real-world materials and actions; others will resemble them or appear to imitate them.[3] Even raw, untransformed recordings of real events may be misinterpreted due to the acousmatic listening context.[4] The relationship between the perceiving subject's interpretive tendencies and a recorded sound are part of this experience of "in-itself-ness." My intention, therefore, is to examine and evaluate the relationship between the perception of recordings and the mental formations of real or imaginary sound sources.

However, there is a conundrum: a sound source usually involves a physical object activated by an agent. The inescapable consequence of using recordings forced Schaeffer to reevaluate the status of physical devices in the studio. Equipment such as tape recorders play back recordings of sound sources—this is self-evident. But does this technical operation in itself transform a tape recorder or, indeed, the recording into a sound source comparable to, for example, a violin, a gong, or a struck sheet of metal? Clarity is needed to prevent simplistic and ultimately unhelpful claims that the tape recorder is a sound source or even a musical instrument (this subject is discussed further in the following pages). It is nevertheless important to note that studio practice demonstrated how an impression of physicality could still emerge from using such equipment, thereby providing access to a world of virtual actions, materials, and agents. In contrast to the 1950s and 1960s, a conceptual vocabulary associated with the virtual is now commonplace. In my references to Schaeffer's Program of Musical Research and its theoretical consequences, it will be clear that terms such as "real" and "virtual," as well as "physical" and "imaginary," are inextricably linked, and any discussion of one will inevitably imply the others. Such is the nature of the dualisms that Schaeffer favored in his thinking.

Schaeffer's concern was with music, or, as he often wrote, the "phenomenon of music." His research program was not concerned solely with the genre of *musique concrète* (a term he abandoned in 1958 without repudiating its initial aims and discoveries). It extends beyond both electroacoustic music as a whole and the impact of media technology to which his theories are commonly applied. It was music as a collection of artistic and social practices that encompass different scientific and intellectual disciplines that interested him. His frequent use of the verb "to generalize" (*généraliser*) in the *Traité des objets musicaux* (*Treatise on Musical Objects*) is, therefore, unsurprising. Schaeffer identified fundamental aspects of how traditional music functions; these would then be applied more generally to suggest their relevance to contemporary musical thought and, crucially, to music created by new forms of technology. This methodology has significant implications for another musical concept closely related to the sound source: the musical instrument. Inevitably, perhaps, in any discussion of sound sources we are forced to consider the meaning of this culturally loaded term. The unavoidable fact for most musicians is that the source of most musical sounds will be a traditional musical instrument. It follows that any evaluation of the sound source must affect our understanding of the musical instrument and, most important, how it actively contributes to the evolution of musical languages. But what happens when a recorded sound bears little resemblance to a known method of sound generation? Can such a recording be reconciled with the musical instrument? Indeed, does it need to be? It is my view that Schaeffer did not in fact abandon the musical instrument. Instead, he generalized the concept and, by transcending its physical nature, enabled its reappropriation for both studio-based and instrumental music. At this point, a language issue is worth considering. For Schaeffer, "making" and "doing" music were central to the musical experience. In "Making Music" (*Faire de la musique*), book 1 of the *Treatise on Musical Objects*, the first two chapters are titled, "The Instrumental Prerequisite" (*Le préalable instrumental*) and "Playing an Instrument" (*Jouer d'un instrument*). Both indicate unequivocally Schaeffer's interest in the instrument, its construction, how it is played, and its active role in the emergence of musical thought. Here the French language also reveals its unique capacity to shape Schaeffer's thinking. The verb *faire* can be translated as "to do" as well as "to make," and book 1's title can also be translated "Doing Music." During the act of translation, decisions are made according to context: "Making Music" was our choice. But to a French-speaker, the acts of *doing* and *making* coexist. The sentence is understood with both meanings. The same is true of the noun *expérience*, which can be translated into English as both "experience" and "experiment." Bearing these points in mind, the following statement, clumsy though it is, should be considered: a new experience/experiment of making/doing music with studio technology involves constructing virtual instruments from recordings. But here is yet another conundrum: in an age in which technology is increasingly prevalent, have traditional definitions of the musical instrument become inadequate? Many contemporary musical languages make use of performance practices such as extended techniques, which simultaneously elaborate and subvert traditional instrumental play. Nonstandard sound sources are also common, as are novel interfaces using software such as Max/MSP or Pure Data. Must we cling obstinately to established organological definitions, which satisfy the classification requirements of museum collections, or do we class everything as a musical instrument? The former strategy is unhelpful for recorded sounds; the latter certainly liberates the term but is intellectually lazy. Extricating the concept of a musical instrument from cultural preconditions renders it practically meaningless. In *Les musiques électroacoustiques*, Michel Chion and Guy Reibel stated adamantly that "the studio is not an instrument."[5] This may be an unpopular comment for many practitioners who are creating music in studios or with laptop computers and are reluctant to sever links (even metaphorical ones) with physical instruments. Nevertheless, for Chion and Reibel the reassuring presence of equipment in the studio did not provide a simple substitute for musical instruments. They recognized that the term "musical instrument," like "sound source," deserves more serious investigation. However paradoxical it may seem, losing the material construction and the physicality of instruments and asserting the primacy of aural perception via studio practice actually encourages greater understanding of the musical instrument as a central and dynamic musical concept.

In the remainder of this chapter, I provide a summary of the first three parts of Schaeffer's Program of Musical Research: typology, morphology and characterology. We will see that Pierre Schaeffer referred to what can only be described as the real-world characteristics and behaviors of material objects to develop his theories. There was a constant two-way process of generalization between the physical and the virtual.

The Program of Musical Research

Schaeffer was in many ways a systems builder. Music emerged from the interplay between binary pairs such as abstract and concrete, sound and sonorous, and culture and nature. To quote from the foreword of the *Treatise*, "We should then see, in this complementariness of naturally given means and cultural structures, the resolution of numerous superficial contradistinctions, between the ancients and the moderns, the arts and sciences, the sound and the musical."[6] The important passage here is the reference to "the resolution of . . . the sound and the musical." Schaeffer sought to understand how the *musical* can be fashioned from the *sonorous*, from the totality of sound that we hear as part of our lived experience. He concluded that musical elements are not restricted to discrete pitches and rhythmic values. Texture, spectral constitution, and dynamic development can be promoted to more important roles in the articulation of musical structure. Such an enlarged vocabulary has implications for the musical instrument.

A system was needed to assist composers in navigating their way through a sonic universe that contains a potentially limitless number of sounds, or *sound objects*, generated during studio practice.[7] These sound objects were initially recorded on shellac discs and later on magnetic tape. Today, composers would almost certainly work with digital sound files. Sounds were removed from their causal context by editing. They might also have been transformed by simple technical processes such as reversal, filtering, acceleration, or deceleration. Even these relatively basic techniques could render the sounds unrecognizable and would, Schaeffer claimed, encourage the listener to concentrate on the totality of the sound's concrete features to discover and abstract musical elements. The objective was to elevate the status of a sound object to that of a musical object. The recording process had an additional advantage: it enabled sounds to be repeated exactly and encouraged the aforementioned acousmatic mode of perception. Given the multitude of sound objects that would result from experimenting in the studio, a system was developed to classify and describe them. The alternative, Schaeffer thought, was simply getting lost or being overwhelmed. But on what basis can classification begin if the musician is working with recordings rather than actual sound sources? Here acute aural scrutiny provided by perception became of paramount importance. The result was Schaeffer's Summary Diagram of Typology (see figure 2.1). However, two caveats must be taken into account. First, some sounds, especially those of long duration, may initially need to be segmented according to articulation or stress. Second, there is the thorny issue of anecdotal sounds, which refer directly to real-world events. Schaeffer's summary diagram is concerned solely with the concrete features of sound objects, not with explicit extramusical associations. Regrettably, due to space limitations, these topics must be disregarded in the present chapter.

TYPOLOGY

Typology is the first stage of the Program of Musical Research and its role is to assist the ambitious enterprise of classifying any sound object. Schaeffer's Summary Diagram of Typology illustrates some thirty types of sound

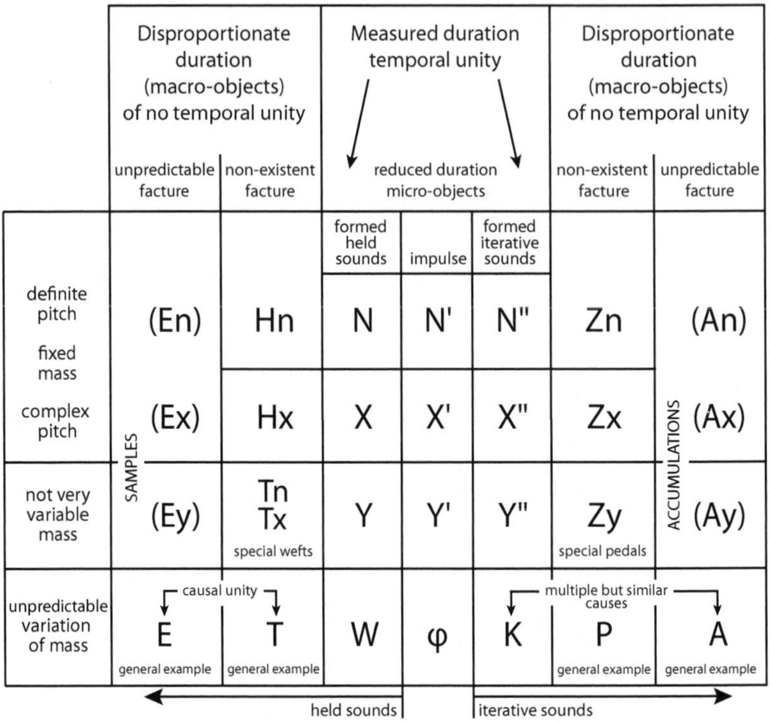

	Disproportionate duration (macro-objects) of no temporal unity		Measured duration temporal unity ↓ reduced duration micro-objects ↓			Disproportionate duration (macro-objects) of no temporal unity	
	unpredictable facture	non-existent facture	formed held sounds	impulse	formed iterative sounds	non-existent facture	unpredictable facture
definite pitch / fixed mass	(En)	Hn	N	N'	N"	Zn	(An)
complex pitch	(Ex)	Hx	X	X'	X"	Zx	(Ax)
not very variable mass	(Ey)	Tn Tx (special wefts)	Y	Y'	Y"	Zy (special pedals)	(Ay)
unpredictable variation of mass	E (general example)	⌐ causal unity ⌐ T (general example)	W	φ	⌐ multiple but similar causes ⌐ K	P (general example)	A (general example)

SAMPLES (left margin) — ACCUMULATIONS (right margin)

← held sounds | iterative sounds →

FIG 2.1 Summary Table of Typology, from Pierre Schaeffer, *Treatise on Musical Objects: An Essay across Disciplines,* trans. Christine North and John Dack, © 2017 by The Regents of the University of California Press. Published by the University of California Press.

object arranged in three groups: *balanced, eccentric,* and *redundant* sound types (see figure 2.1). The clear lines of demarcation in the diagram are in reality rather fuzzy, and classification must be assessed and possibly reassessed according to context. By examining the diagram in detail, one can ascertain Schaeffer's strategy: the entire diagram is based on agency and physicality of real sources—or, and this is where Schaeffer performs an intellectual *tour de force,* their absence. The seven columns deal with aspects of temporality. But caution is needed: duration here is not an expression of chronometric quantity. In the column headings there are references to macro- and micro-objects, as well as to *temporal unity* (or lack of it). Consequently, the classification criteria of the columns are derived from how sounds progress in time when physical objects are excited into vibration. This is then generalized and applied to recorded sounds heard acousmatically.

The balanced sound types in the three upper rows of the three central columns of the Summary Diagram of Typology are of particular importance. Each is characterized by a specific kind of energy required to produce sound. First, a sound body can be activated by a single, short burst of energy resulting in an impulse—the central column. Second, energy can be transferred to a sound body and then maintained in a continuous manner according to its material construction—the column of formed held sounds on the left. Or, third, sound energy can result from a series of several impulse-like bursts or iterations—the column of formed iterative sounds on the right. Thus, the columns radiate outward symmetrically from the impulse. The temporal unity above these columns indicates that the sound types are neither too short nor too long in duration. The listener can grasp the sound object under consideration as one unit.

The consequences of the balanced sound types are twofold. First, Schaeffer recognized that individual sounds that can be apprehended as a unit are likely to become basic elements of a language because they can be compared with one another and can form relationships that lead to more extended structures. As such, they have a special status in music. They are "suitable" (*convenable*), in Schaeffer's terms, and, in broad terms, are equivalent to the notes of traditional and much contemporary music. Second, such sound objects are by far the most common types of sounds produced by activating material objects such as musical instruments.

THE OUTER COLUMNS AND "FACTURE"

Before investigating the outer columns of macro-objects, it is important to note a feature of the Summary Diagram that is not immediately obvious. In the diagram, there are two pairs of adjoining columns. One column is for nonexistent facture, and the other is for unpredictable facture. These pairs are situated symmetrically to the left and right of the three central columns, but they should be superimposed. The diagrammatic arrangement is a consequence of representing several sonic features in two dimensions.[8] As sound objects increase in duration, they no longer fit within the central columns. The columns of nonexistent facture and unpredictable facture indicate a process of bifurcation, which affects both duration and classification: sound objects fit in one *or* the other. For example, an N-type sound object, if extended in duration, may demand reclassification in the box to the left for Hn sound objects. The diagram's spatial arrangement could give the impression that, if it is extended further, it will need to be moved to the left once again to become an En sound object. But this would be incorrect. *Both* of these columns are for macro-objects, indicating that they exceed the temporal unity of the three central columns as described previously. The classification depends not just on duration but also on facture.

At this point, the fundamental concept of *facture* must be explained. Christine North and I decided to retain *facture* in the original French in our translations. Although it is uncommon, the term "facture" can be found in English, usually in a cognate form in words such as "manufacture."[9] Facture is a quality perceived in a sound object that communicates how the sound *might* have been made. In an assessment of facture, there is an implication of energy being applied to an object or medium as that is commonly determined by real-world processes. Although this may seem somewhat vague, it must be emphasized that the listener will assess recorded sounds solely according to their concrete characteristics, but reference to known materials and behavior is part of this. To explain further: let us consider a sound from a physical object such as a musical instrument. The actions of friction, percussion, or the blowing of air through a tube will produce the sound and will invariably display facture. Recorded sounds can be assessed in the same manner, even though in such cases actual sound sources cannot be identified. Facture therefore provides a fundamental evaluative criterion based on agency and physical materiality. The sound objects in the three central columns by definition will display facture. The sole exception is the impulse. Little spectral or dynamic information will probably be perceptible in an impulse because of its brevity. Nevertheless, we are familiar with such sounds, and they display a self-contained logic. By contrast, the column for *non-existent* facture on the left indicates that the sound evolves slowly or even imperceptibly in its spectral components and dynamic development. The attack or onset, which is often a principal means by which a source can be identified, is indistinct; the same is true of its termination. Similarly, the adjacent column for unpredictable facture denotes sound objects with erratic spectral and dynamic evolutions that cannot be predicted as the sound progresses. Such sounds are often processed or synthesized and may deviate considerably from real-world behavior. The two columns to the right of the formed sounds are iterative examples of these sound types. There may be some doubt as to whether a sound object with unpredictable facture fits best in the column to the far left (an Ex type, or *sample*) or to the far right (an Ax type, or *accumulation*). Schaeffer claimed,

"Thus in the outer columns of our diagram extremes meet"; as a result, many sounds of unpredictable facture can be described as either samples or accumulations.[10] As always, context will probably prove decisive.

THE FOUR ROWS

The concept of mass and how it varies underpins the construction of the four rows. In the Summary Diagram, Schaeffer did not refer to pitch as this is conventionally understood. Instead, pitch was generalized to become the criterion called "mass." It is mass that occupies the pitch field, and this can extend from a narrow sine tone to the other extreme: white noise. In the diagram, mass is not arranged in a continuous progression but classed in four basic types. From the top row to the lowest, they are mass that is stable in the pitch field (the two upper rows of *fixed mass*); mass that varies slightly (the third row); and mass that varies unpredictably (the fourth row). The two upper rows of fixed mass are further differentiated by the sound object's spectral composition. If the mass is clearly defined and locatable in the pitch field, it belongs in the top row. However, if it displays noise content, it is classed as *complex* mass and is assigned to the second row. The two lower rows bear scrutiny when considering the boxes created by the intersection with the columns. First, let us examine the third row for sound objects with slightly varying mass. Variation in these sound objects can be ascending or descending in the pitch field. The only difference is that the movement will be continuous for held sounds and discontinuous for iterative sounds. The duration of the impulse will by definition result in little movement in the pitch field. The lowest row is reserved for sound objects, which display unpredictable variation in their mass. The unforeseeable movement in pitch space, accompanied perhaps by erratic dynamic/spectral evolution, demonstrates once again the importance of facture in the task of classification. Such sound objects occur in many electroacoustic compositions, but the lack of facture inevitably conveys a sense of estrangement from real-world causalities. This will have consequences for the listeners' aesthetic appreciation of the work, although it will not necessarily be negative. Furthermore, note the three sound types in the bottom row at the intersection of the three central columns (though, in strict terms, the middle one is an impulse-like fragment with the somewhat enigmatic designation φ). These are classed as *eccentric* sounds whose unpredictable variation in mass disrupts any temporal unity the sound object will display. Despite their locations in the central columns, they are therefore not regarded as balanced sounds.

Naturally, each box of the diagram potentially contains a vast number of sound objects. Merely to designate a sound object with the label N would be inadequate for a composer intent on compiling a repository of sounds. Additional descriptive features are provided by the second stage of Schaeffer's program: morphology. Morphology is described in detail in the Summary Diagram of the Theory of Musical Objects.[11] Unfortunately, lack of space prevents an examination of this diagram. Schaeffer identified seven morphological criteria, although he accepted there were potentially many more. A brief summary of the seven used in his system must suffice. They are mass, harmonic timbre, dynamic, grain, allure, melodic profile, and mass profile. "Mass" was defined in the previous section, and its position in both typology and morphology indicates its importance. "Harmonic timbre" corresponds broadly to a sound's spectrum, while "dynamic" describes the sound's dynamic evolution in time. "Melodic profile" and "mass profile" refer to sound objects that vary in the pitch field. In the case of melodic profile, the whole sound moves in the pitch field, whereas with mass profile, the movement in mass is internal to the sound object. Although it is impossible in this chapter to discuss morphology in detail, two criteria are particularly noteworthy, as they are explicitly connected to real-world events: grain and allure. "Grain" describes the surface texture of a sound, which might be smooth, scintillating, or rough, and often reveals a type of facture and the material from which the sound body is constructed. Grain "leaves it signature on matter," according to Schaeffer.[12] A metal rod rubbed along the edge of a tam-tam would produce a sound object with scintillating grain. It would also indicate quite clearly the physical origins. "Allure" can be regarded as a generalization of vibrato. Schaeffer thought that "allure . . . 'reveals' the energetic agent's way of being, and very broadly whether this agent is living or not."[13] A regular, unchanging allure would imply a mechanical agent, whereas slight fluctuations (as in a violinist's vibrato) would indicate the likelihood of a living musician.

The Summary Diagram of Typology is best thought of as a map for guiding one's way through a multiplicity of sound objects rather than a neat arrangement of pigeonholes into which sound objects can be placed without ambiguity. It is a dynamic system open to flexible application and indicates how sound objects might function, depending on their structural level, and how sounds can be transformed from one type to another.

I should note that Schaeffer identified different musical languages that result from the various types of sound objects identified in the diagram. This needs some explanation. The columns of nonexistent and unpredictable factures contain sound types described as eccentric and redundant. (In strict terms, the sound types around the periphery of the diagram are eccentric; redundant types are in the top three boxes in the columns of nonexistent facture). These macro-objects should not be excluded from music, but their extended duration and the variations of features within the sound encourage the listener to perceive internal mobility. Musical meaning arises from what characteristic is perceived to vary, such as dynamic level and spectral content, as well as the type of variation in terms of speed—whether it is continuous or discontinuous and so on. It is precisely the intrinsic properties of these macro-objects that often resist comparison with real-world events. Sounds of long duration and spectral complexity are, of course, quite common in contemporary urban environments, and their inclusion in musical contexts can make them interesting as aesthetic objects. By contrast, the sound types of the middle three columns (excluding the eccentric sound objects in the bottom row) give rise to different musical languages that can be regarded as generalizations of traditional ones. These are the aforementioned nine balanced sounds. Due to the shorter durations and self-contained nature of these sound objects, they encourage the abstraction of common features such as pitch and spectral evolution. It is the process of abstraction of shared characteristics that is central to one aspect of Schaeffer's theories: permanence of characteristics/variations of values (discussed later). By abstracting a common characteristic, individual, discrete sound objects relinquish their independent status and participate in forming higher-level structures. It is the predisposition of listeners to find salience in such structures, which, moreover, are the inevitable result of sounds from physical sources such as musical instruments. It is at this point that the musical instrument and instrumental thought are, as it were, reappropriated. This is the subject of the remainder of this chapter.

Instrument

The preceding discussion of the roles of physical causality in typology and morphology may be of little more significance than acknowledging a listener's automatic and perhaps even rather naïve response to the evaluation of recorded sound objects. Does such classification and description carry any significance in musical theory other than recognizing that some appear to resemble sounds originating in the real world? The answer, I believe, can be found in the next stage of the Program of Musical Research: characterology. As Chion claims, with characterology the musician returns to the *concrete* and begins to consider not just how characteristics evolve interdependently in individual sound objects, but how they might be combined with others to form low-level and high-level structures in the act of composition.[14]

Chion's *Guide to Sound Objects* contains a subsection titled "The Instrument Found, Lost, and Found Again."[15] This is a succinct commentary on the early days of musique concrète when the musical instrument became, to put it mildly, a rather troublesome concept. It is hardly surprising that during the period of experimentation with turntables and shellac discs, Schaeffer and others continued to relate a sound to a physical sound body even within the context of listening to a recording acousmatically (as discussed earlier). For example, in *In Search of a Concrete Music* Schaeffer referred to his vision of how the composition of musique concrète might be facilitated by an "instrument" constructed of turntables. He wrote, "I've already got quite a lot of problems with my turntables because there is only one note per turntable. With a cinematographic flash-forward, Hollywood-style, I see myself surrounded by twelve dozen turntables, each with one note. Yet it would be, as mathematicians would say, *the most general musical instrument possible.*"[16] His intention was clear: he wanted a device that could produce a collection of perceptibly related sound objects comparable to those produced by traditional instruments. In the case of this generalized instrument, the sounds recorded on the discs can be thought of as substitutes for the individual keys of a piano. Dynamic levels and, to an extent, spectral content could be modified by a mixer. Needless to say, this somewhat bizarre "instrument" was never actually constructed, but it was one of Schaeffer's remarkable thought experiments. It is noteworthy that a musical principle relating physical sound sources, human perception, and musical meaning can be identified. Another example illustrates this point: in the earliest stages of his research, Schaeffer imagined "a scale of bicycle horns."[17] This implies that perception of discrete scale steps can lead to melodic structures as the listener focuses on one or two changing characteristics, such as pitch and duration. Variations in these characteristics is perceptible because other concrete features do not change, ensuring the identity of the bicycle horn remains constant. As a result, Schaeffer postulated the fundamental dualisms of permanence of variation and of value and characteristic, which were combined to give the law—permanence of characteristics/variation of values—that, he asserted, "dominates all musical phenomena."[18] In the case of the bicycle horn scale, *permanence* would be all of the features that enabled the listener to recognize the sounds' common origin. This would provide the consistent set of common characteristics, such as the dynamic envelope and spectral contents, that would facilitate the perception of pitch variations. Traditionally, permanence can be compared to an instrument's timbre. The characteristics that vary and form the melody become values. The other characteristics are secondary features, although they are still important aesthetically. This is an explicitly instrumental model and one to which Schaeffer aspired, even though the means of realizing it through technology eluded him. A better solution to the creation of a family of related sounds was eventually discovered with the invention of the phonogène commissioned by Schaeffer in 1953.[19] A recorded sound on a tape loop was placed on the capstans of the phonogène à clavier. When one depressed a key on a piano-type keyboard, the configuration of the capstans and pinch roller spindles caused tape to run at different speeds, thus changing pitch. It was ingenious as a resolution to the problem, but it proved a fleeting success. Rather than the anticipated unified family of varying sounds, the phonogène revealed that the most salient feature was the mechanical process of acceleration or deceleration. Simply shifting the entire spectrum of a recorded sound up or down in the pitch field does not create a perceptibly convincing movement within a homogeneous family. Even a small increase in pitch on a physical instrument involves subtle changes in the formants of the spectrum, which are easily detected by the ear. Having apparently found the instrument for musique concrète, it was rapidly and, I suspect, reluctantly, lost. Nevertheless, the phonogène was still used in the studio to transform sounds.

How, then, could Chion claim that the instrument was found again? In the chapter from the *Treatise* titled "The Instrumental Prerequisite," Schaeffer described another thought experiment, similar to that of the bicycle horn scale, in which an early man played a gourd. One gourd can produce a series of sounds that can be varied according to dynamic level and attack points in time. Different beaters will produce different sound shapes. Experimentation will create a larger sound repository, but in reality, little can be achieved with one gourd. An expanded vocabulary and probably a rather more sophisticated language can be achieved by playing several gourds of different sizes, thus introducing the register of pitch to which humans are particularly attuned. The permanence provided by the physical source (now a *collection* of gourds) would encourage the musician (and Schaeffer dignified the early man with the title "musician") to develop structures that displayed variety in characteristics such as pitch, dynamic levels, and so on, and these variations could be perceived precisely because they belonged to the same homogeneous gourd sound family. This is an example of *permanence of characteristics/variations of values* derived from physical causality.

Schaeffer conducted numerous experiments with musical instruments to examine the interdependence among characteristics in what are perceived as unified sound families. The best documented is the piano law.[20] Eventually, Schaeffer identified three distinctive features of the musical instrument that can be applied to all instruments, regardless of organological classification. This is "instrumental analysis," and it consisted of Schaeffer's redefinition of timbre and the related concepts of registers and play.

TIMBRE

It is clear from the previous discussions that timbre for Schaeffer differed from the most common current definition. The official (and much criticized) Acoustical Society of America definition from 1994 states that timbre is "that attribute of auditory sensation which enables a listener to judge that two non-identical sounds, similarly presented and having the same loudness and pitch, are dissimilar." This is supplemented by, "Timbre depends primarily upon the frequency spectrum, although it also depends upon the sound pressure and the temporal characteristics of the sound."[21] The reference, therefore, is principally to the spectral content of the sound, although the role of the dynamic profile is acknowledged. Schaeffer accepted the importance of spectral content, which was largely synonymous with his morphological criterion of harmonic timbre. However, he emphasized timbre's role in the perceptual formation of sources by resurrecting an earlier meaning of the word, "as a 'stamp of origin' attached to a particular object to indicate where it came from."[22] The word "timbre" is related by etymology to *tambour* in an explicit reference to source recognition. Schaefferian timbre, therefore, emphasizes the listener's capacity to perceive sounds holistically, taking into account not only the spectral and dynamic developments, but also the specific effects of the attack section. All of these features would create the impression of a source (real or virtual) activated in a particular manner.

Registers are areas of the three perceptual fields of pitch, intensity, and duration. It is in these areas that the variations of characteristics are perceived. But, as Schaeffer discovered (and as our practical experiences has shown to be true), such variations are invariably interdependent, and this has consequences for the perception of unity within a sound family's timbre. For example, identical pitches played at extremes of dynamic level on a traditional instrument will display different spectral components and attack sections. However, such changes are invariably accommodated by the listener, who nevertheless hears the sounds originating from a common source. The same type of unity will not necessarily be perceived if a recorded sound object is played back at different dynamic or pitch levels. In such cases, the lack of physical causality disrupts the interdependence, leading to what will almost certainly be an unconvincing sense of homogeneity (as Schaeffer discovered when using the phonogène).

Play is how sound objects are shaped through duration. There is an obvious reference to how musicians create numerous different kinds of articulation by interacting with the physical construction of musical instruments. We can imagine a musician playing middle C on the violin with a relatively fast-moving bow. Through careful control of the bow, the same note can be shaped with numerous attacks and dynamic envelopes while the left hand controls the rate of vibrato. Even in a musical language based primarily on pitch and duration, the subtle shaping of sounds is precisely what distinguishes individual performers. It is no less important in shaping recorded sounds for studio composers, who must also pay scrupulous attention to how sounds develop over time.

Characterology

The principal task of characterology is to study how sound objects can be perceived as unified clusters or bundles of interdependent characteristics on the model of sounds produced by physical causality. It is at this stage of Schaeffer's program that the activity of composition, properly, is addressed. As each composition will make unique demands on the creation of repositories of sound objects, a detailed exposition of characterology could not be provided in advance. By contrast with typology, where individual sound objects are scrutinized, characterology's task is to gather together sounds to produce a family consisting of related members. An example will make this clear: if a composer decides to create a structure from a succession of discrete pitches (of any tuning system), general consistency among the sounds is required to facilitate pitch discrimination. If the sounds are too dissimilar, they might exist as individual, rather than related, sound objects, weakening any sense of a unified structure. Thus, in a family of *metallic percussion-resonance* sound objects, changing the pitch levels might not guarantee the homogeneity that is needed to make pitch the most salient characteristic. Delicate adjustments, as previously described in registers and play, will probably be required to adjust spectral and dynamic evolutions at extremes of the pitch field. These families of related sound objects were called *genres* by Schaeffer. According to Chion, "*Genre*, therefore, replaces instrumental *timbre*" in the sense of relating sounds to a common origin.[23] Self-evidently, genres are precisely what musical instruments produce, though we must remember that most will produce more than one genre. Violinists can play pizzicato as well as arco. But did Schaeffer, by some sleight of hand, simply replace one concept (instrumental timbre) with another (genre)? What practical purpose does the concept of genre serve? In the provided example of *metallic percussion-resonance* sound objects, it might become clear to the composer that structures displaying stability or a sense of direction are undermined due to gaps in the pitch registers. Consequently, it might be difficult, if not impossible, to make smooth transitions from low-register sounds to those in higher registers. Moreover, the attacks of certain sounds or their spectral content may also require adjustment to maintain the genre's consistency.

Identifying such anomalies involves Schaeffer's stage of *analysis*. The creation of new sound objects to correct these irregularities is *synthesis*. But here we should note that Schaefferian synthesis was founded on acute aural investigation provided by the Program of Musical Research as a whole. (This can be contrasted with synthesis based on predetermined serial schemes.) Fabricating genres in the studio involves precisely the kind of musicality that is required when playing a musical instrument. There are differences, of course. First, this new form of musicality is achieved by using equipment rather than relying on the given features of an instrument. Second, unlike instrumental play, in acousmatic music on fixed media such musicality cannot be expressed by modifying sounds in real time (although real time transformation is now viable with the increased processing power of contemporary digital computers). The composer is now engaged in the making of virtual instruments (Schaeffer called them "pseudo-instruments"), with different, perhaps imaginary, materials and methods of excitation, as referred to earlier in the chapter. Thus, a genre is a generalization of the notion of instrumental timbre, but because it is entirely artificial, the composer can explore the variation of sound characteristics in a multidimensional manner.

The example of a *metallic percussion-resonance* genre was deliberately simple, even rather traditional. Varying discrete pitches and durations can be thought of as a relatively commonplace kind of musical discourse. If several completely different genres were to occupy the same area of the pitch field, then the listener might follow the variations within a particular one with difficulty: virtual instruments will demand virtual orchestration. Schaefferian genres are porous and susceptible to reappraisal according to listening intentions, and this, of course, is their advantage. They are multidimensional perceptual constructs that can be in a state of flux as their individual elements shift and reconfigure. A genre may split as individual sounds that are related in one area of the pitch field begin to diverge as they ascend or descend. Metallic genres can morph into wooden or ceramic genres. Given Schaeffer's insistence on separating the sound event from its causal origins, it is unnecessary to imagine real sound bodies (although such anecdotal reference may be the reaction of some listeners). The success (or not) of creating homogeneity will depend on the composer's control of registers and play as structures are formed that are difficult, if not impossible, to create from real instruments. Consequently, genres can suggest real-world sources; they can extend or subvert them; and they can present us with hybrid or even completely unimaginable sources.

Conclusion

Schaeffer's advice to hear the "in-itself-ness" of sounds does not, in my opinion, mean that he intended this process to be isolated from the listener's knowledge of how materials and objects behave in the physical world. His proposal involved a much more nuanced understanding of the nature of human perception—its interaction with sonic information and the extent to which the sound source and, in particular, the musical instrument, still plays an important role in our comprehension and appreciation of musical languages. I would argue, therefore, that (to repeat Chion's phrase) the instrument was indeed found again through Schaefferian characterology, although this time it was in a virtual form. This rediscovery has implications not only for electroacoustic music but also for music in general.

For example, eccentric and redundant sounds challenge traditional instrumental associations. We should note from the Summary Diagram of Typology that the sound types most closely related to instrumental sounds are placed in the central boxes of balanced sounds (see figure 2.1). It is the extended durations, complex spectral behavior, and nonexistent or unpredictable factures of eccentric and redundant sound types that result in their classification in the outer columns and rows of the diagram. Contemporary instrumental music can furnish many examples of such sounds, frequently achieved by careful orchestration. György Ligeti, Iannis Xenakis, Karlheinz Stockhausen, Luciano Berio, and, more recently, Helmut Lachenmann have composed works in which continuous variations within sounds or unpredictable factures assume important form-creating functions. I would not claim that these composers are directly influenced by Schaeffer's system. Nevertheless, a common concern with the sculpting of spectral and dynamic evolutions can be detected. Any analytical-theoretical attempts to examine compositions using these vocabularies will benefit greatly from Schaeffer's typology and morphology, as well as from his concept of variation/texture. Furthermore, new insights into the communicative aspects of playing an instrument can be developed. This is particularly true of virtuosity and even embodiment. Consequently, during a performance of a piano work—"live" or recorded—a listener is, of course, always aware of the pianist's technique. But it is often only by a conscious effort that the physical construction of the piano is recalled: hammers hitting strings; the instrument's resonance controlled by the keys, pedals, and soundboard. The instrument recedes into the background, as it were, as the structures emerging from the notes themselves demand our attention.

However, such attitudes are not mutually exclusive. There are occasions, such as listening to extended techniques, in which the instrument itself and how it is played come to the foreground as we become acutely aware of the physical actions of the musician interacting with an object, albeit an extremely sophisticated object, that combines aspects of both culture and nature. Single notes played on the piano, for example, will be produced in a different physical manner from fist or forearm clusters. Thus, the musical language will have to accommodate the range of possibilities between N-type and X-type sound objects. The Summary Diagram of Typology illustrates this migration from one area of the sonic universe to another. The implications for the role of the musical instrument not only for realizing known musical languages, but also for developing new ones, are profound. This is perhaps the most significant contribution of Schaeffer's reappropriation of the sound source. His redefined concepts of timbre, registers, and play are rooted in physical causality, but in their generalized states, they can reveal new relationships of pitch, texture, articulation, and color in instrumental music. In electroacoustic music, the use of virtual sources opens up a poetic domain in which genres can change identity to coalesce or splinter. Events in the real world can be alluded to or sounds can behave in ways that defy our understanding. Such access to the world of aural imagination is perhaps Schaeffer's most enduring legacy.

Notes

1 In this chapter I refer to Michel Chion, *Guide to Sound Objects*, trans. Christine North and John Dack, 2009, accessed March 1, 2017, http://ears.pierrecouprie .fr/spip.php?article3597; Schaeffer, *In Search of a Concrete Music*; Schaeffer, *Treatise on Musical Objects*. References in the text are to the English translation; in the notes, these citations are followed by the reference to the original French publication.

2 Schaeffer, *In Search of a Concrete Music*, 13; Schaeffer, *A la recherche d'une musique concrète*, 21.

3 Smalley's concept of surrogacy is relevant here: see Smalley, "Spectromorphology."

4 An acousmatic situation occurs when a sound is heard without visual corroboration of its causal origin. The full significance of acousmatic listening becomes evident when the sound is unrecognizable. The perceiver is then forced to scrutinize the sound *for itself*, without reference to possible causes.

5 "Le studio n'est pas un instrument": Chion and Reibel, *Les musiques électroacoustiques*, 240.

6 Schaeffer, *Treatise on Musical Objects*, xxxvii–ix. "Dans cette complémentarité des moyens naturellement donnés et des structures culturelles, on verrait alors se résoudre nombre d'oppositions superficielles, celle des anciens et des modernes, celle des arts et des sciences, celle du sonore et du musical": Schaeffer, *Traité des objets musicaux*, 10–11.

7 The sound object is a construct, a relationship between subject and object, the listener's perception and the sound under consideration. Thus, it is not the sound body; nor is it the sound signal. A sound heard for itself, by means of the intentional act of reduced listening, disregarding the origin (assuming this can be identified) or its social/cultural meaning, is a sound object.

8 Consistent with his dualistic manner of thinking, Schaeffer uses four pairs of criteria in the construction of the Summary Diagram of Typology. They are articulation and stress, mass and facture, duration and variation, and balance and originality.

9 "Facture" is a common term in fine art. It refers, for example, to the visible effects of brush strokes imprinted in thick oil paint applied to a canvas. The paint reveals a trace of the artist's energetic gesture.

10 Schaeffer, *Treatise on Musical Objects*, 361. "Les colonnes extrêmes de notre tableau se rejoignent ainsi à la limite": Schaeffer, *Traité des objets musicaux*, 454.

11 Schaeffer, *Treatise on Musical Objects*, 464–67; Schaeffer, *Traité des objets musicaux*, 584–87.

12 Schaeffer, *Treatise on Musical Objects*, 438. "Le grain 'signe' la matière": Schaeffer, *Traité des objets musicaux*, 550.

13 Schaeffer, *Treatise on Musical Objects*, 438. "L'allure . . . 'révèle' la façon d'être de l'agent énergétique et, d'une façon très générale, si cet agent est vivant ou non": Schaeffer, *Traité des objets musicaux*, 550.

14 Chion, *Guide to Sound Objects*, 114; Chion, *Guide des objets sonores*, 103.

15 Chion, *Guide to Sound Objects*, 56. "L'instrument trouvé, perdu et retrouvé": Chion, *Guide des objets sonores*, 54.

16 Schaeffer, *In Search of a Concrete Music*, 7. "Me voilà assez en peine avec mes tourne-disques, à raison d'une note par tourne-disque. Dans une anticipation cinématographique, à la manière de Hollywood, je me vois entouré de douze douzaines de tourne-disques, chacun à une note. Ce serait enfin, comme diraient les mathématiciens, l'instrument de musique *le plus general qui soit*": Schaeffer, *A la recherche d'une musique concrète*, 15.

17 Schaeffer, *In Search of a Concrete Music*, 4. "J'imagine une gamme de trompes": Schaeffer, *A la recherche d'une musique concrète*, 12.

18 Schaeffer, *Treatise on Musical Objects*, 31. "Qui domine l'ensemble des phénomènes musicaux": Schaeffer, *Traité des objets musicaux*, 51.

19 There were three phonogènes: the *phonogène à clavier*, the *phonogène à coulisses*, and the *phonogène universel*.

20 Schaeffer, *Treatise on Musical Objects*, 182; Schaeffer, *Traité des objets musicaux*, 234.

21 Standards Secretariat, Acoustical Society of America, *Acoustical Terminology* ANSI S1.1-1994, revision of ANSI S.1.1-1960 (R 1976), approved January 4, 1994.

22 Schaeffer, *Treatise on Musical Objects*, 34. "Comme 'marque d'origine' apposée sur tel ou tel objet pour indiquer sa provenance": Schaeffer, *Traité des objets musicaux*, 55.

23 Chion, *Guide to Sound Objects*, 114. "Le *genre* remplacerait alors le *timbre* des instruments": Chion, *Guide des objets sonores*, 104.

The Fluctuating Sound Object

In this chapter, I want to consider the "sound object" in both ontological and historical terms, paradoxical as that ambition may seem. In its classical sense, ontology is impervious to history since it establishes the transcendental conditions assumed by the unfolding of historical forces. In this view, history is, at most, the location where ontology is either disclosed or occluded, where what was always already present is coyly veiled or boldly revealed. Such a view asserts over and over that incorrigible ontology is outside of history. But what if this play, this hiding and seeking, were not simply the surface effect of an unchanging ontological "real" but the very process by which ontology came into being? If so, the history of the "sound object"—the history of its fluctuations in meaning—might tell us something about the fluctuating ontology of sound, not by disclosing it, but by tracing the use to which its ontology is put.

The Birth of the Sound Object

Origin stories gain currency through repetition, and the origin story of *musique concrète* is no different. It has been told again and again in various histories of the musical avant-garde, in books on the theory and practice of electronic music, in recent works of sound studies, and in critical writings on sound art.

Pierre Schaeffer, the inventor of musique concrète, was fond of repeating it. Let us hear him tell it once again:

> It was around 1948, having had already considerable experience with texts and sound in radio, that I wished to go further, to do a program without words, with music entirely composed of "noises," that is, sounds not made by musical instruments or by the human voice. I was up against a brick wall. When one wants to do something solely with noises, one has to make a drastic choice. For there are two possibilities: either one does or does not tell a story with noises; when one does not, one takes sounds for their intrinsic qualities and then the relationships between them give a kind of music. Actually, I did not then dare to call this "music," for it was too unusual when compared to classical music. Therefore, I finally called it "concrete" music to indicate it was not of traditional conception—instruments, notation, composing—but that it consisted of recorded sounds not produced by especially designed musical instruments or by voice.[1]

The story always follows a well-trodden path.[2] Schaeffer's desire to produce a "symphony of noises" leads him to a musical conundrum: either allow noises to reveal their mundane sources, and thus retain their anecdotal signification, or find a way to work with sounds such that their "intrinsic qualities" become audible and thus amenable to being combined into new "musical" relationships. On the way, two discoveries are made. First, when working with a recording of a bell, Schaeffer notices that, through keen manipulation of the potentiometer alone, one can remove its attack and compensate for its reduction in intensity: "The bell becomes an oboe sound."[3] By means of this discovery—the "cut bell," or *cloche coupée*—the source of the sound suddenly vanishes, and the sound itself becomes capable of manipulation and transformation. Second, by repeating a sound over and over, the sound seems to lose its anecdotal character. Like a word drained of its signification by being uttered again and again, a sound's repetition drains it of reference to its mundane source or cause, thereby disclosing its intrinsic qualities. By producing a special closed-groove phonograph disc, or *sillon fermé*, a sound of short duration could be infinitely repeated, shedding its signification, and then integrated into organized musical phrases. With these two discoveries in hand, the intrepid engineer/composer then goes on to compose his first works of musique concrète.

This story is not only an origin story of the birth of musique concrète. It is also the origin story of the *objet sonore*, or the "sound object." It, too, follows a well-trodden path. Two discoveries in the studio—the cloche coupée and the sillon fermé—facilitate the birth of musique concrète by creating the conditions by which the source of a sound can be distinguished from its "intrinsic qualities." The latter, to speak quite reductively, are designated by the term "objet sonore." The sound object, one might say, separates a sound's "intrinsic qualities" from its indexical signification of its physical-causal source. Of course, such a distinction between sound and source was already common in music theory, where the instrumental source of a sound is distinguished from the tones it produces. But Schaeffer's work in the studio brought this distinction to so-called nonmusical sounds, what Schaeffer sometimes calls "noises." The sound object then replaces the term "note" or "tone" in Schaeffer's new music theory, a theory appropriate for *concrète* compositions.

Most accounts of the twinned origins of musique concrète and the objet sonore—like the one I have just repeated—overlook a peculiar detail in Schaeffer's journals covering the period, published as part 1 of *In Search of a Concrete Music*—namely, the sound object's referent changed quite drastically across the interval between Schaeffer's initial desire to create a "symphony of noises" and his first *concrete studies*. The trajectory of the term over the course of 1948 is revealing. After collecting a wild assortment of sound-producing objects with which to build his "symphony," Schaeffer's writes the following in a journal entry simply dated "March": "Back in Paris I have started to collect objects [*objets*]. I have a 'Symphony of noises' in mind."[4] Here, an "object" refers to a physical-material thing—a source for the production of sound. By April, once Schaeffer had decided to move into the booth of the studio to manipulate his recordings of objets, rather than the objects themselves, the term acquired a modifier. It is now called an "objet sonore," though the term still refers to the physical-material source, not the effect of the sound: "I am amongst the turn-tables, the mixer, the potentiometers. . . . I operate through intermediaries. I no longer manipulate sound objects [*objets sonores*] myself. I listen to their effect through the microphone."[5]

By early May, Schaeffer had begun to work with recordings of trains made at the Batignolles station, which would form the basis of his famous *Étude aux chemins de fer*. The sound object (*objet sonore*) is supplemented with a new term, the "sound fragment" (*fragment sonore*). Unlike the physical-material sound object, a fragment sonore designates a bit of recorded sound, the "effect" emitted from a sound object and engraved into the spiral groove of a phonographic disc: "I lower the pick-up arm as one rhythmic group starts. I raise it just as it ends, I link it with another and so on. How powerful our imagination is! When in our minds we pick out a certain rhythmic or melodic outline in a sound fragment like this, we think we have its musical element."[6] A few days later, Schaeffer exploits the infinite repeatability of the fragment to distinguish it from the sound object, the physical-material cause: "Repeat the same sound fragment twice: there is no longer event, but music."[7] Crystallized by the discovery of the sillon fermé, repetition turns the sound fragment into music by removing the banal and anecdotal traces of its original causal context.

By May 15, Schaeffer's work with both bells and trains had led to a generic conclusion about the sound fragment: "For the 'concrete' musician there is no difference between the cut bell and the piece of train: they are 'sound fragments.'"[8] A sound fragment (*fragment sonore*) is a bit of recorded raw material for the composer to manipulate in the recording booth—a sample. Yet in the very same entry, the objet sonore returns, albeit transformed, to reassert its priority. Schaeffer writes: "I have coined the term *Musique Concrète* for this desire to compose with materials taken from 'given' experimental sound in order to emphasize our dependence, no longer on preconceived sound abstractions, but on sound fragments [*fragments sonores*] which exist in reality, and which are considered as discrete and complete sound objects [*objets sonores*], even and above all when they do not fit in with the elementary definitions of music theory."[9] Here, the objet sonore no longer designates the material-physical cause of the sound in distinction to the effect, captured on disc. It has leapfrogged over the sound fragment to assume a new significance. More than simply a bit of recorded sound or sample, the sound object now suggestively designates something "discrete and complete," an apprehension of fragments sonores that parses the fragment into integral units and (to apply Schaeffer's description anachronistically) attends to the sound's "intrinsic qualities."

Schaeffer would continue to develop his theory of the objet sonore until the publication of his *Traité des objets musicaux*, in 1966, eventually characterizing it as an "intentional object" and offering a phenomenological theory (greatly indebted to Husserl) of its nature and essence.[10] Before getting too far afield, I want to underscore one simple fact. For a few months in 1948, the term "objet sonore" fluctuated in its meaning. While it first designated the physical-causal source of a sound, to be recorded and manipulated in the studio, it ended up designating a sound apart from all reference to its physical-causal source. The "sound object" shifted from a sounded object to an object's sound.

This shift in the reference should be understood as more than just a philological issue about how Schaeffer eventually stipulated the meaning of his terminology. Rather, the term "objet sonore" has a history of usage in French that precedes Schaeffer and that, I would argue, is reflected in his fluctuation. To open up the archive and examine the term's past usage casts this fluctuation in a new light.

Let me offer a few historical examples—samples, if you will—of the meaning of the term before Schaeffer:

1   First, a passage from Jean-Baptiste le Rond d'Alembert's entry on "Pression" in the *Encyclopédie*: "When waves that form on the surface of water encounter some obstacle they break up, dilate, and spread across the stagnant and tranquil water behind the obstacle. Vibrations and, so to speak, waves in the air that form sound [*le son*], spread in the same way; for the sound [*le son*] of a bell or a canon can be heard behind a mountain which hides the sounding object [*objet sonore*] from our view."[11] In this passage, the "objet sonore" is contrasted with the "son." The sound (*le son*) of a bell or a canon can still be heard even when the sounding object (*objet sonore*) is not visible. By distinguishing the sound heard from the source of the sound, d'Alembert draws a sharp contrast not only between seeing and hearing, but also between a sounding object and the sounds it emits. The latter is labeled "son," while the object, hidden from view, is labeled "objet sonore."

2   D'Alembert's usage was preserved far into the nineteenth century. Charles Dunan, a professor of philosophy, published *Théorie psychologique de l'espace* in 1895, which includes the following passage: "There is no immediate and evident connection between a sound [*son*] and a sounding object [*objet sonore*]. The two things are so little bound together that the first is transitory and the second is permanent."[12] Again, the same contrast is drawn between the "son" and the "objet sonore." Whether or not one accepts Dunan's claim about the lack of immediate and evident connection between the "son" and the "objet sonore," his claim specifies the meaning of these terms by noting that the "son" is transitory, while the "objet sonore" is permanent. The transience of sound waves and their perception is contrasted with the permanence of physical entities.

3   There is this little piece of braggadocio from Camille Saint-Saëns's memoirs: "In my childhood, I had a very delicate ear and people often amused themselves by making me name the note [*la note*] produced by this or that sounding object [*objet sonore*], lamp, glass, or receptacle. When someone asked me what note a bell produced, I always responded: 'It does not make a note, it makes several.'"[13] Instead of contrasting the objet sonore with the sound [*son*], Saint-Saëns contrasts it with the note. The objet sonore is included in a series of sound-producing objects, such as lamps, glasses, and bells. In no case is the objet sonore aligned with the sound itself or the tone produced by such objects. Saint-Saëns's passage underscores just how surprising Schaeffer's use of the objet sonore as a replacement for the note is in his *solfège* of musique concrète.

Needless to say, many more examples could be found in the archive. My point is simply to suggest that "objet sonore" had a well-established meaning in French before Schaeffer. It designated the source of a sound and not the sound itself. *Le son, le bruit,* or *la note* designated the latter. Moreover, this older usage is reflected in Schaeffer's diaries. Thus, Schaeffer documents more than just the origin story of musique concrète or the objet sonore as a theoretical entity over the course of a few months in 1948; he also documents the attempt to alter the designation of the term "objet sonore" altogether. Schaeffer is working against the linguistic conventions registered by his initial usage to designate his particular object of study.

This is significant because Schaeffer's writings demonstrate his close attention to the historical use of language, often mining the history of the French language to discover new technical terms or expose the impoverishment of terms to describe sound. One example is the famous definition of "acousmatic" from Larousse that Schaeffer critically considers in the *Traité*.[14] Another appears in the article "Sound and Communication," from 1973.[15] There Schaeffer examines historical definitions of the word "son" and notes an important ambiguity. "Son" does not clearly distinguish the physical vibration produced by an object from the listener's perception; it covers "acceptations as widely varying and objects as distinct as physical or sensorial sound and psychological sound, and even thus do our contemporaries express themselves, passing spontaneously from one sense to the other without giving and warning."[16] In other words, it confuses the distinction between *l'acoustique* and *l'acousmatique* by allowing naturalistic and scientific notions of sound to clutter its phenomenological and psychological parallels. The introduction and redesignation of the *objet sonore* aimed to pry apart the ambiguity of the term "son" by clearly differentiating sound as physical, acoustic vibration from sound as an object of perception alone.

Yet this redesignation of the *objet sonore* leads to an unintended paradox. It resolves the ambiguity of the word "son" only by reintroducing an ambiguity of its own. If we take both the historical meaning and Schaeffer's meaning into consideration, then "objet sonore" appears to designate two distinct things that are often counterpoised: the source of a sound *and* the sound emitted. While the historical contrast between "son" and "objet sonore" kept the latter term squarely aligned with the physical source of the sound, Schaeffer's promotion of the term loosens this constraint and unwittingly expands its meaning such that it ambiguously crosses the threshold between objects and subjects, outer and inner, physics and phenomenology. Perhaps it is simply a problem of trying to get three distinct things classed under two concepts. We can either isolate the sounding object (*objet sonore*) from the sound *qua* vibration and the sound *qua* percept (*le son*), or we can isolate the sound *qua* vibration (*le son*) from the sounding object and the sound *qua* percept (*objet sonore*). But we cannot isolate all three moments without introducing another technical term.

Sound Object, Sonic Object, Sonorous Object

"Objet sonore" has been variously translated into English as "sound object," "sonic object," and "sonorous object." However, the ambiguity of "objet sonore" does not appear to persist in translation. The main reason is that these translations, with a few exceptions, began to appear in English after 1950, primarily in publications concerned with the musical avant-garde, electronic music, and musique concrète. In other words, they derive from Schaeffer's usage. In English, these terms lack the same linguistic history that makes the meaning of "objet sonore" ambiguous.[17]

Again, I offer a few samples from the archive:

1   *Sound object.* The earliest English-language reception of Schaeffer's ideas renders *objet sonore* as "sound object." For example, the word appears in Schaeffer's "Note on Time Relationships," published in English in 1960 in the *Gravesano Review*.[18] However, by the late 1950s, "sound object" was already in use by avant-garde composers.

Vladimir Ussachevsky published an introductory essay about tape as a compositional medium in an issue of the *Juilliard Review* in 1959. One of the founders of the Columbia-Princeton Electronic Music Center, Ussachevsky was heavily involved with "tape music" and had firsthand familiarity with Schaeffer's studio, works, and ideas. He explicitly employs the term "sound object" when discussing the techniques and theories of musique concrète. According to Ussachevsky, composers of musique concrète often "reduce complex sounds to a more simple form" or build up "more complex textures through multiple superimpositions" of simple elements: "Loops of tape, up to a few feet in diameter, containing what is known as a 'sound object,' are often used for this purpose."[19]

Surprisingly enough, Pierre Boulez uses the term in his famous essay "At the Ends of the Fruitful Land . . ."[20] After spending a brief period in Schaeffer's studio in the early 1950s, Boulez harshly rejected musique concrète for, among other things, its lack of rigor. Yet Boulez continued to employ Schaeffer's terminology in print, even while neglecting to mention Schaeffer or musique concrète—a conspicuous slight.[21] He writes, "If we wish to make any progress in the methods of working with sound objects, the idea of the series must be extended to include the primary interactions of temporal phenomena resulting either from the differences between manner of organization arising from the objects themselves or from within a single family of objects deduced one from another." Such a way of using "sound objects" is much more descriptive of Boulez's own application of serial operations to recorded sound, as in his *1st Étude* and *2nd Étude*, than to the "surrealist" method of Schaeffer and Pierre Henry's early collaborations, such as the *Symphonie pour un homme seul* or *Orphée*.

In 1964, the American composer James Tenney devoted a handful of pages in *Meta+Hodos* to Schaeffer and his ideas, specifically engaging with the objet sonore, which he translated as "sound-object." Tenney contrasts the phenomenological and gestaltist theory developed in *Meta+Hodos* with Schaeffer's "operational" approach, which is primarily restricted (in Tenney's characterization) to the "particular medium with which he is working"—that is, tape-based musique concrète. "Schaeffer's definitions refer less to the perceptual events in the music (or rather, in the musical experience)," he writes, "than to the physical or acoustic materials that are manipulated in the process of composition."[22] In *Meta+Hodos* Tenney's understanding of Schaeffer, relying solely on the early *In Search of a Concrete Music* and its diaristic and essayistic formulations, seems to confuse the objet sonore with the fragment sonore. What is fascinating about this little bit of *méconnaissance* is that Tenney and Schaeffer were developing phenomenological approaches to contemporary music simultaneously, but apparently, despite such parallel developments, they did not inform each other's research.

2   *Sonic object.* Before the publication of Schaeffer's *Traité*, the most precise definition of "objet sonore" available appeared in the final chapter of *A la recherche d'une musique concrète*, which Schaeffer co-wrote with the information theorist Abraham Moles. Moles, who spent much of the 1950s working in Hermann Scherchen's Experimental Studio Gravesano, was a frequent visitor to Schaeffer's weekly meetings with his research associates.[23] While Schaeffer's eventual approach to the objet sonore would be grounded in Husserlian phenomenology, Moles continued to develop an information-theoretical approach to sound and new music and published his findings in the book *Thèorie de l'information et perception esthétique* (1958). In the English translation, *Information Theory and Esthetic Perception* (1966), the term "objet sonore" is translated as "sonic object."[24] Moles establishes various laws governing the internal structure of the sonic object, then considers the perception of such objects both in isolation and when organized into larger sequences. The sonic object forms the cornerstone for a listener-oriented music theory intended to bridge the gap among tonal, post-tonal, and electronic music.

3   *Sonorous object.* The most literal translation of "objet sonore," and the most awkward in English, is "sonorous object." It appears throughout Colin J. Norris's clunky translation of Schaeffer's article "Son et communication."[25] In a section that revisits the famous four modes (*fonctions*) of listening (described in the *Traité*), Schaeffer observes the various ways that the sonorous object is perceived according to each mode. In Schaeffer's privileged third mode of *entendre*—inelegantly rendered as "hearkening"—a "number of listeners gathered around a tape-recorder" hear one and the same sonorous object. However, they "do not all hear the same thing, do not select and appreciate it in the same way. . . . And yet, the single sonorous object which renders possible this multiplicity of qualified aspects of the

object, remains in the form of a sort of halo of perceptions to which the explicit qualifications implicitly refer."[26] Here we get a glimpse of Schaeffer's phenomenology: despite the ways that different listeners qualify the sonorous object (i.e., despite their distinct noetic acts), they all refer to one and the same intentional object (*noema*).

Affirming Schaeffer, Rejecting the Sound Object

The term "sound object," in general terms, made its way into English with its Schaefferian sense intact, and most commentators on Schaeffer today do not dispute its meaning. Rather they argue that, by forcing sound under the form of an object, "sound object" promotes the wrong kind of sonic ontology. Sound is not an object but an event, matter, or flux. Some, such as R. Murray Schafer, dismiss Pierre Schaeffer by means of a critical assessment of the sound object. Schafer calls it a "laboratory specimen." His preference is for "sound events," which implies the inseparability of sounds from their contexts because an event is "something that occurs in a certain place during a particular interval of time." Sound events, unlike sound objects, are denatured when removed from that place and time.[27] Others affirm the general outlines of Schaeffer's project but revise the notion of the sound object quite dramatically.[28] I offer a few thumbnail sketches of the latter:

1   Christoph Cox, in his writings on sound art, often argues against the notion that sound is an object in favor of an ontology of sonic flux. In his particular form of philosophical naturalism, which owes much to a Deleuzian-inspired reading of Schopenhauer and Nietzsche, nature is described as a series of differential flows. However, among these various natural flows, the flow of sound is privileged.[29] "The sonic flux," asserts Cox, "is not just one flow among many; it deserves special status insofar as it so elegantly and forcefully models and manifests the myriad fluxes that constitute the natural world."[30] The ontology of sonic flux emphasizes sound's temporality and transitory nature. Sounds are "intangible, ephemeral, and invisible." Such a "flux ontology replaces objects with *events*"—or, rather, undermines them, because "objects" are "merely temporary concretions of fluid processes." At the same time, Cox claims that sounds are "real and mind-independent," reducible neither to secondary qualities relative to their observers nor to properties of the sources that cause or

generate them. To argue for the realism of sonic flows, Cox appeals to Schaeffer. *Les objets sonores*, as patiently argued in the *Traité*, are intentional objects, and Schaeffer's argument for their realism follows the lines of Husserl's argument for the reality of noemata.[31] Cox writes, "Pierre Schaeffer (the father of *musique concrète* and one of the progenitors of sound art) aimed to show in his analysis of the *objet sonore* [that] the sonorous object has a peculiar existence distinct from the instrument that produces it, the medium in or on which it exists, and the mind of the listener." Sounds are "ontological particulars and individuals." At the same time, Cox's appeal is qualified: Schaeffer "misses the mark" by calling sounds "objects," because "sounds are peculiarly temporal and durational, tied to the qualities they exhibit over time. If sounds are particulars or individuals, then they are not as static *objects* but as temporal *events*."

To understand the consequences of Cox's replacement of the sound object with the sound event, it is fruitful to revisit Schaeffer's analysis of *son* (sound) and its ambiguity. As noted earlier, "son" does not clearly distinguish the physical vibration produced by an object from the listener's perception. The introduction of the objet sonore helped dissolve this ambiguity. The Schaefferian sound object is not the physical, acoustical event but the objective correlate of the listener's perception. It is distinct from the physical world and properly studied by the science of acousmatics, not acoustics. But Cox's sound event reverses this situation. His anti-representational critique downplays the role of human perception (negatively characterized as anthropomorphism or "correlationism") in favor of the differential fluxes and flows that "constitute the natural world." The primacy of perception in Schaeffer's account is devalued in favor of a sonic ontology of material, physical, acoustic events—fluxes, flows, and vibrations indifferent to their perception. While Cox appeals to Schaeffer for his realism about sound, he is not very precise about the kind of reality that is affirmed by their competing forms of realism. The reality of intentional objects is not the same as the reality of fluxes of flows. Sound objects-qua-intentional objects are immaterial; Cox's flux ontology is explicitly materialist. In the end, one must wonder what it is about Schaeffer's theory that Cox finds appealing.

2   The sound artist Francisco López often mentions the important influence of Schaeffer's thinking on his work. Recoiling against John

Cage's automatic inclusion of all sounds into the domain of music, López maintains a distinction between sound and music by claiming that music is not simply organized sound (even sound organized by chance); music is, rather, sufficiently constituted by a special mode of listening—that is, Schaefferian reduced listening, which López rebrands as "profound listening." Any sound becomes musical when intentionally auditioned for its own intrinsic properties, no longer functioning as an index or an icon. This happens through the specific act of profound listening. López's work challenges the listener's capacity for profound listening by employing sonic materials that are extraordinarily resistant to it, such as field recordings of rain forests, buildings, and wind. These materials initially resist profound listening because they are so replete with indexical and iconic signs. What López finds of value in these environments is not a complex ecosystem of acoustic communication but, rather, a richness of densely layered sonic matter. "In my conception," writes López, "the essence of sound recording is not that of documenting or representing a much richer and more significant world, but a way to focus on and access the inner world of sounds. When the representational/ relational level is emphasized, sounds acquire a restricted meaning or a goal, and this inner world is dissipated."[32] While affirming "the original 'sound object' concept of P[ierre] Schaeffer," López, like Cox, modifies the terminology. "I prefer the term 'matter,' instead of 'object,' because I think it better reflects the continuity of the sonic entities that is at the basis of the non-representational conception [of sound recording] and also of the very nature of sound environments." Again, discomfort with the term "sound objects" arises from its inability to express the continuous, temporal aspect of sound.

But what kind of matter is sound? It is at this point that we must distinguish Cox from López. Sound, for Cox, is a mind-independent flux or flow that overflows human forms of perception and representation. Cox's materialism evades the human; it is more akin to the vibrational or material fact of acoustic events, which can be registered apart from human perception. In contrast, López considers sound matter from within the state of profound listening. His materialism emphasizes not physics but phenomenology; if sound is a kind of matter, it is inseparable from perception's very own materiality. The materiality of sound, when heard profoundly, is nothing other than the materiality of phenomenality.

These competing views of sonic matter are brought into sharp relief when Cox considers López's *Wind (Patagonia)* from 2007. The piece presents an hour-long recording of wind as it blows across the Patagonian landscape. Like many of López's pieces, the recordings are unprocessed, presenting to the listener—at first glance—something akin to pure field recording. But to hear them as field recordings would be to mishear them, at least if we follow López's intention, because this would attend to the ostensible subject matter of the piece, wind, and thus be inattentive to the "inner world of sound." The titles of many of López's works—such as *La Selva*, *Buildings (New York)*, and *Wind (Patagonia)*—are tantalizing clues that, in the end, he intends for listeners to disregard. If one listens to these works under the spell of profound listening, such indexical and iconic signs are irrelevant. The point is to listen in a way that brackets signification and representation to attend to the "sound matter" alone. But Cox hears something very different:

> The piece as a whole focuses on the very medium of sonic transport—*air*—and highlights the fact that sound is simply the result of pressure changes in that medium. Its subject matter—wind—is the most elemental of all phenomena and the most primeval sonic stuff. Wind is powerful, invisible and ever-changing. To focus on it is to transcend the limits of our ordinary ontology, composed as it is of relatively stable visible objects. For wind is pure becoming, pure flow. It is immemorial, but never the same. And it is nothing but the play of differential forces, differences in air pressure and temperature that generate immense currents, fronts and bursts across the surface of the earth–phenomena that are contracted by our ears (and by the microphone membrane) as sound.[33]

Cox's listening thematizes the "subject matter" of the piece, wind, but not the sounds produced or heard. Instead, the sounds are heard as manifestations (or indices) of the physical phenomenon of pressure changes in the air. They encourage a reflection on the role of air as an acoustical medium for sound and on ears as physiological transducers. His interpretation is less about the specific sound of the wind than the way that wind embodies the general conditions of sound production altogether. Wind plays a dual role: it is both the subject matter of the piece and an instance of the kind of material events that interest Cox. Wind both "models and manifests" natural fluxes and flows. Thus, for Cox, *Wind (Patagonia)* exemplifies his larger philosophical commitments—moving from the motion of the wind to an ontological account about the primacy of events over objects, the sonic over the visual, flux over stasis, and matter over representation.

Ontology Is an Appeal, Not the Real

What are we to make of such qualified affirmation of Schaeffer and such discomfort with the ontology of the sound object? As a replacement for "sound object," "sound event" and "sonic matter" do not offer much assistance. While they shift the focus to sound's temporality, process, ephemerality, and the like, such substitutions seem to miss that fact that Schaeffer quite explicitly considered the temporal continuity of sounds in his analyses of the sound object. In the *Traité*, Schaeffer's exposition leading up to the *Tableau récapitulative de la typologie* (Summary Diagram of Typology) explicitly considers the challenge of finding "suitable" temporal boundaries of the sound object.[34] The sound object can be neither too short nor too long, somewhere between an impulse and a "macro-object." Too short and the object vanishes; too long and it seems to fragment into many objects.

Schaeffer is deeply concerned with the relationship between the sound's transitory temporality and the perception of its unity, and he tries to formulate simple guidelines for parsing sound objects from the flow of the auditory stream. One such rule is the "stress-articulation" rule, which looks for boundaries at moments where there is a break in the energy output of a sound continuum. By so doing, the rule offers a way to parse diverse auditory streams into comparable units (modeled on linguistic phonemes) that do not depend on any knowledge of the source of the sound.[35]

In this respect, Schaeffer's notion of the sound object recognizes the tension inherent in any philosophy of time, balanced as it is between event-like flow and object-like individuation. While Schaeffer's work tends to consider such heady philosophical themes in practical terms—those directed at the production of musique concrète and its solfège—they are also reflected in this passage from Husserl's *Idea of Phenomenology*, which Schaeffer affirmatively quotes:

> If we look closer and notice how in the mental process, say of [perceiving] a sound, even after phenomenological reduction, *appearance and that which appears stand in contrast*, and this *in the midst of pure givenness*, hence in the midst of true immanence, then we are taken aback. Perhaps the sound lasts. We have there the patently given unity of the

sound and its duration with its temporal phases, the present and the past. On the other hand, when we reflect, the phenomenon of enduring sound, itself a temporal phenomenon, has its own now-phase and past phases. And if one picks out a now-phase of the phenomenon there is not only the objective now of the sound itself, but the now of the sound is but a point in the duration of a sound.[36]

Unless one wants to really unpack what is entailed in various ontological commitments concerning sound, the simple replacement of "sound object" with "sound event" or "sound matter" does not mean much. There can be many different forms of materialism or realism; events can be understood in physical or perceptual terms; objects can be intentional or material, and not all objects are reifications. Depending on pragmatic use and context, sound objects flow and sonic flows are objectified.

At a certain point, I find myself weary of the promotion of this or that ontological position about sound. Most ontological claims are less arguments than assertions or commitments. They often smack of circularity, where this or that ontology is adopted to promote foregone conclusions. The reason this occurs—to make my own blunt assertion—is that ontology is secondary, not primary. In contrast to the classical tradition, I do not believe that ontology describes the way the world *is*. Rather, ontologies emerge by capturing the ways that agents and actors understand, totalize, substantialize, and engage with the shared historical, geographic, cultural, scientific, and political situations in which they find themselves.[37] But that does not make ontology irrelevant. Rather, if ontology is secondary, then ontological "arguments" can be extraordinarily revealing. Rather than simply positioning sound objects against sound events and sound matter, such assertions make legible the epistemic and axiological views of those who do the positioning. Is Cox really making an argument that sound has a "flux ontology," or is this flux ontology tacitly assumed to destabilize "the visual" or challenge "music" altogether? Is Schaeffer really making an argument about sound as "objects," or is he asserting their objective status so he can develop his solfège and compositional projects? Is Schafer really making an argument about sound events, or is he committed to their contextual emplacement to promote his environmental and design goals and the values they embody? Is López really making an argument for sound matter, or is he emphasizing the materiality of perception to demote the semiotic significance of sounds? It seems to me that reading the ontology asserted in terms of the values promoted is the more useful strategy.

I, too, have registered my dissatisfaction with the Schaefferian sound object. But the argument I made in *Sound Unseen* was not to promote some alternative ontology of the sound object because it was wrong or inadequate as an ontology of sound in general.[38] Rather than worry about whether sound is an event or an object, I am concerned about the lack of history and mediation in Schaeffer's ontology. To arrive at the sound object requires a long process of production and mediation. To study the methods employed by Schaeffer's research units around the time of the *Traité* is to see how that process involved tape recording, editing, group listening, surveys, typologies, auditory tests, and slew of other mediating acts. Yet at the moment that the sound object is finally produced, that whole production process is rendered inessential and erased from the account: the sound object is simply "disclosed." In a strange case of ontological *Nachträglichkeit*, the sound object is covertly placed back at the beginning of its process of discovery but claimed to have always already been present. This phantasmagoric occultation of production, I would argue, is an artifact of Schaeffer's phenomenological method and commitments, for it has never been clear how phenomenology could reconcile history and mediation with its severe employment of reduction, *Wesensschau*, eidetic variation, and the like. The reduction required to "disclose" the sound object sacrifices its context and history, denaturing the sound object and distorting its "essence." Yet replacement of objects with events or matter can be just as phantasmagoric when it neglects the process of production and mediation behind the emergence of any ontology. The meaning of any sound—whether object, event, or material—is inseparable from its historical moment, site of production, or reception. Rather, sounds need to be recognized as sedimentation of historical and social forces. Ontological assertions and counter-assertions about the sound object or the sound event do little to encourage such recognition.

Notes

1 Malina and Schaeffer, "A Conversation on Concrete Music and Kinetic Art," 255.
2 The primary source for the story is Schaeffer, *A la recherche d'une musique concrète*. The book is divided into two sections of heavily edited journals documenting the discovery and early days of musique concrète, followed by essays and a sketch of a music theory appropriate for musique concrète (cowritten with Abraham Moles).

All quotations from this work are from Schaeffer, *In Search of a Concrete Music*, the recent translation by Christine North and John Dack.

3 Schaeffer, *In Search of a Concrete Music*, 7.

4 Schaeffer, *In Search of a Concrete Music*, 4.

5 Schaeffer, *In Search of a Concrete Music*, 3.

6 Schaeffer, *In Search of a Concrete Music*, 12.

7 Schaeffer, *In Search of a Concrete Music*, 13.

8 Schaeffer, *In Search of a Concrete Music*, 14.

9 Schaeffer, *In Search of a Concrete Music*, 14.

10 Schaeffer, *Traité des objets musicaux*. For a detailed account of Schaeffer's debt to Husserl and its impact on the theory of the sound object, see Kane, *Sound Unseen*, chap. 1.

11 "Lorsque les vagues qui se forment sur la surface de l'eau viennent à rencontrer quelque obstacle, elles se brisent, se dilatent & se répandent dans l'eau stagnante & tranquille qui est derrière l'obstacle. Les vibrations &, pour ainsi dire, les vagues de l'air qui forment le son, se répandent en tout sens; car le son d'une cloche ou d'un canon peut être entendu derrière une montagne qui cache l'objet sonore à notre vue": d'Alembert and Diderot, *Encyclopédie*, 323.

12 "C'est qu'il n'y a aucune connexion immédiate et évidente entre le son et l'objet sonore. Les deux choses sont même si peu liées l'une à l'autre que la première est transitoire, et la seconde permanente": Dunan, *Thèorie psychologique de l'espace*, 52.

13 "Dans mon enfance, j'avais l'oreille très délicate et l'on s'amusait souvent à me faire désigner la note produite par tel ou tel objet sonore, flambeau, verre ou bobèche. J'indiquais la note sans hésitation. Quand on me demandait quelle note produisait une cloche, je répondais toujours: *Elle ne fait pas une note, elle en fait plusieurs*": Saint-Saëns, *Harmonie et mélodie*, 241.

14 "*Acousmatic*, the Larousse dictionary tells us, is the: *Name given to the disciples of Pythagoras who, for five years, listened to his teachings while he was hidden behind a curtain, without seeing him, while observing a strict silence*" [*Acousmatique*, nous dit le *Larousse: Nom donné aux disciples de Pythagore qui, pendant cinq années, écoutaient ses leçons cachés derrière un rideau, sans le voir, et en observant le silence le plus rigoureux*]: Schaeffer, *Traité des objets musicaux*, 91.

15 Schaeffer, "Sound and Communcation." This article, published in the inaugural issue of UNESCO's *Cultures*, was simultaneously published in French. For the original French-language source, see Schaeffer, "Son et communication."

16 Schaeffer, "Sound and Communcation," 65.

17 The one exception I was able to locate appears in William Carpenter's textbook on the principles of physiology, which went through many editions and expansions in from the 1850s until the 1880s. In a chapter on the physiology of hearing, Carpenter puts forth an account of sensation that is heavily influenced by Johannes Müller, writing, "In the Ear, as in the Eye, the impressions made upon the sensory nerve are not at once produced by the body which originates the sensation; but they are propagated to it, through a medium capable of transmitting them. Here too, therefore, we take cognizance by the mind, not of the sonorous object, but of the condition of the auditory nerve; and all the ideas we form of sounds, as to their nature,

intensity, direction, &c., must be based upon the changes which they produce in it": Carpenter, *Principles of Human Physiology, with Their Chief Applications to Psychology, Pathology, Therapeutics, Hygiène, and Forensic Medicine,* 422. Since "sonorous object" is not a term commonly found in the archive or one that rolls off the tongue in English, my best guess is that Carpenter translated it directly from a French source. Regardless of whether the conjecture holds, Carpenter preserves the older French usage. The cause of the sound or sounding body—that is, the "sonorous object"—is distinct from the "condition of the auditory nerve," which is the real basis for our ideas about "sounds." The sensation of sound is much more closely tied to the physical state of the relevant nerves than to the "sonorous object" that, through a medium, stimulates the nerves in the first place.

18 Schaeffer, "Note on Time Relationships."

19 Ussachevsky, "Music in the Tape Medium," 9.

20 Boulez, "At the Ends of the Fruitful Land . . . ," 28. This is an English translation of the original article, "An der Grenze des Fruchtlandes," *Die Reihe* 1 (1955), 47–56.

21 The slight is especially egregious, given that *Die Reihe* was widely understood to be a journal partisan to German *elektronische Musik*, which had severe aesthetic and ideological differences with its rival musique concrète.

22 Tenney, *Meta+Hodos and Meta Meta+Hodos,* 25.

23 For records of these meetings and Moles's involvement with Schaeffer, see Tournet-Lammer, *Sur les traces de Pierre Schaeffer.*

24 Moles, *Théorie de l'information et perception esthétique*; Moles, *Information Theory and Esthetic Perception.*

25 Schaeffer, "Son et communication"; Schaeffer, "Sound and Communcation."

26 Schaeffer, "Sound and Communcation," 62.

27 Schafer, *The Soundscape,* 131.

28 In addition to Christoph Cox and Francisco López, whose work I address later, one could also consider Michel Chion and Salome Voegelin for their simultaneous affirmation of Schaeffer and discomfort with his ontology of the sound object: Chion, *Sound,* chap. 11; Voegelin, *Sonic Possible Worlds,* chap. 1.

29 See Kane, "Sound Studies without Auditory Culture."

30 Cox, "Sonic Thoughts," 126.

31 For a discussion of this argument, see Kane, *Sound Unseen,* 30–33.

32 López, "Environmental Sound Matter," 4.

33 Cox, "Sound Art and the Sonic Unconscious," 25.

34 Schaeffer, *Traité des objets musicaux,* 432–34.

35 For a good presentation of this "rule," see Pierre Schaeffer, Guy Reibel, and Beatriz Ferreyra, *Solfège de l'objet sonore,* compact disc no. 3, Institut National de l'Audiovisuel–Groupe de Recherches Musicales, Paris, tracks 19–22.

36 Husserl, *The Idea of Phenomenology,* 8–9. Quoted in Schaeffer, "Sound and Communcation," 79.

37 For an exposition of this argument, see Kane, "Sound Studies without Auditory Culture"; Lynch, "Ontography."

38 See chapter 1 of Kane, *Sound Unseen.*

II | Aural Reification, Sonic Commodification

Listening with Adorno, Again

Nonobjective Objectivity and the Possibility of Critique

Theodor W. Adorno has a problem when it comes to sound studies. He is a towering figure in the philosophy of music, but this focus works against him in the context of the emergent discipline: music, while hardly irrelevant to sound studies, is nonetheless peripheral. The marginalization of music has come about for two, somewhat contradictory reasons. The first reason is to emphasize the generality of the disciplinary object: all sounds rather than a special category of them. The second is to avoid encroaching on other disciplines and their expertise. For example, ethnomusicologists rightly assert their knowledge of particular musical systems and the cultures in which they are embedded. An approach to Adorno's relevance to sound studies will have to confront his commitment to music and simultaneously to seek out avenues—or, more likely alleyways—of generalizability, or at least portability. If we go this route, a second problem arises: are Adorno's insights into music of more than historical interest? If not, then why bother to generalize or transport his work at all? Adorno's writings are notoriously allusive and often maddeningly opaque. Nonetheless, we can make some definitive statements about Adorno and music, and they do not suggest that his relevance is self-evident. While he allowed for and in fact insisted on their dialectical intermingling, Adorno nonetheless always split music into two distinct spheres: the serious and the light.[1] The former he also qualified as "autonomous"; the latter, as "entertainment," "functional," or "popular" music (as his *leichte Musik* is sometimes translated). As for serious music, Adorno's densely argued defense of Schoenberg and his concomitant critique of Stravinsky in *Philosophy of New Music* (1949) appears as a fight without stakes today.[2] Further, his notion and valorization of "structural listening"—listening that takes in every aspect of a piece of music and enacts a totalization that Adorno deems "adequate" to the composition—has been criticized as both wrong and wrongheaded.[3] Similarly, his view of popular music as utterly administered, standardized, and complicit with capital tends to run counter to our own sympathies. Marking in advance the rise of academic cultural studies, Adorno already knew in his essay "On the Fetish-Character in Music and the Regression of Listening" (1938) what we would think in this regard. Here is his withering assessment: "In America, it is just the so-called liberals and progressives whom one finds among the advocates of light popular music, most of whom want to classify their activity as democratic."[4]

In opposition to such misguided advocacy, Adorno would insist that popular music was not only harmful but "objectively untrue."[5] Setting aside the embrace of popular culture in academe, we are still likely to find such an assessment confounding. The category of judgment seems unsuitable. How could such music be true or false—especially if we disregard lyrics and attend only to melody, harmony, rhythm, and other non-semantic, non-referential elements? Adorno himself consistently characterized true art as "nonconceptual" in a conscious adoption of Kant's notion that beauty pleases "without a purpose."[6] As for music, Adorno put the case more strongly, remarking in the posthumously published *Aesthetic Theory* that the "aconceptuality" of music "is obvious."[7] By definition, the "aconceptual" would appear to be nonpropositional as well, such that attributions of true and false make little sense according to the standard logic. As for a more suitable category, good-versus-bad music is a game that we are hardly likely to play. Instead, we tend to assume a Humean, pre-critical aesthetics: first, there is a variety of tastes (*chacun à son goût*); second, determinate criteria for valorizing some tastes over others do not exist (*de gustibus non est disputandum*).[8] Hume himself regarded taste as grounded in the human constitution and ultimately derived from utility, with the relative diversity of tastes accounted for by variety within that constitution and conditioning factors such as national character. We can easily reimagine Hume's approach in more modern psychological or sociological terms, including Marxist notions of ideology. For example, this position is not far from Pierre Bourdieu's functionalist notion of *distinction*: matters of taste, including taste in music, are markers of class and serve to reinforce class identity.[9]

While Adorno frequently expressed similar views, he deemed them superficial in relation to the deep work of both serious and popular music under capitalism. In this chapter, I examine why and how Adorno makes truth claims about music and, more important, what he means when he characterizes those claims as "objective." In part, mine is a hermeneutic quest driven by the oddness of assertions such as the objective untruth of popular music, as well as a diagnostic examination of the alienating effect that Adorno's judgments have on us. Getting a better grasp on what Adorno had in mind may shed some light on our own preconceptions and assumptions. Yet my motive is not so much getting Adorno right as getting at whether his take on sonic objectivity can and should be reconsidered. Broadly, does Adorno's way of thinking still have something to offer us in approaching today's changed political economy and media ecology? In this political economy and media ecology, music—both serious and light—while still important, has a diminished role in terms of valorization and market share. In more narrowly disciplinary terms, can tracing this particular thread of intellectual history lead to new alleyways for sound studies to explore?

Varieties of Objectivity

The collection *Stichworte: Kritische Modelle 2* (Keywords: Critical Models 2), which Adorno edited, included his own contribution on the conceptual couple "Subject and Object" (Zu Subjekt und Objekt). This was in 1969, the year of Adorno's death. If you are looking for finality regarding a topic that exercised Adorno throughout his career, you will be disappointed. In "Subject and Object," the author is eager *not* to provide clear definitions of the terms. Instead, he shows the convolutions of their relation. From the outset, Adorno declares that defining the terms lands us in "an aporia," for "in a way, the concepts of subject and object—or rather, the things they intend—have priority before all definition."[10] Notwithstanding, Adorno does not deem this aporia incapacitating. On the contrary, he advises that we take up "the words 'subject' and 'object' as the well-honed philosophical language hands them to us and as a historical sediment—not, of course, sticking to such conventionalism but continuing with critical analysis."[11] The essay "Subject and Object" is consistently Adornian in that it urges historicizing and critique and in that it treats its concepts as both essential to critical analysis and complex and "dialectical," if not irreducibly paradoxical. To take a complementary example: the opening section of *Negative Dialectics* is dedicated to preserving the entanglement of terms that Heidegger "evades by usurping a standpoint beyond the difference between subject and object"—that is, through his insistence on Being, a notion that he "overstretches into a sort of nonobjective objectivity."[12] Similar engagements are found in *Aesthetic Theory*, and not only in the section titled "Subject and Object."[13]

Adorno's style reflects these convolutions of subject and object. This willfully heightened tension between hermeneutics and rhetoric is exacerbated by a complication of translation. Three German terms in Adorno's writings are rendered as "objectivity": *Objektivität*, *Sachlichkeit*, and *Gegenständlichkeit*. The first, while ordinary enough in both this form and in the noun *Objekt* or adjective *objektiv*, is also the most technical: a part of philosophical parlance, as in *objektiver Geist* (objective mind or spirit). The term *objektiver Geist* is Hegel's, although Adorno frequently, and often with alarming casualness, mentions "objective spirit" in his writings. For example, discussing the "schizophrenic deportment of Stravinsky's music," which he deems "a ritual that means to outbid the coldness of the world," Adorno claims that "his work makes itself a match for the insanity of objective spirit."[14] That his use of the term in *Philosophy of New Music* was surely not clear to all of his readers is verified by his discussion in an appendix to the work entitled "Misunderstandings," in which Adorno responds to reviewers and critics of the first edition. Adorno here remarks that he has "implicitly applied to music a concept of objective spirit that asserts itself over and above the heads of individual artists as well as beyond the merits of individual works," before going on to state the concept is "as foreign to everyday consciousness as it is self-evident to my own spiritual experience."[15] If only his critics did not "lack the concept of objective spirit," they would have grasped what for Adorno is so obvious that he sarcastically asks for pardon in making it explicit: he does not think that Stravinsky is psychotic; he thinks that Stravinsky's music imitates and "in a sense" masters—the qualification indicates that this mastery is actually a capitulation—"collective psychotic tendencies."[16] Society is mad, not the composer, and there is no way to reduce this madness to the psyche or subjectivity of the individual artist in question.[17]

A thorough account of what Adorno understood by the term "objective spirit" would require a lengthy detour into the history of German idealism and, in particular, Max Horkheimer's exegeses of the tradition as foundational for the Frankfurt School: Kant's critical enterprise, which placed things-in-themselves off limits and emphasized the constructive role of the subject in the production of knowledge and perception; Fichte's more thoroughgoing idealist and subjectivist turn; Schelling's retrieval of objectivity in his natural philosophy; and Hegel's attempt to overcome dialectally the dichotomy of subject and object.[18] For Hegel, objective spirit named at a given moment in the unfolding of "spirit" the totality of originally subjective constructs that had become externalized and confronted the subject as such: the nexus of laws, norms, cultural values, practices, and so forth. Or, as Fredric Jameson, in a memorable turn of phrase, characterized Hegel's term with intentionally Adornian pathos: "the great absolute web of all the error and delusion and passionate conviction held together and believed and spoken at any moment in human history."[19] In Hegel, the moment of "objective spirit" is preceded by that of "subjective spirit" and is eventually, through the work of the dialectic and so-called determinate negation, sublated positively into "absolute spirit." As Max Paddison remarks, Adorno's own use of "objective spirit," while clearly Hegelian in terms of intellectual history, remains somewhat elusive. The term "spirit," or *Geist*, is not meant to have numinous overtones—on the contrary—although these are with difficulty exorcised. Paddison himself offers this understandably vague and capacious definition of spirit: "The concept is difficult to pin down with any precision, and has to be understood in the dual sense of 'totality' and of 'historical tendency.' For Adorno *Geist* (as 'progress of spirit') comes to stand for 'historical consciousness' (*Bewußtsein*) and, at the same time, 'rationality' (*Rationalität*) and the historical tendency towards increasing 'rationalization' (*Rationalisierung*) in Western society."[20] Following Hegel, Adorno attributes "objectivity" (*Objektivität*) to spirit so understood—that is, it stands over and against human subjects, albeit, as noted, spirit in this sense must be grasped in dialectical terms as a sediment, to use a favorite Adornian term, of subjectivity.

By contrast, *Sachlichkeit* names a delusion of objectivity, a matter-of-factness and detachment that denies and represses the subjectivity inherent in the objective. It is an identification with objective spirit that is inadvertently uncritical and affirmative. *Sachlichkeit* could be translated as "realism" or even "impartiality," although "objectivity" is the usual rendering in Adorno's texts. This is likely because the standard English translation of the visual artistic movement Neue Sachlichkeit is "New Objectivity," and Adorno is often openly or allusively referring to this movement and its rejection of expressionism when he uses the term.[21] *Sachlichkeit* is to a large extent a gloss on another favorite—and peculiar—term of Adorno's: *Objecktivismus*, or "objectivism." This is a label that Adorno pins on Stravinsky, for instance. Bemoaning an artistic endeavor that aims to expunge all traces of subjectivity in its name, Adorno writes about the composer's music:

> Objectivism, then, turns out to be what it shudders at, the horror of which is its entire content to demonstrate; it is the vainly private preoccupation of the aesthetic subject, a trick of the isolated individual who strikes up a posture as if he were objective spirit itself. Were objective spirit indeed identical with the individual, such art would still not be legitimate, for the objective spirit of a society that has been unified by means of an arrogated domination in opposition to its subjects has become transparent untruth in itself [*denn der objektive Geist einer durch angemaßte Herrschaft gegen seine Subjekte integrierten Gesellschaft ist durchsichtig geworden als unwahr an sich*].[22]

Clearly, Adorno's notion of truth and falsity—or, rather, his notion of truth and untruth—is not so much propositional as existential, moral, or, perhaps, simply definitional: a society unified by domination alone is not a society at all. An art that would be true to such a society—acquiescing in the crushing of the individual by objective spirit—would simply faithfully recapitulate such moral "untruth." However, there *is* a propositional element at work: objectivism is not truly objective; at heart, it is falsified or repressed subjectivity. Adorno, in a related if different vein in *Negative Dialectics*, accuses Heidegger of "objectivism" insofar as the philosopher interdicts the "thinking subject," deducts "entity as well as the categories of abstract thought," and focuses on Being: "an unknown quantity which nothing but the pathos of its invocation lifts above the Kantian concept of the transcendent thing-in-itself."[23] Ironically, in Heidegger's objectivism the subject remains manifest as pathos, whereas objects are, in a sense, conjured away. Being is "something added to the individual entity [*tritt zum einzelnen Seienden hinzu*]," and it turns "the fact that things point beyond themselves into a substrate . . . thus making that fact itself like a thing."[24] In short, Heidegger "pursues dialectics to the point of saying that neither the subject nor the object [is] immediate and ultimate; but he deserts dialectics in reaching for something immediate and primary beyond subject and object."[25] We should note that Heidegger in Adorno's assessment does achieve the insight that neither subject nor object is immediate and ultimate, yet he abandons this insight for a mystification rather than remaining within their paradoxical and necessary entanglement.

At this juncture, we might justifiably wonder what these "individual entities" or "things" to which Adorno refers are. While he was deeply aware of the Kantian distinction between phenomena and noumena—between *Phänomen* and *Ding an sich*—and of the Heideggerian construction *das Seiende*, or "entity," Adorno frequently refers in a seemingly casual way to "things," "entities," and "objects" (*Gegenstände*). He also has recourse to the adjective *gegenständlich* and the abstract noun formation *Gegenständlichkeit*. The latter two are generally translated as "objective" and "objectivity," respectively, although neither captures the distinction at hand. Thus, when Adorno accuses Heidegger of indulging in "nonobjective objectivity" in *Negative Dialectics*, what he writes is "ungegenständliche Objektivität": an illusory objectivity, set askew of objects *qua* concrete materialities. While much could be said about Adorno's critique of Heidegger, I will focus on a similar instance of "nonobjective objectivity" from the lecture on "Function" in the *Introduction to the Sociology of Music*. This instance shifts us toward the relation of sound and listening to objects and objectivity in Adorno's thought and, importantly, includes general claims about sound and listening as such—that is, including but not limited to music.

Form and the Anthropology of Listening

Adorno's overarching claim about the function of popular music is a variation on the Frankfurt School's critique of the culture industry *tout court* as standardized, managed, and administered. Popular music provides industrial workers with an "ersatz" experience of what they no longer have.[26] In tandem with this compensatory function, apparent entertainment prepares consumers for their place in the current regime of labor. The contradictory nature of popular music is simultaneously to fulfill humans "in themselves"—granted in falsified form—and to train them "for consent."[27] In short, popular music offers distraction, respite, and a hollowed-out dream of freedom; at the same time, it offers nothing of the sort, recapitulating and reinforcing the conditions of Fordist production at the point of consumption. Indeed, popular music blurs the line between consumption and production, and consumers are in fact grimly aware of the trap. Serious music in its autonomy and withdrawal, however, opens up a route for distance and critique. In spite of this, Adorno remarks that serious music is also deceptive:

> The deceptive moment that lies in great music too, the autarky of an inwardness split off from objectivity and practice [*die Autarkie einer von Gegenständlichkeit und Praxis abgespaltenen Innerlichkeit*] and compensated in works of art by the truth content of their externalization in a structured objectivity [*die in den Kunstwerken kompensiert ward durch den Wahrheitsgehalt ihrer Entäußerung zur gefügten Objektivität*]—this moment, in functional music, is unreservedly transferred to ideology.[28]

When "objectivity" is first mentioned in this sentence, we have *Gegenständlichkeit*: severed from the world of objects (loosely defined), serious music produces an interiority that is illusorily autonomous. To put it prosaically, such music turns us away from *reality*, a term that Adorno does not hesitate to use elsewhere, and from action in or on that reality. This division from "objectivity" *qua Gegenständlichkeit* and the presumably consequent cleavage from practical activity grounds a sham inwardness and autarky. It is what we might call extreme *subjectivism*, and one that is as "untrue" at heart as the objectivism of Stravinsky or of Heidegger.

The next time "objectivity" is mentioned in the sentence it is *Objektivität*: the compensation of great works of music is *externalization* of their "truth content" as *structured objectivity*. Adorno's claims here echo what he will later assert in *Aesthetic Theory*: that art has become an autonomous realm of the social division of labor and yet, as such, will always recall and reflect that very division. Artworks exist in a world apart from reality yet are constructed from that very stuff and mediated by the social and its contradictions. In the terms of the *Introduction to the Sociology of Music*, we might say that the truth *content* of great music is its *form*, and this form is what Adorno characterizes in terms of *Objektivität*. How exactly Adorno understood this equation is a topic of considerable debate and consternation in the secondary literature on Adorno's musical aesthetics. The important point to grasp is that serious music confronts the listener with structures that are irreducible to subjectivity and interiority; they are external and objective, which does not mean that they are anything but mediately related to objects (*Gegenstände*). The lingering question is how the parallel between objective structures (social and musical) works and how they are coupled—

the one reinforcing the other. Adorno posits what we could call, in strict terms, *isomorphism*. His implicit answer to the question of what holds this together is *objective spirit*, which encompasses both and that Adorno, as noted, characterizes as a totality.[29] As for popular music, while clearly deemed ideological, the crux is form or structure and not lyrical content. So, for example, repetition and standardization in music recapitulate not only the general commodity form but also the conditions of administered production. Elements such as syncopation and dissonance mimic freedom and spontaneity but are always recaptured by the overarching administered and standardized thrust. Like great, serious, or autonomous music, light, popular, or functional music splits off from *Gegenständlichkeit* and produces interiority—in this case, an interior of affects and imaginings—but the compensation in this case is not truth but untruth: reality at first appears to have been escaped, but what is worse is that reality reappears in the objective structure in falsified—that is, unrecognized—form. The movement of externalization in this case is not of structured objectivity but, rather, of *reification* (as Adorno will later explicitly indicate when he refers to popular music as "*radikal verdinglichte Musik*," or radically reified music).[30] Serious music recapitulates objective spirit, but at best in a critical mode; popular music recapitulates objective spirit, ever affirming and reproducing its contradictions.

Adorno makes two claims about listening or hearing (*das Hören*) to clarify and justify his notions of the function of popular music. These claims he characterizes as "anthropological."[31] To be clear: this adjective refers not to the realm of culture but, rather, to that of human nature and physiology. The first claim is that listening or hearing is inherently passive:

> The ear is passive [*Das Ohr ist passiv*]. The eye is covered by a lid and must be opened; the ear is open and must not so much turn its attention toward stimuli as seek protection from them. The activity of the ear, its attentiveness, probably developed late, along with the strength of the ego; amid universally regressive tendencies, late ego traits will be the first to get lost.[32]

Among all of the senses, Adorno claims that the "ear was the one sense organ to register stimuli without an effort."[33] Moreover, while the ear can become active, *das Hören* easily reverts to its archaic passivity and is in this regard essentially different from the other senses in terms of the relationship to labor: "This [viz., essential passivity] set it apart from the permanent exertion of the other senses, which are coupled with the processes of labor because they are always laboring themselves."[34] The physiological thus entwines with social: the ear is particularly suited to its historical, ideological function. This passivity of hearing—its regressive physiological core—both enables the consumption of music to function as respite and escape *and* reinforces the paradoxical passivity of the laboring subject.

These assertions are dubious. There are, of course, physiological differences in the ways that the human eye and ear, for example, are open to stimuli. Yet how much can one legitimately extrapolate about agency based on these differences? Indeed, languages commonly have ways to mark active and passive perception for both senses, albeit the German *Hören* is by itself ambiguous.[35] One could claim, following Adorno, that these distinctions postdate the evolution of the senses. Such a claim would be highly speculative, to say the least. Would it not make far more sense to argue that early hominids must have been better active listeners than their modern counterparts? Moreover, how many other senses are we really talking about? Adorno does mention smell, but he focuses almost exclusively on contrasting the aural with the visual. This contrast fits with what Jonathan Sterne has called "the audiovisual litany": a series of juxtapositions that are meant to be essential and ahistorical—Adorno's "anthropological"—but turn out to be doubtful discursive constructs.[36] These claims, in other words, are historical artifacts or what Adorno himself might label "sediments." Adorno's discussion of seeing and hearing in his lecture on "Function" fits perfectly Sterne's observation that "assertions about the difference between hearing and seeing usually appear together in form of a list" and that they "begin at the level of the individual human being (both physically and psychologically)" before moving on "to construct a cultural theory of the senses."[37] While Adorno tirelessly critiqued the distorting, affirmative ahistoricism of much sociology, in this case it seems we should level the charge against him instead. Nonetheless, a critical approach to the audiovisual litany and to Adorno's claims would refuse the opposition of the "anthropological" to the "cultural" or "historical" and would insist instead on the interrelation of these categories of analysis. And while fully disentangling may ultimately be impossible, opting for one side or the other because it simplifies matters is precisely what Adorno would have cautioned against in *Aesthetic Theory*, in "Subject and Object," and elsewhere in his oeuvre.

Although we should be suspicious of Adorno's naturalization of some of the differences between hearing and vision—and at the same time admit that there are obvious physiological differences—we might still hold on to the distinction that he uses between active and passive perception.[38] This is a common enough distinction, after all, embedded in ordinary language. To sharpen the point: could we not, following Adorno, track and analyze various modalities of agency that relate sound perception to the world of objects (*Gegenstände*) and, importantly, how these modalities might be coupled with or favored by different modes of production, consumption, and—as Adorno's thought prognosticates—prosumption? Adorno leads us precisely in this direction and back to the question of objectivity with his second anthropological claim: a fundamental characteristic of hearing is its "nonobjectiveness" (*Ungegenständlichkeit*).[39] As Adorno explains:

> The phenomena [the sense of hearing] transmits are not phenomena of things in extraesthetic experience. Hearing neither establishes a transparent relation to the world of things, a relation in which useful work is done, nor can it be controlled from the standpoint of this work and its desiderata.[40]

> Die Phänomene, die er [der Gehörsinn] übermittelt, sind in der außerästhetischen Erfarung nicht solche von Dingen. Weder stellt das Gehör eine durchsichtige Beziehung zur Welt der Dinge her, in der nützliche Arbeit sich ereignet, noch ist es von dieser und ihren Desideraten her zu kontrollieren.[41]

Earlier in the same essay, Adorno had posited the non-objectiveness of music and musical perception: "Music is nonobjective and not unequivocally identifiable with any moments of the outside world. At the same time, it is nonetheless commensurable, however indirectly, with the outside world of social reality. It is a language, but a language without concepts [*Musik ist ungegenständlich, mit keinen Momenten der äußeren Welt eindeutig zu identifizieren, dabei indessen höchst artikuliert und bestimmt in sich selbst, und dadurch doch wieder, sei's noch so vermittelt, der äußeren Welt, der gesellschaftlichen Realität kommensurabel. Sie ist eine Sprache, aber eine ohne Begriffe*]."[42] Subsequently, Adorno makes this into a more general claim about listening, as indicated by his use of the term "extra-esthetic." Adorno habitually uses this term for everything that does not fall under the category of artistic perception, which here includes both serious and light music. A translation that cleaves to the original syntax makes this clearer: "The phenomena that it [the sense of hearing] mediates are not in extra-esthetic experience those of things." In other words, Adorno is not simply claiming that music is non- or aconceptual and therefore at best equivocally referential. It is not just that the sounds of music do not refer us to the world, including the social world, unlike the lines and colors of figurative painting. This would be a banal observation about the non-iconic nature of musical expression in general, some mimetic instances notwithstanding. Rather, he is asserting that music *does* have a relation to that world and reality, although further—and crucially—hearing in general entails a detached, indirect, and uncertain relationship to perceptual objects (*Gegenstände*) not only as mediated and externalized social reality but from the outset. Let me insist: Adorno is putting forward "nonobjective" not as the equivalent of "subjective" but, rather, as an adjective that asserts the equivocal relation between the listening subject and its objects (which are, notwithstanding, *objects* and not figments).

Adorno in this instance uses *Dinge* and *Gegenstände* interchangeably, and both terms contrast with *Phänomene*. The latter appear as aural images of objects, so to speak, and recall not only phenomenology, with its insistence on the intentionality of perceiving consciousness, but also Kant's distinction of phenomena and noumena. Adorno implies that objects or things are in a way accessible to perception. He implies that they can be separated from phenomena either as the content of conscious intentionality or as subjective artifacts. Finally, as far as vision is concerned, he insinuates that the relation between phenomenon and thing is relatively clear or "transparent." As for hearing, it does not enjoy such a "see-through" (*durchsichtig*)—to translate Adorno's German rather more literally—relation to the things. We might think it ironic that Adorno uses a visual figure to express himself here. A deconstructionist tactic would be to hold this figure out as catachrestic—of course hearing is blind—and have done with it. Yet perhaps "see-through" is not a figure at all but, rather, a productive tautology that exposes an essential difference. When we see things, we see objects and the medium we *see through*. When we hear things, what we hear are sounds and not the objects, although we may certainly infer causality.[43] The difference has to do with attribution: we attribute colors, for example, to objects. In old philosophical parlance, we may ultimately deem color a secondary quality or an idea in our minds rather than a primary quality or inherent aspect of an object, such as shape, as John Locke argued (and a distinction that George Berkeley, forwarding a more radical idealism, considered spurious—for Berkeley, all qualities are in our minds).[44] In updated parlance, we might say that color is a mental construct. Either way, we still make the *attribution* of the quality to the object.[45] Sound and hearing would not work this way.

Sonic Ideology?

While Adorno does not elaborate helpfully on what he has in mind, his discussion of the nonobjectivity of hearing does have analogs in recent philosophy. Thus, Casey O'Callaghan remarks that sounds do not seem to us to be qualities of sounding objects; nor do we talk about them this way. O'Callaghan's argument is in the Anglo-American or analytical philosophical tradition, and while he does not use the term "ordinary language philosophy," he frequently invokes the ways that we habitually talk about sounds—at least in English—as guides to how sound should be understood. Yet language potentially seems to block understanding as well, because for O'Callaghan part of the problem of grasping the ontological status of sounds stems from bias in our conceptual apparatus and terminology: "visocentric thought" is confounded by the seemingly odd and ungraspable characteristics of sounds.[46] Sounds "in auditory experience" neither appear—and the very term "appear" suggests a figurative or analogical approach to sound using vision—as proper objects in themselves; but neither do we "hear them to qualify ordinary objects in the way that visible attributes do."[47] Colors appear *stuck onto* objects—or perhaps, more honestly, as inseparable qualities of them. Similarly with shape: it would ring absurd to state that cubes emit the sight of a six-sided geometrical figure. Sounds do not seem to stick onto objects in this way. Moreover, they seem to have their own qualities, which we can consider secondary—that is, dependent on perception: pitch (precise or not), intensity or loudness, and that grab-bag category of timbre.[48] And at least by analogy or figuratively, they seem to have traditional primary qualities such as mass, extension, and volume. But if we are to approach sounds as objects, then grasping their temporal dimension seems crucial. To be a sound as such seems to require a distinct beginning, middle, and end—or what in more technical acoustic terms are called the phases of attack, sustain, and decay.[49] Ultimately, O'Callaghan argues for a definition of sounds not as objects but as events that occur close to sounding objects.

There are limitations to O'Callaghan's approach, which he labels "sonic realism." Adorno obviously would have taken this as instance of philosophical objectivism: affirmative and insufficiently dialectical. What elements of the social, historical, and subjective are embedded in this sonic real? Still, O'Callaghan's notion of sounds as events distal to the listener and proximate to—although never merging with—sounding objects does help make sense of Adorno's compressed claim. It is difficult, moreover, to find any philosophical account that simply makes sound an attribute of objects and listening thus into a type of—transparent or not—object perception. The only exception that I have found is Robert Pasnau, who argues that our "standard view about sound" is "incoherent" because, on the one hand, "we suppose that sound is a quality, not of the object that makes the sound, but of the surrounding medium," and, on the other, "we suppose that sound is the object of hearing."[50] To resolve this supposed incoherence, Pasnau suggests that we reject the first assumption of the standard view and instead "continue to treat sound as the object of hearing, and we should think of sounds as existing within the object that 'makes' them."[51] Sound would be more analogous to color than to light: we should not identify "sound with the vibration of air molecules (or any other medium)" but, rather, identify "sound with the vibrations of the object that has the sound."[52] The notion that sounds are simply "sensible properties of objects" along with "color, shape, and size"—and that we ought to ignore ordinary language and begin talking this way—strikes me as tellingly counterintuitive. The first part of the so-called standard view was not generated out of a desire to avoid the radically subjectivist claims of Berkeleyan idealism (as Pasnau would have it). It is not that "rather than make the eccentric claim that sounds are in our minds, we chose to put them in the air, safely mysterious and irreducible."[53] The philosophical view came about because there is something to the claim that O'Callaghan makes for the asymptotically proximal separateness of sound and sounding object—or, for that matter, Adorno's nontransparency and equivocalness of listening and *Gegenstände*. Thus, we do say that a bird is blue or streamlined, and we do not say that "a bird is tweet." Most obviously, the temporal, event character of the bird's sound is elided in such an attribution. Less obviously, we sense that sound is not an attribute of the object in the same way that color or size are—indeed, that it is not an attribute of the sounding object at all, although it just as clearly bears some relation to it.

Yet if we grant Adorno some truth when it comes to the detachment or indirect relation of hearing to the "world of things," his subsequent assertion about labor is seemingly farfetched. In what way does the nontransparent relation of hearing or of listening to objects make sound ill-suited to the control of production? Consider a simple counterexample: hammering a nail involves not only tactile and visual labor, but sonic feedback or what Michel Chion has called the audio-phonatory loop to aid in determining whether the head has been struck correctly and the progress of the operation.[54] In a different vein, sonic signals such as bells and whistles have served to organize industrial production. Nonetheless, we might still entertain the possibility that different senses have different relations—without excluding complex interrelations of the senses, as my example of hammering suggests—to labor, to production, and to consumption, and that the nontransparency of listening might help account for some of these differences. Ultimately, Adorno is more convincing when he posits that it is this lack of a transparent relation of hearing to objects that constitutes the precondition of music becoming art or what he calls "the sensual a priori [*das sensuelle Apriori*]" of music: "In a way, what turns music into a work of art equals its turning into a thing—a solidified text, quite simply. But in the mass function of radically reified music this very aspect disappears [*Kommt, was Musik zum Kunstwerk macht, in gewisser Weise dem gleich, daß sie zum Ding—ganz einfach: zum fixierten Text—wurde, so verschwindet in der Massenfunktion der radikal verdinglichten Musik gerade dieser Aspekt*]."[55] In other words, the possibility of music becoming a *thing*—self-subsisting, autonomous, exterior, objective—depends on the loose, uncertain coupling of hearing and objects in the world. Yet this uncertain coupling simultaneously facilitates the vitiation of music—its becoming an entertainment commodity—under capitalism: it is also the ground of music's peculiar manner of reification, for which the German term is the more prosaic *Verdinglichung*. Such so-called music is not a thing but appears as such—it has become thingified—until we analyze and critique the very processes by which this has taken place.

Does this mean that commodified music lacks a "relation to reality" (*[eine] Beziehung auf die Realität*)?[56] On the contrary, while passive hearing for Adorno does not "objectify" (*objektiviert*) such music—the verb indicating not that the listener would hold the aural aesthetic object at a distance but, rather, that he or she would actively synthesize music as an object—this passivity becomes a way to smuggle into the "domain of imagination" via the contraband of "musical phenomena" (*musikalischen Phänomene*), various "feelings," "motive impulses," and "dynamic schemata" in a *non-concrete* form.[57] This is where the nonobjectiveness of hearing is fundamental, and the term used to express the non-concreteness of reified musical forms is that they are without *Gegenständlichkeit*. As we have seen, for Adorno such concreteness, or *Gegenständlichkeit*, is only *equivocally present in the relation between listening and the world, yet this equivocal presence, when produced in aesthetic experience*—when synthesized as a thing—*is nonetheless objectively there*. When the "sensual a priori" of listening is joined with the commodity form, however, the products of the culture industry, when consumed, appear as—and, in fact, are—a break from labor and even administer a dosed amount of precapitalist enjoyment or resistance. At the same time, they function to instill in non-concrete ways attitudes and mental habits—what we, with Bourdieu, might call *habitus*[58]—that adjust workers to the conditions and relations of production. For Adorno, this is most clearly grasped in the domain of rhythm: "In the mechanical rigor of their repetition, the functions copied by the rhythm are themselves identical with those of the production processes which robbed the individual of his original bodily functions."[59] At heart, commodified music is not ideological because it provides moments of irrational release from rationalized labor; it is ideological because the form of these moments of release are training and disciplining. As Adorno asserts in relation to music's nonconceptual character and how such nonconceptuality as a quasi-language both unbinds and binds music to social reality: "Its definiteness fits it for a collective model of disciplined conduct; its conceptlessness guarantees that awkward questions about the goal of the discipline cannot even arise."[60] In other words, musical sounds are more insidiously ideological than images because their equivocal relation to reality makes them difficult to nail down and thus to critique.[61] This accounts for the question mark that accompanies my section heading "Sonic Ideology," for insofar as it is conceptless—detached from language as a semantic vehicle and from visual iconography—can we speak of musical ideology at all? Or perhaps we find ourselves more profoundly within ideology, with the reminder that etymologically "idea" can mean the appearance of a thing as well as pattern or form. What is certain is that, for Adorno, what troubles the very possibility of critique makes critique all the more necessary.

Nontransparency and equivocalness are fundamental aspects of aurality for Adorno, grounded in its nonobjectiveness. Let me summarize what I have characterized as Adorno's core claims about listening and especially how these claims relate to objectivity—keeping in mind that "objectivity" signifies variously in Adorno's writings. First, Adorno posits that listening is nonobjective (*ungegenständlich*). This lack of objectivity (*Ungegenständlichkeit*) means that listening has an equivocal, "nontransparent" relation to objects (*Gegenstände*). We might say that sounding objects and sound objects do not fully coincide for Adorno. Second, at least in the case of music, this nontransparent relation, while mediated through artistic subjectivity on the production side and the listener's subjectivity on the consumption side, *carries with it both the relation and the equivocality*. This includes a difficult-to-pin-down but no less certain relation to social realities, or what

Adorno tends to call "objective spirit." In short, while music may be non-objective in one sense, it is objective in another: both the material and the social are *objectively embedded or sedimented in it*. This *Objektivität* is not to be confused with *Gegenständlichkeit*. In fact, it is the nonobjectiveness, or *Ungegenständlichkeit*, of listening that underwrites the peculiar objectivity of music as "speech": as something that tells us about the world—and that acts in that world—without concepts. Following Adorno's suggestion, I have described this as the insidiousness of music, which is based for him on core characteristics of sound perception. Popular music is ideological but not in ways that can be clearly, unequivocally unmasked, for it does not wear a mask at all. As Adorno puts it, making a telling comparison, music is "not as easily nailed down as are the crass falsifications of reality in films for instance. . . . Its ideology eludes unmasking by skeptics."[62] Critique has as its target not only what he sees as the "anthropological" passivity of listening—the predisposition of the listener to acquiesce that commodified music takes advantage of—but *also and importantly that music yields its "objective" content as form.*

On the whole, "form" in Adorno's writings is not specific or elaborated enough to make his relevance to current sound studies certain, and gnomic statements from his mature aesthetic thought such as "form is sedimented content" are more suggestive than self-evident.[63] We might here compare Adorno's invocations of form with the project of Pierre Schaeffer, which was unfolding at the same moment, to produce a "morphology" of "sound objects"—that is, a formal description of sounds considered in phenomenological terms as entities divorced from sounding objects, applying what Schaeffer called "reduced listening."[64] Much like my casual characterization of what Adorno would have deemed the flaws of analytical philosophy, he doubtless would have seen Schaeffer's project as uncritical and insufficiently dialectical and, indeed, as itself a peculiar form of objectivism: an attempt to bracket off sound and listening from technological, historical, and social mediations in order to consider them in themselves—that is, an impossibility. While we are familiar with the attacks of poststructuralism and especially of deconstruction on phenomenology, which proceeded in part by undermining the supposed self-presence and transparency of the voice, we should recall that the Frankfurt School, including Adorno, was deeply critical of phenomenological claims and methods.[65] Yet Adorno would have benefited in equally dialectical terms from a serious encounter with Schaeffer's attempt to provide a rich formal description that could be joined to social and historical analysis and to critique. This encounter did not take place, but it would be more than an interesting thought experiment to imagine the consequences. More to the point, if we are willing to consider nonobjective objectivity a working concept, we might begin to consider whether what Adorno claims about music could be extended to other media, to other sounds, and to other sonic forms.

Notes

1 See Hamilton, *Aesthetics and Music*, 171–74.
2 See Adorno, *Philosophy of New Music*, the whole of which focuses on the case for Schoenberg and against Stravinsky. Dates provided in parentheses refer here and throughout to the original date of publication.
3 "Structural listening" is alternatively translated as "structural hearing." Adorno attributes this to the "expert" in his typology of "musical conduct" and describes it as "entirely adequate hearing" in which "the fully conscious listener . . . hears the sequence, hears past, present, and future moments together so that they crystallize into a meaningful context": Adorno, *Introduction to the Sociology of Music*, 4–5. Adorno's conception has been criticized most notably by Rose Rosengard Subotnik in "Toward a Deconstruction of Structural Listening: A Critique of Schoenberg, Adorno, and Stravinsky," in Subotnik, *Deconstructive Variations*, 148–76.
4 Adorno, *Essays on Music*, 311. It is doubtless statements such as these that have made attempts to rehabilitate Adorno for (postmodern) academics a persistent challenge, despite the efforts of some scholars. See, e.g., Thomas Y. Levin's account of Adorno's early and profound encounter with the gramophone as medium of mass culture and reification—an account that aims in part to thwart simplistic characterizations of Adorno the "myopic mandarin" versus the sympathetic Benjamin: Levin, "For the Record," 23.
5 Adorno, *Introduction to the Sociology of Music*, 38.
6 Adorno, *Aesthetic Theory* (University of Minnesota Press), 141.
7 Adorno, *Aesthetic Theory* (University of Minnesota Press), 120.
8 Hume lays out his empiricist argument in the essay "Of the Standard of Taste," in Hume, *Selected Essays*, 133–54.
9 This is the overarching argument in Bourdieu, *Distinction*.
10 Theodor Adorno, "Subject and Object," in Arato and Gebhardt, *The Essential Frankfurt School Reader*, 498.
11 Adorno, "Subject and Object," 498.
12 Adorno, *Negative Dialectics*, 85, 90.
13 See Adorno, *Aesthetic Theory* (University of Minnesota Press), 163–75.
14 Adorno, *Philosophy of New Music*, 127.
15 Adorno, *Philosophy of New Music*, 165.
16 Adorno, *Philosophy of New Music*, 167.

17 Adorno's criticism of those who mistakenly think he is analyzing and pathologizing Stravinsky rather than the "objective spirit" embedded in his art is similar to his more elaborated criticism of Freudian aesthetics: Adorno, *Aesthetic Theory* (University of Minnesota Press), 8–13.

18 For an account of this genealogy, see Abromeit, *Horkheimer and the Foundations of the Frankfurt School*, 112–16.

19 Jameson, *Late Marxism*, 50.

20 Paddison, *Adorno's Aesthetics of Music*, 114–15.

21 See Crockett, *German Post-Expressionism*, xix.

22 Adorno, *Philosophy of New Music*, 157; Adorno, *Philosophie der neuen Musik*, 195–96.

23 Adorno, *Negative Dialectics*, 98.

24 Adorno, *Negative Dialectics*, 106; Adorno, *Negative Dialektik*, 110.

25 Adorno, *Negative Dialectics*, 106.

26 Adorno, *Introduction to the Sociology of Music*, 27, 49.

27 Adorno, *Introduction to the Sociology of Music*, 50.

28 Adorno, *Introduction to the Sociology of Music*, 50; Adorno, *Dissonanzen/Einleitung in die Musiksoziologie*, 232.

29 Adorno's "totality" thesis is frequently remarked and explicated in the secondary literature. See, e.g., Brian O'Connor's account of both the philosopher's take on totality and critical responses to it: O'Connor, *Adorno*, 26–44. Note also Paddison's mention of "totality" in his gloss on "objective spirit": Paddison, *Adorno's Aesthetics of Music*, 114.

30 Adorno, *Dissonanzen/Einleitung in die Musiksoziologie*, 233.

31 Adorno, *Introduction to the Sociology of Music*, 51.

32 Adorno, *Introduction to the Sociology of Music*, 51; Adorno, *Dissonanzen/Einleitung in die Musiksoziologie*, 232.

33 Adorno, *Introduction to the Sociology of Music*, 51.

34 Adorno, *Introduction to the Sociology of Music*, 51.

35 To take just two examples: obviously there are the contrasting couplings in English of hear and listen and see and watch. They match the French distinctions between *entendre* and *écouter* and *voir* and *regarder*.

36 Sterne, *The Audible Past*, 15.

37 Sterne, *The Audible Past*, 14–15.

38 However, we should also take care not to reify aspects of the distinction between active and passive and to attend to how this distinction becomes "fuzzy" in the case of listening, as Rey Chow argues in her contribution to this volume.

39 Adorno, *Introduction to the Sociology of Music*, 51; Adorno, *Dissonanzen/Einleitung in die Musiksoziologie*, 233.

40 Adorno, *Introduction to the Sociology of Music*, 51.

41 Adorno, *Dissonanzen/Einleitung in die Musiksoziologie*, 233.

42 Adorno, *Introduction to the Sociology of Music*, 44; Adorno, *Dissonanzen/Einleitung in die Musiksoziologie*, 224.

43 But on the "causal vagueness" of sound, see Chion, *Sound*, 108–12.

44 See Locke, *An Essay Concerning Human Understanding*, 135–41. Berkeley's argument with Locke, including discussion of sound as a quality, is in George Berkeley,

"Three Dialogues between Hylas and Philonous," in Berkeley, *Philosophical Writings*, 151–242. Don Ihde refers to the Lockean distinction between primary and secondary qualities as an instance of the dominant philosophical tradition of "visualism" that he hopes to decenter through he phenomenology of sound: see Ihde, *Listening and Voice*, 12–15. On this topic, see also Biancorosso, "Sound," 264.

45 In constructivist philosophy, see, for example, Humphrey, *Seeing Red*.

46 O'Callaghan, *Sounds*, 8.

47 O'Callaghan, *Sounds*, 8.

48 On the problematically vague notion of timbre, see Chion, *Sound*, 173–74.

49 I will leave aside potential arguments about drones and varieties of noise that do not seem to fit neatly with this assertion about the temporality of most, if perhaps not all, sounds.

50 Pasnau, "What Is Sound?," 309.

51 Pasnau, "What Is Sound?," 316.

52 Pasnau, "What Is Sound?," 316.

53 Pasnau, "What Is Sound?," 324.

54 Chion, *Sound*, 93–95.

55 Adorno, *Introduction to the Sociology of Music*, 51–52; Adorno, *Dissonanzen/Einleitung in die Musiksoziologie*, 233.

56 Adorno, *Introduction to the Sociology of Music*, 52; and Adorno, *Dissonanzen/Einleitung in die Musiksoziologie*, 232.

57 Adorno, *Introduction to the Sociology of Music*, 52; Adorno, *Dissonanzen/Einleitung in die Musiksoziologie*, 233.

58 See Bourdieu, *The Logic of Practice*, 52–65.

59 Adorno, *Introduction to the Sociology of Music*, 52.

60 Adorno, *Introduction to the Sociology of Music*, 44

61 It is, of course, tempting to compare what Adorno says about "discipline" in relation to music with Foucault's bio-power theses. In general, Foucault posits models of disciplining that either appear generalizable (the Panopticon as a model for internalized discipline and self-surveillance in modernity) or spread through professional discourse (sexuality). There is little discussion of mass-mediation or cultural production to speak of, let alone of the commodity form. Nonetheless, there would appear to be affinities between the two thinkers in terms of their emphasis on administrative apparatuses.

62 Adorno, *Introduction to the Sociology of Music*, 44.

63 Adorno asserts, "If art opposes the empirical through the element of form—and the mediation of form and content is not to be grasped without their differentiation—the mediation is to be sought in the recognition of aesthetic form as sedimented content. What are taken to be the purest forms (e.g., traditional musical forms) can be traced back even in the smallest idiomatic detail to content such as dance": Adorno, *Aesthetic Theory* (University of Minnesota Press), 5.

64 The culmination of Schaeffer's thought about the morphology of sound objects is in *Traité des objets musicaux*, 389–459. Brian Kane has examined how, following the phenomenological model, Schaeffer's sound object is less a concrete object than a "phantasmagoria": see Kane, *Sound Unseen*, 15–41.

65 There is a common Hegelian genealogy that doubtless could be rooted out here. An interesting and appropriate point of comparison would be the deconstruction of phenomenology in Derrida, *Voice and Phenomenon*, and Herbert Marcuse, "On Science and Phenomenology," in Arato and Gebhardt, *The Essential Frankfurt School Reader*, 466–76. It is worth noting that for Derrida the circumscription of the sonic field to voice and for Adorno to music might have led them preemptively away from sound and sounds as "objects." Moreover, what we might have been tempted to treat as Schaeffer's naïveté from a "theoretical" standpoint now appears to us as a robust and variegated treatment that, in a sense, redresses an imbalance in favor of objectivity.

Spectral Objects

On the Fetish Character of Music Technologies

"Commodity fetishism? I love that idea!" It is 2012. I am in Northern California, in a car with Matt Ward, then president of Universal Audio, a company that specializes in reproducing old analog audio-recording hardware, both as period-accurate reissues of the equipment and as computer software. We are discussing musicians' lust for old equipment and their fierce arguments, which populate online discussion boards, such as the question of whether software models of hardware instruments and technologies will ever sound "as good as the real thing." I ask Ward why he thinks musicians are so invested in the technologies his company produces. We go through the usual reasons: some musicians have experience with the old technology from working in studios; they already know how to use it and want to own it themselves without paying inflated prices for vintage equipment. Some lust after the equipment because they know it was used on their favorite recordings.[1] And some are just learning the craft of sound recording but want to purchase a well-known tool with the hope that it has a little bit of magic inside that will rub off on them.[2]

When I tell Ward that scholars have a name for this last phenomenon—commodity fetishism—and explain the basics of the concept, he is amused. It explains so much, and yet it does not explain away the phenomenon. Wendy Chun calls commodity fetishism a kind of false causality. She writes, "A fetish allows one to visualize what is unknown—to substitute images for causes. Fetishes allow the human mind both too much and not enough control by establishing a 'unified causal field' that encompasses both personal actions and physical events. Fetishes enable a semblance of control over future events—a possibility of influence, if not an airtight programmability—that itself relies on distorting real social relations into material givens."[3] In other words, in the fetish, relations among people crystallize in things and the effects attributed to them.

What is a critic to do with the commodity fetishism of instruments? To leave it undisturbed would be to naturalize and affirm the workings of capitalism. To explain it away as misrecognition or false consciousness would be to ignore instruments' roles in musicians', makers', and audiences' relationships to sound. It would be to treat sonic culture as something that can be falsified. In this chapter, I offer two accounts of the fetishism of instruments. One is theoretical: I outline it through a mix of reference to Marxist work on commodity fetishism and scholarship in the new organology, "a systematic study of the natures, uses, degrees of agency, and ends of instruments in different fields and at different times."[4] The other refers the theory back to my ongoing ethnographic and media-analytical work on musical instruments and audio technologies for signal processing, as well as to other studies of commodity fetishism and music by authors such as Louise Meintjes and Paul Théberge.[5] By attending to the spectrality of instruments in both senses of the term "spectral"—their sounds and the aspects of their social character that remain intangible to the senses—I argue that we must understand commodity fetishism as a real force in sonic culture, as opposed to a form of false consciousness that must be demystified. At the same time, I show that the "objectness" of the sound of particular instruments is, ultimately, unavailable to the senses. Rather, the fetishism of instrumental sounds always gestures toward a set of relations that lie beyond the instrument itself.

Spectral Objectivity, or Commodity Fetishism in Sound

To understand commodity fetishism in sound, we have to define our terms carefully. Despite the common (and, in my reading, misguided) emphasis on their ephemerality, sounds themselves can be commodities.[6] But like all commodities, they can become commodities only through social practice and in specific contexts and relationships. Recent work on synthesizer presets, ringtones, and stock movie sound effects suggests different ways to approach this problem.[7] But musical technologies are especially interesting, since in this case *both the object and the sound it makes becomes part of the commodity fetish*. In other words, is a Stradivarius violin or 1958 Fender bass prized because of the sound it makes or because it is a Stradivarius or a Fender? To answer this question in the abstract, we need a brief detour through theories of commodity fetishism and instruments.

Here Michael Heinrich's explication of Marx's *Capital* is helpful because of how he and his translator parse the German term *gespenstige Gegenständlichkeit*. Although it is traditionally rendered in English as "phantom objectivity," Heinrich prefers the phrase "spectral objectivity" because commodity fetishism is something more than a false apprehension of a commodity; on the contrary, he says it expresses "an actual situation:"[8]

> The value of commodities is an expression of an overwhelming social interaction that cannot be controlled by individuals. In a commodity-producing society, people (all of them!) are under the control of things, and the decisive relations of domination are not personal but "objective" (*sachlich*). This impersonal, objective domination, submission to "inherent necessities," does not exist because such thing(s) themselves possess characteristics that generate such domination, or because social activity necessitates this mediation through things, but only because *people relate to things in a particular way—as commodities*.[9]

"Under the control of things" may seem like a harsh way to put it, but even for noninstrumental vocal music, there is a robust infrastructure that subtends any form of musical production, ranging from the air as a medium through which sound travels to the architectures within which music is made and the component technologies of the instruments and sound-processing devices. Without making claims for music technologies in all times and places, it should be clear that modern music technologies have emerged in the broader context of capitalism and within a capitalist music economy. Instruments and sound-processing devices are bought and sold for profit. Music making and consumption operate according to a range of market logics, however distorted. Although state sponsorship of some music is an exception, even then the goal is as often as not some kind of intervention in the international markets for music and musicians. All this is to say that we Westerners tend to live in a musical world that is at once ideologically individualistic, as ideas of talent, genius, and expression suggest (ideas to which I return later), and in which individual activity depends on accumulations of labor and collections of objects working in concert.

Heinrich is useful for another reason, and that is his choice of the phrase "spectral objectivity." Regardless of whether it is in fact a better translation of Marx's phrase into English than "phantom objectivity," the other meanings of the term "spectral" are immensely useful for thinking about commodity fetishism and sound. "Spectral" is also the adjectival form of the noun "spectrum," which describes the range of component frequencies that make up a sound.[10] The distribution of different frequencies and their relative intensities are said to compose the timbre of the sound, as distinct from its pitch or loudness. Timbre is the dimension of sound that explains how a violin and a piano playing the same note at the same volume can still sound entirely different from each other. While timbre (or "tone color") is notoriously difficult to define, it is also the key to the fetishism of instruments.[11] To speak of an instrument's spectral objectivity is thus to simultaneously reference the web of social relations in which it exists and the sonic history of which it is a part. I intentionally distinguish these phenomena from the sounds the instrument makes, because instruments cannot make sounds independently of their playing—this is true even for automated instruments like player pianos or sequenced synthesizers. For musicians who play stringed instruments, this is embodied in the old cliché, "The tone is in the hands." At the same time, certain instruments come to be associated with certain performance styles, genres, and timbres. People want certain kinds of instruments because they want certain kinds of sounds—or, at least, to plug into those histories of sound. The (sonic) spectral objectivity works only because of the (social) spectral objectivity of the instrument.

This is most obvious in cases where people get it wrong, believing in the instrument as a singular cause of the sound. Even Theodor Adorno, as he criticizes the pursuit of timbre, or a signature sound, in his essay on musical fetishism, falls into this trap when he denounces the "cult of the master violins. One promptly goes into raptures at the well-announced sound of a Stradivarius or Amati, which only the ear of a specialist can tell from that of a good modern violin. . . . Moments of sensual pleasure in the idea, the voice, the instrument are made into fetishes and torn away from any function which could give them meaning."[12] As is often the case, even if his political aesthetics are open to critique (a point not worth rehashing here), Adorno has described a vital dimension of modern mediatic music culture. A great deal of musical pleasure for both musician and listener is in the sound of the music quite apart from the structure of the work or its larger meaning. This is made apparent in the work of social psychologists such as Daniel Levitin, who has shown that test subjects can identify many well-known songs by snippets so short that the only audible aspect of the song is its timbre (and maybe pitch). It is also made apparent in reviews of new music, especially electronic music, on sites such as *Pitchfork* that describe the tonal palette or spatial feel of new records.[13]

But Adorno misses his own point when he says that "the ear of a special-ist" can distinguish a Stradivarius from a good modern violin. No, it can-not. By any measure, the category of "Stradivarius violin" contains a wider range of differences than the differences between Strads and other kinds of violins.[14] As Emily Dolan shows, the very elevation of the Stradivarius co-incides with the increasing standardization of symphonic instrumentation and repertoire in the nineteenth century and the creation and expansion of a market for old violins. The same pattern can be found today, as (not quite as) old guitars, drum machines, or drum sets come to be associated with certain music and musical sounds.[15] Even software instruments now conform to this pattern, as when a representative of Native Instruments explained that the company's software synthesizer Massive remained in version 1 because of its importance to the genre of Dubsteb.[16] As music genres' repertoires become canons, the instruments associated with them begin to take on additional forms of value, which in turn feed back into their spectral objectivity in both senses of the term "spectral."

In new media studies, much has been made of the term "prosumer" to describe the elision of categories of production and consumption, or profes-sional and consumer, in the age of digital technologies.[17] Conceptually, this is not so far from Adorno's claim that relations to instruments as keys to partic-ular sounds or tones "are the same relations as exist between the consumers of hit songs and the hit songs."[18] What Adorno missed is that this is a feature of the historical capitalism of the music he loved just as much as it was a feature of the contemporary capitalism of the music he despised. Musicians' fetish for instruments is a long-term trend in the history of instruments and not something that arises with the mass media. Its current form is outlined well by Paul Théberge, who writes that, over the 1980s and 1990s, the musi-cal instrument industry became increasingly dependent on a range of digital "tech" industries—especially those that produce microprocessors, storage, and software—which in turn accelerated the rate and quantity of music instrument acquisition and replacement among practicing musicians. In other words, making music became a form of consuming technology. While this had always been the case on some level, the industries and practices surrounding digital technologies ramped up the speed and intensity of consumption. He writes, "By becoming 'consumers of technology,' many musicians have been able to take advantage of the enormous productive potential of new digital technologies. At the same time, however, they have witnessed the incursion of capitalist relation(s) upon their creative practices at the most fundamental level."[19] In other words, musicians' relationships to instruments are shaped by the capitalistic contours of their specific moment. It is not only digital signal processing that is at play here: containerization in shipping, printed circuit boards, CNC (computer numerical control) and CAD (computer-aided design), and other new processes of design and manufacture all shape the current consumer environment for musicians. In anachronistic terms, musicians have always been "prosumers"—producers and consumers at the same time—as evidenced both by the markets in prized instruments and in their quests for tone. But the past three decades have witnessed an acceleration and intensification of market logics and cycles of acquisition and replacement for whole subsets of the music-making and recording industries.

Musical instruments are thus spectral objects in the richest possible sense: when operated, they produce a range of distinctive timbres that are available to the senses. Those operations stand in for whole histories of aesthetics and social relations, to the point that it is possible to hear aspects of the sounds that are not even there, as in the fantastical trained ear that can distinguish a Stradivarius from another make of violin. This is why it is not enough to simply reword "allows one to . . . substitute images for causes," as Chun writes," as "substitute *sounds* for causes." To study commodity fetishism in the sonic domain is to ask after the causes of the sound. And causal listening, as Michel Chion has written, is the most deceptive form of listening. All sounds have multiple causes.[20] They index webs of relations and context as much as things coming into contact with one another and transmitted through a medium.

Spectral Instrumentality

We can now return to Universal Audio's business. Ward and I agree that Universal Audio is at least in part in the business of commodity fetishism, because the company produces devices, sounds, and interfaces all at once. Universal Audio goes even further, producing potted histories of the technologies it sells online, thereby educating its potential user base about the mystique it intends to invoke in its design and marketing choices. One part of the company's business involves building hardware copies of paradigmatic sound-processing devices used in the 1960s and 1970s. Universal Audio also produces software replicas of analog audio devices. The graphical interface on its software screen looks like a photo of the hardware, and the algorithms beneath the surface model every part of the circuits, down to the level of components. The user "grabs" images of knobs with the mouse to turn them. Even with the added flexibility afforded by software, Universal Audio shies away from introducing new capabilities, apart from maybe making a monaural unit into a stereo one or adding presets.

Although Universal Audio is exceptionally committed to a notion of faithfulness to originals, it is hardly alone. Native Instruments in Berlin got its start modeling old Hammond organs and analog synthesizers in the software domain. Line6 in Los Angeles builds tools for guitarists based on models of classic instruments, amplifiers, and effects but goes more for the sound than the old interfaces. If you acquire a comprehensive software package for music recording, composition, or performance, it is likely to come with software models of old instruments and signal processing devices as part of the bundle. Its own operating parameters are likely to be skeuomorphic, as well, presenting users with knobs and faders as if they were sitting before a giant mixing desk, providing at once a degree of legibility and an illusion of control. In her discussion of software interfaces, Chun argues that interfaces are "driven by a dream of individual control: of direct personal manipulation of the screen, and thus, by extension, of the system it indexes or represents. . . . Interfaces offer us an imaginary relationship to our hardware."[21] Between a mouse click and an action on the screen lie countless digital instructions deliberately obscured from the end user, along with the labor that went into making the computer, mouse, and screen and the elaborate standards and protocols that allow them to work with one another consistently, to work with other systems, and to appear seamless in the experience of use. Yet it is not simply about hidden labor.

Whether we judge it to be real or illusory, a feeling of agency and control is crucial to rendering sensible what is otherwise unavailable to the individual's senses: the web of relations and histories of which the sound partakes. But since we are talking about sound technologies taking on different interfaces, we must also account for the fact that interfaces address sense modalities differently. People who use an analog mixing board can use all of their fingers to control it and can find their way around by touch as well as by looking. Desktop and laptop software is generally confined to keyboard shortcuts and mouse clicks and requires a more fixed gaze on a screen. Touchscreen interfaces bring back more fingers and promise greater immediacy, but currently they do so without much haptic feedback, thereby also demanding the musicians' gaze. In all of these cases, the skeuomorph helps to create a sense of equivalence.[22] This may be especially important for sound, since if listeners cannot tell modern violins from Stradivarius violins, their chances of distinguishing a well-designed digital model of a compressor or delay from the hardware by sound alone is also quite low. The rhetoric and representation of the model becomes part of the model itself.[23]

In the experience of use, operational control stands in for whole sets of relations and histories that otherwise are not immediately available to the user's senses. This is true of software, as Chun notes, but it also true of any technology for making sound or music. Barry Blesser and Linda-Ruth Salter make the connection explicitly in their discussion of artificial reverberators that Blesser worked on in the 1970s. Blesser designed one of the first commercial digital simulations of a room, and here is how he and Salter describe operating that simulation in practice: "Once a spatial parameter is connected to a knob, button, or key, [from the perspective of the person operating it] a reverberator becomes effectively indistinguishable from a musical instrument, played in real time by a musician." In music technologies, media collapse into instruments—or, rather, the line between instruments and media grows fuzzy.[24]

We are used to thinking of instrument design as interface design when an instrument is digital, such as a synthesizer or sampler. But all instruments have interfaces. The apparent immediacy of an acoustic instrument conceals just as much labor, craft, and standardization as a software interface or digital signal processor. Alongside a set of pedals, a piano key operates a hammer, mediating and modulating the percussive dimensions of the instrument. The taut head of a tabla presents itself as a target for the player, with vastly different tones available depending on where and how fingers strike the surface. The fingers are meant to hit one end of the keys on a mbira, not the other, just as Western string musicians know that the strings on members of the violin and guitar families are meant to be played between the bridge and the nut (though many have violated that rule for interesting effect). As with the example of software, all of these mechanisms obfuscate all manner of labor, learning, and decisions.

The pitch and temperament compromises built into a piano keyboard or cut into a guitar's fretboard come from sustained collective reflection on the differences between the physics of sound and the cultured ears of musicians and listeners. This is no accident, for reference pitches and tuning standards are some of the oldest continuous controversies over standards in Western culture. For instance, in *Harmonious Triads*, Myles Jackson chronicles the politics of pitch in nineteenth-century Europe, which were intensely bound up with nationalism but also with the broader spread of international standards for the purposes of commerce.[25] Standardized pitch provides a basis for musical complementarity, but so do a whole other set of protocols. Members of the violin or brass family—or the drums in the "kit"—exist in a relation of complementarity with one another within specific genres, shown in Emily Dolan's history of orchestration, Matt Brennan's forthcoming history of the drum kit, and Georgina Born and Joe Snape's study of Max patches, where even "limitless" music software quickly refers back to common standards and practices.[26] This is even true *within* instruments. A synthesizer, drum set, or computer is a kind of system based on a set of relations that are at once social, physical, commercial, and customary, but so, too, are acoustic instruments such as acoustic guitars.[27] The chain of physical causes and effects are more readily apparent to the untrained observer, but they are no less real: move the bridge on a stringed instrument even a little and you will probably have to adjust the neck and retune the strings to achieve the same intonation as you had before the move.[28]

The decisions built into instruments have real ramifications for musicians, from the finer points of technique to the injuries one can suffer from playing too much or incorrectly. During the same trip to Northern California in 2012 that took me to Universal Audio, I spoke with Roger Linn in his living room. He was seated near a piano and not far from an electric guitar connected to a pedal and then a computer. Linn made his mark as an inventor of electronic instruments. After designing one of the first sampling drum machines—in other words, a drum machine that used the sounds of recorded drums rather than synthesizing its own drum sounds—he developed the concept for the MPC (MIDI Production Center), which became the most important instrument for rap and hip hop besides the turntable.[29] At the time of my visit, Linn was hard at work trying to create a properly "expressive" digital instrument. By "expressive," he meant that it would have the qualities of a stringed instrument as used by a trained musician, where even subtle gestures are mapped to variations in pitch, timbre, or loudness. Gazing over at the piano and guitar, he lambasted them both from the standpoint of interface design. For both, the hand gestures change when the musician wants to change key. In other words, the skills are not transferrable. From the standpoint of modern interface theory, old instruments are unnecessarily difficult to learn and lack sound ergonomics. But while he criticized old instruments for their inaccessibility, Linn criticized new digital instruments for their lack of expressivity, because—he argued—they do not offer musicians sufficient control to produce sophisticated melody, harmony, and timbral variation in real time.[30]

Historically, virtuosity has been described as an expressive relationship to an instrument achieved *in spite of* the difficulties inherent in learning that instrument. This suggests a contradiction in the scenario Linn set out: while expressivity is held up in theory as the value that will most set new instruments apart from their limits, expressivity may be the value that most functions in setting *social* limits for new instruments and circumscribing the category of musicianship itself. In my discussions with instrument makers, expressivity is consistently held up as a value—none of the people I have interviewed have argued against it or for an alternative term. But when pressed as to its meaning, the point of reference is always a set of established techniques for playing *another* instrument (usually violin, piano, or guitar), not a definable quality. Even references to abstractions such as "virtuosity" depend on understandings and instances of musicians' relationships to existing instruments rather than abstract categories of practice. For instance, Christopher Dolan and Daniel Koppelman argue that instrument designers need to distinguish between control and virtuosity to promote expressiveness in new instruments. To this end, they propose using motion-tracking technologies to study how musicians play existing instruments and to use virtuosi on existing instruments as models for virtuosity on new instruments.[31] To have their expressivity properly evaluated and improved, the reasoning goes, new instruments must be tested on people who are good at playing old instruments. The strategy is inherently conservative: the skills needed to be a great MPC player cannot be divined by watching a great electric guitarist; the skills needed to be a great electric guitarist cannot be divined by watching a great trombonist. Linn encapsulates the contradiction in our interview: while he criticizes new instruments for not being expressive like old instruments, musicians have used his MPC and its descendants to make music that has different rules for meaning and expression and different criteria for expression and expressiveness.[32] Virtuosity and skill across the history of instruments is an endless chain of nonequivalence.

In musical practice, skills developed on an instrument require skills with an interface *and* the system to which it is connected, whether we are talking about a set of energy transfers built into assemblies of metal, bone, and wood or about electronics and plastic. A fretboard, a keyboard and a GUI are all interfaces of a sort.[33] Playing an instrument is a form of embodied knowledge—a knowledge won with hours and years of practice, a "second nature."[34] Embodied knowledge mediates the standardization that went into the instrument's interface. When I pick up an electric bass guitar, my hand movements are now second nature, even though long ago they were a struggle. After years of playing, my body seems to conform to the instrument, even though it feels like the instrument is conforming to my body or my will. Phenomenally, this is not so different from typing out this sentence on a keyboard, where again my body has conformed to a standard—a standard that was originally developed for an system entirely different from a computer. The conformity results in the actual transformation of the body, as dramatically shown in Lochlann Jain's history of repetitive stress injuries.[35]

From the outside, gestures such as these can appear effortless to the casual observer because the labor behind them is obscured in the design of the instrument and the skill of the musician. When observing skilled musicians perform (or people skilled with any technology), we might say that they are *in instrumentality*. This is to say, they are in a relationship to the instrument in which intention and action conform to each other, where certain prior actions and knowledges are relegated to a background status so that the musician may "sustain a certain direction," to use Sara Ahmed's terms.[36] But what happens when we confront instruments outside this moment of performance? They can be experienced as tools of learning or as partial objects, but they may also be experienced as magical in their own right.

In her classic ethnography of a South African recording studio, Louise Meintjes tells a story of a singer named Joana mistaking a MIDI clock that synchronizes all of the studio's different devices for a sound-container. "The MIDI clock does not actually house the sounds to which Joana refers," Meintjes writes. "For her, there is a whole sonic world packed into that sleek machine. . . . It is a world to which Joana can point, but that she cannot enter herself. It is invisible but sensed to be of enormous proportion."[37] This specific case illustrates a general condition: when people do not have access to the inner world of an instrument—because of knowledge, experience, power differences, custom—they are more likely to attribute to it a vast, complex inner world.

In part, this is a deliberate design feature, and an old one at that. My recording teacher Mark Rubel calls this dimension of instruments "psychocosmetic." The ornate scrolls and flourishes of the violin family; the branded headstocks of the guitar family; the shiny, smooth surface of a piano; the finishes on wood or brass; the blinking LEDS of a drum machine—all of these allude to the magic within, the agency held inside the thing, just beyond a person's fingertips. Writing about the recording studio, Meintjes captures the futurism that enrobes so many electronic instruments today. For her, the studio space is

> constructed and experienced as magical and as a fetish by music-makers who work within it. By typifying the space as magical, I mean that it is remote from the ordinary and that through the art of illusion and the capacity of the imagination, it seems to house a natural force . . . that when tapped produces compelling art. By thinking of the studio as fetish, I reify it into an object that can procure for those who have earned access to it the services of that force, or "spirit," lodged within it.[38]

Hanging on walls at music stores, leaned up against the chairs on a stage, assembled into racks, or organologically classified at museums, instruments can suggest some kind of spirit when separated from their moments of making or use. It is perhaps more appealing to believe that magic lies in instruments than in people's labor because of the ways in which music and musicianship are mystified and separated from everyday life; because of the appearance of effortlessness that attends so much good performance; and because of the distance most people will have from most instruments in their lived experience.

In the fantasy lives of musicians and artists, we can also see a connection between instrumentality and spirit or magic. A quick search of the phrase "It's like an instrument" yields a steady drone of artistic longings attached to equipment. Like Blesser's parameter-assigned-to-a-knob, magic manifests in machinery the moment that parameter control and efficient operation yield inspiration and hidden resources for art. One genre of comments comes from communities of musicians online who are discussing equipment, sometimes as users and sometimes as reviewers. A reviewer for a microphone writes, "The mic is a pleasure to sing through, it's like an instrument for singers like a guitar is to a guitarist." A user of digital reverb software called ValhallaShimmer writes, "I see Shimmer as a special effect—it has so much character it's almost like an instrument." Another musician, writing about a sequencer (which controls other instruments but does not make any sounds on its own) says, "It's almost like an instrument in itself when you start doing things like assign knobs A + B to control when things happen relative to other things."[39]

Artists, too, use this terminology. The artist Jim Andrews writes about the interactive visual art program Aleph Null, "It takes practice to tease the really good stuff out of it. It's like an instrument that way." Note that the good stuff is teased out by the user but resides in the thing itself. In an interview with ART iT magazine, Janet Cardiff and George Bures Miller describe an installation the same way:

ART iT. If you don't know where the sensors are, it seems natural to explore [*Experiment in F# Minor* (2013)] through movement, to see whether you can control the intensity by waving your arms in one direction or another. The work sucks you into performative behavior. With the walks too, there's a mechanism of unconsciously entering a different zone of behavior.

JANET CARDIFF. You see how unlimited it could be. It's like an instrument.

GEORGE BURES MILLER. That's the problem for us. We're always discovering these things that could be unlimited.

CARDIFF. With *Pandemonium* (2005), for which we installed robotic percussive beaters in the cells of the Eastern State Penitentiary Museum in Philadelphia, we discovered that was like an instrument too. You could have made any piece of music with it. You could invite percussionists in and say, here's an instrument, what do you want to do with it? There's all these offshoots that would be great to follow through. Our problem is we have too many ideas and not enough time.[40]

"You see how unlimited it can be": this turn of phrase marks the moment where description calls forth fetishism. The limitlessness—"you could have made any piece of music with it"—is the fantasy of that "natural force that produces good art" to which Meintjes gestures.

Conclusion

It is not accidental that people attribute magical powers to instruments at some distance from the moments of their use: either the moment of observation from a distance where embodied practice is not fully possible or the moment of reflection from a distance of time. In *Queer Phenomenology*, Ahmed writes about what is revealed when "technologies are no longer ready for action." An experience of being unable to use a thing—or at a distance from the moment of use—leads to attribution of properties to the thing itself. Writing about failure, using Martin Heidegger's example of a hammer, she says that it "might then lead to 'the object' *being attributed* with properties, qualities and values. In other words, what is at stake in moments of failure is not so much access to properties but attributions of properties, which become a matter of how we *approach* the object. . . . The moment of 'non-use' is . . . the same moment in which objects may be judged insofar as they are inadequate to a task, the moment when we 'blame the tool.'"[41]

This may also be the moment when we credit the tool for the sound. Drawing on Ivan Illich's philosophy of technology, Christopher Small has famously argued against the prevalent notion that some people possess innate musical ability while others do not. Instead, he shows how this idea both represents the limits of the modern educational system and functions to limit democratic cultural participation.[42] But here we can extend his ideas in a slightly different direction. The idea that one needs a particular instrument to get a good sound is not, as Adorno suggests, merely an index of a novice's ignorance and false consciousness masquerading as aestheticism (although it certainly *could* be that in some cases). It may also be, as Meintjes suggests, an index of a musician's search for greater meaning and relationality in musical practice. The deep feeling that an instrument brings magic or power to musicians, rather than they to it, is a residuum of this more general way of thinking. This agential inversion of musician and instrument defines the role of commodity fetishism in sound.

Like all technologies, sound technologies' actual contours are available only in their entelechy. Without a player, an instrument's sonic powers sit at rest. Without a phone call, you can know only so much about a telephone. Yet it is precisely in this moment of rest—in anticipation or retrospection of use—or when an instrument is in the hands of someone else that its fetish character is most effective, for this is where it most fully points to a set of social relations that are otherwise unavailable to the senses. Instrumentality recursively transforms contingent effects, themselves barely perceptible, into new kinds of causes. In apprehending sound technologies' spectral objectivity, we eavesdrop on this process.

Notes

I thank Carrie Rentschler, Vicki Simon, Jim Steintrager, Rachel Bergmann, and Burç Kostem for comments and Emily Dolan and Louise Meintjes for conversations that led to some of the ideas in this chapter.

1 Matt Ward, interview by author, February 17, 2012.
2 Matt Ward, interview by author, February 17, 2012.
3 Chun, *Programmed Visions*, 50.
4 Tresch and Dolan, "Toward a New Organology," 281.
5 These categories are actually quite fluid, but explaining the fluidity is beyond the scope of this paper. Meintjes and Théberge are discussed in detail later.
6 For a critique of the ephemerality of sound thesis, see Sterne, *The Audible Past*, 15; Sterne, "The Theology of Sound." For an example of a sound in commodity form, see Gaines, *Contested Culture*; McLeod and DiCola, *Creative License*.
7 Gopinath, *The Ringtone Dialectic*; Théberge, *Any Sound You Can Imagine*; Wright, "The Wilhelm Scream."
8 Heinrich, *An Introduction to the Three Volumes of Karl Marx's Capital*, 72.
9 Heinrich, *An Introduction to the Three Volumes of Karl Marx's Capital*, 75, emphasis in original.
10 This, too, has a history: see Mills, "Deaf Jam."
11 See Dolan and Rehding, *Oxford Handbook on Timbre*.
12 Adorno, "On the Fetish-Character of Music and the Regression of Listening," 295.
13 Levitin, *This Is Your Brain on Music*. Almost any *Pitchfork* review of electronic music will do, but here is a choice quote from a review of Tim Hecker's *Love Streams*. "Hecker's palette has evolved in other ways, too. 'Obsidian Counterpoint' opens the album with a blippy stream of arpeggios, an explicitly electronic sound that is unusual for his work. Throughout, his sounds seem tugged in two directions at once, as though caught between the digital and the physical. In 'Music of the Air,' a buzzing, droning synthesizer patch bobs in unpredictable motions like a handful of jewel-colored flies. Toward the end of 'Bijie Dream,' a harpsichord-like sound mutates into something resembling a steel pan, a far cry from Hecker's typically Arctic-inspired palette": Philip Sherburne, "Tim Hecker *Love Streams*," *Pitchfork*, April 7, 2016, https://pitchfork.com/reviews/albums/21635-love-streams.
14 Dolan, "Mendacious Technology"; Wilder, "Patina and the Role of Nostalgia in the Field of Stringed Instrument Cultural Production."
15 Bennett, *On Becoming a Rock Musician*. See also Ian Dunham, "From Kitchy to Classy: Reviving the Roland TR-808," *Sounding Out! The Sound Studies Blog*, June 9, 2014, https://soundstudiesblog.com/2014/06/09/808.
16 Wellmer, "Machines to Hear for Us."
17 Maxwell and Miller, *Greening the Media*, 20; Ritzer and Jurgenson, "Production, Consumption, Prosumption."

18 Adorno, "On the Fetish-Character of Music and the Regression of Listening," 295.

19 Théberge, *Any Sound You Can Imagine*, 255; see also 244–45.

20 Chion, *Audio-Vision*, 26.

21 Chun, *Programmed Visions*, 62, 66.

22 Victoria Simon's forthcoming dissertation on touchscreen interfaces describes this relationship in greater detail. A skeuomorph, following Katherine Hayles, is "a design feature that is no longer functional in itself but refers back to a feature that was functional at an earlier time": Hayles, *How We Became Posthuman*, 17.

23 I pursue this further in Sterne, "The Software Passes the Test When the User Fails It."

24 Blesser and Salter, *Spaces Speak, Are You Listening?* 91.

25 Jackson, *Harmonious Triads*.

26 Dolan, *The Orchestral Revolution*; Waksman, *Instruments of Desire*; Weintraub, *Power Plays*. See also Georgina Born and Joe Snape, "Max, Music Software and the Mutual Mediation of Aesthetics and Digital Technologies," working paper, Oxford University; Matt Brennan, "The Drum Kit: A Social History of the Instrument That Changed Popular Music," unpublished ms., University of Edinburgh.

27 Gura, *C. F. Martin and His Guitars*.

28 Jackson, *Harmonious Triads*.

29 On the MPC, see, e.g., Butler, *Unlocking the Groove*; Rose, *Black Noise*.

30 Roger Linn, interview by author, February 13, 2012.

31 Dobrian and Koppelman, "The 'E' in NIME."

32 Butler, *Playing with Something That Runs*; Demers, *Listening through the Noise*.

33 Kursell, "Visualizing Piano Playing."

34 Bourdieu, *The Logic of Practice*.

35 Jain, *Injury*.

36 Ahmed, *Queer Phenomenology*, 31.

37 Meintjes, *Sound of Africa!* 89.

38 Meintjes, *Sound of Africa!* 73–74.

39 Pete Pell, reviewer's comment on the Sterling Audio ST66 Large Diaphragm Tube Condensor Microphone, Musician's Friend sales website, https://www.musiciansfriend.com/pro-audio/sterling-audio-st66-large-diaphragm-tube-condenser-microphone; Aniston, user's comment on "Valhalla Shimmer or EOS?" thread, KVRAudio music software forum, https://www.kvraudio.com/forum/viewtopic.php?t=302426; Gosh, user's comment on "Sequentix Cirklon" thread, Muff Wiggler modular synthesis forum https://www.muffwiggler.com/forum/viewtopic.php?p=933082&sid=c75363c58507ef9674cb8b3bac00fc8c. All accessed March 2, 2014.

40 "Jim Andrews," artist profile on Rhizome.org, http://classic.rhizome.org/profile/jimandrews/?page=2#activity_stream; "Janet Cardiff and George Bures Miller: Part II," *ART iT*, September 27, 2013, https://www.art-it.asia/en/u/admin_ed_itv_e/k15n0uprnfsy6i3capt9. Both accessed March 2, 2014.

41 Ahmed, *Queer Phenomenology*, 49, emphasis in original.

42 Small, *Music, Society, Education*.

III | Acousmatic Complications

Listening after "Acousmaticity"

Notes on a Transdisciplinary Problematic

The Inner Voice, Revisited

In his early works such as *Voice and Phenomenon* and *Of Grammatology*, Jacques Derrida, as is well known, undertakes a critique of a foundational feature of Western philosophy having to do with the voice. The point of Derrida's critique is not so much the ascendency of the voice over writing as the tendency, as he shows through a meticulous analysis of the writings of Edmund Husserl, to attribute to the voice qualities of an inalienable inner meaning that seems immediately present to itself (as in the phenomenon of hearing oneself speak). According to Derrida, the voice has been the privileged carrier by default of that ineffable something that is referred to variously as the spirit, the soul, the mind, and the like. The fact that this ineffable something is assumed to be there, as though diaphanously, without mediation, is what he calls the Western metaphysics of presence, which is built on an idealization and universalization of the voice as a transcendent operation of pure auto-affection.

The appeal of such auto-affection to Husserl is its apparent self-sufficiency. He is drawn to the familiar phenomenon whereby, in hearing oneself speak, one seems to be moving in a spontaneous, continuous, and unified circuit, with the ear and the mouth forming a single, closed loop. For Husserl, it is when one hears one's own voice *in silence*—that is to say, in a solitary mental state, without going through the detour of the tongue and the mouth, the kind of externally mediated communication that he calls indication—that the inner voice is at its purest.[1] The essence of this "voice that keeps silent" is the result of what Husserl calls a phenomenological reduction. Derrida's strategic move to open this inner voice loop is worth repeating: "Hearing-oneself-speak is not the interiority of an inside closed in upon itself. It is the irreducible openness in the inside, the eye and the world in speech. *The phenomenological reduction is a scene.*"[2]

Jean-Luc Nancy, echoing Derrida but putting the emphasis on the act of sounding, describes this scene of hearing oneself speak in this manner: "To sound is to vibrate in itself or by itself: it is not only, for the sonorous body . . . to emit a sound, but it is also to stretch out, to carry itself and be resolved into vibrations that both return it to itself and place it outside itself."[3] As Mladen Dolar comments, "The Derridean turn has thus . . . turned the voice into a preeminent object of philosophical inquiry, demonstrating its complicity with the principal metaphysical preoccupations."[4] Derrida's point, it should be stressed, is not exactly to leverage writing against voice; rather, it is to argue that the voice, which (as a result of the phonocentric bias) seems readily self-same and self-present, is actually the effect of a prior—and ongoing—temporal series of inscription, an arche-writing that leaves traces (imprints of differentiation). Despite its lure of immediacy, the voice, even when it is heard in the solitary mental state, is not originary but already an artifact, a variant in a chain of emissions involving duration and spacing. Insofar as Derrida's utopian project of grammatology is meant to be a science of signs supposedly to be "founded" between signs' retention and escape, appearance and disappearance, the voice belongs as much in grammatology as does writing.[5]

If we were to approach philosophy as an ethnographic exercise, Husserl's investment in the inner voice could be analogized to a type of nativism. The attempt to salvage a virginal voice, as yet untouched and, by implication, untouchable by outside or foreign influences, reminds us of certain anthropological endeavors to seek out and preserve primitive cultures. (Think of Derrida's well-known critique of Claude Lévi-Strauss's reading of the Nambikwara in *Tristes Tropiques*.) Is the inner voice not like that putatively authentic native whose contamination through contact with the outside world worries those who want to keep her in her pristine, in-digenous condition? This longing for the origin in the form of the voice that keeps silent, far from the madding crowd, is what Derrida has taught us to deconstruct.

Although Derrida's reading of Husserl is not informed by sound repro-duction technology, it was probably not a coincidence that the problematic of the inner voice, the essence of the phenomenological reduction, emerged at a time when the voice as such had become eminently reproducible with the invention of machines such as the phonograph. As Amy Lawrence re-minds us, "Nearly all of Edison's proposed uses for sound recording are linked to the reproduction of the voice—in elocution, pronunciation, pres-ervation of family histories . . . , dictation, lectures, and recording phone calls. . . . Thus, almost before the phonograph had been invented, its spe-cial mission as preserver of the voice was set out for it. The ideology of the apparatus to a great extent pre-existed the invention of the apparatus."[6] This important correlation between voice and reproductive technology is also underscored in *Sound Unseen: Acousmatic Sound in Theory and Prac-tice*, in which Brian Kane suggestively prefaces a discussion of Husserl with a discussion of the arrival of the phonographic voice.[7] A landmark study of Western philosophy's responses to sound and voice *after* Edison invented the phonograph (i.e., in the age of sound's and voice's mechani-cal recordability and iterability), Kane's book demonstrates in remarkable historical detail how a phenomenological approach to sound such as Pierre Schaeffer's—an approach that began with an interest in ordinary objects of sound but culminated rather in the ideality of a sound object that is not reducible to ordinary objects—is fundamentally indebted to the philoso-phy of Husserl.[8]

Supplementing Derrida's reading of Husserl with Kane's analysis, we could argue that the inner voice, which Derrida places at the core of Western metaphysics, is *a post- appearing in the guise of a pre-*: a virginal self-presence that is recovered, so to speak, precisely when the voice has become—because of the irreversible happening of sound recording—ceaselessly repeatable, copyable, and dispersible. Douglas Kahn summarizes this ep-ochal transition succinctly:

> No longer was the ability to hear oneself speak restricted to a fleeting moment. It became locked in a materiality that could both stand still and mute and also time travel by taking one's voice far afield from one's own presence . . . The voice no longer occupied its own space and

time. *It was removed from the body where, following Derrida, it entered the realm of writing . . . where one loses control of the voice because it no longer disappears.*[9]

The Curtain

The contemporary conceptualization of "acousmaticity"—of listening un-accompanied by the sight of sound's source—has become popularized through the sound and audiovisual work of Schaeffer and Michel Chion.[10] However, acousmaticity should also be conjoined to the aforementioned trend-setting philosophical scene, in which the phenomenological effort to re-essentialize (or *re-nativize*) the voice encounters its politicized resistance in the form of deconstruction. The consequences of this scene are far-reaching. For although Husserl's voice nativism or voice primitivism, if it may be so called, has been debunked (by Derrida and his followers) for its idealist presuppositions, the technique of phenomenological reduction remains profoundly influential. Involving the move of *bracketing off* the given (in Husserl's case, nature's or some other factual existence), this technique has implications on a number of intellectual, aesthetic, and mediatic fronts, in ways that go considerably beyond the more esoteric circles of phenomenology and deconstruction.[11] In Schaeffer's and his followers' theorization of the so-called acousmatic situation, for instance—I think here of Chion, Dolar, Nancy,[12] Slavoj Žižek, and others, myself included, in their reflections on sound and voice—we are confronted with just how salient and powerful phenomenological reduction can be as a method. How so?

As is typical of modern uses of antiquity (Freud's use of the legend of Oedipus being a foremost example), what is interesting in the Schaefferians' adaptation of the legend of the Pythagorean sect and its pedagogical practice (whereupon the pupils were separated from their master by a hanging so that they learned by hearing the master's voice but not by seeing his face) is a certain dramatization.[13] What exactly is being dramatized? In what is commonly understood as sound's boundlessness—its all-encompassing ambience, its ability to envelope the listener as though in a continuum—Schaefferians install—or, more properly speaking, underscore—the crucial mechanism of a divide (a break or caesura). In their rendition of the Pythagorean sect's practice, even as the interplay between presence (sound/voice) and absence (face/body) remains key, *what is epistemologically decisive is the part played by the curtain.* This simple prop enables the master's voice, generalizable first as voice and then more broadly as sound, to spring forth in isolation as an object. As Kane suggests, this phantasmatic object's emergence in the acousmatic situation is akin to the inner voice's emergence (as a self-same presence) in the phenomenological situation; the Schaefferian *acousmatique* and the Husserlian *epochē* are two moments sutured together.[14] As the source of sound is obscured because it is withheld, the listeners are compelled to notice the sonic object's immanent logic, a logic that is not reducible to, or accountable through, external factors.

A bit more needs to be said about this legendary curtain. Before the emergence of the object, the curtain separates. If it serves as a means of concealment, it does so by way of *a cut through space*, a cut that institutes at once a boundary and a new beginning, conjuring at once a barrier and a novel coming-through. While in the realm of phenomenology the curtain functions as (a symbol of) the interruption—the bracketing—of a given (or assumed) way of thinking, in the realm of contemporary sound and music the curtain is the site where technology, together with its ideological effects, is to be located.[15] We may go as far as to say that the curtain is the very *hinge* where the Husserlian bracket meets, not only Derridean deconstruction, but also the recording machine, as Schaeffer himself notes: "In ancient times, the apparatus was a curtain; today, it is the radio and the methods of reproduction, with the whole set of electro-acoustic transformations that place us, modern listeners to an invisible voice, under similar circumstances."[16] And, whereas the Husserlian bracket does its work by closing things down, sound recording does its work in the opposite direction, by opening things up. Between the phenomenological reduction that represses (among other things, the historical arrival of sound recording), and the phonographic supplementation that liberates (e.g., by freeing sound from previous traditions of abstract [note] music), the conceptual grounds have radically shifted. A whole new way of thinking has come into play, resonating game-changing effects.

The curtain, in other words, is nothing short of a stand-in for a process of structuration, a geometric way of tracking thought, wherein things acquire a kind of autonomy, a new recognizability, after they have been bracketed off—removed from traditional settings or severed from presumed origins. Between the nativist conservation of a metaphysics of (voice's) self-presence and the deconstructive-reproductive multiplication of such self-presence into infinite (sonic) traces, we hear echoes of other modernist philosophical gestures: Martin Heidegger's line across words, Derrida's coinage of *sous rature* (i.e., the move of putting "under erasure"), and, in an arguably affined but otherwise divergent operation, Michel Foucault's depiction of the modern production of madness by way of confinement (i.e., spatial partitioning).[17] When lined up alongside these other instances, acousmaticity comes across less as a mechanism of obstruction than as an event involving a threshold artifact, a means of bringing things into focus. As Kane suggests, "By defamiliarizing everyday practices of listening, the acousmatic reduction makes these modes perspicuous . . . [or] brings these modes of listening into audibility."[18]

Beyond sound and music, we are reminded of other aesthetic experiments—the Russian Formalists' techniques of defamiliarizing poetry and narrative, early filmmakers' deployments of montage, Bertolt Brecht's epic theater and its alienation effects, Marcel Duchamp's "ready-mades" derived from *objets trouvés*, and so forth—that similarly depend on techniques of *bracketing-off-cum-estrangement* to make customary phenomena leap forward in a new frame. Does not the Schaefferians' adaptation of antiquity, too, belong in this larger history of modernism and its conceptual-aesthetic attempts at reflexivity and renewal? The "given" to be bracketed off could be anything: nature, convention, habit, or any jaded way of perceiving and doing things. The signature modernist move is that of letting a known object—be it phenomenological, imagistic, theatrical, sculptural, sonic, or vocal—become freshly noticeable through a deliberate, artful suspension of the given, so much so that the beholder, whose perception is roughened in this process, is forced to come to terms with a different and often disturbing order of things.[19]

In Bits and Pieces: Sonic Objecthood

By naming the acousmatic situation, the Schaefferians have thus established, in tandem with other modernist endeavors, a special kind of object, one that is essentially a (cut) fragment, for which the whole (a coherent, organic unity), for one reason or another, is irrecoverable. "The fragment is the intrusion of death into the work," writes Theodor Adorno. "While destroying it, it removes the stain of semblance."[20] If this reflection on the fragment holds validity, the question remains as to why what Adorno calls death—presumably, the state of disintegration that absolves the fragment of the culpability ("the stain") of mimesis, of having an identity or being like something—seems to intrude so readily in modernity. Chion provides a rejoinder to Adorno when he remarks on the intimate link between the acousmatic voice and those who are dead. In both cases, voices have been cut off from bodies: "Ever since the telephone and gramophone made it possible to isolate voices from bodies, the voice naturally has reminded us of the voice of the dead. And more than our generation, those who witnessed the birth of these technologies were aware of their funerary quality. In the cinema, the voice of the *acousmêtre* is frequently the voice of one who is dead."[21] Is not Chion suggesting here a certain *historicity* borne mutely but not accidentally by sound as fragment? This historicity manifests as a collective imprint of things having been torn out of their integrated contexts—of things having had their "stain of semblance" removed, as Adorno puts it—and (re)appearing in isolated and funerary form. These qualities of fragmentariness and deadness are emblematic of such things' (in this case, sound technologies') participation in modernity; as Chion mentions, sonic objects such as the telephonic or gramophonic voice frequently remind us of such qualities. The cultural complexity of this state of affairs, whereby objects, and objectivity per se, become knowable primarily through the condition of being disconnected, disembodied, and dead, cannot be overstated.[22]

From the listener's perspective, this state of affairs is evident in the considerable list of sound- and music-receiving apparatuses (and the experiences they enable) since recording became possible.[23] From the phonograph, gramophone with its loudspeaker, radio, and turntable playing vinyl records at different speeds to the portable transistor radio, cassette tape recorder, Walkman, Discman, and electronic devices such as iPods, smartphones, tablets, and laptops, sounds—and let us assume that these are sounds we choose to listen to—have been coming to us in bits and pieces. From being captured in the grooves of an old-fashioned LP to being downloadable from companies such as Apple Music, sound increasingly tends to reach us without our seeing where it originates, and what we can see—the mechanical or electronic equipment—is typically not the cause or the source of the sound. Even when one seems to know the source, as it were, the source is never one thing: is it the composer; the performer (with her vocal cords, instruments, recording studio, and sound-editing procedures); the station or channel playing a piece of music; or the device with which one streams, downloads, plays, and listens to the sound being transmitted? This ever-widening gap between the relatively straightforward event of listening (i.e., of sound reception for those who are not hearing-impaired) and the proliferating multitude of causes and sources, a multitude that renders the question "where are these sounds coming from?" by and large meaningless, is one reason acousmaticity has become such an indispensable concept.

This is not to mention all of the sounds that come to us not by our choosing—music in public places such as elevators, restaurants, malls, gyms, supermarkets, and airports; tunes and advertisements we have to listen to while being put on hold when phoning businesses and institutions—and that nonetheless punctuate, indeed permeate, global urbanized existences. There are also the GPS devices that help us navigate. Even when they sound like humans (with different national and gendered accents), the simulated voices giving us directions on the road, like their counterparts talking to us from electronic screens big and small, are among the most advanced configurations of fragmented sonic objects, of sounds as *bytes*. In these intimate yet inhuman daily encounters, the basic formulation of the acousmatic—as sound whose cause or source is not visibly present or accessible—remains on the mark. In fact, acousmaticity has become such a regular feature of contemporary social interactions that it is difficult to imagine everyday life in a different format. The curtain, to wit, has thoroughly restructured and redefined human perceptual experiences and the collective imaginaries arising therefrom.[24]

Although non-acousmatic sound arguably still exists—and it is easy enough to give examples from nature, such as birds chirping, dogs barking, trees falling, and so forth *within one's view*—it is important to ponder the fact that contemporary listening itself, rather than a pristine activity, function, or capacity, has long been acclimatized to acousmaticity (of which the infinite mass of sound fragments released with the virtually nonstop generation of "smart" devices is only one conspicuous example). If we accept that such listening is now often trained, and perhaps generated, by acousmatic situations of various kinds, a more daunting set of questions ensues. How do we conceptualize listening after we have grasped the pervasive extent of acousmaticity? Should we think of acousmatic listening as universal or as particular? As independent of or as co-evolving with technology? As automated, reflexive, or both? These questions demand some answers, however provisional they may be.

Double-Voiced or Double-Listening?
Some Hints from Literary Studies

What does it mean to hear or listen to something? A random list of ordinary examples may include some of the following: a doctor listening to a patient's heartbeat through a stethoscope; an entomologist listening to cicadas' chirping; a linguist catching the tones of a tonal language; a musician discerning the different parts and instruments of a musical composition; a mechanic figuring out a car's trouble by the sound of its engine, and so forth. These mundane instances foreground what may be called a sensory-cognitive paradox even for trained specialists and skilled technicians: is listening an activity, or is it a form of passivity? The fact that "to listen" is, in the English language at least, both a transitive and an intransitive verb suggests that the line between the two states may not always be so clear and that "to listen" straddles action and reaction. To borrow from Jean-Luc Nancy's comparison between sight and sound: "In terms of the gaze, the subject is referred back to itself as object. In terms of listening, it is, in a way, to itself that the subject refers or refers back."[25] The acousmatic situation, in which the source of sound is hidden, further compounds the intrigue: is listening in such a situation a matter of doing something, or is it not, more precisely speaking, a sensorially truncated mode of receiving something—a matter of something happening to the listener in discontinuous form? Should listening be aligned with what we call *consciousness*, in which case all of the old-fashioned humanistic values of understanding and interpretation based on subjectivity would need to remain valid, or should it be aligned with a mechanistic or electronic *sensor*, for which sounds, whether in the form of refined classical music, recorded human voices, or raw street noise, are signals, pieces of data to be decoded and assimilated? How do we talk about listening as what takes place between or aside from these usual poles of categorization?

One approach has been to return listening to a kind of embodied materialism. A relatively early example of such an approach is in Roland Barthes's well-known essay "The Grain of the Voice," in which the language of the body becomes the singular aspect of a vocal deliverance.[26] Barthes writes, "The 'grain' is . . . the materiality of the body speaking its mother tongue; perhaps the letter, almost certainly *signifiance*"; such *signifiance*, he continues, "cannot better be defined, indeed, than by the very friction between the music and something else, which something else is the particular language (and nowise the message)."[27] Finally, Barthes asserts,

"The 'grain' is *the body in the voice* as it sings, the hand as it writes, the limb as it performs."[28]

In a full-fledged version of such embodied materialism, the divisions among sounds, listening, instruments, and their capacities for sonority and resounding tend to dissolve altogether, giving way instead to an alignment of mutually *touching* matrices of resonance. An exquisite instance of this type of theorization is found in Nancy's *Listening*, a work that makes the case for sound as a sensation distinct from, and other to, the kind of sense (i.e., meaning) based in the logos and, with it, logic and language. On the inextricable codependence between emission and reception, Nancy is insistent: the resonance or "sonance" of sound, he writes, is an expression we should hear "as much from the side of sound itself, or of its emission, as from the side of its reception or its listening: it is precisely from one to the other that it 'sounds.'"[29] Accordingly, the subject of listening (i.e., the subject who listens), he argues, is neither a phenomenological nor a philosophical subject, and perhaps is not a subject at all, except as "the place of resonance, of its infinite tension and rebound."[30] The most unforgettable lexicon from Nancy's discussion is that of *timbre*. He defines this as the resonance of a stretched skin and the expansion of this resonance in the hollow of a drum, which he in turn associates with a pregnant woman's belly, that cavity where a new life forms that first listens on the inside and then arrives at the outside with a cry. For Nancy, timbre—and, by implication, *subjectless listening*—is "above all the unity of a diversity that its unity does not reabsorb."[31]

Notwithstanding the subtlety and sophistication of Nancy's analysis, a disquieting question looms: is not his materialist approach to sound another form of nativism, primitivism, and origination myth, this time localized in the (female) body rather than, as in the case of Husserl, idealized through the mind?

And what if, contra Nancy, the subject is not so quickly dissolved? How otherwise might listening be conceptualized? Grammar—indeed, language—offers some provocative, if unexpected, assistance here. First is the illumination made by the proverbial active and passive voices, which break up actions into source and target (e.g., "I tell" as opposed to "I am told"). Interestingly, in the case of listening, "active" and "passive" seem readily reversible or become fuzzy: "I tell" is more or less equivalent to "I am heard," while "I am told" is another way to say "I hear." Second, and perhaps more perplexing, *what is the pronoun that best describes the listener in relation to what she hears?* Does the listener function in the capacity of an "I" with respect to the sound coming at her? Does not the listener also function as a "you," an addressee? Can the listener be conceived as an "it" or a "them"?

In linguistics, pronouns belong to a class of nouns known as shifters because of the ambiguous character of their significations.[32] Although pronouns are seldom invoked in the study of sound, by virtue of the fact that a certain relationship with an other is explicit or implicit in the activity or experience of listening, the question about pronouns seems appropriate—indeed, logical—even if it is irresolvable. Does the pronouns' ambiguity in this case imply that the *places* that listening might *mark*—or shall we say touch? pass through? remember? differentiate?—as it proceeds are unfixable, interchangeable, or nonexistent? Does not such shiftiness or fluidity of place become ever more acute when listening is mediated by various apparatuses of recording, transmission, and simulation? Think of karaoke, the popular form of entertainment in which, in order to sing along, one is supposed to lip sync with a song by following the lyrics displayed on the screen. Is the listener in this case an active "I" (the one singing and performing by lip syncing), a "you" (the one addressed and sung to by the song), or an "it" or "them" (*anyone* participating and mimicking in tandem with the sounds "coming from" the machine, the performance on the screen, the composer of the music, the author of the lyrics, and so forth)?

The question raised by pronouns in acousmatic listening—that is, listening in a surround of sounds and voices whose sources or causes are unseen, unavailable, or altogether irrelevant—is perhaps paradigmatic of a conceptual, aesthetic, and mediatic ecology considerably more expansive than that covered by the specialized terrains of sound and music studies. Accompanying the endless (re)producibility of acousmaticity in the contemporary world—among *musique concrète* practices, avant-garde experiments, high-tech inventions and their spinoffs, and all of the commercial exploitations of sound as fragments—is also, as we notice, the evisceration of a viably unified and authoritative point of command, of what some might call a transcendental subject position. How might such evisceration be articulated in conjunction with processes of listening?

Across disciplinary boundaries, scholars of literature have been grappling with a parallel set of questions for quite some time. In the realm of modern fiction, for instance, the ambiguity or instability of the narrative voice—encapsulated in the classic narratological question "Who is speaking?"—has long been deemed a key feature of modern literary form. As the type of narrator traditionally presumed to be omniscient gives way to so-called unreliable narrators, issues of origination, authorship, authority, and trust are played out with existential and political ramifications. To what extent could such literary scholarship be shared—or, perhaps, adapted—for a comparative study of the voice in the realm of sound theory? To what extent might literary studies be regarded, if somewhat belatedly, as partaking of the transdisciplinary discourse about acousmaticity?

To give a prominent example: in his reading of Fyodor Dostoyevsky's novels and stories, the literary critic Mikhail Bakhtin defines the enunciated word as the locus of an intersubjective struggle. According to Bakhtin, Dostoyevsky's texts exemplify a noteworthy quality: even when only one voice is apparently speaking, a multitude of voices can be *heard*; different people's opinions and attitudes have been internalized, are anticipated and responded to in advance or controverted at the moment of utterance.[33] The co-presence of clashing voices in the Underground Man, Raskolnikov, Prince Mishkin, the brothers Karamazov, and numerous other narrators and characters, a co-presence that is usually implicit—detectable in the mute, yet also garrulous, chasms between perception and expression, between hearing and speaking, between reported speech and direct speech—leads Bakhtin to describe the word in Dostoyevsky as double-voiced or polyphonic. Bakhtin's intervention serves to amplify the voice's inherent heterogeneity, its anxious "sideward glance" at and quarrel with others in the midst of enunciation.[34] Insofar as the double-voiced or polyphonic utterance is, rather than a space of unison and harmony, an echo chamber, an opening for a strife for dominance, the voice (as enunciation) in Bakhtin's reading is partial, interferential, and internally split. Double-voicedness or polyphonicity signifies not neoliberal inclusion or peaceful coexistence (as is sometimes assumed) but, rather, a politics of antagonism, insubordination, and dissent.

Just as Jacques Lacan describes the voice as "the alterity of what is said,"[35] so does Bakhtin's work highlight the voice's permeable and far from tranquil borders. Double-voicedness or polyphonicity, as made evident in Dostoyevsky's fiction, suggests that a word may be emitted in one way but is usually heard and received in plural, oftentimes conflictual or incommensurate, ways. Indeed, a word's (or language's) emission and reception never entirely coincide because different speakers and listeners, whose interactions are traversed by different lived temporalities, are involved. The appearance of a word in the form of a singular vocal emission is always underwritten (and under-spoken) by other voices; even when silent, these other voices are audible and can exert a powerful impact. Such fundamentally nonsynchronized and nonsynchronizable workings of the voice make up the richly open-ended, if silently deafening, dynamics of a novelistic world such as Dostoyevsky's.

What remains germane from Bakhtin's discussion is the pressing concern of the voice as non-unified because it is *un-closable*: as a phenomenon, the voice is always inflected with otherness, with the pressures of temporal or vocal exteriority. Going a step further, I would venture that, although he focuses attention on the voice (as an object of study), *what Bakhtin has contributed is a de facto theory of acousmatic listening*. The reason is simple: for the voice to be apprehended as double or polyphonic, it has to be heard as such—it has to be heard as coming from ambiguous or uncertain causes or sources. Rather than the double-voiced emission, as Bakhtin so carefully delineates it, it would have been more accurate to speak of the double- or multiple-listening "ear"—that is, a listening that carries in its mode of receptivity a capacity for discerning contending wills, desires, intentions, and implications; a capacity, in short, for handling divergences *aurally*.

In the field of fiction, such a theory of listening—even though listening itself is seldom given the spotlight—is embedded in the narrative convention known as the free indirect style. The "free indirect" intermixing of different voices in storytelling—for instance, by taking the syntax and verbal tenses from one, and the tones and pronouns from another, to form a particular utterance—marks crucial literary-historical transitions, as was evident in the writings of eighteenth- and nineteenth-century Western European novelists such as Johann Wolfgang von Goethe, Jane Austen, and Gustave Flaubert. It is easy to see how the basic feature of reporting another's speech, so fundamental to narration, carries with it the potential for dispute, negotiation, compromise, and subordination. How can one report another's speech act in such a way as to transmit not only its content, but also its tone and affect, its emotional and stylistic attributes? Rather than producing an exact overlap with what is being reported (even if this were possible), the persona doing such reporting—often the narrator or the author—enters a delicate situation in which, to keep some distance from what is reported, she may need to assume an ironic, sarcastic, or analytical stance. Such competition with another (or another's) speech act, competition that can have the effect of throwing that speech act's stylistic characteristics (or what might be called its immanent logic) into sharp relief, amplifies nothing other than the co-presence of multiple, discordant, or quarrelsome voices (and, we should add, *listenings*).[36] For some, such vocal and tonal (and, we should add, *aural*) intermixing announces a progressively democratized society, one that has become tolerant of disagreements and conflicting opinions. For other, more skeptical observers, this apparent intermixing signals modernity's transformed (and more genteel) ways of exerting authority and power, and the evolving, though usually unspoken, rules, codes, etiquette, and politics of socialization. Sponsoring the latter view, one literary historian goes as far as to suggest that, as a mechanism of social control, the free indirect style, in which voices (and, we should add, *listenings*) materialize in the interstices between the lines, as it were, may be considered a kind of stylistic Panopticon.[37]

As in the case of Bakhtin's study of the voice in Dostoyevsky, however, the name "free indirect style" may be part of the problem here. Insofar as such naming focuses on the externalizable instance of emission (such as voice, speech, or style) as its object, listening tends always to be given short shrift (as my parenthetical insertions in the previous paragraph indicate). The labels "double-voiced word" and "free indirect style," in this regard, are as misleading as they are instructive, precisely because they distract attention from—indeed, cover up—the very factor without which the voice could not have been double or polyphonic: listening. For sound and voice to work productively among and across the disciplines in the foreseeable future, therefore, it cannot simply be a matter of amassing comparable concerns in established fields such as philosophy, literature, music, film, and sound studies. More critically, it will need to be a matter of coming to grips with the persistently under-acknowledged, yet indisputable and ineluctable, part played by listening—together with all the epistemological issues that arise with specific acousmatic situations—in the making of sonic and vocal objects.

Notes

1 For this essay, the texts by Husserl that are relevant are *Ideas for a Pure Phenomenology and Phenomenological Philosophy*; *The Logical Investigations*; and *On the Phenomenology of the Consciousness of Internal Time*.

2 Derrida, *Voice and Phenomenon*, 74, emphasis added. The quote is from chapter six, "The Voice That Keeps Silent," which is especially illuminating for my thinking in the present chapter. (In his chapter, Derrida often references Derrida, *Edmund Husserl's* Origin of Geometry: *An Introduction*). For a helpful discussion, see Lawlor, "Translator's Introduction." For discussions of logocentrism and phonocentrism

in other major authors, discussions that constitute Derrida's deconstruction of the premises of Western philosophy, see Derrida, *Of Grammatology*.

3 Nancy, *Listening*, 8. Nancy goes on to elaborate the notion of presence in sound as "not the position of a being-present" but, rather, "a *coming* and a *passing*, an *extending* and a *penetrating*. Sound essentially comes and expands, or is deferred and transferred": Nancy, *Listening*, 13.

4 Dolar, *A Voice and Nothing More*, 38.

5 Derrida's focus on his project of grammatology also meant that he had to sidestep or seemed oblivious to some interesting issues. In his reflections on sonic experiences in everyday life, Michel Chion makes the perceptive observation that, despite emphasizing the importance and specificity of "self-hearing" in *Voice and Phenomenon*, Derrida nonetheless fails to address the oddness of the situation in which external perceptions and internal perception of "self-hearing," while being bound to one another, do not merge: see Chion, *Sound*, 94. In a nutshell, "self-hearing" for Derrida remains a matter of hearing oneself *speak* (and with it, the philosophical and literary effects of the voice), whereas for Chion, "self-hearing" involves the sonic circuits among hearing and various *embodied* functions and activities, circuits in which the voice does not necessarily play a privileged role.

6 Lawrence, *Echo and Narcissus*, 11–12. Lawrence offers an informative discussion of the close links between sound recording and the reproduction of voice: see Lawrence, *Echo and Narcissus*, 1–32.

7 Kane, *Sound Unseen*; esp. 180–95.

8 See, e.g., Schaeffer, *In Search of a Concrete Music*; Schaeffer, *Traité des objets musicaux*; Schaeffer, *Treatise on Musical Objects*. See also "Pierre Schaeffer's *Treatise on Musical Objects* and Music Theory," the interesting chapter by John Dack, in Schaeffer, *Treatise on Musical Objects*, xxix–xxxiv.

9 Kahn, *Noise, Water, Meat*, 8, emphasis added.

10 See, e.g., Schaeffer, *In Search of a Concrete Music*; Schaeffer, *Traité des objets musicaux*; Schaeffer, *Treatise on Musical Objects*. For references to the acousmatic in Michel Chion's analysis of Hitchcock's *Psycho*, see Chion, *The Voice in Cinema*, 140–51. Chion's analysis also appears in a modified translation under the title "An Impossible Embodiment," in Žižek, *Everything You Always Wanted to Know about Lacan*, 195–207; a long note is included on Schaeffer's retrieval in the 1950s of the ancient term "acousmatic," supposedly the name given to a Pythagorean sect "whose adepts used to listen to their Master speaking from behind a hanging, so that, it was said, the sight of the sender would not distract them from the message": Chion, "An Impossible Embodiment," 206. For related interest, see the various sections in Chion, *Sound*, and Chion's chapter in this volume.

11 For reasons of space, this point will need to be elaborated on a separate occasion.

12 Nancy, *Listening*, 3.

13 For an account of the complex details about Pythagoras and his different groups of disciples, see the chapter "Myth and the Origin of the Pythagorean Veil" in Kane, *Sound Unseen*, 45–72.

14 "Just as the Husserlian theory of the object allows Schaeffer to define the sound object, the phenomenological *epochē* allows for a definition of *l'acousmatique*. The two moments are sutured together": Kane, *Sound Unseen*, 22.

15 Schaeffer, *Traité des objets musicaux*, 93, quoted in Kane, *Sound Unseen*, 24.

16 Schaeffer, *Traité des objets musicaux*, 91, quoted in Kane, *Sound Unseen*, 24.

17 Because of Foucault's acute awareness of the inherent relations between thinking and spacing, Michel Serres argues for reading his work on madness as geometrical: see Serres, "The Geometry of the Incommunicable." For related interest, see also Didi-Huberman, "Knowing When to Cut."

18 Kane, *Sound Unseen*, 30.

19 For a more extended discussion of these modernist conceptual-aesthetic attempts at interrupting the given, see the chapter "When Reflexivity Becomes Porn," in Chow, *Entanglements*, 13–30.

20 This metaphor for works of art from Adorno is cited at the beginning of Gretel Adorno and Rolf Tiedemann, "Editors' Afterword," in Adorno, *Aesthetic Theory* (Athlone), 361. The editors go on to offer the productive and negative associations Adorno attached to fragmentariness in his various works: Adorno and Tiedemann, "Editors' Afterword," 362.

21 Chion, *The Voice in Cinema*, 46. For a fairly recent fictional treatment of this link between sound media technologies and the dead (in the expanding popular genre of New Age connectivity), see "Be Right Back," dir. Owen Harris, *Black Mirror*, series 2, episode 1, aired February 11, 2013. Part science fiction and part sentimental drama, the episode features a woman who talks with her dead husband by way of chat room software and cell phone and eventually brings him back through biochemical maneuvers as a "live" partner who is programmed to "replay" (or respond) to her verbally and physically but not emotionally.

22 To this extent, I tend to disagree with Kane's critique that Schaeffer is producing a phantasmagorical version of the Pythagorean story through a *metaphysics* (under-stood in a pejorative sense) of the sound object. Describing how Schaeffer, despite stressing the importance of phenomenological experience and using concrete materials for his sound objects early on (as in his search for a concrete music), became increasingly focused on ideal objects in his mature works, Kane argues that Schaeffer is ultimately Husserlian in his mode of theorization. Accordingly, because the existence of an ideal, originary object is affirmed as prior to experience, experience can serve to reveal but not sully pure objectivity with vulgar contingencies of history and matter: see the informative discussions in Kane, *Sound Unseen*, chaps. 1–4. For the gist of his critique of Schaeffer, see, e.g., Kane, *Sound Unseen*, 17, 34, 60. My disagreement with this reading has to do primarily with the larger, modernist conceptual-aesthetic context in which, as I have been arguing, Schaeffer's work should be situated. Schaeffer is hardly the only theorist or artist to think of art making the way he does. I also believe that boundaries between so-called ideal and concrete objects are often blurred *in practice*. No concrete object can be completely devoid of ideality, and no ideal object can "make sense" without some concrete mani-festation. The use and revitalization of myth is an excellent case in point of such

indistinction. To give a familiar sonic example, consider the legend of the Sirens. Modern and contemporary adaptations and searches—from James Joyce's use of the nymphs for an episode in his novel *Ulysses* and Franz Kafka's rendition of them as silent in the short story "The Silence of the Sirens" to emergency alarm signals deployed in modern cities around the world and the research expedition carried out by contemporary German media experts at the Galli Islands, off the Amalfi Coast in Italy, to verify the location and sources of the Sirens' songs—are worlds apart from the ancient narrative context in which the Sirens first appear. In the historicity of such adaptations and searches—literary, scientific, mediatic, or archaeological—the Sirens as such seem to be both concrete and ideal objects, functioning at once at the everyday and the metaphysical (or phantasmagorical) levels. For a discussion of the Galli Islands expedition, see Ernst, *Sonic Time Machines*, 49–69.

23 For an authoritative study, see Sterne, *The Audible Past.*

24 For related interest, see Maitra and Chow, "What's 'In'?," especially the section "From Gulf to Gulf to Gulf," which discusses the ephemeral, low-resolution digital music videos circulated among sailors trafficking in the oceans around India, the Middle East, and Africa. The fragmentary networks generated in the process are excellent instances of the contemporaneity of sound's acousmaticity.

25 Nancy, *Listening*, 10.

26 Barthes, "The Grain of the Voice."

27 Barthes, "The Grain of the Voice," 182, 185.

28 Barthes, "The Grain of the Voice," 188, emphasis added.

29 Nancy, *Listening*, 16.

30 Nancy, *Listening*, 21–22.

31 Nancy, *Listening*, 41. For a fascinating exploration of the status of sound and listening in relation to pregnancy, see the chapter by Jairo Moreno and Gavin Steingo in this volume.

32 For a discussion of shifters and pronouns in relation to the arrival of new sound technologies such as the phonograph, see Kane, *Sound Unseen*, 182–86.

33 See esp. the detailed analyses of the internal dialogicality of Dostoyevsky's "discourse" in Bakhtin, *Problems of Dostoyevsky's Poetics*, 181–269. As Nancy writes, "*Écrire* in its modern conception—elaborated since Proust, Adorno, and Benjamin, through Blanchot, Barthes, and to Derrida's *archi-écriture*—is nothing other than making sense resound beyond signification, or beyond itself. It is *vocalizing* a sense that, for classical thought, intended to remain deaf and mute": Nancy, *Listening*, 34–35. Although Nancy has not included Dostoyevsky and Bakhtin on his list of modern writers attuned to this sense "beyond signification," his description certainly echoes the Russian authors' notions of double-voicedness and polyphonicity to some extent.

34 Bakhtin, *Problems of Dostoyevsky's Poetics*, 196 and passim.

35 Quoted in Nancy, *Listening*, 28.

36 For related interest, see the discussion of Russian novels in Vološinov, *Marxism and the Philosophy of Language*, esp. pt. 3, 107–59.

37 See the succinct discussion in Moretti, *The Bourgeois*, 94–100.

The Skin of the Voice

Acousmatic Illusions, Ventriloquial Listening

The Voice behind the Face

The turning point of Julie Dash's acclaimed independent short film *Illusions* (1982) takes place in a fictional Hollywood studio's sound booth.[1] Dash's film is shot in black-and-white celluloid and edited in the classical film style of 1942, the year in which it is set. The film's statuesque protagonist Mignon Dupree, the studio's sole female producer's assistant—a light-skinned African American woman who is passing for white—is working overtime to oversee the postproduction of a film. The sound technicians inform Mignon and her boss that they have a problem: the sound operator lost the sync while filming one of the musical numbers, a jazzy love song, and as a result the picture and music tracks do not match. Upon viewing the rushes, Mignon remarks, "Leila Grant [the star] looks like she's chewing marbles while somebody else sings." Since the usual solution, to reshoot the scene with Grant following the song, is not an option, the senior sound engineer devises an unorthodox solution: he asks Esther Jeter, the young black female singer who provided the original backup vocals, to return to the studio and sing along with the actress's moving lips.

When the recording begins, all eyes, including Esther's—she has been instructed to "watch the screen"—are locked on the actress on-screen as she sashays around a bedroom in a satin gown and feather boa, mouthing the words to the song that Esther sings (Ella Fitzgerald's *Starlit Hour*, in another act of doubling/dubbing). The disparate acts joined together to create the illusion of screen unity, in both Dash's film and the film within Dash's film, are captured in two symmetrical frontal medium shots of Esther and Leila Grant. Both women move their lips in tune with Fitzgerald's song, and while Esther's face is at first knit in concentration, she gradually begins to mimic Grant's expressive facial gestures. By the end of the scene, Esther no longer seems to be looking directly at the screen. Captured in profile, she sings with ecstatic abandon, having fully inhabited the imaginary role of star.

Mignon is not looking at the screen, either. When the camera pans across the inhabitants of the sound booth shortly before the end of the recording session, the two white sound men are captivated by Grant's image on the screen, but Mignon looks the other way at Esther, her brow furrowed in an inscrutable expression. We only learn later, during an exchange between Mignon and Esther, who has recognized Mignon's ethnic heritage, that this moment "behind the scenes" has been a moment of unmasking for Mignon. Esther tells Mignon that when she goes to the cinema and hears her own voice coming out of an actress's mouth, she shuts her eyes and imagines that she is on the screen in a satin gown. Mignon recognizes the pathos in Esther's cheerful comment: the act of witnessing the seamless concealment of Esther's voice by Leila Grant's face reminds Mignon of how her own racial concealment perpetuates the veiling of black women's labor by the cinematic apparatus. Mignon's disillusionment paves the way, as Judylyn Ryan notes, to a counter-hegemonic manifesto, "when Mignon, ventriloquizing Dash, proclaims her new determination to 'use the power of the motion picture.'"[2] Her goal? To work against the Hollywood system to tell "real" stories—to "represent real characters that people can identify with."

Although *Illusions* is a fiction film, its aims are anti-illusory. Dash unmasks the façade of Hollywood-style fiction, showing that the romantic ideals of whiteness that unfold on-screen are held in place by the invisible realities of black labor. Intriguingly, image and sound play the roles of villain and protagonist in the story of Mignon's enlightenment, which invites the reading that Hollywood's subordination of the sonic to the visual lies at the heart of its injustices. Such, for instance, is the reading of *Illusions* offered by the feminist film scholar Patricia Mellencamp, who likens the concealment of Hollywood's racialized politics of labor to the camouflaging of sound in the process of synchronization. She argues, "The seamless union between image and sound, face and voice, with voice subservient to face (as black women are in film to white women) . . . paradoxically seals the dominance of face, of the visible."[3] In her disavowal of Hollywood-style fiction to pursue "real" stories about "real" people, Mignon is an avatar of Dash, who has devoted much of her career to producing historical dramas, biopics, and documentaries about the African American experience. Dash's creative trajectory is understandable, since the documentary film genre seeks not only to represent real social actors but also to reverse the audiovisual hierarchy of fiction film, foregrounding the spoken word over the image and, by association, reality over illusion.

The reality principle and democratic impulse associated with liberating minoritized voices from veiling or distortion are a central concern of this chapter. Using the vocal conventions of documentary as an illustrative example, I suggest that the realist pursuit of vocal equality, which restricts the relationship between veiling and power to a visual register, also restricts our understanding of the complex ways in which veiling and unveiling operate in relation to sound and listening. To specify the nature of these auditory illusions, I introduce a term that emphasizes the racialized and gendered perceptual frames that mediate the production and reception of vocal sounds: "the skin of the voice." Using this term, which I evolve in conversation with recent feminist and postcolonialist scholarship on the political economies of sound, I examine how cinematic applications of "acousmatic listening" free from the distortions of vision, as advocated by the composer Pierre Schaeffer, can end up concealing the invisible logics that separate voices into those that are forcibly embodied as an objectified surface and those that are disembodied as a protective disguise. I propose that, to confront and deflect these discriminatory perceptual habits, it is necessary to cultivate an attunement to the seam between the embodied origins of voices and the illusory, surrogate bodies that voices conjure into existence. To this end, I offer a reading of an experimental documentary film in which the artist Mounira Al Solh develops an audiovisual idiom for expressing the ventriloquial basis of vocal sounds as well as the political significance of a *ventriloquial* mode of listening.

Illusions invites the feminist reading that Mignon must *look away* from the illusion of Leila Grant's face to *hear* Esther's voice without distortion. The scenario of this film rehearses a familiar refrain of sound studies, which is that the perceptual and cultural privilege accorded to the image in modern Western art forms foils and even defiles the study of sound on its own terms. Cinema plays on this dynamic when it attributes the sounds we hear to causes the film makes us believe in: the attribution of a black woman's singing voice to the screen image of a white woman in Dash's *Illusions* is just one instance of the ideologically loaded possibilities of this perceptual sleight of hand. In this regard, Dash's film offers a variation on the film sound scholar Rick Altman's argument that the study of Hollywood film must begin by looking past the image—a mere ventriloquist's dummy—to its true sonic source.[4] But to what extent are this argument, and the remedy it proposes (looking past the image to hear sound objectively), helpful in apprehending the "reality" of Esther's voice? I propose a different line of thinking that foregrounds the ventriloquial basis of vocal sounds, as well as the perceptual biases that predetermine the success of the vocalic bodies that voices conjure, habituating to them as a screen, or outing them as a skin. At stake in this approach is an apprehension of the discriminatory habits of listening to vocal sounds, as well as the limitations of acousmatic listening as a means of undoing these habits.

The notion that the veiling or distortion of hearing by vision can be countered only by another act of veiling—averting the eyes—is at the basis of Schaeffer's theory of the sound object. An engineer and composer by training, as well as the founder of *musique concrète*, Schaeffer proposed that acousmatic sound, defined as a sound that is heard without its causes being seen, could enable a non-preconceived, "reduced" mode of listening. Schaeffer's interest in the technique of reduced listening, also known as acousmatic listening, was technical rather than ideological. Michel Chion explains: "Reduced listening takes the sound—verbal, played on an instrument, noises, or whatever—as itself the object to be observed instead of as a vehicle for something else."[5] He continues: "Schaeffer thought that the acousmatic situation could encourage reduced listening, in that it provokes one to separate oneself from causes or effects in favor of consciously attending to sonic textures, masses, and velocities."[6] In a recent book on acousmatic sound, Brian Kane paraphrases Schaeffer's theory as follows: "A sound object only truly emerges when a sound no longer functions *for another* as a medium, but rather is perceived *as such.*"[7] In other words, Schaeffer believed that he could cultivate an "objective" attunement to sound, including vocal sounds, by denaturalizing or defamiliarizing the distorting lens that visual context habitually imposes on sound and, furthermore, by "fixing" the sound in the manner of an object. As the editors of this anthology note, a phonographic stylus stuck in a closed groove, permitting the listener to study the same sound over and over under acousmatic circumstances, was the paradigmatic realization of Schaeffer's concept.

It is interesting to note that the originary sound object that inspired Schaeffer's technique involved a ventriloquial illusion whose effects were not only technical (in fact, the illusion prefigures technical mediation) but also thoroughly ideological. Chion observes that the term "acousmatic" derives from "the name assigned to a Pythagorean sect whose followers would listen to their Master speak *behind a curtain*, as the story goes, so that the sight of the speaker wouldn't distract them from the message."[8] According to this legend, the uninitiated disciples, known as *acousmatiques*, were allowed to look upon their master as full members of the sect only after spending five years in silence listening to him speak from behind the curtain. The purpose of this technique was to ensure obedience by *disciplining* the disciples to hear the subjective content of the master's voice as objective truth. Writing about the same Pythagorean illusion, Mladen Dolar suggests that the master's technique can be seen as a symptomatic response to a logocentric auditory culture. Dolar argues that in the Western philosophical tradition, which is bound by the imperatives of logocentrism, voices are obliged to shed their corporeal encumbrances (these include the embodied traits of accent, timbre, and tone, as well as involuntary utterances such as laughter, coughing, sighs, and so on) to convey their proximity to *logos*, or divine reason. The ritual of listening to their master lecture from behind a veil may therefore have served to train the disciples to hear his voice as a divine utterance—a "vanishing mediator" whose corporeal content (*phonê*) evaporated in the act of utterance (*logos*).[9]

The question then arises: would the lifting of the curtain not spoil the illusion of mastery, revealing the master to be a mere mortal? Dolar's answer is that the five-year ritual of acousmatic listening would have habituated the disciples to the *sound* of their master's voice, permitting it to function as a virtual screen or veil even after the actual screen concealing his body had been lifted.[10] Counter to the technique it inspired, the Pythagorean ritual of acousmatic listening actually would have *prevented* the listeners from "fixing" and regarding the traits of their master's voice in the manner of an object. If we take the master's voice as the originary sound object, then, the sound of his voice "as such" is not the outcome of disillusioned listening liberated from the distortions of vision. Rather, this sound is *itself* an auditory illusion, curtain, or ideological veil—one that conceals the particularity of its embodied source and subject-position in order to evoke the authority and aura of a divine presence. To put it somewhat differently, the "objective" effect of the master's voice is the result of a ventriloquial illusion that summons what Steven Connor calls an imaginary "vocalic body." The vocalic body, writes Connor, "is the idea—which can take the form of dream, fantasy, ideal, theological doctrine, or hallucination—of a surrogate or secondary body, a projection of a new way of having or being a body, formed and sustained out of the autonomous operations of the voice."[11] In summoning an imaginary body of metaphysical proportions, the master's voice functions as a manner of invisibility cloak that conceals its actual origins, using the power of sound to countermand the evidence of sight.

The idea of the vocalic body as invisibility cloak in this originary scene of acousmatic listening vividly illustrates the often imperceptible but thoroughly ideological practices of perceptual disciplining that cloak the subjective, embodied origins of *certain* idealized voices, framing their traits as divine or disembodied. But if the Pythagorean master's voice points to how white, male voices come to function as a screen despite their visible corporeality, then *Illusions* dramatizes the opposite: the equally imperceptible disciplinary practices that forcibly relocate voices whose traits depart from this norm in a racialized and gendered body. Esther Jeter also attempts a ventriloquial illusion in that her singing voice conjures an idealized vocalic body that obscures attention from her own black body—a dynamic that cinema only visualizes after the fact by attributing her voice to the face of a white woman as the epitome of an idealized and objectified femininity. However, the film is haunted by the failure of this illusion: the prospect of a (racialized) body whose skin threatens to assert its vocal presence, "outing" or disacousmatizing the body even in its visual absence.

In a revealing historical anecdote, Jennifer Lynn Stoever notes that in the late nineteenth century, white opera reviewers often advocated "blind listening" as a technique for listening to black female opera singers, suggesting that closing one's eyes would enable white listeners to judge black vocal performers more objectively, without being skewed by their visible blackness. However, this technique seldom worked. To the contrary, Stoever observes that white listeners persisted in perceiving the voices of black female opera singers as both hypersexualized and technically inferior to those of their white counterparts.[12] The musicologist Nina Sun Eidsheim has emphasized that there is no technical basis for the type of perceptual bias described by Stoever. Her own research on vocal morphology in the context of American operatic singing concludes that there are no more similarities in timbre within a so-called racial group than there are differences among groups. Eidsheim attributes the discriminatory tendency in operatic listening to *"acousmatic blackness,"* or *"the perceived presence of the black body in a voice that otherwise meets all the standards of a professional classical voice."*[13] By this, she means that even under acousmatic circumstances, the absent, visibly "other" bodies of black singers were conjured up as a perceptual phantom projected by listeners onto their vocal timbre.

Esther's voice calls up the racialized perceptual biases that mediate both the production and the reception of vocal sounds—biases that acousmatic listening cannot necessarily remedy. These disciplinary perceptual processes interweave the racial gaze and its aural counterpart, or what Stoever calls "the listening ear," in a collusive relationship.[14] As a matter of fact, Dash's use of Ella Fitzgerald's voice to represent a black female singer whose voice passes as that of a white woman is a wishful revision of American film and music history. In the 1930s and '40s, it was not unusual for black vocalists to sing specialty numbers for dramatic films, but the film historian Marsha Siefert reminds us that these numbers were often cut when the films were distributed in the American South for fear that their "natural voices and singing styles might also mark their ethnicity and therefore might limit the market for the film and sound track sales."[15] In fact, it was far more common for songs in film musicals featuring black casts to be dubbed by white, classically trained singers: a famous example is that of Marilyn Horne, a white, classically trained mezzo-soprano opera singer who was hired to sing the lead female vocals in Otto Preminger's film *Carmen Jones* (1954), dubbing for the African American actress Dorothy Dandridge, who was herself an accomplished musical performer. This technique both drew on and reinforced a racialized hierarchy of musical styles, between the mannered and cultivated style of opera singers and the so-called spontaneous or natural style of jazz and pop singing.[16] Dubbing was thus used in Hollywood films as a means of audibly "whitewashing" the visual presence of black bodies, producing an effect that the film music historian Jeff Smith calls "a kind of phantasmic body that registers visually as black but sounds 'white' in terms of the material qualities of its 'voice.'"[17]

The contrasting attunements of the acousmatic listeners described by Chion and Dolar, on one hand, and by Stoever, Eidsheim, and Smith, on the other, illustrate an insidious and ideologically fraught perceptual tendency that I sum up as follows: idealized voices are heard as a *screen* that resists objectification even when their bodies are visible, whereas minoritized voices are circumscribed in advance as an objectified *skin*—even when they are acousmatic. My reference to the voice as skin adapts and extends Rey Chow's use of the term "skin tones" to describe how accented voices are not only heard but subject to a type of visual scrutiny that probes and reads them as a racialized visual surface. Chow points out how the conjoined visual and audial connotations of "skin tones" are activated in a postmodern version of Esther Jeter's vocal makeover: the situation of South Asian and East Asian offshore call center workers who must imitate the vocal mannerisms, styles, and accents of their American customers to be understood by them.[18] I would add that we can better apprehend the complexly political operations of sound and listening if we attend to the ways in which sound—and specifically, the voice—functions as a protective veil or skin, as well as the moments in which that auditory illusion fails and is exposed, denuded. Indeed, the restriction of "veiling" to a visual register to arrive at a more discerning mode of listening—the technique to which Schaeffer subscribes—can have the unexpected effect of concealing the ways in which listening stands in for and conjoins with vision as a means of discrimination, or a way of separating subjects from objects in the field of sound.

In the next section, I briefly turn to scholarly debates surrounding the voice in documentary. While this may seem somewhat of a departure from my discussion so far, the purpose of my turn to documentary is to consider the genre's vocal conventions—which documentary scholars typically frame as a realist corrective to fictional illusions—as another instance of how anti-illusory cinematic forms can end up concealing the discriminatory perceptual frames of voicing and listening, even when they aim to achieve the opposite. My main contention is that the liberatory impulse driving innovations in documentary's vocal modes maintain an unproductive focus on the fundamental visuality of the acousmatic veil. Feminist criticisms of one of documentary's most derided sonic inventions, "Voice of God" narration, which takes inspiration from the Pythagorean technique of lecturing from behind a veil, offer a case in point. These critiques, and their proposed vocal alternatives, exemplify how realist attempts to achieve vocal parity using the disillusioning techniques of disacousmatization or acousmatization fail to account for the different degrees and types of auditory scrutiny to which idealized and minoritized voices are subject, as well as the ventriloquial illusions to which they have recourse. This analysis of documentary lays the foundation for my reading, in the final section of this chapter, of a ventriloquial mode of cinematic looking-listening that makes perceptual adjustments to offset the discriminatory frames of vocal production and reception.

Documentary (Dis)illusions

Documentary's difference from fiction film is frequently articulated in terms of its reliance on sound rather than the image. The speaking voice is regarded as a reality principle that brings sobriety and grounding to the flights of fancy that the image might otherwise encourage. Bill Nichols captures this sentiment in *Representing Reality* (1991), a classic of documentary studies, when he writes:

> Documentary film often builds itself around the spoken word. Works from Frank Capra's Why We Fight series (1942–45) on the reasons for United States involvement in World War II to Ken Burns's *The Civil War* (1990) would be subject to endless interpretation if we had nothing but their extraordinarily diverse and historically intriguing images to guide us. Commentary points us toward the light, the truth . . . Fiction attends to unconscious desires and latent meanings. It operates where the id lives. Documentary, on the other hand, attends to social issues of which we are consciously aware. It operates where the reality-attentive ego and superego live.[19]

Even though Nichols has been criticized for associating progressive ideologies with aesthetic features, and himself goes on to deconstruct and complicate this polarization of reality/documentary versus illusion/fiction, documentary scholars continue to associate *voice*—that is, the spoken word—with the pursuit of democracy, disillusionment, and truth.[20] The proposed alternatives to documentary's most vilified device, Voice of God narration, evidence the enduring power of these associations. Critics of this device attribute its effects of distortion to a visual illusion and have accordingly sought alternatives to this convention that visualize the sources of idealized speaking voices. At the same time, feminist documentary scholars have recuperated the veil of acousmatic anonymity as a means of drawing attention to the voices of minorities free from the distortion of the image. I propose that these parallel attempts to unveil the "truth" of sound conceal a larger concern: that the capacity for illusion and deception rests not only with the image but also with sound.

Voice of God narration is the name given to the distinctive type of disembodied voice-over commentary associated with "classical" documentary films of the 1930s and '40s. This type of commentary is usually described in terms of its prototypical features, exemplified by the vocal commentary for the *March of Time* newsreel series—for example, "a white, male, middle-class and anonymous voice," according to Stella Bruzzi; "detached, authoritarian, male," according to Jeffrey Youdelman; and "disembodied . . . stentorian, aggressive, assuming a power to speak the truth of the filmic text, to hold captive through verbal caption what the spectator sees" and "omniscient, omnipresent," according to Charles Wolfe.[21] Since these descriptions note the absence of the cause or source of Voice of God commentary in their emphases on anonymity, detachment, and disembodiment, this mode of documentary narration can be called an example of what Chion, adapting Schaeffer, calls an "acousmatic voice."[22] Indeed, the origins of the word "acousmatic" in the myth of the Pythagorean teacher lecturing from behind a veil are strongly evocative of documentary's etymological root in the Latin *docere*, in its emphasis on pedagogy and the transmission of knowledge by "telling" unencumbered by the distractions of "showing."

The convention of Voice of God narration exemplifies how contemporary audiovisual forms adapt and mutate the ancient Pythagorean technique to disguise the particular, subjective source of certain privileged voices (namely, those of white, middle-class, educated men) in an authoritarian cloak of universality. Documentary scholars have championed two types of democratic alternatives to Voice of God narration. The first type includes vocal conventions such as the recorded conversation, dialogue, and the "talking head" interview that synchronize voices to their "real" or originating bodies as a means of unmasking their location. This practice was pioneered by practitioners of direct cinema and cinéma vérité in the 1950s and '60s who rejected voice-over narration in favor of visualizing verbal events. Although these conventions have been critiqued for actively promoting the illusion of authenticity and immediacy, they remain in widespread use in contemporary documentary practices. What is more, they have garnered critical appreciation for invoking the particularity of embodied speech, or, to quote Jeffrey Ruoff, "the material texture and richness of unrehearsed speech, the grain of the voice."[23] These values are positively opposed to the negative values of objectivity and univocality associated with the idealized male acousmatic voice in Voice of God narration.

The second alternative consists of voice-overs that, while disembodied, are nonetheless believed to foreground the particularity of speakers' embodiment in their tone, gender, ethnic identity, and mode of address.[24] Bruzzi, for instance, praises films that employ women's voices in subjective, experimental ways (e.g., first-person narration) that undercut the emphasis of Voice of God narration on authority, detachment, and omniscience by embodying the virtues of indefiniteness, idiosyncrasy, and personal exploration.[25] In this regard, Bruzzi is one among several documentary scholars who has extended Kaja Silverman's advocacy of the acousmatic voice as a feminist documentary device. Silverman celebrates the work of feminist filmmakers who borrow the veil of acousmatic anonymity as a means of claiming the authority of speaking subject for women's voices. She argues that the presence of a female acousmatic voice defamiliarizes the gendered articulation of power typical of classical Hollywood cinema, in which acousmatic authority is reserved for male voices, whereas female voices are "pinned" to bodies and thereby subject to the distortion of "to-be-looked-at-ness."[26]

We can thus categorize the democratizing tactics adopted by critics of Voice of God narration as (1) the attempt to disacousmatize voices, especially idealized voices, by revealing/unveiling their bodies; and, reciprocally, (2) the attempt to recuperate the veil of acousmatic anonymity for minoritized voices. Both tactics interpret the acousmatic veil in literal terms as a *visual* screen. Thus, the powerful effects of offscreen commentary are claimed as a way for minoritized voices to be *heard*, free from the visual distortion of being turned into an image. Through an inversion of the same logic, the incontrovertible effects of Voice of God narration are countered by visualizing the sources of authoritarian or "expert" voices. The goal, as Bruzzi puts it, is to problematize claims to an unproblematic or universal truth. "Narration," she writes, "could therefore be seen as a mechanism deployed to *mask* the realization that this mode of representation, and indeed its inherent belief in a consistent and unproblematic truth, are perpetually on the verge of collapse, that commentary, far from being a sign of omniscience and control, is the hysterical barrier erected against the specter of ambivalence and uncertainty."[27]

What is salient in Bruzzi's analysis of narration is that she cautions against too literal an interpretation of the acousmatic mask or veil of classical documentary narration, describing it instead as a structure of disavowal. Her analysis unintentionally sheds light on the ventriloquial illusions involved not just in Voice of God narration but in *all forms* of documentary narration, including the talking head or subjective, first-person commentary. However, when we take into account the centuries of auditory habituation that connect the Pythagorean *acousmatiques* and documentary listeners, we can also see how these illusions might have discrepant degrees of success. Following Bruzzi's logic, we may venture this proposition: idealized voices may continue to exert their powers even *after* their sources have been exposed or disacousmatized. The embodied traits of a mid-Atlantic, middle-class, educated, deep male voice can thus be made to seem weightless, almost immaterial, summoning a metaphysical vocalic body that supplants the evidence of the eyes. Conversely, voices that depart from this zero degree of speech may be disacousmatized *despite* being disembodied; the audible evidence of their race, gender, class, and education can envelop and weigh them down, summoning their bodies in absentia even when their sources are withheld from view. Under these circumstances, the realist documentary discourse of sound's distortion by the image can itself become a veil or "hysterical barrier," to repurpose Bruzzi's term. The specter that is warded off is twofold: that the speaking voice is as capable of illusory flights of fancy as the image, and that discriminatory habits of (looking and) listening determine which of these illusions pass as reality.

The "real" source of Esther Jeter's voice in *Illusions* is an interesting limit case that reveals the contradictions of the critical consensus I have described. In a politically correct sense, the synchronization of Esther's voice to Leila Grant's face is a falsehood—a visual distortion that demands disillusioning corrections of the kind that documentary filmmakers have pursued. But in a more perverse sense, the "false" synchronization is true to the auditory illusion that Esther is attempting (and failing) to produce: the illusion of a voice that *sounds* white, and which seeks to deflect the visible evidence of her own black body. Esther's voice ostensibly emerges from her body, but it conjures up what Connor calls an imaginary vocalic body that may "contradict, compete with, replace, or even reshape the actual, visible body of the speaker."[28] This dematerializing vocalic body promises an auditory screen of relative anonymity, allowing Esther to elude the experience of being heard and objectified as a skin. Neither a corrective disacousmatization nor a redemptive acousmatic solution would allow us to properly apprehend the enigmatic embodiment of this vocal performance or the perceptual biases that it acknowledges and seeks to circumvent.

In the final section of this chapter, I turn to *Paris without a Sea*, a short experimental documentary film by the Lebanese artist Mounira Al Solh, as a counterpoint to Dash's *Illusions*.[29] I would like to hold this film alongside the predominantly visual interpretations of the Pythagorean veil that have inspired the realist turn to acousmatic voicing and listening among feminist film critics and documentary scholars. Al Solh neither proposes averting our gaze to grasp minoritized voices objectively nor recuperates the cloak of visual anonymity for these voices. Instead, she brings a concrete audiovisual expression to Connor's concept of the vocalic body as a type of auditory veil ("a surrogate or secondary body, a projection of a new way of having or being a body, formed and sustained out of the autonomous operations of the voice"). What is more, she finds an unusual way to subvert the discriminatory perceptual habits that virtually unveil and denude some voices as a means of keeping them in their place while permitting others to function as a dematerializing screen body that consolidates their privileged social position. The absurd ventriloquial performance at the center of Al Solh's film uses the simple but effective technique of reversal to school us in a ventriloquial mode of listening—one that confronts the ways in which the disciplining of the ear and eye hold larger social hierarchies in place.

Ventriloquial Displacements

Paris without a Sea is provocative to think with alongside Dash's *Illusions* because of the irreverent way in which Al Solh connects the two chimerical registers of the voice's skin—objectified surface and performative cover-up—with the broader symbolic economies of voicing in documentary and fiction. Al Solh is Lebanese and works between Beirut and Amsterdam, as well as between the idioms of documentary and performance art. Migration, translation, appropriation, and miscommunication are central themes in her work. Trained as a painter, Al Solh incorporates a variety of media in her cinematic language, including drawing, performance, puppetry, and role-playing. In her hands, all of these media become ways to navigate the world as an Arab woman whose movements and artistic expressions are further restricted by the realities of conflict and its aftermath.

In *Paris without a Sea*, Al Solh comes up with an ingenious solution for occupying the world vocally in ways that her own body does not allow: she steals the voices of Beiruti men, as though to proclaim that a voice always speaks from elsewhere than one's body. This short film is part of a multimedia project that revolves around a group of Beiruti men, including Al Solh's father, who swim daily in the Mediterranean, no matter the weather. Al Solh speaks wistfully of the ability of the men to sun themselves shirtless and to strip off their clothing and jump into the water. She compares their daily escape to her own mobility as an art student in Amsterdam, but with one important difference. She writes, "It is as if they emigrate every day to somewhere else through the water, without really leaving their country. They are out of place, yet still immersed in it."[30] Al Solh attempts to access the eminently embodied yet out-of-body experience of this masculine public sphere by conducting interviews in Arabic and French with the men right after they emerge from the water. Her interview questions turn the men's love for swimming into an avenue for a dialogue on more intimate topics, such as courtship, religion, romance, and gender. Caught off-guard (and on camera) by Al Solh's polite but playful questions, the men answer in disarming ways that nonetheless reveal their male privilege. One young man admits, for instance, that his mother washes the laundry that he discards after his daily swims. Another, asked by Al Solh how he would respond if his girlfriend—by his own poetic admission, the "love of my life, the veins in my body"—asked him to give up the sea and move to the mountains, answers, "No way! The sea is more important. . . . Go to the mountains by yourself. . . . If she tries to deprive me of the sea?! The sea is part of my eyes!"

Al Solh finds an unusual way to imagine what it might be like if their gender roles were reversed. She dubs the men's answers in her own voice, replicating their intonations and their laughter, their bravado and their embarrassment. This simple technique is both comical and subversive: Al Solh remains offscreen so that her soft, feminine voice not only issues the questions but also answers them, appearing to emanate incongruously from the naked, sunburned torsos of the men, many of whom are clad only in swim trunks and goggles. English subtitles, rendered in two different colors, assist Anglophone audiences in telling the questions from the answers, but since both are voiced by Al Solh, the effect is that of a ventriloquist's performance in which Al Solh projects her voice from offscreen onto the men's onscreen bodies. The performance is humorous because it is unconvincing. Although Al Solh syncs her speech as perfectly to the men's moving lips as Esther Jeter does to Leila Grant's in *Illusions*, the effect is absurd, not naturalistic. Al Solh superimposes two vocal conventions associated with documentary realism—the talking head interview and the acousmatic female voice—by projecting the latter over the former. In the process, she also undoes the reality effects of these seemingly naturalistic conventions, inviting us to engage with them both as advanced Pythagorean illusions. This has an estranging effect on our habits of looking and listening. Where we would ordinarily hear documentary voices as indexes of bodies, Al Solh urges us to listen for how voices call surrogate vocalic bodies into being and how the reality effects of these vocalic bodies are differentially mediated in every cultural context by the twinned operations of a racialized, gendered gaze and its aural counterpart, the listening ear. The realism of documentary's vocal conventions, she suggests, can leave these perceptual frames undisturbed.

The unexpected reversal of hearing Al Solh's voice emerge from the men's torsos brings a concrete audiovisual expression to the perceptual adjustments required to work against these mediating forms. Al Solh effectively uses the cinematic play of sound and image to claim the protective cover of acousmatic displacement for her voice in the very same movement in which she (doubly) denudes the men as an objectified skin, transforming them from speaking subjects into a ventriloquist's dummies. By the end of the video, it becomes clear that Al Solh is speaking from a place, and calling into being an embodiment, that is unavailable to her *except* as a vocal performance. She ends her video by once again ventriloquizing the second of the men mentioned earlier. Asked whether he can imagine a city without a sea, he declares, "I'd die! . . . There's no city without a sea. It's just that maybe the sea is far . . . you might need to travel thousands of kilometers to get to it." This heartfelt statement becomes a poetic metaphor for Al Solh's voice, in which it is delivered. Speaking through her proxy, Al Solh tells us that using her voice as anything but a protective skin that is both immersed in her body and out of place would be like living in Beirut without a sea. To partake daily of that performance, that displacement, she insists, is as important to her as swimming in the sea is to the Beiruti men.

What makes this humorous spectacle sobering is that Al Solh asks us to understand her absurd ventriloquial performance as a necessary and even natural precondition of speaking and being heard in a logocentric, Eurocentric, and patriarchal society. Her film produces a Brechtian alienation or estrangement effect similar to that which Chow argues is achieved when actors memorize and reproduce lines of dialogue in a foreign language whose grammatical meaning is unknown to them: the actor's body is displaced as the de facto "origin" of the voice and instead appears as a ventriloquist's dummy that is animated by a force that comes from without and not within.[31] Al Solh's ventriloquial performance invites a mode of listening that is attentive to the ways in which voices displace their origins, as well as the hierarchizing social forces that animate the desire for this displacement and shape the phantasmic forms that these desires take. Indeed, Al Solh invites us to actively practice a *ventriloquial* mode of listening as a necessary and even natural mode of listening to vocal sounds. Ventriloquial listening brings a political dimension to the technical ritual of acousmatic listening that is especially pertinent in the context of vocal sounds. Acousmatic listening, as advocated by Schaeffer, attunes the listener to the traits of a voice, independent of its causes. Ventriloquial listening displaces the listener's attention from the visible causes of a voice (its embodied origins), attuning them instead to the invisible racialized and gendered perceptual frames—those forces that "come from without and not within"—that shape the production and reception of vocal sounds.

To listen ventriloquially is to behold the bifurcation of a voice's origins and its surrogate forms as one might behold performances of ventriloquists projecting their voices onto dummies. A ventriloquial listener becomes perceptive to the *seam* between the embodied origins of voices and the surrogate bodies that voices conjure into existence. They take note of when the illusion succeeds, magically animating the dummy, and when the illusion fails, reasserting the thingness or the matter of the dummy body. Ventriloquial listening asserts the ideological work involved on the part of both the performer and the audience of these vocal and perceptual illusions. It trains listeners to notice and work against the training of their senses by coercive social forces that operate disparately to "out" the origins of some voices, unraveling their auditory illusions and grounding their vocal traits in embodied matter, or that conversely transform the material traits of other voices into a vanishing mediator, seamlessly allowing the illusion to persist.

Conclusion

"Every emission of the voice is by its very essence *ventriloquism*," writes Dolar.[32] While Dolar points to the inherently acousmatic, veiled origins of every voice, Stoever, Eidsheim, and Chow point to the equally veiled perceptual frames that mediate the prospects of these ventriloquial illusions through their analyses of "the listening ear," "acousmatic blackness," and "skin tones." Listening, as Eidsheim notes, "does not connote passive reception of information and is not a neutral activity. Rather, in listening we participate in social processes both embedded in and producing cultural forms."[33] I have foregrounded the perceptual frames that mediate the production and reception of acousmatic voices by introducing the interrelated concepts of "the skin of the voice" and "ventriloquial listening." As a conceptual frame, the skin of the voice frames the voice as both an auditory phenomenon and a visual surface that can be read, profiled, and objectified and pinpoints how hearing is complicit in *and* complexly intertwined with vision in distinguishing between idealized and "other" voices.[34] I have argued, using this term, that idealized voices are perceived as an acousmatic screen—that is, as detached and displaced from their source—even when they emerge from a visible body, while minoritized voices are heard and objectified as a skin, even when their bodies are invisible. This term not only moves us beyond the persistent dualisms between sound and image, and *logos* and *phone*, that frame discussions of acousmatic listening, but also points to the ideologically inscribed perceptual processes that interweave the habitual operations of looking and listening.

Reconceptualizing the voice as skin also suggests that the voice can displace itself from its embodied source and relocate to an "other" imaginary place even without the assistance of a visual barrier. While Esther Jeter uses a surrogate white body to claim the protective veil of acousmatic displacement that her own voice has been unfairly denied, Mounira Al Solh's surreal projection of her own voice onto surrogate male bodies behaves as a supplement that paradoxically strips the veil from voices that enjoy its protection. I have read these films together in an effort to point out how Al Solh develops an audiovisual idiom that invites us to listen ventriloquially to *every* voice as an acousmatic performance that estranges and disguises the body from which it emanates. The closing image in Al Solh's film, of her father, towel slung over his shoulder, squinting into and adjusting a pair of binoculars, is a visual echo of Mignon Dupree's piercing but unfathomable look at Esther in the recording booth. It is a fitting reminder of the varying levels of scrutiny that different voices—whether speaking or singing, gendered or accented, embodied or disembodied—must "pass" for their illusions to succeed. Ventriloquial listening can function as a type of perceptual adjustment that attends to and actively works against these differential frames of scrutiny so that we may indeed grasp every voice as an acousmatic performance emerging from and contending with asymmetrical social conditions.

Notes

1 Julie Dash, dir., *Illusions*, film, Women Make Movies, New York, 1983.

2 Ryan, "Outing the Black Feminist Filmmaker," 1322.

3 Mellencamp, *A Fine Romance*, 235.

4 Altman, "Moving Lips."

5 Chion, *Audio-Vision*, 29.

6 Chion, *Audio-Vision*, 32.

7 Kane, *Sound Unseen*, 25.

8 Chion, *The Voice in Cinema*, 19, 19n5. Chion attributes the anecdote regarding the *acousmatiques* to Denis Diderot and Jean le Rond d'Alembert's *Encyclopédie* from 1751.

9 Dolar, *A Voice and Nothing More*, 15.

10 See Dolar, *A Voice and Nothing More*, 67–68. Dolar speculates that, like the eponymous character in *The Wizard of Oz*, the Pythagorean master is capable of exercising his divine powers over his listeners only as long as the source of his voice remains hidden. But while the wizard is revealed to be a "pitiable old man" once the veil is lifted and his voice is disacousmatized, the master's five-year acousmatic ritual wards off the castrating effects of exposure. Thus, the master's voice becomes a "phonic phallus" that allows the fantasy of his power to persist.

11 Connor, *Dumbstruck*, 35.

12 Stoever, *The Sonic Color Line*, 114–15.

13 Eidsheim, "Marian Anderson and 'Sonic Blackness' in American Opera," 647. Eidsheim writes that reviewers of American opera from the late nineteenth century to the mid-twentieth century have persisted in attributing a "distinctly black" timbre to the voices of black female opera singers, a tendency that may have led to the typecasting of these singers in roles such as maid, slave girl, or gypsy.

14 Stoever, *The Sonic Color Line*, 79.

15 Siefert, "Image/Music/Voice," 60.

16 Smith, "Black Faces, White Voices," 37.

17 Smith, "Black Faces, White Voices," 37.

18 See Chow, *Not Like a Native Speaker*, 7–9. Chow reads the failed attempts of these workers to disguise the *sound* of their unseen but audible embodiment as a form of vocal disfigurement akin to the botched effects of skin-whitening treatments. Both resort, she argues, to self-defacement in order to rectify a mode of self-expression that is falsely deemed defective.

19 Nichols, *Representing Reality*, 4.

20 See, e.g., Bruzzi, *New Documentary*. Since the publication of the first edition of her book, Bruzzi has been a vocal critic of Nichols's chronology of the various modes of documentary, which, she argues, produces false dichotomies between ideologically regressive and progressive documentary approaches based on films that share formal features.

21 Bruzzi, *New Documentary*, 57–58; Youdelman, "Narration, Invention, and History," 9; Wolfe, "Historicizing the 'Voice of God,'" 151.

22 Whether such a voice can be described as an *acousmêtre*—or, indeed, whether this concept is applicable to documentary—is an open question. Chion's analysis of the *acousmêtre*, defined as a disembodied cinematic voice that activates a tension between onscreen and offscreen space in the form of an "acousmatic zone," is restricted to fiction films, and he disavows the capacity of documentary voices to activate an acousmatic zone; see Chion, *The Voice in Cinema*, 22. The coordinates and implications of an acousmatic zone in documentary could profitably be discussed in alignment with Eidsheim's account of "acousmatic blackness," and I hope to address them on another occasion.

23 Ruoff, "Conventions of Sound in Documentary," 30. See also the analysis of these conventions in contemporary biographical and indie-rock documentaries in Sexton, "Excavating Authenticity."

24 See, e.g., Wolfe, "Historicizing the 'Voice of God'"; Youdelman, "Narration, Invention, and History"; Bruzzi, *New Documentary*.

25 Bruzzi, *New Documentary*, 64–65.

26 Silverman, *The Acoustic Mirror*, 165.

27 Bruzzi, *New Documentary*, 59, emphasis added.

28 Connor, *Dumbstruck*, 36.

29 Mounira Al Solh, dir., *Paris without a Sea*, video, https://vimeo.com/40821360 (password-protected).

30 Mounira Al Solh, "The Many Metamorphoses of Mounira Al Solh," interview by Nat Muller, *Ibraaz*, June 27, 2013, accessed February 1, 2016, http://www.ibraaz.org /interviews/82.

31 See Chow, "After the Passage of the Beast," 42.

32 Dolar, *A Voice and Nothing More*, 70.

33 Eidsheim, "Marian Anderson and 'Sonic Blackness' in American Opera," 665.

34 For this chapter, I am bracketing the haptic dimensions of voicing and listening but I discuss them at greater length in my introduction to a special issue of the journal *Discourse* on "Documentary Audibilities" that I coedited with Genevieve Yue: see Rangan, "Audibilities."

IV | Sound Abjects and
Nonhuman Relations

The Acoustic Abject

Sound and the Legal Imagination

Modernity, the authoritative *Oxford Handbook of Sound Studies* states, "has brought about developments in science, technology, and medicine and at the same time increasingly new ways of producing, storing, and reproducing sound."[1] Indeed, in modernity sound becomes more "thing-like . . . measured, regulated, and controlled."[2] Maybe so. Yet as the current paradigmatic shift toward hyper-objects, object-oriented ontologies, new materialism, thing theory, and animal studies indicates, the very concept of an object—alongside narratives of subjectification based on "epistemic virtues" such as objectivity—has never been more uncertain.

One of the epistemologies that is often overlooked in discussions of sound and yet is indissolubly entwined with liberal notions of subjectivity and, by implication, the sensory mediation of the subject to the object world is law. This is not to say that musicologists, ethnomusicologists, and other scholars of music ignore law altogether. For example, for the past decade a substantial literature has emerged in response to the legal implications of the digital revolution and hip hop's rise to hegemony. Yet the primary concern of works such as Patrick Burkhart's *Music and Cyberliberties*, Joanna Demers's *Steal this Music*, and Kembrew McLeod and Peter DiCola's *Creative*

License is more with the chilling effect copyright law's ever more aggressive intrusion into every aspect of creative practice has on the future of the democracy and the public sphere than with sound's increasingly marginal status as a result of the collapsing of the idea-expression dichotomy at the heart of copyright doctrine brought about by a flurry of *de minimis* cases.

On occasion, sound also features in legal scholarship. For instance, Bernard Hibbits, in a discussion of the "sound of law," surveys a large number of cultural and historical contexts in which sound occupies a prominent role in law's metaphorology.[3] For his part, Desmond Manderson, possibly the legal scholar who has written most prolifically on the relationship between music and law, suggests that music's role in law resembles that of a "structural device," a metaphor, a point of historical comparison, or a frame of reference.[4] A similar analogy between music and law also informs Sara Ramshaw's study of New York bebop in *Justice as Improvisation*. Like bebop, she boldly claims, justice is a "species of improvisation" that entails a "negotiation between abstract notions of justice and the everyday practice of judging."[5]

Although imaginative, the crux with this literature is that sound's deep entanglement with law and legal practice is either narrowly and unambiguously framed in instrumental terms as a means serving legal ends or, alternatively, figured as a question of regulation of undesirable sonic practices such as noise pollution. By contrast, in the pages that follow I substantiate a concept of sound that questions both the means-to-ends logic and the objectification of sound in the legal imagination. My argument is twofold. Instrumentalist and objectifying discourses of law's sound, I suggest, not only neutralize sound as a mere medium and in the process uncritically perpetuate sound's absence from musico-aesthetic and legal constructions of subject-object relationships, but they also foreclose the possibility of engaging sound's agency *in specific legal ways*. Sound, as I will show in the second prong of my argument, using two rather graphic examples of the place of hate speech, "noise," and music in constitutional law and international criminal law, has injurious potential and hence might be considered more as a doing than a mere medium for vocal utterance. But, paradoxically, for us to speak legally about this elusive yet viscerally, vibrationally "real" of sound and its ability to shape, subject, terrify, and obliterate, sound itself would need to be expelled from the realm of juridical reason.

This aporia of speaking about an object that must be ejected from the realm of the speakable to instantiate a speaking subject is at the center of Julia Kristeva's concept of abjection. Readers familiar with Kristeva's sono-linguistic elaboration of Lacan's theory of subject formation in terms of an ontological oscillation between the prosodic-rhythmic realm of the semiotic and the denotative sphere of the symbolic might expect here a discussion of her adumbration of the unitary subject as the result of the Law (of the Father), understood as a system of social domination. In what follows I will resist such a move as a simplistic identification of the social and the legal and will focus instead on the potential of Kristeva's concept of the abject for rethinking the place of sound in law *as a specific epistemology and practice* that not only shuns sound (even as it constantly evokes it) but exploits sound's liminality as a necessary condition of its own distance from the object world. Put differently, on the one hand, law naturalizes sound as being inextricably intertwined with the subject: as voice, as verbal utterance, and as an expression of the self's innermost intentions. At the same time, however, sound is also barred from forming a durable basis for instantiating a (legal) subject. The "strange privilege of sound in idealization," the "indissociable system" of φωνή (voice) and subject that Jacques Derrida made the center of his critique of phonocentrist presentism, in law dissolves in the same breath that the oath has been sworn, the testimony has been given, the plea has been entered.[6] Sound, in law, not only leaves no trace; it never attains the status of an object to begin with. Yet far from jeopardizing the possibility of a subject-object relationship at the heart of modernist (formalist or realist) jurisprudence's claims to rationality and thus from undermining law's very legitimacy as a sui generis epistemology, this sonic limbo, this aporia must be seen as law's very condition of possibility, as the possibility of law, despite *and* because of sound's absence, to be itself.

On the Edge: Julia Kristeva and the Abjection of Sound

Kristeva's *The Powers of Horror: An Essay on Abjection* (1982) has what one might call an "acoustic dead angle." Although much of its two hundred or so pages are about sonic phenomena such as language and poetry, sound in its raw materiality hardly ever figures. Usually read as an elaboration of Lacanian psychoanalysis and as an extension of Kristeva's earlier writings on language and literature, *The Powers of Horror* instead might be interpreted itself as being an act of abjection—of sound. As a reminder, the novelty—if one may call it that—of Kristeva's theory of abjection consists in having shifted Freud's concept of primary repression from that of a subject's forbidden desire for a particular relation to a given object to that of the repression of the antecedent ambiguity of the subject-object relation itself. Hence, in contrast to Freud's return of the repressed, things such as uncontrollable body fluids, cadavers, or milk curd do not evoke specific traumas as much as they recall the fragility of the borders separating the inside from the outside. It is these unstable boundaries that form the space proper of what Kristeva famously calls "signifiance."

The latter term—along with other original Kristevan portmanteaus such as "genotext" and "phenotext"—was subsequently adopted by Roland Barthes and developed into a theory of the musical voice that played a significant role in the formative period of New Musicology. Irrespective of Barthes's influence, however, musicological readings of Kristeva's concept of abjection—which is intimately linked to the theory of signifiance—have remained surprisingly scarce. There are some noteworthy exceptions, though. For instance, in a wide-ranging classic of the field, Lawrence Kramer has sought to revive classical music's waning appeal not by fetishizing its role as an anchor of enlightened subjectivity but by embracing music's inescapable and irredeemable abjection.[7] Kramer arrives at this conclusion by way of an intricate argument that bears closer scrutiny because of its significance beyond the realm of classical music—and, indeed, the musical realm generally—for the argument of this chapter about the sonic abject in the legal imagination.

Since the mid-eighteenth century, Kramer writes, music has been closely tied to what he calls a "logic of alterity."[8] Much of New Musicology's initial project (including, prominently, Kramer's own work) has centered on figuring this "logic" as the "opposition of form and sensuous plenitude," or as the "rational" containment of excessive, "oriental," "effeminate" sonority. But the opposition between the unitary identity that the Enlightenment self recognizes and the others it depends on for the construction of that identity is not only an imaginary one, as Lacan would say, articulated within specific musical terrains and serving cultural institutions that continually reproduce this opposition; it also rests on a "systematic contradiction in the identification of self and other." The "othering" that is articulated in the "opposition of form and sensuous plenitude" intensifies further when music as a whole comes to stand as the Other. It is then, Kramer argues, that this othering of music begins to decenter the process by which musical form constructs a musical self, for if "the self speaks through music when form contains (limits and encloses) sonority, then formally articulate music cannot stand as other. Yet the very presence within music of a position between form and sonority presupposes that something in music must be other."[9]

Unsurprisingly, Kramer never quite frees himself from the binary of self and other that he identified as being at the heart of music's "logic of alterity." Over the breadth and length of his article, the eponymous abject hardly ever comes into view. For sure, Kramer advocates an auditory stance, or what he calls "performative listening," which "subsumes the logic of alterity but can never be subsumed by it."[10] He also envisages a type of "pragmatic" experience in which "presymbolic involvement, symbolic understanding, and keenness of pleasure or distress can all coexist, precisely because there is no imperative to reconcile them or order them hierarchically." Yet such incantations of a "more contingent logic of postmodern musical experience" do not bring us a single step closer to the instability of the subject-object relationship, that strange *je ne sais quoi* that is said to be at the heart of music and that the reflexive self must discard to be itself.

The problem is not Kramer's alone. The difficulty of locating this "something in music" that is other also troubles emerging work on the cultural production of the abject in popular art forms. Thus, in a discussion of country music—a genre of music often decried for its alleged aesthetic plainness and right-wing political sympathies—Aaron Fox argues for country's "alchemical" transformation from a state of abjection as "bad" music to an object of intense desire, or, as Kristeva might have put it, to the abject that "is edged with the sublime."[11] In a slightly different vein, Nataša Pivec finds that in the intense, in-your-face music videos of the rock artist Marilyn Manson, various material, spatial, and symbolic forms of "dirt" are employed tactically to subvert "hegemonic masculinity."[12] What unites this scholarship beyond, or precisely because of, its Kristevan echoes, is something far more concrete than abjection though. It is the assumption that various forms of identity—masculine, country, working class, and so forth—are already in place and that as such they can be deconstructed, restructured, or redeemed by harnessing the abject, by stabilizing the inescapably fragile boundaries between self and other by aesthetic means. Thus it is that country music's abjection—its plebeian flouting of the rules of political correctness or liberal gender politics—is being subsumed under what Fox calls "a cultural logic" through which "bad" is sublimated into "good."[13] The abject sublime becomes readable within social logics of race, class, and gender that may confirm or contest identities without, however, the concept of identity itself being questioned.

In fairness, throughout Kristeva's oeuvre a similar reluctance may be sensed to engage the sonic at the same level of theoretical rigor as in her readings of Céline, Mallarmé, and Joyce. Thus, all assertions to the contrary of "signifiance" being an "unlimited and unbounded generating process" and enabling a "passage to the outer *boundaries* of the subject," whenever she invokes music, such open-endedness is renounced in favor of binary oppositions. For instance, the primary signifiers within the semiotic and the symbolic—the two "modalities" of signifiance—are organized in opposites: rhythm and intonation are situated within the realm of the semiotic or chora; music and melody, in the symbolic order.[14] At the same time, however, the relationship of these terms among one another is anything but obvious. Thus, one cannot be but struck by the near-inscrutability of claims such as the one that Céline's declared intention of mining the emotional depths by "imparting to thought a certain melodious, melodic twist" constitutes the moment when "melody alone reveals, and even holds, such buried intimacy" and when the worship of emotion "slips into glorification of sound."[15] Whence this total metonymy of melody and sound, redolent of romantic ideas of mellifluous excess undermining the rationality of musical form? Why this constant oscillation between the pre-symbolic intimacy of music and its containment in melody? And what is one to make of the perplexing assertion, in her pioneering *Revolution in Poetic Language*, that music is a nonverbal signifying system that is "constructed exclusively on the basis of the semiotic," when elsewhere we are told that the semiotic consists of non-signifying pulsations of rhythm?[16] Finally, what is the meaning behind the suggestive, if unlikely, claim that, in Céline, Joyce, and Artaud, music and rhythm merge into a strange sort of polyphony that is meant to "wipe out sense"?[17]

Kristeva's blistering analysis of Céline's work in the last pages of *Powers* may provide some clues. In it, Kristeva berates Céline's project—modernism's project—to let language "fly off its handle" as a failed project. On the one hand, Céline is to be applauded for having downgraded the "logical or grammatical dominant of written language," but on the other hand, he undermines that effort by means of transformations situated at the deeper, "semiotic" level through devices such as segmentation, preposing, displacement, ellipsis, and, most crucially, intonation. Usually thought of as a mere acoustic instantiation of the language system, intonation, especially for Kristeva, exists prior to enunciation, producing language and, of course, the subject of enunciation itself—through the symbolic integration of rejection and death drive in the first place.[18] For all of his vulgar, hate-filled verbal convulsions—thus, Kristeva's crushing verdict—Céline is a "grammarian who reconciles melody and logic admirably well."[19]

Clearly, Kristeva's sonic imagination is a rather impoverished one. Contrary to the grandiose title—"From Content to Sound"—of the chapter quoted earlier, much of her work might be said actually to take us in the opposite direction: from sound to content. Kristeva fails to embrace sound's abjection because her perspective on sound has already been filtered through a discourse that assigns to "rhythm" a subordinate position as the Other of more hegemonic parameters such as "melody." By blindly reproducing the othering implicit in the common repertoire's placing of rhythm at the bottom of the hierarchy of parameters, Kristeva fails to query musical form's control of the musical order over and against sonority and visceral excess. Kristeva's sonic world is firmly integrated into the symbolic order.

Still, although musicians and music scholars may find it difficult to relate Kristeva's sweeping terminology to the specifics of musical grammar and practice, they might recognize in her writing something of the intensity with which previous generations of thinkers have tackled the *je ne sais quoi* of sound, a quest that has been renewed with unprecedented vigor in sound studies. Although this field may be credited for having provided during its formative period a much needed corrective to the dominance of vision as the sensory core of Western epistemology, current sound scholarship has since moved into what Jonathan Sterne and Mitchell Akiyama call its "postsonic" phase.[20] Stretching the sonic spectrum to its outer limits— to unwanted, aesthetically disparaged, unbearable, repulsive, deafening, or barely audible sound—researchers are increasingly questioning "axiomatic assumptions regarding the givenness of a particular domain called 'sound,' a process called 'hearing,' or a listening subject." Good examples of such scholarship are David Novak's *Japanoise*, a study on Japan's underground Noise scene, or Brendon LaBelle's evocative *Lexicon of the Mouth*, partly a compendium and partly a philosophical essay on orally produced abject sounds such as sloshing, belching, and puking.[21] But in doing so, these and other authors do not simply open up new topics of investigation; they also alter conventional object-centered methodologies. In tandem with this shift toward the edges of the sonic spectrum, sound is being repositioned from an object of knowledge to a way of knowing. Inspired by Steven Feld's influential concept of acoustemology, the cultural study of sound stands in for a type of knowledge production about the world that does not a priori presume essences such as "human," "animal," or "sound" and that, as a consequence, also refuses to recognize the subject-object framework structuring the relationship of such essences in traditional epistemology. Acoustemology, Feld suggests, accepts the "conjunctions, disjunctions, and entanglements among all copresent and historically accumulated forms" as what holds the world together.[22]

Perhaps the most promising direction sound studies has taken in recent years, however, is toward a deeper understanding of sound *as* abjection—that is, as an obliterating force deployed in situations of extreme violence such as war or torture. Thus, Suzanne Cusick, in a seminal piece on sound and music in detention facilities used in the U.S. "war on terror," has probed the de-territorializing effects of sound and music during, or as, a technique of torture and the all-encompassing damage it inflicts on the perpetrators, their victims, the public, and even music itself.[23] Meanwhile, J. Martin Daughtry introduced the term "abject acoustic victims" to refer to Iraqi detainees who were being hooded during interrogation by their U.S. captors and whose exposure to extremely loud sounds deprived them of sensory control of their surroundings, trapping them "in a resonant acoustic territory within which they were not and could never be citizens."[24] The point, then, about such "belliphonic sounds" (another Daughtry coinage) is not only that they strip their victims of their entire being by casting the abject back on bodies that, under normal circumstances, would eject them as extreme, painful, or unpalatable. Occupying "intracorporeal acoustic territories," the breakdown of subject-object boundaries created by such weaponization of sound also opens up entirely new possibilities for radically reshaping conventional Enlightenment notions and rules of identity formation focusing on the autharchic body, feeding what Steve Goodman calls the "ecology of fear" in their wake.[25]

But acoustic boundary violations are not confined to the association with real or threatened physical violence. Less traumatic (albeit by no means any less morally debilitating) is the way more aestheticized manifestations of the sonic abject invade, stretch, and explode the confines of what Didier Anzieu, a student of Lacan, calls the "skin ego," causing revulsion, disgust, and outrage in their wake.[26] Steven Connor, in a series of texts that draw on this and other related terms introduced by Anzieu such as the "acoustic envelope," explores the role of sound in upsetting the conventional notion of the skin as a mere outer shell that separates the outside (other) from the inside (self).[27] On this account, the tympanum is not what Derrida famously derided as the "organ . . . of absolute properness"—that is, of the distinction between what is proper to oneself and what is the realm of the Other.[28] Quite to the contrary: skin as a whole, not just the eardrum, assumes resonant, acoustic qualities.[29] Skin is the space of nowhere par excellence and as such it belongs neither to the subject nor to the object. This is why this void frequently invites a different form of the sonic abject. As Lisa Coulthard points out in an essay on "dirty sound" in New Extremism (which includes films by the likes of Lars von Trier and Philippe Grandrieux), images and sounds of abjection, dissociation, and disturbance materially implicate or immerse audiences in what one might call a complicity of sublime acoustic violence.[30]

The Silence of the Law

The question, then, becomes a broader one for the assertion of this chapter that sound is not an object but an abject of law. If the abject is what "does not respect borders, positions, rules," and if, as shown earlier, scholars consider sound one of the privileged sites of abjection by dint of its ability to de-territorialize and reterritorialize self and other, what work does the sonic abject do in the legal imagination?[31] Why is it that the law is suffused with acoustic metaphors and procedures that are central to its functioning, such as the doctrines of hearsay and viva voce, but that the law at the same time goes to extraordinary efforts to keep sound at bay? Why do legal practitioners and legal scholars, faced with an ever growing presence and awareness of sounds both wanted and unwanted in areas from environmental pollution and conflicts over land to debates about cultural heritage and intellectual property rights, turn a deaf ear to sound? In the second half of this chapter, we will see that the life of the law—its identity, formal integrity, self-referentiality, and, most important, claims to autonomy and neutrality—are contingent on the abjection of sound. The law, as Stanley Fish famously puts it in his controversial essay "The Law Wishes to Have a Formal Existence," is "continually creating and recreating itself out of the very materials and forces it is obliged, by the very desire to *be* law, to push away."[32]

We will return to Fish's essay in more detail later, but first we must begin, in proper legal fashion, with a case. In September 2006, a Rwandan pop singer named Simon Bikindi was put on trial at the International Criminal Tribunal for Rwanda on charges of incitement to genocide. In 1994, Rwanda (and a largely passive world audience) became witness to one of the worst genocides of the twentieth century, in the course of which more than half a million Tutsi and tens of thousands of moderate Hutu were murdered in fewer than one hundred days. A key role in the mass slaughter was played by Radio Télévision Libre des Mille Collines (RTLMC), a station that flooded the Rwandan airwaves with Tutsi-baiting rhetoric and Bikindi's songs. Although for much of its duration the trial looked and sounded more like a "musical trial" than a criminal trial—the tribunal frequently finding itself tuning in to Bikindi's music, hearing evidence from musicologists, and even listening to Bikindi himself as he sang his final statement—it was not for his songs that Bikindi was eventually convicted but for two inflammatory speeches the singer gave from a truck in which, to the sound of his own music, he exhorted the public to go out and exterminate all Tutsi. In a way, then, Bikindi's voice and music might be said to have provided the soundtrack to the genocide. But why is it, James Parker wonders in his pioneering *Acoustic Jurisprudence: Listening to the Trial of Simon Bikindi*, that the tribunal never explicitly engaged the materiality of sound permeating the "judicial soundscape"?[33] And, at the same time, why is the law "never without the problem of sound"?[34] At bottom, Parker concludes, the main reason for the tribunal's sonic obtuseness is the crude, instrumentalist conception of mass media, music, and the voice. In the chamber's opinion, these merely functioned as language's handmaiden. For instance, RTLMC was seen as a vehicle for disseminating and amplifying messages of hatred but never as an agent of violence. For its part, music was to be understood as separate from song, as instrumental backing and as such irrelevant to the "content" or lyrics of the song.

The voice is a different matter. On the one hand, voice is to speech what "music" is to the lyrics of a song; it is speech's natural embodiment and material form, and as such it is extraneous to thought. But at the same time, voice figures in a more ambiguous role, drawing together vocalization, thought, intent, and even technology (RTLMC, the public-address system, and so on) into a perilous, even tautological metonymy, or what Parker calls an "expressive chain."[35] What enables this chain and ultimately secured Bikindi's conviction, Parker argues, is a peculiar conflation of the jurisprudential reasoning underpinning the doctrine of incitement, on the one hand, and the legacy of phonocentrism as defined by Derrida, on the other. In essence, the tribunal treated Bikindi's speeches as an "expression" of individual criminal intent. Yet the concept of "expression" is so deeply enshrined in a host of legal doctrines—from the law of evidence and the law of criminal procedure to copyright law—that it no longer requires justification, particularly in relation to the law's most taken-for-granted, "natural" entity, the voice. This is why the court had no difficulty in merging voice and subjectivity in its effort to lend plausibility and weight to the finding that, in making these speeches, Bikindi not only had genocidal intentions but that, as such, these intentions can clearly be deduced from his vocal utterances. Thus, ultimately, what is essentially an ontological problem—the "problem of sound"—here comes down to a question of juridical convenience. Eschewing sound by separating the sonic materiality of the voice from its enunciative outcome is simply a sophisticated "jurisprudential technique" for silencing the voice precisely "in the process of 'giving voice' to speech."[36] Through the "substitution of the language of voice for that of subjectivity," sound is sacrificed to evidentiary reliability and, ultimately, to the stability of the subject.

While the court's decision to abstract meaning and intention and their expression in spoken (or even sung) language from sound and thereby also to deny sound's agency to inflict bodily harm clearly highlights the paucity of law's sonic imagination, it amounts to more than technique. Jurisprudential technique, Fish might weigh in, is anything but a sign of legal trickery or a lack of self-reflexivity. Quite the contrary, it is the "trick by which law subsists."[37] What makes law the law, then, of necessity entails the abjection of sound.

In her *Excitable Speech: A Politics of the Performative*, Judith Butler faces a similar conundrum. Like Parker, Butler seems to imply that the judicial attribution of injurious speech to a singular subject is a matter of basic linguistics or a mere "grammatical requirement of accountability."[38] And although she, like Parker, sees such attribution as little more than a "juridical constraint on thought," she might also find herself at odds with Parker in that she rejects any attempt at judicial censoring of injurious speech as curtailing the possibility of political opposition to such speech. More usefully, however, Butler also seeks to broaden the question of agency in hate speech by attending to the role of the non-constative foundation of speech as transcending the utterer-utterance divide underpinning the concept of efficacious, violence-inducing speaking. In a familiar, Derridean move, she denies to the utterer any claims to antecedence to the utterance. Much as "auto-affection" does not characterize a being that is already itself, the injuriously speaking, morally, and juridically accountable subject first needs to be produced through a prior configuration in which the question of "who is accountable for a given injury precedes and initiates the subject, and the subject itself is formed through being nominated to inhabit that grammatical and juridical site."[39]

This leaves us with the question of what agent might replace the doing subject now demoted to an aftereffect of a prior grammatical and juridical configuration. It will come as no surprise that, throughout her analysis, Butler studiously avoids the "problem of sound"—except once, as metaphor. Discussing a case in which the U.S. Supreme Court pondered the question of whether the Ku Klux Klan–style burning of a cross on the front lawn of an African American family in St. Paul, Minnesota, constitutes protected speech under the First Amendment (*R.A.V. v. City of St. Paul*, 505 U.S. 377 [1992]), she touches on the relationship the ruling establishes between the "noncontent element (e.g. noise)" and the "content element" of speech. Delivering the opinion, Justice Antonin Scalia revisits the "fighting words" doctrine of constitutional law according to which speech acts unprotected by the U.S. Constitution are those that "are no essential part of any exposition of ideas, and are of such slight social value as a step to truth that any benefit that may be derived from them is clearly outweighed by the social interest in order and morality" (*Chaplinsky v. New Hampshire*, 315 U.S. 568 [1942]). This wording, Scalia argues, would appear to legitimize the absurd claim that "the unprotected features of the words are, despite their verbal character, 'nonspeech' elements of communication."[40] Thus, to shield any act of speech communication from government interference, Scalia, in a remarkable twist of formal legal reasoning, invokes an analogy with sound. "Fighting words," he writes, are "analogous to a noisy sound truck." In other words, by distinguishing between a medium ("noise truck,") and an expression ("idea," "message"), the sound of a speech act may well be considered injurious, but the message it conveys may not. And while injurious acts such as "noise" may be regulated (e.g., by noise ordinances), "the government may not regulate use based on hostility—or favoritism—towards the underlying message expressed."

The ruling thus might be said to fit a square peg into a round hole. It elevates an otherwise punishable act of destruction (on someone else's private property, no less) to a protected expression of a viewpoint. Or, as Butler puts it, by assuming a connection between the signifying power of the burning cross and what may or may not constitute its speech-like character, the burning of the cross, now construed as free speech, is no longer a doing, an action, or an injury. It is only an "expression" that, although repugnant, is to be tolerated precisely for that reason.[41]

But ambiguity remains. On the one hand, sound, construed by *R.A.V.* as a container of speech, is demoted to the rank of a mere nuisance to be prevented by means other than by proscribing the content of the speech it houses. Such sound, then, can be ejected from "order" and "morality" and their foundation in speech into a space from which it cannot exert any discursive power. Devoid of agency, it simply endures in a state of abjection. But on the other hand, the same sound, now stripped of its unproductive, violent force, reemerges in purified and, in a sense, inaudible form to support the unhindered flow of free speech.

Such is, precisely, the ambiguity of the sonic abject. And it is the same ambiguity that constitutes the very possibility of the law's "formal existence." This is what Justice John Paul Stevens must have had in mind when, in a dissenting opinion, he offered an alternative to what he calls the majority's "absolutism in the prohibition of content-based regulations" of speech. The difference between injurious and free speech, he argued, can be established not formally but by interpretation—that is, in context.[42] A word, for instance, says Stevens, quoting the legendary Justice Oliver Wendell Holmes, "is not a crystal, transparent and unchanged" but the "skin of a living thought" that may vary in "color and content according to the circumstances and the time in which it is used."[43] Ignoring the racial undertones of Holmes's adumbration (duly critiqued by Butler), yet being mindful of the ambiguities of skin as a site of identity formation, it is worthwhile to examine the concept of "context" a little further and how Butler ties Stevens's opinion back to her theory of hate speech and discursive power. In Butler's Foucauldian understanding of symbolic violence, the relationship between an injury and the act of a subject is not a causal one between a doer and a deed; it is more a "kind of discursive transitivity."[44] This more performance-like process is best grasped by attending to the moments, sites, and techniques of power in and through which it is enacted—in short, by attending to Stevens's "context."

Stevens's contextualist dissenting opinion and Butler's performative-constitutivist reading of it are no doubt incisive and thus indicative of the kind of readings critical legal studies routinely bring to bear on the style of reasoning espoused by formalists such as Scalia. While rhetorically virtuosic, such readings might argue, Scalia's opinion in R.A.V. equally could be seen as logically questionable, if not downright politically expedient. Indisputably, the Scalia opinion is both. But the reverse seems equally true. Both Butler's "discursive transitivity"—that is, the notion that the lethal power of contemporary acts of injurious speech is the cumulative effect of iterative uses of past "fighting words"—and Stevens's accommodation of "cultural" contingency raise a number of troubling questions. What qualities invest some sounds with more agentive, injurious potential than others?

At what point does the line between medium and "expression" get blurred to the extent that it becomes possible to consider sound itself as injurious? And vice versa: what happens when the words are injurious but the sound is not? Can Bikindi's songs be exonerated from being categorized as hate speech simply because their light-touch, pop sound might seem to predestine them for uses that are radically opposed to mass killings? But have we not heard of marching bands playing "happy" tunes while the innocent were being commandeered to the quarries? And what about the sounds of Islamic piety that provide the acoustic backdrop to all those death squads currently roaming the Middle East?[45] Is music abject only when it is loud, continuously playing, or dissonant or when it operates by association, such as when Wagner's "Ride of the Valkyries," in Francis Ford Coppola's *Apocalypse Now*, blares from helicopters dropping napalm bombs on unsuspecting Vietnamese villagers?

Conversely, what productive, regenerative force might inhere in those poignant moments in which expressions of pain and suffering burst forth from the bodies of traumatized victims of violence and disrupt the legal protocol—for instance, during the trial of Adolf Eichmann, when the Holocaust survivor K. Zetnik collapsed on the witness stand? Does such a dramatic moment or "mute cry," as he himself later called it, prove the trial a failure, as Hannah Arendt famously argued? Or is the mute cry rather what Shoshana Felman calls a "necessary failure," one that not only exposes the trauma but, more significantly, "creates a new dimension in the trial, a physical legal dimension that dramatically expands what can be grasped as legal meaning"?[46]

In a similar vein, Sonali Chakravarti argues that the particular tone, modulation, and cadence of an individual's voice—or what she calls the "kinetic dimension of anger"—expressed by a victim of violence during proceedings of restorative justice such as the South African Truth and Reconciliation Commission can open up new avenues for political agency and civic engagement.[47] Although courts tend to shun such overtly emotional expressions, giving victims the opportunity to let go of the restraint imposed by the ideology of reasoned discourse as the basis of truth when sounding their deepest feelings instantiates a political practice of listening in relation to judgment that goes beyond catharsis. Such sounding becomes constitutive of justice.

Clearly, if one person's minuet can be another's funeral march, the basis on which such "expressions" can be judged as being either injurious or protected speech becomes a very fragile one—and one, to boot, that the law constantly has to stabilize. But this effort to achieve "formal existence" does not operate by suppressing interpretation, context, and morality. Rather, it operates, as Fish eloquently puts it, by telling two stories, "one of which is denying that the other is being told at all."[48] Translated into this chapter's concern with the "sonic abject," one might conclude, silencing sound by denying it the status of an object of legal discourse (at least in cases involving doctrines based on distinctions among "expression," "idea," or "act") is the *conditio sine qua non* and, if we are to believe Fish, the very reason for law's remarkable resilience (e.g., in bringing perpetrators such as Bikindi to justice). By the same token, however, it is not too far-fetched a counterclaim to suggest that the unease with the "problem of sound" articulated by Parker, Butler, and Stevens also partakes of what Fish calls a "feat of legerdemain."[49] The interpretive, contextualizing stance advocated by critical legal scholarship, when it comes to sound, must present itself as "common sense," beyond contingency and interpretation. What better way to do this than to abject sound?

Notes

1   Bijsterveld and Pinch, "New Keys to the World of Sound," 4.
2   Bijsterveld and Pinch, "New Keys to the World of Sound," 5.
3   See Hibbitts, "'Coming to Our Senses.'"
4   Manderson, *Songs without Music*, 49.
5   Ramshaw, *Justice as Improvisation*, 2.
6   Derrida, *Of Grammatology*, 23.
7   See Kramer, "From the Other to the Abject."
8   Kramer, "From the Other to the Abject," 35.
9   Kramer, "From the Other to the Abject," 36.
10 Kramer, "From the Other to the Abject," 65.
11 Fox, "White Trash Alchemies of the Abject Sublime"; Kristeva, *Powers of Horror*, 11.
12 Pivec, "Drags, Drugs and Dirt," 123.
13 Fox, "White Trash Alchemies of the Abject Sublime," 59.
14 Kristeva, *Powers of Horror*, 17.
15 Kristeva, *Powers of Horror*, 190.
16 Kristeva, *Revolution in Poetic Language*, 93.
17 Kristeva, *Desire in Language*, 142.
18 Kristeva, *Powers of Horror*, 196.
19 Kristeva, *Powers of Horror*, 192.
20 Sterne and Akiyama, "The Recording That Never Wanted to Be Heard and Other Stories of Sonification," 556.

21 See Novak, *Japanoise*; Labelle, *Lexicon of the Mouth*.

22 Feld, "Acoustemology," 12.

23 See Cusick, "You Are in a Place That Is out of the World . . ."

24 Daughtry, *Listening to War*, 107.

25 Goodman, *Sonic Warfare*, 107.

26 See Anzieu, *The Skin-Ego*.

27 See Connor, *The Book of Skin*.

28 Derrida, "Tympan," xvii.

29 See Erlmann, *Reason and Resonance*.

30 See Coulthard, "Dirty Sound."

31 Kristeva, *Powers of Horror*, 4.

32 Fish, "The Law Wishes to Have a Formal Existence," 181.

33 Parker, *Acoustic Jurisprudence*, 3.

34 Parker, *Acoustic Jurisprudence*, 2.

35 Parker, *Acoustic Jurisprudence*, 114–18.

36 Parker, *Acoustic Jurisprudence*, 122–23.

37 Fish, "The Law Wishes to Have a Formal Existence," 195.

38 Butler, *Excitable Speech*, 50.

39 Butler, *Excitable Speech*, 46.

40 Butler, *Excitable Speech*, 386.

41 Butler, *Excitable Speech*, 56.

42 Butler, *Excitable Speech*, 427.

43 *R.A. V. v. City of St. Paul*, 505 U.S. 377 (1992), 427n5; see also Holmes, *The Essential Holmes*, 287.

44 Butler, *Excitable Speech*, 47.

45 Shirin Jaafari, "How ISIS Uses Catchy, Violent Tunes for Propaganda," December 18, 2014, https://www.pri.org/stories/2014-12-18/how-isis-uses-catchy-violent-tunes-propaganda.

46 Felman, "A Ghost in the House of Justice," 38.

47 Chakravarti, *Sing the Rage*, 149.

48 Fish, "The Law Wishes to Have a Formal Existence," 200.

49 Fish, "The Law Wishes to Have a Formal Existence," 184.

The Alluring Objecthood
of the Heartbeat

A heartbeat: nothing is more decisive to confirming a human life, its sonic form relaying this antenatal address to a listener for whom it constitutes a vital index—quite literally. This sonic form, a delicate thud of a sound competing in the listener's attention with the complex sonorous world of the mother's—her heartbeat, louder and more assertive; respiratory whirls; vascular murmurs; placental blood flow; and digestive growling—may well constitute a sound object *par excellence*. It compels multiple listening modes and corollary techniques for which phenomenology offers possible vocabularies, categories, and mappings of relations vis-à-vis subjects (consciousness, perceptual systems, and so on).

Aided by a Pinard horn, a midwife listens intently to the sounds issuing from the mother's abdomen, her audile efforts directed toward the fetus's heartbeat, the main focus of her auscultation.[1] At that very instant, the heartbeat exists in the interior of the midwife's sensory and perceptual experience, constituting a presentation *in* (not merely *to*) her consciousness—what Franz Brentano calls an "immanent objectivity."[2] Brentano's student Kazimierz Twardowski would redistribute this objectivity beyond the midwife's consciousness, arguing that consciousness maintains content even while the object is assigned a place outside of it. Husserl, finally, would relocate both content and object back to the "immanent realm" of Brentano.[3] There, the transcendental ego hoards for itself the essence of its object—this ante-natal heartbeat—in the isolated splendor of its eidetic reduction, leaving to the sound object little or nothing of its own.

This is no indictment of phenomenology, for in order to fulfill her mon-itoring and diagnostic responsibilities, the midwife's listening must be *subtractive* and its object must be *intentional*—hence, embodying two clas-sic phenomenological attitudes. Attaining this object in its most focused specificity as sound phenomenon—rather than a bundle of its qualities (à la empiricism) or as pure biological matter (à la naturalism)—the midwife operates within a pragmatic and vernacular phenomenology necessary for the sustenance and reproduction of human life in her community. This vernacular phenomenology, however, anchors a science that jettisons in-flexible distinctions between the sensible and the intelligible. Thus, the Husserlian aspiration to a purely intellectual delivery of the object's *eidos* to consciousness gives way to the allusive character of the sensory.

We will argue in this chapter that the allure of the fetal heartbeat reg-isters antenatal listening as a primary form of aurality.[4] Such primacy is not limited to its temporal position within development—the (phylogenic) human capacity for hearing or the "ontogeny of audition" in Western science—but extends to fundamental ontological and epistemic questions at the heart (no pun intended) of antenatal existence.[5] In particular, we are interested in the status of sound as an object both within human percep-tion and beyond its sensual qualities.

As a way into these questions, we offer examples from the Colombian case in dialogue with recent Amazonian anthropology.[6] We offer alterna-tives to a prevalent view of antenatal sound, as articulated in the following quotation and echoed across psychoanalytic, feminist, and phenomenolog-ical discourse: "In the amniotic ocean, all of us are unified by the furtive yet helpless condition of eavesdropping, unable to identify what we hear when this operation is enacted in another space, entirely beyond our experience as unborn beings."[7] But rather than simply upturn this hauntology and defuse its universalism, we examine antenatality with ears attuned to acoustemol-ogies organized outside unyielding distinctions between individuals—the "two beating syncopated hearts" of fetus and mother, or as part of the "split subjectivity" of the mother.[8] Amid these ontological arrangements, notions of sound as object and relation come under interrogation.

Our primary task in this chapter is to ask quite simply what kind of rela-tion or object sound is. And we argue, by way of conclusion, that *a sound is an object* (or, more precisely stated, that a fetal heartbeat is an object). That such a claim is so surprising and uncommon is, of course, quite ironic, given the title of this volume. Nonetheless, in light of insistent claims for sound's inherent relationality and processualism, arguing for a conceptualization of sound *qua* object is, we believe, necessary.

More than One, Less than Two

Views of human pregnancy index fundamental social orders everywhere.[9] These views cover a vast range, from the natural to the supernatural, from crisis to normality, and from transition to transfiguration. In Western societies and under the impetus of scientific and economic interests, pregnancy increasingly has become identified with risk and the imperative for biomedical care.[10] Pregnancy compels societal control and monitoring precisely because it constitutes an event that cannot be fully controlled.[11]

Perhaps no dispositive has more decisively shaped such monitoring in recent times than the use of ultrasound. As Rayna Rapp puts it, we live in an "age of monitored reproduction" in which obstetrical clinicians use ultrasound's "instant visualizations to measure, date, position, and intervene in pregnancies, while 'reassuring' their patients that their fetuses are developing in a normal matter."[12] This visualization does important sensory and psychological work for the mother. It helps close whatever distance may be perceived between the mother and fetal movement issuing as if from "nowhere," beginning around the sixteenth week. But it also, paradoxically, creates the experience of the fetus as a distinct and separate entity from which a modicum of psychological separation emerges.[13] This distancing is in some sense instrumental, because it might reduce trauma in the case that something goes wrong with the pregnancy and the woman then has to decide whether to "end or continue the pregnancy."[14] In either case, ultrasonic visualization regulates and channels the object-subject relation fundamental to any pregnancy: that of mother and fetus.

The processes of gestation and birthing have long provoked debates concerning the character of psychic individuation. Consider the psychoanalytic *locus classicus* of the maternal voice. Under Didier Anzieu's notion of the *envelope sonore*, because the baby's body is "a resonant cavern whose noises are all the more disquieting . . . since they cannot be localized," the maternal voice constitutes a "sound envelope."[15] This envelope, argues Kaja Silverman, constitutes a fantasy that, as elaborated by Julia Kristeva, posits intrauterine life as a prototype for the double enclosure of (1) the fetus in the mother; and (2) the mother as a "receptacle" that is "fused or confused with her infant."[16] Kristeva's notion of the chora "is more an image of unity than one of archaic differentiation; prior to the absence and an economy of the object, it figures the oneness of mother and child" for which "pregnancy is the ultimate prototype."[17] The maternal voice is forced "to the inside of the sonorous envelope," Silverman explains, distancing the mother from the symbolic order and implying the "perceptual immaturity and discursive incapacity" of interiority.[18] For Kristeva, "The whole image of the child [is] wrapped in the sonorous envelope of the maternal voice . . . [in] a fantasy about biological 'beginnings.'"[19] Kristeva's acoustemology is thus partial: the infant listens to the sounds issuing from only one voice—the mother's.[20] Here, the infant is understood as the passive beneficiary of the sound world issuing within and from outside—this passivity reflects Kristeva's acceptance of biomedical notions of the fetus as an inchoate being in the process of cognitive development. Just as the fetus is suspended in the resonant amniotic fluid of the womb, so, too, does the mother's voice envelop the infant: the maternal voice extends and expands the womb.

Much is at stake in these emerging spatial configurations in pregnancy. To bring out the ambivalence of the mother as a being who is at once an enclosure and enclosed, Kristeva plays on the double meaning of the French word *enceinte*, which can be translated as both "pregnant" and "protective" (as in a protective wall or enclosure). If motherhood implies singular difference and a resistance to signification, it does so partly because the mother becomes mute ("[motherhood] no longer hear[s] words or meanings; not even sounds"), losing "communital [*sic*] meaning" in what Kristeva refers to as "Oriental nothingness . . . what, in the eyes of a Westerner, can only be regression."[21] Imagine, then, the mother-fetus dyad as a monad—walled off from others who both protect it and maintain a distance from it. But imagine also the fetus, which, as Michel Chion writes, "'hears' the sounds that accompany variations in pressure on the bodily walls, as well as two cycles of heartbeats, that of the mother and its own."[22] The fetus, in this rendering, constitutes a monad that "hears" dyadically (the scare quotes are Chion's), while the mother is a peculiar dyad paradoxically barred from that sonic environment. In this account, "hearing" is differently constituted for the fetus "plunged in a liquid environment [that] does not experience or discriminate sensations in the same way as an adult, if only because lacking both familiarity and the words to do so."[23] This biological, bio-linguistic, and biomedical ontogeny of audition posits prenatal aurality as "covibration"—not as hearing proper, which requires air as its medium—but as the osteo–transmission of aquatic sound that, besides being monophonic, constitutes an archaic trans-sensorial form of rhythmic pressures.[24] There is no "auditory window" through which the sound of the fetus passes; instead, the entire sonic world "covibrating" with the fetus remains a possibility of meanings "yet to come." This particular aural economy renders the mother-fetus as "more than one, less than two."[25]

Following Françoise Dolto, Chion remarks that both the fetus and the early infant are unable to filter "the sonic whole in order to extract the useful signal."[26] In phenomenological terms, one might say that Chion's conceptualization constitutes a *sonic objectivity without sound objects*. That is, the fetus and early infant inhabit a pre-individuated environment in which subjectivity cannot possibly emerge: a sonic plenum of total auditory immersion, or what Stefan Helmreich has called "a zone of sonic immanence and intensity: a *soundstate*."[27] As a corollary, then, it would follow that without the *intentionality* of subjects, there can be no objects. Yet some form of objectivity remains insofar as something hears from within the depths of the amniotic whirl of sound.

The psychoanalytic notion of the mother's distributed or "enveloping" subjectivity in pregnancy—along with what we begin to envision as a diffuse perceptual field, a kind of "phenomenological 'in-between,'" in Nicholas Smith's expression—does not contradict understandings of the fetus as "communicative and relational."[28] What matters most in the psychoanalytic framework is the expansiveness of the sphere of communication. The question remains: what and where does this phenomenology of pregnancy stand "in-between"? In this peculiar objectivity without objects, what form might subjectivity take—if it takes any form at all—in the constitution of that objective world, *sensu* Husserl? Why does pregnancy always seem to teeter on the edges of both the immanence and the transcendence of life?

Quasi-Life

The egological underpinnings of the feminist critique represented by Kristeva, for example, find a limit in the inability to listen across the broader spectrum of antenatal soundings. Similarly, as tantalizing as Chion's and Dolto's admission of an objectivity without objects is, their insistence on a radical difference between antenatal and postnatal sound worlds (i.e., the fetus or early infant's inability to "extract the useful signal" and of its exclusively covibrational aurality) forecloses the possibility of any relation beyond linguistic meaning and bodily communication. And while there are proponents of the idea that, rather than a breach between pregnancy and birth, there is a sensorially manifested continuum that bridges ante-natality and postnatality, a similar claim operates: a fetus is always already a human life in process; it is ontologically one and the same thing but at varying stages along a single temporal line.[29]

It has long been noted that conceptualizations of pregnancy and fetal development are not everywhere the same. For Beth Conklin and Lynn Morgan's interlocutors in the Wari' communities of Brazil, for example, fetal development is considered "a process that requires the ongoing par-ticipation of people other than the mother. Flesh and bones—the solid parts of the fetal body—are literally created out of semen and nourished by it."[30] Thus, many Wari' women hold that sex during pregnancy is crucial.

Indeed, alternative ontological claims exist for which sound and aurality play a key role. Afro-Pacific Colombian communities hold that, in the event of death, kin and close friends of the deceased child must observe extreme care in what they say, lest the child communicate to divinities on her or his return to heaven. The faculty of hearing remains operational for two to three days following death. This does not constitute merely a reflexive residual hearing, but a full-fledged capacity to listen, given their status as beings closer to divinity than "regular" living people, as well as the ability to actually "extract the useful signal" from the presumed sonic plenum of antenatal existence. Such listening denotes *intentionality without an inten-tional subject* in any traditional sense, a correlate to the sonic objectivity without objects referred to earlier.

More than simply a form of postmortem animism (a "belief" that even the dead are animated; that even the dead are "alive"), the notion that listening continues beyond death indexes a fundamentally different con-ceptualization of time and space, redolent of lowland Amerindian peoples' notion of death as a "quasi-event" (*quase-acontecimento*).[31] The term speaks to a set of paradoxical simultaneities accompanying death. First, the dead cannot experience their own death as an event, since death presumes the end of consciousness. Death, on this view, is the ultimate non-experience of the deceased person, a radical corporeal breach, and a mark of absolute finitude. Second, death is only ever *for* the person who undergoes it; no one can live anyone else's death—a point frequently made by phenomenolo-gists of many stripes. But contra phenomenology, death in Amerindian cosmology is in fact experienced in the manner by which the dead remain among the living, haunting their existence. Death is not a state. It is the becoming nonhuman of the human; the transformation of the human soul, and the acquisition of superhuman status, ontologically distinct from and higher than the relation of living humans and divinities.[32]

The quasi-event is not that which almost happens or an event in-between, but that which happens in these multiple and paradoxical ways at once, holding life and death in heightened tension. The quasi-event emanates from the intersection or superposition of "creatural" and "creative" time, following Deleuze's distinction between "actual" and "virtual" time.[33] Creatural time constitutes "the medium through which creatures coordinate their perceptions, actions, and reactions. The time of the creature *qua* creature, the time of its birth and growth, its living and acting, its aging and death—this is the time in which nothing becomes."[34] Creative time, in contrast, is "the time of events which do not themselves 'have' time, and that in particular have no present." Events here "give rise to time," reversing "the traditional relation of time and event."[35]

Creative time, "absolute, original time," Peter Hallward concludes, "explodes the limits of creatural temporality."[36] Creatures, however, arrive to it "in the image of a unique and tremendous event, an act which is adequate to time as a whole": birth or death.[37]

We might take Viveiros de Castro to conceive of the quasi-event as the multiple perspectives produced in the juxtaposition of death as *act* and *event*. But there is more. For one, among indigenous Amazonian peoples, fear and enmity are directed against *the dead* and not, as in many Western societies, toward *death* itself. For another, both the living and the dead are the particular perspectives each has on the other, while each one, in a way, is composed out of the juxtaposition of act and event. Finally, the event of death speaks to a primordial temporality out of which the event of the human and the nonhuman emerges: it is a cause and consequence of speciation.[38] In Viveiros de Castro's recounting, humans and nonhumans share a common primordial immortality, which was shattered when, according to myth, someone accidentally heeded the call of death, even though this someone was warned not to heed any sound.[39] Mortality and audition are correlates. And in the Afro-Colombian case, aurality characterizes the continuum from antenatality to postmortem existence.

We approach antenatality in the Colombian Afro-Pacific as the obverse of the Amazonian conception of the dead; we propose thinking about antenatality as a quasi-event and of the life that takes place therein as a *quasi-life*. Here the nodes are divinities, the not-yet-born, and the living. The fetus is regarded as the direct incarnation of divine power. It is not only a Being; rather, it is that which subsumes "being and non-being, existence and inherence."[40] The anthropologist Anne-Marie Losonczy observes that among Afro-Pacific people in the province of Choco, "Conception is a 'divine matter' that comes from Above and therefore introduces God as mediator between man and woman [and] positions the origin of children in another place: extra-human but wholly positivized. This origin is positioned in the same space as that of the divine creation of the first men."[41] Indeed, across the Afro-Pacific region, "giving birth has been related historically with the unpredictable and mysterious."[42]

Aurality figures centrally in Afro-Pacific conceptualizations of pregnancy. Not quite a divinity but higher up ontologically than humans already born, the fetus possesses one gift above all: the power to hear.[43] This does not mean that, as in biomedicine, the inner ear is fully "developed" by the twentieth week of pregnancy, hearing being the first sense faculty to form, or that after twenty-eight weeks there is consistency in "blink-startle responses to vibroacoustic stimulation . . . indicating maturation of the auditory pathways of the central nervous system," as described by the American Academy of Pediatrics.[44] Instead, Afro-Pacific peoples regard the capacity to hear as the capacity to *listen in* to the living. Mindful of this protean aurality and of the powers of the extra-human, the living exercise caution in what they say around pregnant women, should their words be conveyed to the divinities, who listen to the child directly but to the living only indirectly.

The vernacular phenomenology of the midwife plays a central role. The yet-to-be-born child becomes known as such only after the midwife has confirmed her or his existence. This, of course, is carried out by her auscultation of the fetal heartbeat. Heard by the midwife, the heartbeat marks the entrance of the fetus into the public life of the community, as well as the beginning of the sonic precautions taken by the community to safeguard their well-being. The heartbeat announces the presence of a quasi-life that dwells simultaneously in the realm of divinities and among the living.

The fetus is both a corporeal and incorporeal aggregate in the human and nonhuman (divine) enmeshment from which human speciation occurs. As such, it presents a kind of pre-cosmological condition, rendered in myth as "a geometrical locus where the difference between points of view is at once annulled and exacerbated."[45] The divine and the human constitute figure and ground for each other.

The View from Perspectivism

The reversibility of perspectives forms a general cosmological matrix. Perspectivism differs radically from the hegemonic Euro-American view—sometimes referred to as "naturalism"—according to which all entities share a basic material form, but only some entities are endowed with interiority, agency, or what some would call a "soul."[46] Naturalism underpins contemporary debates surrounding definitions of the beginning of life, with some arguing for the existence of a soul at the very moment of conception and others understanding fetal personhood in terms of its degree of sentience. As a broad category, naturalism also shapes socially progressive feminist views of fetus and mother individuation, as we saw earlier.

Quite unlike naturalism—in which humans are connected to nonhuman entities through a shared materiality but in which only humans are considered to have genuine interiority—in perspectivism all entities are bestowed with a similar interiority but inhabit radically different bodies. Here, the Christian preoccupation with a fetus's soul is moot, since anything—a jaguar or a peccary, even a tree or a stone—can have a "soul."

In his ethnography of two Urarina communities in the Peruvian Amazon basin, Harry Walker brings insights from perspectivist anthropology to bear directly on questions of pregnancy and childbirth.[47] Most Urarina women give birth in a small hut (*jata*) fashioned from palm leaves. This hut or enclosure attenuates an infant's movement from the protective space of its mother's womb into the world at large, from a "state of contained suspension in amniotic fluids into the cold open air."[48]

After ten days, the infant is transferred from the birth hut to a hammock. This rite of passage is highly ritualized, the most crucial aspect of which is a series of chants sung by a shaman. These chants cannot be understood according to Western notions of musical transience or processual performativity. Rather, Walker remarks, "The songs and chants that accompany a newborn baby's emergence from the birth hut are in many ways as physically real and tangible as its gifts of body ornaments and artifacts."[49] He continues, "It is not simply the fact that words are objectlike, for artifacts such as the hammock and its rattle come closely to resemble a powerful form of song." As the shaman sings about turtles, jaguars, and the sun, for example, he does not simply refer to these beings; he "brings about some form of interaction" with them, even "touching them"—as a local schoolteacher and one of Walker's key interlocutors put it.[50]

The hammock serves a similar function to both the birth hut and womb before it, providing a cozy space for the vulnerable body. Walker emphasizes the importance of the "protective role of sound" for the duration of the infant's time in the hammock.[51] A rattle is attached to the hammock, and this instrument is "played" to and by the infant through its perpetual swaying. The sound of the rattle is known as a "baby lullaby" (*canaanai joororoa*), implying that with this rattle the caregiving tasks of the mother are deferred to an artifact.

As is the case with perspectivism, for the Urarina personhood is not limited to humans. Any entity can establish personhood based on relations of caregiving, protection, and accessorization. For example, "Calabash trees are adorned with animal skulls in the hope that the gourds they produce will be bigger, fatter, and harder."[52] Here, the calabash tree is considered an infant that requires protection. In the Urarina communities studied by Walker, a thing may be attributed a perspective—and, indeed, a life (*ichaoha*)—because it has a "mother" or "owner" (*neba* or *ijiaene*).[53] One task of a mother or owner is to accessorize her "child"—whether this means fashioning a rattle for her infant or adorning her calabash tree with skulls.

The importance of accessorization has its origins in intrauterine existence. The main argument of Walker's book is that Urarina cosmology is predicated on a "sense of security and mutuality that is sometimes imagined as the *intimate coexistence of fetus and placenta in the protective space of the womb*, a founding state of proximity and mutual permeability that in some ways they seek to re-create."[54] All of the forms of accessorization and attachment that Urarina people seek to establish from the very moment of natality onward—the birth hut, the hammock, and various types of adult relationships with people and things—is propelled by the loss of intrauterine protection.

Taking a cue from Peter Sloterdijk's philosophy of "spheres," Walker suggests that the fetus's first relationship is not with the mother but, rather, with the placenta, an argument already anticipated by feminist theorists such as Luce Irigaray.[55] For the Urarina with whom Walker worked, the "quintessential companion is thus a kind of membrane, a semipermeable zone of mediation between the subject and the outside world." But here it is important to note the crucial injunction, in Urarina culture, to bury the placenta in a way that removes it from view but that also allows it to be "found" by the shadow soul of the person after death.[56] In conclusion, "Separation from the placenta launches a desire for reunification that persists throughout a life, testimony to the fact of being alive and enmeshed in relations of proximity but also, crucially, difference from others. For to be fully rejoined with the original companion means no longer to be a true person, a real, living human being—hence the widespread notion that such a reunion is for the dead, for the souls of the deceased."[57]

There is a rhyming structure of antenatality and death, where the separation from and return to the placenta bookends the protracted period of full personhood known simply as a life.[58] Beyond the Janus-faced thresholds of life, personhood is obliterated through reunion.

Without questioning Walker's ethnographic claims, we nonetheless ask whether the fetus—even in its intimate companionship with the placenta—is conceived by his Urarina interlocutors as fully *unified* with its surroundings. Nowhere does Walker entertain the possibility (nor does he inquire about it with his interlocutors) that the fetus might hear beyond and through the placenta. It is indeed possible, if not necessarily likely, that this fetus would listen into the world of the wholly living, as we noted earlier with the Afro-Colombian example. The fetus, then, in addition to its propinquities to placenta and womb, might also be said to stand in a relation of minimal distance. This interpretive possibility is to some extent already implied by Walker when he writes that the placenta figures as a "semipermeable zone," where the term "*semi*permeable" seeks to denote the fetus's ambiguous relationship with the exterior world—its simultaneous attachment to *and* withdrawal from the membrane that surrounds it.

The Objecthood of Sound: Aporia, Speculation, Allusion

The term "semipermeable zone" belies an ambiguity at the heart of much antenatal thinking: what does "semi" mean here? Does it suggest that, as a zone of mediation between fetus and world, the placenta is only partially permeable and only partially not? If so, what is this "not" that remains before or after permeability?

The ambiguity of the term "semipermeability" is attributable, in part, to theoretical imprecision. But it also suggests a more profound dilemma, or even an aporia. Walker is not alone in reaching this aporia. Kristeva's use of the French term *enceinte* designates the contradiction, from the perspective of the mother, of being both the wall enclosing the mother-fetus relation and walled off from the relation. David Toop's conjuring of our amniotic existence as eavesdroppers who cannot identify what we hear relies on a characterization of the sonorous in terms of a "sinister resonance." Husserl, too, would be pushed past the grounding tenets of his egological phenomenology when confronting the particularities of the antenatal realm. In his late fragments, Husserl wrote that the infant, the newly born, is "already an experiencing I at a higher level, it already has its acquisition of experience from its existence in the mother's womb, it already has its perception with perceptual horizons."[59] Yet, he hastened to add, this very same ecological phenomenology gives way to a "genetic" and "intersubjective" perspective and, ultimately, to a "generative phenomenology" that recognizes that "the constitution of the world began long before me and us, and it continues long after I and we have died."[60] Chion, finally, describes antenatality as a sonic environment of objectivity without objects. More generally, he notes, "Sound is not graspable outside of a dialectic between the place of the source and the place of listening."[61] For Chion, then, sound can only ever be in the genitive case: sound is always *of* a listener and an object. Yet sound is not identical with the listener who hears it or the object that produces it. The difficulty in ascertaining the object-like aspects of sound vis-à-vis its non-object-like aspects compels Chion to conclude that "sound *is* this contradiction."[62]

All of these examples recall an ancient paradox.[63] Plato's Meno argued that it is impossible to learn something new, because either one knows something or one does not.[64] Put formally: (1) if one knows what one is searching for, there is no need to search; (2) if one does not know what one is searching for, then inquiry is impossible; (3) therefore, searching is either useless or impossible. This paradox implies that any knowledge one may have is already acquired and merely recollected and that it is impossible to acquire new knowledge. This implies, in turn, that a person is essentially static and cut off from the parts of the world of which she is not already a part.

Semipermeability, enceinte, and various other figures described in this chapter follow the first two steps of Meno's argument, leading to the aporia. But whereas Meno concluded that learning something new is impossible, contemporary thinkers of sound seem to arrest the paradox and annihilate it. Whereas Meno would say that the fetus cannot learn anything about the outside environment that it does not already know, Walker's notion of the placenta as a semipermeable membrane allows him to have his cake and eat it, too. Why? Because a semipermeable membrane *simultaneously* joins and separates the fetus from the outside world, thus neutralizing the aporia of *first* knowing something and *then* trying (unsuccessfully) to learn something new. Chion's argument is structurally the same as Walker's, since for Chion any sound one may hear is both dependent on someone hearing it *and* it is an independent entity. On this view, a sound cannot exist prior to the hearing of it because sound requires being heard as a condition of its existence. But then, Meno would ask, how would one ever hear a sound that one does not already hear? And while Meno would affirm the impossibility of hearing a sound that is not already heard, Chion would take this "impossibility" as the very condition of possibility for sound *qua* contradiction ("sound *is* this contradiction").

While Meno says that you either know or you do not know, contemporary theorists of sound effectively say that you know and you do not know. In concluding this chapter, we would suggest two other possible paths beyond this aporia.

First, consider the question of how we would ever learn what the fetus is hearing. The dominant view among Western medical practitioners seems to be one of profound agnosticism. Barring something ridiculous such as playing excessively loud music directly toward the fetus for long periods of time, the "educated" view seems to be one of slightly restrained freedom, because ultimately who really knows what or how the fetus hears? And who really knows, this scenario seems to suggest, what the "life" of the fetus really is or means? We know it is some kind of "life" (in the sense that any living organism, even a microbe, is alive); we know that it can sense; but beyond that, the biomedical line seems to go, who can really say?

The Afro-Colombian communities discussed here engage the lack of positive knowledge by following it to its other, inverse conclusion. "Who knows?" becomes "What if?" Unlike the radical agnostic, who asserts that we *cannot* know which speculations about pre- and afterlife are true, Afro-Colombian midwifery seems to suggest that we *can* know that *anything* could be true.[65] We repeat: *anything* could be true. To restrain speech around pregnant women because it is feared that the fetus may have a direct connection with the divine is thus a kind of vernacular Pascalian wager on the possible condition of antenatal existence. That humans cannot have full knowledge of the antenatal condition generates *more* anxiety for Afro-Colombian communities rather than less. The question "Who knows?" is not merely a hypothetical one that results in the freezing of thought and action. Rather, it is ushered in as an incessant although unanswerable challenge.

Our second move considers the question of the fetal heartbeat. Rather than consider this sound as both an entity in itself *and* dependent on the heart's producing it, as well as the midwife's hearing it, we propose that each sound beat is indeed an object. It is not a physical object but an object or entity in the sense that the sound is what it is, beyond any perspective, index, or determination.[66] If this is so, then Meno is correct, in a way: we *cannot* "know" precisely what the sound object is, because no object can ever be fully known by, transformed, or translated into any other.

But even without fully knowing something, one can, of course, have a sense of the sound object and a taste of what it is or might be. To "know" something may entail knowing it in all its details, but it may, alternatively, mean simply having "some sense of what it is."[67] It is not a matter of speaking of something or not: "We all know a way of speaking of a thing without quite speaking of it: namely, we *allude* to it. Allusion occurs in thinking no less than speaking."[68] By this logic, speaking about a tree, or a handwritten letter, or a heartbeat that lies beyond my knowledge "is neither a successful statement about a thought nor a failed statement about a thing. Instead, it is an allusion to something that might be real but which cannot become fully present."[69]

Let us recapitulate the four possible solutions to Meno's question about how one acquires knowledge about which one does not already know:

1   It is *sensu stricto* impossible. This was Meno's own answer. It parallels the form of radical agnosticism we saw vis-à-vis biomedical notions of pregnancy.

2   With reference to pregnancy in particular, a series of contradictions seem to propel thought rather than freeze it. The fact that the mother is both connected to and walled off from the fetus results in a zone of free exchange; an amniotic world without subjects results in information movement in every direction.

3   One is required to speculate, since anything could be true. (Quentin Meillassoux would add that what exists beyond my knowledge could change dramatically at any moment.)

4   One can allude to a reality that is deeper than anything one can ever have access to.

These answers gain full force only when we recognize that they are simultaneously epistemological and ontological. To recognize that something *is* a sound is to recognize that sound's existence beyond my phenomenological intention toward it. This sense of "recognition" is to some extent latent in much sound theory, but there is a strong tendency to bracket the existence of sound *qua* real object or to drain it by making its existence dependent on one's hearing it. In most scenarios, either of these two approaches (i.e., bracketing or draining) works completely fine: although the sound object is always deeper than one's experience of it, although it always withdraws from intentional consciousness, one usually does not detect this withdrawal and is happy to engage superficially with its sensual qualities.

Allure is a specific kind of experience in which one notices the object's withdrawal. At such moments, the object breaks off from the qualities to which perception attends and makes one aware that it is more than what can be experienced of it.[70] What could be more alluring than that thud generated by a newly formed heart? As an indication of quasi-life, the fetal heartbeat registers as an ungraspable, tremendous event. To acknowledge the existence of that sound object—to release it from the perceptual hoarding of classical phenomenology—is precisely to recognize it, in its splendid autonomous existence, as ungraspable. But the second step is no less important: listening carefully, cautiously, for a sound we seem to know about but that we cannot know.

Notes

1 For studies and commentary on medical auscultation, see Foucault, *The Birth of the Clinic*; Rice, *Hearing and the Hospital*; Sterne, "Mediate Auscultation, the Stethoscope, and the 'Autopsy of the Living.'"

2 Harman, "On Vicarious Causation," 21.

3 Harman, "On Vicarious Causation," 23.

4 We opt for the expression "antenatal" instead of the more common term "prenatal," which gives priority to events temporally prior to birth, or "perinatal," which refers to the period before and after birth. "Antenatal" includes not only the temporality prior to birth but also a kind of spatial "standing before" the events that precede birth. As we will see, even the temporal aspects we consider cannot be contained in a single timeline before birth implied in the term "prenatal."

5 See Chion, *Sound*.

6 Our investigation is part of a larger comparative project on antenatal acoustemologies and ontologies among Afro-Colombian midwives in the country's Pacific region, as well as birth attendants in South Africa's townships.

7 Toop, *Sinister Resonance*, x.

8 Diski, *On Trying to Keep Still*, 106. See Young, "Pregnant Embodiment."

9 We borrow the expression "More than One, Less than Two" from Marisol de la Cadena's rendering of Marilyn Strathern's "partial connection," a "relationship composing an aggregate that is 'neither singular or plural . . . a circuit of connections

rather than joint parts'": de la Cadena, "Indigenous Cosmopolitics in the Andes," 347. See also Strathern, *Partial Connections*.

10 See Lundgren, "The Experience of Pregnancy."

11 See Bergum, *A Child on Her Mind*.

12 Rapp, "Real-Time Fetus," 608.

13 See Hubbard, "Personal Courage Is Not Enough."

14 Rapp, "Real-Time Fetus," 621.

15 Anzieu, *The Skin-Ego*, 162–63.

16 Silverman, *The Acoustic Mirror*, 102, 107.

17 Silverman, *The Acoustic Mirror*, 102. See also Kristeva, *Desire in Language*.

18 Silverman, *The Acoustic Mirror*, 103.

19 Silverman, *The Acoustic Mirror*, 101.

20 Silverman, *The Acoustic Mirror*, 106.

21 Kristeva, *Desire in Language*, 249, cited in Silverman, *The Acoustic Mirror*, 108, 112. Kristeva's comparison of motherhood with "Oriental nothingness" is not insignificant. For more on Kristeva's deployment of non-Western "natives" as constitutive negatives, see Chow, "Where Have All the Natives Gone?"

22 Chion, *Sound*, 12.

23 Chion, *Sound*, 12–13.

24 Chion, *Sound*, 13.

25 Seeking to affirm the central figure of the mother's embodied subjectivity and experience, a number of feminist scholars question the psychoanalytic concern with lack and propose instead the notion of "split subjectivity": see Kristeva, *Desire in Language*; Young, "Pregnant Embodiment."

26 Chion, *Sound*, 13. Dolto, along with Melanie Klein, Esther Bick, and Donald Winnicott, provide the basis for viewing the fetus "as communicative and relational": Smith, "Phenomenology of Pregnancy," 18. Complex bio-semiotic systems such as those explored by Terrence Deacon and, more recently, Gary Tomlinson, in which meaning accrues in ways other than linguistic, may offer further possibilities for research: see Deacon, *The Symbolic Species*; Tomlinson, "Sign, Affect, and Musicking before the Human."

27 Helmreich, "An Anthropologist under Water," 624, emphasis added.

28 Smith, "Phenomenology of Pregnancy," 16.

29 Smith, "Phenomenology of Pregnancy," 18, citing Piontelli, *From Fetus to Child*.

30 Conklin and Morgan, "Babies, Bodies, and the Production of Personhood in North American and a Native Amazonian Society," 671.

31 See Eduardo Viveiros de Castro, "A morte come quase acontecimento (completo)," 2009, accessed May 31, 2016, https://www.youtube.com/watch?v=nz5ShgzmuW4.

32 For ethnographic background, see Viveiros de Castro, *From the Enemy's Point of View*, esp. chap. 7.

33 Hallward, *Out of this World*, 147. See Deleuze, *The Logic of Sense*. Viveiros de Castro's work has a distinctive Deleuzian cast: see Viveiros de Castro, *Cannibal Metaphysics for a Post-Structural Anthropology*.

34 Hallward, *Out of this World*, 146.

35 Hallward, *Out of This World*, 146–47.

36 Deleuze, *Proust and Signs*, 17; Hallward, *Out of this World*, 147.

37 Deleuze, *Difference and Repetition*, 89.

38 Viveiros de Castro, *Cannibal Metaphysics for a Post-Structural Anthropology*, 65.

39 Viveiros de Castro, "A morte come quase acontecimento," 7:55–9:00.

40 Deleuze, *The Logic of Sense*, 7.

41 Losonczy, "Del ombligo a la comunidad," 49–50.

42 Navarro Valencia, *Cuerpos Afrocolombianos*, 179–80.

43 Unborn children are considered sexless, like "little angels," adopting Christian angelological doxa. It is in fact the midwife who, should she wish to respect the corporeal marks of gender (i.e., female or male genitalia), completes the gendering of the child by cutting the umbilical cord according to precisely specified lengths: two fingertips in length for boys and three for girls. The midwife is considered a giver of sex (*dadora de sexo*): see Losonczy, "Del ombligo a la comunidad," 50.

44 American Academy of Pediatrics: Committee on Environmental Health, "Noise: A Hazard for the Fetus and Newborn," 724.

45 Viveiros de Castro, *Cannibal Metaphysics for a Post-Structural Anthropology*, 68.

46 See Descola, *Beyond Nature and Culture*; Latour, *We Have Never Been Modern*.

47 Walker, *Under a Watchful Eye*, 14.

48 Walker, *Under a Watchful Eye*, 36.

49 Walker, *Under a Watchful Eye*, 35.

50 Walker, *Under a Watchful Eye*, 55.

51 Walker, *Under a Watchful Eye*, 41.

52 Walker, *Under a Watchful Eye*, 42.

53 Walker, "Baby Hammocks and Stone Bowls," 99.

54 Walker, *Under a Watchful Eye*, 14, emphasis added.

55 See Irigaray, *I Love to You*; Irigaray, *To Be Two*; Sloterdijk, *Spheres, Volume 1*; Walker, *Under a Watchful Eye*, 221.

56 Losonczy discusses placenta burial practices among Afro-Colombians from the Choco region: see Losonczy, "Del ombligo a la comunidad."

57 Walker, *Under a Watchful Eye*, 212.

58 This rhyming structure is widely distributed across many cultures. In a completely different context, Veit Erlmann notes that "auditory resonance may well have enabled Descartes to rehearse the fragile proximity of reason and sensation. As material *sympathia*, resonance reminds us of our past history of intrauterine dependency; as culture, such resonance holds the promise that we might make ourselves anew each time we listen, realizing our prenatal potential to become, at some point in our postnatal lives, reasoning minds who resonate with their own bodies and those of others": Erlmann, "Descartes' Resonant Subject," 27.

59 Husserl, *Husserliana XIII–XV*, 604, as quoted in Smith, "Phenomenology of Pregnancy," 35.

60 Smith, "Phenomenology of Pregnancy," 36; Husserl, *Husserliana XIII–XV*, 199.

61 Chion, *Sound*, 105.

62 Chion, *Sound*, 210.

63 This exploration of knowledge and ontology vis-à-vis Meno (and riffing on Harman) was first developed in Steingo, "Vital Signs/Life Writing."

64 Plato, "Meno," 70.

65 Here, we are loosely following, but taking many liberties with, Quentin Meillassoux: see Meillassoux, *After Finitude*.

66 For a careful elaboration of this position, see Harman, *The Quadruple Object*.

67 Harman, "On Vicarious Causation," 67.

68 Harman, "On Vicarious Causation," 215.

69 Harman, "On Vicarious Causation," 215.

70 See Harman, "On Vicarious Causation."

On Nonhuman Sound—
Sound as Relation

A touch of anthropomorphism, then, can catalyze a sensibility that finds a world filled not with ontologically distinct categories of beings (subjects and objects) but with variously composed materialities that form confederations.

—JANE BENNETT, *Vibrant Matter*

STS brings nonhumans and humans into the same analytical framework through a form of reductionism that leaves concepts like agency and representation unexamined. As a consequence the distinctively human instantiations of these become stand-ins for all agency and representation. The result is a form of dualism in which humans and nonhumans acquire mixtures of thing-like and humanlike properties.

—EDUARDO KOHN, *How Forests Think*

Miss La Trobe stood there with her eye on her script. . . . Her little game had gone wrong. If only she'd a back-cloth to hang between the trees—to shut out cows, swallows, present time! But she had nothing. She had forbidden music. Grating her fingers in the bark, she damned the audience. Panic seized her. Blood seemed to pour from her shoes. This is death, death, death, she noted in the margin of her mind; when illusion fails. Unable to lift her hand, she stood facing the audience.

And then the shower fell, sudden, profuse.

No one had seen the cloud coming. There it was, black, swollen, on top of them. Down it poured like all the people in the world weeping. Tears, tears, tears.

"O that our human pain could here have an ending!" Isa murmured. Looking up she received two great blots of rain full in her face. They trickled down her cheeks as if they were her own tears. But they were all people's tears, weeping for all people. Hands were raised. Here and there a parasol opened. The rain was sudden and universal. Then it stopped. From the grass rose a fresh earthy smell.

—VIRGINIA WOOLF, *Between the Acts*

I compose this chapter subjected to the clamorous sounds of torrential rain falling on the roof of the room in which I write. I am assailed, pummeled, by these sounds. The room is a 1980s conservatory built with wooden struts and a polycarbonate roof, and hard rain falling on this structure produces battering sounds of great intensity that transduce the energetic intensity of the rainstorm itself. The modulating intensities of the rain and rain sounds preoccupy and overwhelm me; drops of rainwater force their way through the ageing roof's cracks, dripping onto my skin as well as the floor next to me. The sounds both animate and excite me, with my close-ness to and near-immersion in the torrent, yet they also bring me down, reminding me of summer's fragility and impermanence. I find I can move into and out of awareness of, attunement to, the sounds—as a companion entity or process.[1] But I cannot block out the rain sounds; I am ineluctably situated in relation to them, subjectified by them, albeit with a certain free-dom of reverie, of enjoying a range of potential affective responses. Sitting alone, the sounds, index of the storm, make of me a responsive companion—to them and to the storm.

I am passing through and sharing in the same dramatic moments as the body of rain and, indeed, the wide, cloud-blackened skies over Newn-ham, Cambridge. I sense that I am also sharing these intense, threatening but enlivening moments with others, sequestered like me in their homes, across the neighborhood. We are, in this sense, a fragmentary collectiv-ity assembled by the storm. On finding it difficult to work, I can move to another place within the house. As I move—crossing the room, down the hallway, into the kitchen, upstairs—the changing qualities of the sounds register our changing relation, rain, rain sounds, and I, as well as the mate-rial constitution and acoustic properties of each space I enter. In this way, I can orchestrate my experience, create out of the drama of the torrent a sonic diversion, an aesthetic form. It feels both that I have certain controls, through my attunement, my bodily movements, my orchestration, and that—without obvious escape—I have no alternative but to submit, involuntarily, to the demand that I enter into relation with the overwhelming sounds. I am, in these real senses, subjectified by the nonhuman sounds.

How should we conceptualize sound? Does the conceptualization of sound as an object reify and detach what are inherently fluid and relational sonic processes? Departing from the concept of the sound object, in this chapter I pursue sound's multiple mediations, its embeddedness in events, socialities, sites, and affective and material processes, including those of the human body.[2] By abandoning the language of the sound object, I contend, we become attuned to the hybrid, human-and-nonhuman assemblages through which sound is both produced and experienced.[3] This exercise, through sound, connects to recent thinking that places the nonhuman in symmetrical relation to the human, for sound is both coproduced nonhumanly—as an apparently independent physical process, "object," or "actor"—yet also transubstantiates perceptually, affectively, and culturally into human experience. What will become obvious in pursuing this assemblage-ecological sense of sound is how powerfully and pervasively sound acts *on* the human rather than merely being modulated by the human. A second element of the chapter addresses a *subcategory* of sound as hybrid assemblage: what I am calling nonhuman sound. With nonhuman sound I draw attention to those kinds of sound that do not originate in human intentional acts or in humanly directed technological mediations (e.g., recorded sounds or sounds produced by digital data). Thus, along with the sounds of animals and other species and the environmental sounds of rain, wind, rustling leaves, running water, earthquakes, and so on, nonhuman sound includes the mechanical and electronic sounds emitted as an incidental effect of the functioning of technologies (cars, planes, fridges, fans, etc.). This subcategory is of interest because it doubles consideration of the contributions of nonhuman entities and processes to sound itself. In defining nonhuman sound in this way I do not mean to privilege or romanticize it, as should be obvious from the focus on sound as hybrid assemblage in the central part of the chapter. Nor do I aim to resurrect the preoccupation with the sources or origins of sound characteristic of earlier debates on the sound object. Rather, I aim to explore what the *difference* evidenced by this subcategory adds to our understanding of the relational nature of all sound.

The question of the affective subjectification of humans by nonhuman sound is, then, one theme of this chapter.[4] Another rain event, one with powerfully affective and subjectifying qualities, is portrayed in my third epigraph, a scene from Virginia Woolf's final novel, *Between the Acts* (1941). The senses enlivened by the rain in Woolf's extraordinary, epiphanic evocation of a "sudden and universal" rainfall are touch and smell, whereas in my autoethnography of the rainstorm, sound is to the fore. In her introduction to Woolf's novel, Gillian Beer portrays the ominous atmosphere in which Woolf was writing: "She imagined, planned, and wrote it through the last days of a peace that seemed at times like a national hallucination, and into the period when England daily expected invasion. As she wrote and revised, the bombers passed nightly overhead."[5] Here, in the context of war, nonhuman sound becomes the harbinger of mass violence: the collective subject, England, is interpellated by the expectation of invasion produced by the nightly sound of bombers.[6]

....

In my opening paragraphs, through the cases of rain and bombers, I have drawn attention to nonhuman sound. Generally, nonhuman sound is not a focus of human attention. To become aware of it requires an attunement, a shift from perceptual background to foreground, whether it is high-volume environmental sound or the more continuous ebb and flow of low-level hushes, hums, washes, and clusters of sonic events (trees rustling, planes and trains passing, fridge humming, flies buzzing, house creaking, cars revving, birds calling, construction work proceeding, and so on). Nonhuman sound exists as a constant, potentially affect-laden companion to quotidian life.

What is gained conceptually by attending to such nonhuman sound and the nature of its relation to us? What does this add to our understanding of sound? I pursue these questions as they point to an approach to sound as relation. I do this, in part, by relating two autoethnographic incidents—one ordinary, the other life-changing. The first, my involuntary immersion in the sound of the rainstorm, concerns the relations conjured up between nonhuman and human and centers on the idea of overwhelming nonhuman sound proffering, as its historical correlate, subjectivities. The second, a story of my attempt to sing with and subsume the nonhuman sound of a smart bed on which my mother lay dying, revolves around a three-way relation set in motion between my dying mother, the hum of her bed, and me. The story highlights my efforts to ease, transform, the dying process by encompassing the demands made on my mother by the bed hum through the entraining capacities of my voice. Of the two incidents, the first highlights a passing event, a responsive engagement conjured up between rain sound and myself, whereas the second is enfolded within a long-term situation saturated with affective social relations and concerns an experimental intervention to moderate an ongoing sonic experience, reshaping an established dyad into a new, three-way relation.

Sound's capacity to overwhelm has been variously sourced by previous writers to humanly directed, high-volume sound: in Julian Henriques's reggae-sound-system derived idea of sonic dominance; Suzanne Cusick's research on the violence of sonic torture; and Steve Goodman's ontology of vibrational force.[7] All three writers make bold conceptual moves into the borderlands where, through intentional (often musical) human acts, extreme volume inflames somatic, bone- and viscera-shaking sympathetic vibration. Such work has been less concerned with the affordances of nonhuman sound, particularly those of insistent low-level sonic processes and events.

A focus on the relation between nonhuman sound and experience has the potential, I suggest, to offer insights quite different from the more common focus in sound studies on the technological mediation of music and sound. In addressing the nonhuman production of sound, I edge ineluctably onto a much wider terrain situated at the intersection between two prominent debates: on the one hand, discussions of the nature of sound itself; on the other, a spectrum of theoretical debates that have gathered pace conjointly in the humanities and social sciences under the headings of materiality, the new materialism, and the nonhuman turn, each concerned with how we should conceive of the nonhuman.[8] Influenced by such unassimilable figures as Arjun Appadurai, Bruno Latour, and Bill Brown, at base the nonhuman turn, as Richard Grusin puts it, "is engaged in decentering the human in favour of a turn toward and concern for the nonhuman, understood variously in terms of animals, affectivity, bodies, organic and geophysical systems, materiality, or technologies."[9] Despite Grusin's liberal list, bringing sound into dialogue with these debates is profitable in resisting the pervasive equation across this work of the nonhuman with objects or things.[10] Sound, I will argue, acts as something of a limit case for discussions of materiality and the nonhuman. It does so in two ways. If sound has been theorized and ontologized as an object, then recent studies that probe its labile materiality, discussed below, point in new and more fertile directions. But sound also demands an additional step, for which I later turn to the philosopher Alfred North Whitehead: that we develop an account of sound that involves a radical reconceptualization of subjectivity while transcending what he called the bifurcation of nature.

Nonhuman sound, in the guise of environmental sound or noise, has, of course, featured in a number of ways in the development of the fields now coalescing as sound studies. Most obviously, it features in the tradition of acoustic ecology initiated in the 1970s by R. Murray Schafer, who coined the concept of the soundscape and ushered in scholarship and activism based on location recordings,[11] as well as encouraging the work of field recording-based sound art and environmental sound artists.[12] It features also in the experimental tradition after John Cage, which dissolves the boundaries between music and sound, often working with the sonorities of everyday environments beyond the concert hall, a "conceptual frame in which music and context set each other into relief, mobilizing silence to incorporate the noise of all that is outside music."[13] Nonhuman sound has, then, become an aesthetic resource in the varieties of experimental performance, environmental sound, field recording, and sound installation art that have extended both traditions. In parallel, nonhuman sound has been prominent in historical research that traces the advent of scientific and governmental discourses on noise and noise abatement in relation to urban environmental sound and in the burgeoning anthropology of sound, from research on the soundscapes of marine science expeditions and hospitals to studies of human adaptations to and interventions in the acoustic ecologies of Middle Eastern megacities and Papua New Guinean rain forests.[14] In a good deal of this scholarship, in the couplet "human subject-nonhuman sound," it is the first term that is privileged. There is a certain anthropocentrism in the way this asymmetry is set up, with nonhuman sound providing a kind of object, ground, context, or wild on the basis of which the active figure of the human subject, or culture, does its perceptual, creative, or civilizing work.[15]

It is reactions against this anthropocentrism that lie behind the tension between my two opening epigraphs, taken from seminal contributions to the debate over the nonhuman by Jane Bennett and Eduardo Kohn. Bennett and Kohn are united, along with many of the influential writers cited earlier, in attempting to combat anthropocentrism by redressing social theory's erstwhile egregious neglect of the creativity of nonhuman entities and processes. Yet despite this unity, they diverge on the vexed question of the anthropomorphic tendencies of arguments about the nonhuman in anthropology and science and technology studies. In Bennett's "vital materialism," a "touch of anthropomorphism" is deemed a small price to pay in order to grasp the "true reciprocity between participants of various material compositions," a reciprocity that points to Bennett's central ethico-political injunction: "Give up the futile attempt to disentangle the human from the nonhuman. Seek instead to engage more civilly, strategically, and subtly with the nonhumans in the assemblages in which you, too, participate."[16] She continues, "Too often, the philosophical rejection of anthropomorphism is bound up with a hubristic demand that only humans and God can bear any traces of creative agency."[17] In contrast, for Kohn, an "anthropology beyond the human" must radically rethink existing posthumanist approaches—notably, those offered by Bennett and Latour—because they propose an unsatisfactory "analytic of mixture," one that merely equalizes "the imbalance between unfeeling matter and desiring humans by depriving humans of a bit of their intentionality and symbolic omnipotence at the same time that [it confers] on things a bit more agency." The result, Kohn claims, is that "the alignment between humans, culture, the mind, and representation, on the one hand, and nonhumans, nature, bodies, and matter, on the other, remains stable."[18]

A large part of the difficulty in arbitrating between these perspectives, I want to suggest, lies in how the argument is supposed to be resolvable in the abstract, a priori, without reference to the specific qualities of the nonhuman entities or processes at issue. Against this background, I propose in what follows that current research on sound can be employed in generative ways in the debates over the nonhuman to elucidate the challenges posed by anthropocentrism and anthropomorphism, while attending to these challenges in turn advances our understanding of the particular nature of sound. One sign that sound studies has achieved the status of a field is the accelerating appearance in recent years both of numerous works on hearing and listening and of a scattering of texts problematizing the nature of sound. Looking across these contributions, it is possible to distinguish those that come down primarily on the side of the listening subject from those that dwell more on the material analysis of sound. I want to review three symptomatic studies that exemplify these distinctive perspectives, each offering a variant of a relational analysis of the "objects" and "subjects" of sound.

The materialist strain is well represented by Casey O'Callaghan's *Sounds: A Philosophical Theory* (2007). O'Callaghan proposes a "realist theory of sound" informed by the natural sciences. In it, sounds are "the immediate objects of auditory experience": audible, non-mental events "constituted by the *interactions* of objects and bodies with the surrounding medium."[19] Sounds as events "take time, occur at distal locations, and involve a medium," so that the "audible qualities of sounds thus are medium dependent."[20]

O'Callaghan is interested in causality: thus, "[sound] waves stand in causal relations. Waves are produced or generated by their sources," yet the waves caused by sound events do not themselves constitute sounds.[21] Rather, sound "is a relational event that involves the object and the medium."[22] Central to his argument is the claim that sounds exist independently of human perception of them; indeed, he proffers a theory "that situates sound in the world independent of the subjects of auditory experience." There is, he contends, "a distinction between genuinely hearing or perceiving a sound and enjoying an auditory experience, since it is possible to have an auditory experience without perceiving anything at all," as in the case of those suffering from tinnitus or auditory hallucinations.[23] Nonetheless, his theory aspires to ground "a complete account of the metaphysics of sounds [including] the phenomenology of auditory experience."[24] What O'Callaghan offers, then, is an object- and event-centered theory of sound that resists anthropocentric and anthropomorphic assumptions and, importantly, that is relational within its physicalist remit. In his account, sound is a physical process initiated by a sound event, which causes energetic waves that are both dependent on and propagated through a medium.[25] But he stops short of including in his relational account the contributions of hearing subjects.

At the other end of the spectrum are those writers—from anthropology, cultural and media studies, sound art scholarship, and musicology—whose work focuses broadly on hearing or listening.[26] Many of these studies are empirically informed, often taking account of the copious technological, architectural, and place-based mediations of sound as they bear on listening and in some cases addressing also the encultured and embodied nature of sonic experience. While O'Callaghan brackets human experience, this body of work weighs in the opposite direction: it tends to bracket the material processes of the production of sound and is susceptible to anthropocentrism, as is evident in Jean-Luc Nancy's influential treatise *Listening*.

Nancy's text centers on the idea that resonance both links sound and listener and calls the subject of listening into being. In his terms, sound is "made of referrals: it spreads in space, where it resounds, while still resounding 'in me' . . . (we will return to this 'inside' of the subject; we will return to nothing but that)."[27] As Brian Kane comments, "As the correlate of the sonorous object, one would *expect* to find a sonorous subject. . . . Nancy calls *his* subject 'a resonant subject' because both the object and subject of listening, in his account, resonate. And they resonate because the object and subject of listening both share a similar 'form, structure or movement,' that of the *renvoi*—a word whose translation as 'reference' obscures its double meaning as both a sending away (a dismissal) and a return."[28] Nancy is insistent that this correlation distinguishes the listening subject from the essential, preexisting subject of phenomenology: "The subject of listening is always still to come, spaced, traversed, and called by itself, *sounded* by itself. . . . The subject of the listening or the subject who is listening (but also the one who is 'subject to listening' in the sense that one can be 'subject to' unease, an ailment, or a crisis) is not a phenomenological subject, . . . [and] is perhaps no subject at all, except as the place of resonance."[29] Further developing the relation between sound and self, Nancy equates sound with the subject's "presence to self": "As we have known since Aristotle, sensing [*sentir*] (*aisthesis*) is always a perception [*ressentir*], that is, a feeling-oneself-to-feel [*se-sentir-sentir*]. . . . A *self* is nothing other than a form or function of a referral: a *self* is made of a relationship *to* self, or of a presence *to* self."[30] He continues, "To be listening will always . . . be to be straining toward or in an approach to the self (one should say, in a pathological manner: *a fit of self* . . .). When one is listening, one is on the lookout for a subject, something (itself) that identifies *itself* by resonating from self to self."[31] This is presence to self "in the sense of an 'in the presence of', . . . not a being . . . , but rather a *coming* and a *passing*, an *extending* and a *penetrating*."[32] Through listening, Nancy aspires simultaneously to re-conceptualize the very formation of subjectivity.

Yet if Nancy intends to register the materiality of sound through the prominence accorded to resonance as a quality of both sound and listening, this is a highly attenuated account of the material nature of sound, and it fails to mask the anthropocentrism evident in his repeated return to self and subjectivity. At the same time, by identifying the ways in which sound engenders the subject(s) of listening, Nancy captures something of my experience in the opening vignette of being subjectified by the clamorous nonhuman sound of torrential rain. He points, moreover, to how becoming "subject to listening" is potentially always a collective experience, for given the "actual physics of sonorous reverberation,"[33] its capacity to move through and across human and nonhuman bodies, sound, as he puts it, is "tendentially methexic (that is, having to do with participation, sharing, contagion)."[34]

A third position in recent scholarship on sound weaves a space between these object-centered and subject-centered orientations, advancing a more complex relational account. I refer to *Sonic Virtuality: Sound as Emergent Perception* (2015) by Mark Grimshaw and Tom Garner. The book develops the model of the "sonic aggregate" to "describe all the components that together create the potential for the perception of sound to emerge." It divides those components into two groups: the exosonus (or material and sensuous elements) and the endosonus (or immaterial and non-sensuous elements).[35] What is attractive about Grimshaw and Garner's model is its ambition to encompass the full spectrum of material and human processes that together compose both the physical existence and the experience of sound. The stress on potential and emergence is important for Grimshaw and Garner; it is their way of trying to overcome the limitations of a model like O'Callaghan's in its inability to explain the diversity of individual experiences of the "same sound," as well as the existential reality of auditory hallucinations. To these ends, drawing on Brian Massumi's interpretation of Gilles Deleuze and on Alva Noë's *Action in Perception* (2004), they argue that "the detail of [sonic] experience is not represented in consciousness but is accessible to it" such that "the content of experience is virtual." In Noë's words, "Qualities are available in experience as possibilities, as potentialities, but not as complete givens. Experience is a dynamic process of navigating the pathways of these possibilities."[36] In this way they aim to account for "observable variations between listeners in response to sound wave stimuli." Their conclusion is that "sound is not a physical phenomenon but a perceptual entity, arising within the mind"; if this were not the case, then "variation between listeners' experiences . . . could not be satisfactorily explained."[37]

En route to this conclusion, and more fully than O'Callaghan, Grimshaw and Garner register via the exosonus a series of material processes that participate in the production of sound, all of them contributing to the sonic aggregate. They include the creation of sound waves and their modification by the particular qualities (humidity, wind, temperature, level of pollution) of air as a medium, and the transduction that occurs when their acoustical energy is converted into electrical energy by the hair cells of the inner ear; a series of additional mediators—notably, the architectural design of the space in which sound waves propagate—and the presence and placement of other materials and objects within that space, all of which transform sound waves by their capacity to "absorb and reflect acoustical energy at different levels and to greater and lesser extents, depending on the frequencies present in the sound wave"; the location of the listener along with her or his movement within the acoustic space; and the physiology and shape of the inner and outer ear, as well as the filtering and delaying effects of the torso and head—that is, how "human anatomy shapes, in

individual ways, the acoustical energy prior to its transformation to electrical energy."[38] At issue are a series of physical mediators, some of which
are also transducers—as the energy of sound waves is both conveyed and
transformed across human and nonhuman materials and media.[39]

In the endosonus, in contrast, and drawing on theories of embodied
cognition, Grimshaw and Garner include components that "are not primarily sensory. . . . They might be initiated by sensation but they can be
initiated in other non-sensory ways" by imagination, expectation, memory,
or emotion.[40] Here they are at pains to navigate a path between "free will"
and determinism. Rejecting the view that "elementary meanings are inherent in sound waves," they point to the role of such factors as implicit memory as they contribute to "the virtual cloud from which one occasion of actualization takes place that is the emergent perception of sound."[41] In this
way, in contrast with Nancy, Grimshaw and Garner privilege the individual
human as the locus of "actualization," underplaying the element of "methexis" or commonality in sonic experience. Moreover, favoring cognitivist
accounts of human experience, they treat terms such as "memory" and
"emotion" as variables abstracted from any socially or culturally embedded
or historicized account of human subjectivities.

It is by tracing the articulation or mutual mediation between material
and sensory processes, on the one hand, and human capacities for imagination, memory, and emotion, on the other, that Grimshaw and Garner
contend that sound should be theorized as "emergent perception." Their
great achievement is a relational and processual model that encompasses
both the material production and human perception of sound. Sound in
their account is definitively not an object; indeed, they problematize any
dualism of object and subject. Yet anthropocentrism is resilient: despite
identifying the contributions of a chain of mediators of sound, their model
comes down finally on the side of human perception—albeit that its "emergence" is materially conditioned. But through a differently weighted ap-
praisal of relations between exosonus and endosonus, one that accords
less privilege to the human subject as *the* locus of sound's emergence,
Grimshaw and Garner's account need not be tilted this way. In this light,
with their emphasis on the plural material and immaterial mediations
that make up the sonic aggregate, Grimshaw and Garner offer the linea-
ments of a non-anthropocentric, non-anthropomorphic theory of sound—
even if the term "aggregate" seems an overly static one for this inherently
temporal, fluxious relay of mediations. Indeed, this is why the Deleuzian
term assemblage—given its dynamic qualities and its anti-essentialist

and anti-organicist entailments—is preferable to aggregate in relation to sound. By advancing a model that encompasses a chain of nonhuman and human mediations and transductions (see note 39) that may or may not be set in motion by an original event (see note 25), sound is captured in all its difference from the human. It is, then, the particular nature of sound that allows it to resist the "analytic of mixture" and the reductions that plague debates about the nonhuman. Because of its materiality/immateriality, sound invites relational analysis, and this is stronger when it takes account of the hybrid multiplicity of the sonic assemblage as a temporalized relay of nonhuman and human mediations. The point is to resist Grimshaw and Garner's reduction of the framework that they themselves elaborate by insisting that the nonhuman *remains nonhuman* even as it enters into those relations with the human that constitute the sonic assemblage.

If sound is immanently composed of mediations in the ways set out by Grimshaw and Garner, then this augments my previous theorization of music's mediation. In a series of writings I have proposed that music has no essence "but a plural and distributed material being," and that we should conceive of music as "as an aggregation of sonic, social, discursive, visual, technological, corporeal and temporal mediations: as a musical assemblage, where this is defined as a characteristic constellation of such heterogeneous mediations."[42] Faced with the arguments in this chapter, the crucial shift is that (musical) sound appears to consist all the way down (as it were) of nothing but mediations—indeed, of nonlinear, recursive mediations of mediations—of varying scale: from energetic waves propagated through the air, to the pinnae and torsos of players and listeners, to the inter-corporeal choreography of the string quartet or rock band, to the musical expectations and affects rippling through an audience, to the large-scale social and architectural mediations characteristic of the rock stadium gig or orchestral concert hall performance.

By elevating the contributions of human perception over the nonhuman, Grimshaw and Garner work against a central tenet of Whitehead's philosophy. It is therefore ironic that they cite Whitehead, employing his concept of prehension to refer to a "pre-epistemic grasping of the sensuous" that is, they imply, decidedly human.[43] But this misunderstands Whitehead, since prehensions are not limited to humans and describe a "kind of generalized perceptive interrelation."[44] In Whitehead, the concept of process—"defined as *the becoming of actual occasions*"—grounds "a unitary philosophy of radical immanence (with nothing 'outside' of nature)," one that foregrounds "the *continuity* that exists between high-grade human experience, at one extreme, and the subject matter of physics, at the other."[45] Since "it is the process of becoming which is given priority in Whitehead's ontology, the terms 'object' and 'subject' lose their usual sense—'subject and object are relative terms.'"[46] As Paul Stenner explains, this stance entails "a radical *relational* re-thinking of the old bifurcated subject/object dualism," but, crucially, "it does not demand its abandonment." Rather, Whitehead's scheme "multiplies the subject/object dualism and distributes it throughout the entirety" of nature.[47] Subjectivity, then, is at play in the actualization immanent in every actual occasion; each actual occasion implies an emergent (human or nonhuman) subject "lending form or pattern to the objects implicated in its momentary field of activity."[48] In Whitehead's words, "The Quaker word 'concern' . . . is [well] fitted to suggest this fundamental structure. The occasion as subject has a 'concern' for the object. And the 'concern' at once places the object as a component in the experience of the subject, with an affective tone drawn from this object and directed towards it. With this interpretation, the subject-object relation is the fundamental structure of experience."[49] For Whitehead, experience is the process of a subject prehending its objects, whereby "the 'potentiality' immanent in the objects is 'actualized' in the form of a real co-creative becoming concrete (*concrescence*)"—a "conjunctive synthesis."[50] Whitehead therefore generalizes the concept of experience beyond the human domain and considers all entities in nature capable of subjectivity, to whatever minimal extent. In these terms, not only humans but nonhumans participate in emergent subjectivity, prehension, and experience. If Grimshaw and Garner followed Whitehead, they would not privilege human perception when weighing the contributions of nonhumans and humans to sonic experience. Their anthropocentrism infects their interpretation of even as resolutely non-anthropocentric a writer as Whitehead.

At the same time, prehension belongs among a group of concepts coined by Whitehead in order to overcome the "bifurcation of nature": the chasm that he argues divides the world into "two systems of reality," experience and the natural sciences, the subjective and the objective, "the nature apprehended in awareness and the nature which is the cause of awareness."[51] Whitehead's targets here are the processes of abstraction that underpin natural scientific accounts of the world. The concept of fact, he argues, "is the ideal of physical science . . . the triumph of the abstractive intellect. . . . [But] connectedness is the essence of all things. . . . It follows that in every consideration of a single fact there is the suppressed presupposition of the environmental coordination requisite for its existence. This environment, thus coordinated, is the whole universe in its perspective to the fact."[52] Elsewhere, he adds,

> The reason why the bifurcation of nature is always creeping back [in] is the extreme difficulty of exhibiting the perceived redness and warmth of the fire in one system of relations with the agitated molecules of carbon and oxygen, with the radiant energy from them, and with the various functionings of the material body. Unless we produce the all-encompassing relations, we are faced with a bifurcated nature; namely, warmth and redness on one side, and molecules, electrons and ether on the other side.[53]

His exhortation is therefore that we withstand scientific abstraction by discerning through "sense-awareness" all those relata, including affective and aesthetic dimensions of experience, that "together form the whole complex of related entities" that constitute an event—even if such knowledge has in principle an "unexhaustive character," for "nature as perceived always has a ragged edge."[54] In this way Whitehead points toward the necessity of an "expanded" or "radical empiricism" in the sense "of taking relations to be as real and as fundamentally given to experience as discrete objects or sense-data."[55]

My reading of the contributions of the three studies of sound detailed above points toward the perspective I am advocating, the contours of which I have developed by reference to Whitehead. My intention is to open up a conceptual space in which we understand sound, including nonhuman sound, as an inherently relational and "mediational" phenomenon that overcomes dualistic understandings of subject and object and that, in Whitehead's terms, itself participates in subjectivity. As we have seen from the different facets illuminated by Nancy and Grimshaw and Garner, sound as a hybrid assemblage composed of a relay of material and immaterial, nonhuman and human mediations baffles any purification of subject from object, mind from body, and individual from collective experience. One implication of this stance, fueled by my autoethnographic vignettes, is to insist that we notice and valorize the affective and aesthetic experiences afforded even by nonhuman sound. Another is to move beyond the privileging of musical sound as *the* catalyst of the engendering and transformation of subjectivity.[56]

Of course, if we are able to become attuned to the affective and aesthetic qualities of nonhuman sound today, this is in no small measure an effect of the historical transformations of sonic experience consequent on the fore-grounding of these qualities in those expansive lineages of environmental sound art, field recording, and sound installation art that I mentioned ear-lier. Thus, against the purifications of the "abstractive intellect," not only aesthetics and affect but also historical processes of change or "temporal relations"[57]—in this case, music- and art-historical processes—enter into the expanding relata to be brought into consideration. The challenge posed by the bifurcation of nature, then, is to enrich our understanding by aspir-ing to bring all that impinges on the sonic assemblage into our analysis, learning to discern more of the "all-encompassing relations," as Whitehead puts it, entering into sound as experience. Through my second autoethno-graphic incident, I aim to discern the many relations in which nonhuman sound is enmeshed as it becomes musicalized within heightened human relations of care.

....

I am sitting with my mother; she is at home in her bed two days before her recent death, late evening. For years she has been increasingly disabled and ill, brought low by chronic pain, blindness, and Parkinson's disease. A month ago she became bedridden; now she has been in a coma for five days, probably after a stroke, with increasing difficulty breathing and long lapses (minutes) without breath. She is heavily sedated by what is called palliative care (the use of constant intravenous opiates).[58] The nurses and doctor say: hearing, responsiveness to sound, is the last working sense, the last to leave the body, in the dying process. My mother, having gone blind seven years before, had no doubt developed the compensatory hearing acu-ity of the visually impaired.[59] She told me only months ago that through-out her life she had a synesthesia in which certain sounds (words, names, numbers) conjured up mental images of color. Moreover, her professional life was as a psychoanalyst, so she was herself an expert listener of a kind, through the media of words, bodies, projections, and introjections. In recent months, given that she could no longer read, one of the greatest pleasures we shared were interludes in which, as she rested, I read aloud to her books suffused with life memories: the autobiography of Fellini, for whom my brother acted in *Satyricon*; a proto-feminist novel penned in the 1960s by a close friend. Once, this being read to led her to exclaim,

"Sometimes I wonder: who is the mother now, and who the daughter?" In the last few days, I have been playing her favorite music to her (Schubert songs, Mozart opera); sometimes her eyes opened and eyebrows rose, her masklike face palpably enlivened, although she remained unconscious. But now this responsiveness has gone, and her breathing is erratic.

I have become increasingly attuned to the dull, buzzing "note" emitted by the smart hospital bed on which she lies. There is no escape from this mechanical hum. It pervades the room and, aware of the keenness of her hearing, it troubles me, since by absorbing her hearing space it seems to demand attention, to enfold her within a dyadic relation: she prostrate, the bed and its hum cocooning her, entraining her to a dead, featureless flatness. Tonight I decide to interrupt this deadening dyad, to introduce myself as a third relatum: to hum along with and harmonize the bed's note. I develop soft, slow, unfolding modal phrase-arcs, ending in sounded, exaggerated breaths, and deep sighs. In this way I activate a three-way relation between the bed hum, my mother, and myself. It is my attempt musically to overcome and encompass the nonhuman sound, rendering it the bass drone, while tempting my mother, by inviting affective mimesis, to breathe and sigh via the mediation of my own hums, breaths, and sighs—a *counter*-entrainment to the dull note. At the same time, in my effort to reach her through my duet with the bed sound, I am trying also to elide or transcend the boundary between us, that separates us as two organisms, to become closer, even to make us one, in this way assisting her fragile, compromised physiology through the co-presence marked by sound, breath, and affective vocal movements, as well as by proximity and touch (her hand in mine).[60]

And the signs were that she *was* affectively entrained by the duet and by touch: that she heard me, knew me, and felt me, my concern, my empathy, and my closeness to her near death. For there were instants when it seemed that my mother breathed and sighed in the spaces that I left at the end of phrases to elicit her response, so that together, momentarily, the three of us—bed sound, my mother, myself—achieved a form of sound- and breath-based call and response, each prehending the other. I was my mother's only daughter; for nine months, given inaccessible siblings, I had been traveling to care for her, to create an environment in which her dearest wishes—to stay at home and die at home without pain—could be achieved. There were passing storms and recriminations as I pressured her to adopt new ways of living that would make this possible. Yet in these last days I believe she knew, through sound's affective mediation and entraining powers, that we were still engaged together in this project, this dying process, beyond words and even beyond her conscious life. For me, the experience of being able still to be in sonic and sensory attunement with her, affectively touching and merged via the call-and-response of my keening hums and sighs, and hers in turn, was precious.

This story turns on an "experiment with subjectivity" afforded by sound and music in which affect, empathy, and entrainment play a considerable part. One source for understanding such an occasion is the work of Gabriel Tarde, with its insistence on how subjects are open to affecting and being affected, such that the fabric of the social results from collective flows of affect, a logic of semiconscious suggestion.[61] Another is the neo-Spinozist philosophy of Moira Gatens and Genevieve Lloyd, when they contend that "the awareness of human collectivities— . . . of bodies in relation—is not merely a cognitive awareness . . . [but] shot through with emotion. . . . Sociability is [therefore] inherently affective [and] the incorporation into collectivities which [also] determines our individuality involves affective imitation—dynamic movements of emotional identification and appropriation."[62] A third is Teresa Brennan's account of the contributions of entrainment to the transmission of affect across individuals and groups.[63] Yet my story compounds these perspectives, adding a focus on the affective powers of sound. Sound, it suggests, should be theorized as affording a particular kind of sensory or even haptic empathy,[64] a type of resonant, vibration-imbued touching—a sonic touching that can double the "mental touch" of affective empathy.[65] It points to the potential, through such sonic touching, for the emergence of what might be called a *transindividual subject*—such that the "individual [is] not bounded, but opened out to others through a . . . porous and permeable membrane."[66] It should also be apparent that these ideas augment Nancy's insights into the ways in which, given the "physics of sonorous reverberation," sound is both mediated by and moves across human and nonhuman entities, animating a collectivity of listening subjects. It should be obvious, finally, how much this body of thought resonates with Whitehead's non-anthropocentric reconceptualization of subjectivity—as irreducible to individual consciousness, and as participating in those creative processes of experience or conjunctive synthesis that compose what he calls actual occasions. Subjectification, the engendering of subjectivities, is at once an immanent component and an outcome of these transindividual processes of experience, which bring human and nonhuman participants into relation and result in the actualization of "novel unities."[67]

There is nothing inherently wrong with an approach to the analysis of sound that focuses exclusively on either the sound object or the listening subject. But the approach that I want to advocate suggests the possibility of troubling the bifurcation of nature—notably, the separation of scientific description from an appreciation of the affective and aesthetic qualities even of nonhuman sound as it enters into historical relations that endow it with such qualities. This is certainly a challenge. It entails seeking, as Whitehead suggests, to attune oneself to the multiple relations constituting an event, while recognizing that they can only ever be elements of a series of yet more complex nexuses or "systems of relations." Imagine an experiment in which we redescribe the history of art music as an instance of the bifurcation of nature in which a privileged "music," as the transcendent subject or locus of experience, is purified from mere background noise (or nonhuman sound) as object, ground, context, or wild. This may be why refiguring nonhuman sound as itself possessing the potential to be a catalyst of subjectification, of engendering aesthetic and affective experience, is productive—since it contributes to the ongoing destabilization of that and other bifurcations and purifications, human from nonhuman, subject from object, culture from nature, and so on. In this chapter I have drawn attention to the nonhuman sound of rain and the hum of a bed, setting them within "all-encompassing relations" that I have attempted autoethnographically to discern, precisely in order to highlight and affirm their potential and that of other nonhuman sounds as participants in novel events yet to come. Rather than push these sounds to the background or screen them out—like those aspects of the sounds of a concert, and of the concert as actual occasion, that are positioned so as not to be part of the "music itself"—it may be that advancing a different kind of relation to nonhuman sound, as I have tried to do, redresses the historical violence of that positioning, along with a series of other, correlative denials of relation.

Notes

My thanks to Harriet Boyd-Bennett, Martin Daughtry, Kyle Devine, Andrew Goffey, Mick Halewood, Chris Haworth, Gascia Ouzounian, Joe Snape, Christabel Stirling, the editors, and an anonymous reviewer for feedback. More particularly, I am grateful to Andrew Barry for the inspiration of Whitehead, and to Paul Stenner for close guidance on Whitehead's thought.

Epigraphs: Bennett, *Vibrant Matter*, 99; Kohn, *How Forests Think*, 91; Woolf, *Between the Acts*, 107.

1 Cf. Haraway, *The Companion Species Manifesto*; Haraway, *When Species Meet*.
2 On music's mediation, see Born, "On Musical Mediation"; Born, "Music and the Materialization of Identities"; Born, "Music: Ontology, Agency, and Creativity." With the concept of mediation I refer to the bidirectional transmission, translation, and transformation of one relatum (e.g., sound) by another relatum (e.g., technologies, discourses, socialities, sites, and spaces). Musical sound, I have suggested, is experienced as enmeshed in specific constellations of mediations. The basic concept of mediation is clarified by Bruno Latour's distinction between intermediaries, "what transports meaning or force without transformation," and mediators, which "transform, translate, distort, and modify the meaning or the elements they are supposed to carry": see Latour, *Reassembling the Social*, 39. Citing Antoine Hennion's *La passion musicale*, Latour suggests that "a mediator . . . creates what it translates as well as the entities between which it plays the mediating role. . . . The layering of intermediaries is replaced by chains of mediators": Latour, *We Have Never Been Modern*, 78.
3 Cf. Whatmore, "Materialist Returns."
4 Subjectification refers at base to the engendering and modulation of subjectivities. By thinking affect and the shaping of subjectivity together, I do not invoke an ontological reading of affect, nor of the link between sound and affect (recently criticized by Brian Kane: see Kane, "Sound Studies without Auditory Culture.") Previously, I developed a reading of affect that was indebted to Gabriel Tarde and Teresa Brennan as their work is taken up by Lisa Blackman, a reading that involves a rejection of the dualisms of individual and social, mind and body, psychology and sociology (Born, "Music and the Materialization of Identities"; Blackman, "Reinventing Psychological Matters"; Blackman, *Immaterial Bodies*). Such an approach is compatible with a commitment to charting the sociocultural differences and historical changes in the affective modalities of music and sound (Born, "Listening, Mediation, Event.") Kane locates such a commitment in the "auditory culture" paradigm, and the distinction he draws between a universalization of certain ontologies of sound (attributed to Cox, Hainge, and Goodman) and research on the "ontological commitments . . . of particular subjects or communities" (Kane, "Sound Studies without Auditory Culture," 2) recapitulates anthropology's ongoing debate over its "ontological turn" (Henare et al., *Thinking through Things*; Carrithers et al., "Ontology Is Just Another Word for Culture"), while highlighting the need for a distinction between what I have called the analytical ontology (our own, as analysts) and the ontology of the people/culture/scene we are researching (Born, "On Tardean Relations," 232–33). Affect, then, can offer an analytical perspective that is responsive to culturally and historically nuanced research (e.g., Navaro-Yashin, "Affective Spaces, Melancholic Objects"; Navaro-Yashin, *The Make-Believe Space*). Bringing these ideas together, I

draw on Blackman's discussion of subjectification as it is inflected by a retheoriza-
tion of affect, including her use of Félix Guattari's "transversalist conception of
subjectivity" (Guattari, *Chaosmosis*, 4), which, against psychological approaches,
explores the role of material and immaterial processes in practices of subjectification,
recognizing that "the subject is always more than human and more than one"
(Blackman, *Immaterial Bodies*, 59). Later, I pursue these matters by reference to
Alfred North Whitehead's account of subjectivity, which shares a number of features
with Guattari's: that it does not equate subjectivity with consciousness or individuality;
that the subject is not conceived as the source but as the outcome of experience; and
that it is "radically non-anthropocentric" (Sehgal, "A Thousand Subjectivities," 5).

5 Beer, "Introduction to *Between the Acts*," ix.

6 I include the sounds of bombers in the category of nonhuman sound in that, as
noted previously, they are unintended mechanical sounds emitted as an incidental
effect of the functioning of technologies.

7 See Henriques, "Sonic Dominance and the Reggae Sound System Session"; Henriques, *Sonic Bodies*; Cusick, "Music as Torture/Music as Weapon"; Cusick, "You Are
in a Place That is Out of the World . . ."; Goodman, *Sonic Warfare*.

8 On materiality, see Miller, *Materiality*; Bennett and Joyce, *Material Powers*. On the
new materialism, see Bennett, *Vibrant Matter*; Coole and Frost, *New Materialisms*;
van der Tuin and Dolphijn, *New Materialism*; Connolly, "The 'New Materialism' and
the Fragility of Things." On the nonhuman turn, see Grusin, *The Nonhuman Turn*.

9 See Appadurai, *The Social Life of Things*; Latour, *Politics of Nature*; Brown, "The
Secret Life of Things"; Brown, "Thing Theory"; Grusin, *The Nonhuman Turn*.

10 See, e.g., Brown, "Thing Theory"; Bennett, "The Force of Things"; Bennett,
"Thing-Power."

11 Schafer, *The Soundscape*.

12 For example, Lane and Carlyle, *In the Field*.

13 LaBelle, *Background Noise*, 14.

14 On urban environmental sound, see Thompson, *The Soundscape of Modernity*; Bijsterveld, *Mechanical Sound*. On the soundscapes of marine science expeditions, see
Helmreich, "An Anthropologist Under Water." On the soundscapes of hospitals, see
Rice, *Hearing and the Hospital*. On the acoustic ecologies of Middle Eastern megacities,
see Hirschkind, *The Ethical Soundscape*. On Papua New Guinean rainforests, see
Feld, *Sound and Sentiment*; Feld, "Aesthetics as Iconicity of Style"; Feld, "Waterfalls
of Song."

15 The work of Steven Feld comes close to escaping this asymmetry through his abid-
ing attention to his Kaluli interlocutors' knowledge of and aesthetic and affective
engagements with environmental sounds such as those of waterfalls, flowing rivers,
birdsong, and the incidental sounds of daily work activities: see Feld, *Sound and
Sentiment*; Feld, "Aesthetics as Iconicity of Style"; Feld, "Waterfalls of Song."

16 Bennett, *Vibrant Matter*, 102, 116.

17 Bennett, *Vibrant Matter*, 120.

18 Kohn, *How Forests Think*, 40.

19 O'Callaghan, *Sounds*, 69, 56.

20 O'Callaghan, *Sounds*, 70, 56.

21 O'Callaghan, *Sounds*, 25.

22 O'Callaghan, *Sounds*, 70.

23 O'Callaghan, *Sounds*, 13.

24 O'Callaghan, *Sounds*, 125.

25 Patrick Feaster notes the challenges posed by, for example, digitization and digital sound synthesis to any definition of sound, like O'Callaghan's, that has it originating in an event "constituted by the *interactions* of objects and bodies with the surrounding medium." As Feaster writes, data can produce sound even when they do not derive from any prior "real" sound, and he calls this process "eduction:" the "elicitation of sound 'from a condition of latent, rudimentary, or merely potential existence':" Feaster, "Phonography," 146–47.

26 For examples from anthropology and cultural and media studies, see Bull, *Sounding Out the City*; Bull and Back, *The Auditory Culture Reader*; Erlmann, *Hearing Cultures*. For examples of scholarship related to sound art, see Carlyle and Lane, *On Listening*; Voegelin, *Listening to Noise and Silence*. For examples from musicology, see Demers, *Listening through the Noise*; Dillon, *The Sense of Sound*; Eidsheim, *Sensing Sound*.

27 Nancy, *Listening*, 7.

28 Nancy, *Listening*, 9; and Kane, "Jean-Luc Nancy and the Listening Subject," 445.

29 Nancy, *Listening*, 21–22.

30 Nancy, *Listening*, 8.

31 Nancy, *Listening*, 9.

32 Nancy, *Listening*, 13.

33 Kane, "Jean-Luc Nancy and the Listening Subject," 445.

34 Nancy, *Listening*, 10.

35 Grimshaw and Garner, *Sonic Virtuality*, 166–78.

36 Noë, *Action in Perception*, 178.

37 Grimshaw and Garner, *Sonic Virtuality*, 112.

38 Grimshaw and Garner, *Sonic Virtuality*, 168–69.

39 Limited space permits me only to advance the suggestion that transduction, which has generally been presented without reference to theories of mediation in sound studies, might be considered a subcategory and a special form of more general processes of mediation. Transduction has been developed for sound studies mainly by Stefan Helmreich: see Helmreich, "An Anthropologist under Water"; Helmreich, "Listening against Soundscapes"; Helmreich, "Transduction." Identifying a range of prior uses of transduction, Helmreich elevates the concept to the status of an "analytic" ("Transduction," 229n3). He defines it as the transmission, "transmutation and conversion of signals across media" ("Listening against Soundscapes," 10); or, more fully, "Transduction names how sound changes as it traverses media, *as it undergoes transformations in its energetic substrate (from electrical to mechanical, for example)*, as it goes through transubstantiations that modulate both its matter and meaning. When an antenna converts electromagnetic waves into electrical signals and when those are converted via a loudspeaker into patterns of air pressure, we have a chain of transductions, material transformations that are also changes in how a [sound] signal can be apprehended and interpreted": Helmreich, "Transduction,"

222, emphasis added. If mediation refers to the transmission and transformation of one relatum (e.g., music, or sound) by another relatum (e.g., technologies, bodies, discourses, socialities, sites) (see note 2 above), while such processes *can* be focused at the level of the transformation of energy, as in Helmreich's account of transduction, they are not limited to this.

40 Grimshaw and Garner, *Sonic Virtuality*, 170–71.

41 Grimshaw and Garner, *Sonic Virtuality*, 173.

42 Born, "Music: Ontology, Agency, and Creativity," 138–39, drawing on Deleuze, *Foucault*; De Landa, *A New Philosophy of Society*.

43 Grimshaw and Garner, *Sonic Virtuality*, 165.

44 Halewood, *A. N. Whitehead and Social Theory*, 30.

45 Stenner, "A. N. Whitehead and Subjectivity," 99; Stenner, "James and Whitehead," 105.

46 Whitehead, *Adventures of Ideas*, 176, cited in Halewood, *A. N. Whitehead and Social Theory*, 29.

47 Stenner, "James and Whitehead," 106.

48 Stenner, "James and Whitehead," 106. More fully, "The ultimate facts of immediate actual experience are actual entities [or occasions], prehensions, and nexūs [the plural of nexus]. . . . [T]he first analysis of an actual entity . . . discloses it to be a concrescence of prehensions [and] every prehension consists of three factors: (a) the 'subject' which is prehending . . . ; (b) the 'datum' which is prehended; (c) the 'subjective form' which is *how* that subject prehends that datum": Whitehead, *Process and Reality*, 20, 23.

49 Whitehead, *Adventures of Ideas*, 176, cited in Stenner, "James and Whitehead," 106.

50 Stenner, "James and Whitehead," 106.

51 Whitehead, *The Concept of Nature*, 30–31. On the fertility of Whitehead's philosophy in its commitment to questions of subjectivity, and on how the exclusion of subjectivity is definitive of the bifurcation of nature, see Stenner, "A. N. Whitehead and Subjectivity." As Stenner argues with regard to affect theory, targeting Nigel Thrift's *Non-Representational Theory* (2008), "In recent 'radical' social theory, it seems the baby of subjectivity is at risk of being thrown out with the bathwater of representationalism": Stenner, "A. N. Whitehead and Subjectivity," 93.

52 Whitehead, *Modes of Thought*, 8–9.

53 Whitehead, *The Concept of Nature*, 32.

54 Whitehead, *The Concept of Nature*, 50.

55 Massumi, "Too-Blue," 177. The idea of radical empiricism comes from William James, *Essays in Radical Empiricism*, a key influence on Whitehead. Brian Massumi advocates a radical empiricist approach in a paper that addresses the nature of color beyond the bifurcation of nature. In it he insists that "humanities disciplines . . . can be argued to be realist, empirical enterprises generating modes of validity specific to their manner of result—provided that the definition of empirical reality is generously broadened": Massumi, "Too-Blue," 177.

56 Cf. Cumming, "The Subjectivities of 'Erbarme Dich'"; Cumming, *The Sonic Self*; Clarke and Clarke, *Music and Consciousness*.

57 Whitehead, *The Concept of Nature*, 51; Born, "On Tardean Relations."

58 It is my conviction that palliative care is today a euphemism for actively assisted dying, since liquids are withdrawn from patients, who die, as my mother did, from the avoidable effects of dehydration.

59 For an astonishing first-person account of the heightened sensory significance of hearing among people who go blind, one that turns on the forms of knowledge produced by deciphering the tonalities of the sounds of rain falling on different materials, see John Martin Hull, "Rain," September 9, 1983, http://www.johnmhull .biz/Touching%20the%20Rock.html. I thank Gascia Ouzounian for this reference.

60 Blackman reports that the psychiatrist R. D. Laing was interested in entrainment as a form of transindividual communication evident in such forms of bodily affectivity as the synchronization of breathing: Blackman, *Immaterial Bodies*, 85.

61 Cf. Blackman and Venn, "Affect," 9; Tarde, *On Communication and Social Influence*.

62 Gatens and Lloyd, *Collective Imaginings*, 77.

63 Brennan, *The Transmission of Affect*.

64 See Marks, *The Skin of the Film*.

65 Blackman, *Immaterial Bodies*, chapter 3.

66 Blackman, *Immaterial Bodies*, 61.

67 Stenner, "James and Whitehead."

v | Memory Traces

The Sound of Arche-Cinema

This small hole [there] is where water comes out gurgling after there has been something like a week of rain, and this probably explains why all those animals were painted around that hole.

—WERNER HERZOG, *Cave of Forgotten Dreams*

This moment in *Cave of Forgotten Dreams*, to which, as if mimicking the mechanics of gurgling, I will return, matters as a point of departure because it signals the perhaps otherwise unforeseeable role that the emergent field of "archaeoacoustics" will play in this treatment of the status of sound in film theory, especially as film theory has been inflected by the recent techno-philosophical innovations of Bernard Stiegler. I am thus proposing that if the cinema can invent its own concepts—can, in effect, theorize—then its theory of sound, especially as an instance of cinema before the cinema, will necessarily present itself in a film that purports, as we say, to "go there," to go where its *arkhé* repeats in a theater near you— perhaps even the one in your hand.

It is now typical in cinema studies to date the end of Grand Theory (a formula designed to weaken if not repudiate the influence of the French theoretical fusion of Marx and Freud) in the last two decades of the twentieth century. Missed here is an approach to the encounter between cinema and theory that derives from Gilles Deleuze's two-volume study, which dates from the mid-1980s. This angle, which grasps theory as immanent to the medium of cinema as opposed to applied to it from above, continues to resonate even while it is putatively passé. It has influenced Alain Badiou directly and Stiegler somewhat more obliquely. In what follows, it is Stiegler's intervention—specifically his notion of what, following Jacques Derrida, he calls "arche-cinema"—that will set the analytical agenda. As the title of this chapter indicates, I am especially concerned with thinking about the status of sound in the concept of arche-cinema as an expression of solidarity (however inconstant) with the partisans of sound studies, but more important as a theoretical opening into what, if we are to believe Deleuze and Badiou, the cinema *itself* has difficulty thinking. A full airing of what is at issue here will have to be deferred, but it seems to me that the problem of sound—not simply the form and content of the soundtrack, but sound, as Aden Evens says, as "a problem posing itself while working itself out"—haunts the Deleuzean problematic.[1]

The concept of arche-cinema has been unwinding in Stiegler's corpus since the early volumes of *Technics and Time* and perhaps nowhere more insistently than in volume three, subtitled, "Cinematic Time and the Question of Malaise" (*Mal-être*). To appreciate what is at stake in this concept, it helps to recall how its avatar, "arche-writing," emerged in Derrida's critique of phonocentrism on the pages of *Of Grammatology*. If I insist on this, I do so because the production of the concept is not only retraced by Stiegler, but this very gesture matters to its articulation with the cinema, especially a cinema thought to be thinking. The relevant passage from Derrida reads:

> I would wish rather to suggest that the alleged derivativeness of writing, however real and massive, was possible only on one condition: that the "original," "natural," etc. language never had existed, never been intact and untouched by writing, that it had itself always been a writing. An arche-writing whose necessity and new concept I wish to indicate and outline here; and which I continue to call writing only because it essentially communicates with the vulgar concept of writing. The latter could not have imposed itself historically except by the dissimulation of the arche-writing, by the desire for a speech displacing its other and its double and working to reduce its difference. . . . It threatened the desire for the living speech from the closest proximity, it *breached* living speech from within and from the very beginning.[2]

This formulation is deployed to tease apart the motif of usurpation drawn on by Ferdinand de Saussure to explain the toxic effects of writing on speech. In effect, if usurpation is possible, then it has always already taken place. By stressing the notion of a (con)founding breach within living speech, Derrida motivates his appeal to a "writing" more primordial than the vulgar distinction between speech and writing, a writing whose engagement with "spacing" (breaching) places it at a beginning more fundamental than time itself. Although such a beginning touches directly on what is meant by logical priority, the *proteron*, it also gestures—and the point is not often noted—toward a Spinozist principle of immanent eternity. In other words, immanent to life itself is an event that has never not been taking place, the event whose advent echoes in the becoming of the "new concept" of arche-writing.

As this summary suggests, Derrida produces arche-writing in a rather traditional philosophical way: in asking after the presuppositions of Saussure's argument, he discovers the need for a more forceful account of what animates and sustains this argument, an account that transgresses by stating the limits of the problematic within which the argument came to matter. However, where Derrida parts ways with philosophy is that he is not here seeking to *ground* usurpation. Instead, by gesturing beyond or before the problematic in relation to which grounding makes sense, Derrida is opening up a space within which to entertain the possibility of thinking what is foreclosed both by the hierarchy of speech and writing *and* by the distinction between arche-writing and vulgar writing. Arche-writing thus gestures toward the problem of the problematic itself. Where did it come from, and why does its still matter?

It is important to stress this because, as I have proposed, this same (although not identical) impulse realizes itself in Stiegler's concept of arche-cinema as formulated in his essay "The Organology of Dreams and Arche-Cinema." As stated, his intervention must be understood as occurring within and around the proposition that the cinema is more than an occasion for thought. Put differently, that cinema thinks not in the sense of a Turing machine (i.e., as a convincing simulation of thinking) but in the sense of expressing, epiphylogenetically (to use Stiegler's term), the cognitive faculty of memory itself.

But a crucial precaution is in order. During the alleged heyday of Grand Theory, the ideological effects of the basic cinematographic apparatus, as they were conceived by Jean-Louis Baudry (among others), were also understood to work, to take effect, not because they coincided with convictions already held about society, but because they took effect in generating the *experience* of the value of such convictions. The cinema called into position the bearer of convictions in general. Thus, it served as an analogy of thought or psychosomatic experience as a whole. It is against the backdrop of this context that the originality and provocation of Stiegler's approach can be measured. Although the terminology is foreign to him, one can say that *his* question reads (and the relation to Derrida is commented on explicitly): if it is possible for the cinema to serve as an analogy for the thinking that occurs in remembering, then this analogy has always already taken place. In fact, if an analogy has always already been in place, then the concept of analogy is not a terribly useful one for thinking the relation between cinema and thought. Something more primordial is afoot, and like Derrida, Stiegler deploys the prefix "arche" to gesture toward it.

In *Technics and Time, 3,* this gambit is pursued in a tenacious and forceful reading of Kant. Specifically, in comparing the two versions of Kant's "transcendental deduction" (one from the 1781 version of the first critique; the second from the 1787 version of the same), Stiegler teases out a telling shift that discloses an early, if somewhat inchoate, commitment to epiphylogenesis in *The Critique of Pure Reason.* Deftly drawing attention to Kant's own relation to his two texts, the latter one presented as a "mere clarification" of the earlier, Stiegler summarizes Kant's argument this way:

> We must examine the conditions under which schema and the role image [an apparently innocuous terminological shift between the two transcendental deductions] plays in it are constituted. Kant posits that schema precedes image; my claim is that they are co-emergent—that is to say, that they share a transductive relationship. Image and schema are two faces of the same reality, constituting a historical process conditioned by the structure of epiphylogenesis—the general system of tertiary retentions form the *medium of consciousness,* its "world" as the spatialization of the time of consciousness past and passing as *Weltgeschichtlichkeit.*[3]

As the italicized phrase implies, what Kant struggles with is the fact that the relation between the two editions of the *Critique* forms, or gives expression to, a medium that operates on the content of the difference between image and schema—specifically, a difference thought to be merely didactically motivated—that Kant knows he does not know anything about. The gesture to "epiphylogenesis" here brings this discussion into sync with Stiegler's approach to cinematic time in *Technics and Time, 3,* insofar as this approach stresses the way the distinctive treatment of time within the cinema—compression, metalepsis, extension—gives structure and texture to what Edmund Husserl called "internal time consciousness."

What brings these formulations into relation with the thematics of arche-cinema is that cinema as an epiphylogenetic medium instances time in a manner that is not an analog to consciousness but, rather, structures consciousness insofar as its structure is thinkable only through the long march of tertiary retention within it. Put differently, if, as Sigmund Freud said in *Beyond the Pleasure Principle*, consciousness arises on the site of a memory trace, then the cinema has become our designation for the institutional locus of the human encounter with this preemption of consciousness by memory. In effect, the flashback is not a technique, it is a technics and its pervasiveness as a formal device in narrative cinema (whether Western or not) is a symptom of this fact. Indeed, one could argue that this is part of what is demonstrated in Stiegler's extended interpretation of Federico Fellini's *Intervista* from chapter 1 in *Technics and Time, 3*, a text that also has recourse to the notion of "flashback" as a section title.[4]

Crucial to the argument of "The Organology of Dreams," as the title states, is Stiegler's commitment to unpacking tertiary retention in relation to oneiric space. The problem here is not simply the ontological and logical priority of memory, but the primitive and foundational character of unconscious memory, the "unknown known" to invoke Donald Rumsfeld. Put differently, what Stiegler is "spelunkulating" here is the sense in which the cinema thinks, to paraphrase Lacan's rewording of Descartes, where thought does not think to think. Clearly, this is an extension of the Deleuzean paradigm that takes cinema's theory of itself to a "whole n'other level," both structurally but, perhaps even more important, historically. In effect, and this is what makes Stiegler's appeal to Marc Azéma's work so urgent, he is trying to grasp in what sense the cinema belongs to human dreaming within the frame of what Donna Haraway names the "Chthonocene," and it is here that he legitimates his appeal to arche-cinema, but now in a quasi-paleontological register that, as he points out, Derrida never risked. Although shortcuts such as the following are foredoomed (and for good reason), one might propose that there stands between Stiegler and Derrida a disagreement about the ontological historicity of media.

Let me now justify my recourse to the preposterous neologism "spelunkulating." Azéma is a researcher of the Paleolithic period and a filmmaker. What interests him, and this is expressed in his co-written essay, "Animation in

Paleolithic Art: A Pre-echo of Cinema," is the notion that in cave paintings—most notably, at Chauvet and Baume Latrone (and a certain baseline Euro-centrism is never properly interrogated here)—one can see clear evidence of the effort, to represent not merely animals (including human hands), but animals' movement.[5] In one of his several short films demonstrating his thesis, Azéma presents stick drawings (abstractions) of cave figures in two distinct positions followed by brief sequences in which he traces the lines that sketch the movement from one position to the other. On this basis he argues that Paleolithic artists were figuring the cinema—that is, a me-dium (here rock) through which life could be tracked in all its dynamism. Stiegler, for his part, rewords this figuring as dreaming, but he complicates the point by insisting not that cave art is some sort of historical *precursor* to a later representational technology, but that prior—in a logical sense—to both cave art and the cinema is an arche-cinema of dreaming, a dreaming that not only brings the projection of movement into the world, but that gestures ahead of the world in a moment of pharmacological stimulation. The cave is a locus of speculation, of wagering on what the world might be capable of, what it might risk. It is not where speculation might be situated, but it is a figure of oneiric speculation, a site, then, of spelunkulation.

Concerned as I am with the question of sound as it bears on the concept of arche-cinema, it is worth considering in what way and to what degree Azéma's notion of the "pre-echo" might haunt the relation just sketched between his thinking and that of Stiegler. To tease out what is potentially generative about this formulation, I turn to another collaborator of Azé-ma's, someone who, like Stiegler, has grasped the significance of his work for cinematic theory and practice: Werner Herzog and, specifically, his film of/on/in the Chauvet cave, the highly acclaimed *Cave of Forgotten Dreams*. Azéma does not appear on-screen, as do other of Herzog's collaborators—significant figures in French and German archaeology—but his name ap-pears prominently in the credit sequence, and his thesis regarding Paleolithic animation and the cinema is advanced directly within Herzog's film. In the voice-over narration—written and spoken by Herzog—Herzog con-cludes a set of observations about the striking anatomy of a multilegged bison by musing that it is "almost a form of proto-cinema" and that, more generally, the cave figures suggest "an illusion of movement like frames from an animated film." As Azéma has made short films in which this thesis is graphically demonstrated, it is clear that Herzog is deeply aware of the provocative resonance between his project—filming the prehistory of the very medium of the cinema—and Azéma's. Less clear but equally important is the way this convergence prompts one to use Azéma's text as the communicating vessel through which to put *Cave of Forgotten Dreams* in correspondence with "The Organology of Dreams and Arche-Cinema."

What stands out immediately here is the motif and concept of the dream, a detail that invites attention to how it plays out in Herzog's film, which, as his title makes plain, is concerned with "forgotten dreams"—that is, psychic events that have an odd, even troubled relation to retention, whether primary, secondary or tertiary. Freud, of course, insisted that while everyone dreams, not everyone remembers his or her dreams—this is part of what he understood by primary repression—but Herzog's provocation is not recuperated so easily. Again, in the voice-over narration at the very moment of denomination—that is, when the film's name invaginates the diegesis—Herzog says that the cave images are "memories of long-forgotten dreams," implying that they are indeed instances of what Stiegler calls "epiphylogenesis" but thereby inviting us to consider that the relation between memory and forgetting may be more complicated for Herzog than appears at first glance. One senses this in the semantic tangle of the utterance itself, where we have images of memories, of dreams that have been long forgotten. Coupled with the deictic "these" (as in "*these* are images"), we already have in play both the images in the frame and the images comprising the frame. Again, the precise relation between dream images (whether forgotten or not) and the cinema is difficult to discern here, much less state. What, one might wonder, is an image of a memory of something forgotten? Or, in a more spelunkulative vein, *where* are such images? Are they *in* the film we are watching? Are they *of* the film we are watching? Both? Neither? Although there would be a great deal to say about the fact the film was shot in 3D, it at least bears noting that this "technical" (merely?) fact bears directly and suggestively on the "where" of these images as screened.

Herzog, as is characteristic of his persona, further complicated matters when, in the wake of the premier of the film at the Ritzy Cinema in London, responded to a question from the audience about the dreams he had while making the film by insisting, "I do not really dream," adding, "Maybe this is why I make films," a set of formulations that invites one to entertain two hard-to-reconcile hypotheses: one in which film is something that happens in the space left vacant by absent dreaming, in which case the film exists *instead* of the dream; or the other, that film is a compensation for a deficit that nevertheless attaches it to the dream that has not really taken place. In the first case, the film is *other* than the dream; in the second, it is the dream in *another* form. Perhaps even a forgotten dream? To add yet a final wrinkle, in the film, in a sequence to which I return, Herzog invokes dreaming as an essential counterweight to mere information, observing that a laser-scanned digital representation of the cave—his metaphor for this representation is "the phone directory of Manhattan"—prompts his urgent question, "But do they dream?" Heard in unison with his assertion that he does not really dream, this would imply that his objection to the phone directory is either false or insincere.[6]

What intrigues me here is not the question of what Herzog means by dreams (recall that in 1984 he made the film *Where the Green Ants Dream*), or even whether he sees the cinema as constitutive of an organology of dreams. Instead, what intrigues me is his ambivalence and the problem of whether this ambivalence gives expression to something active within and corrosive of the cinema-dream matrix. Further, and this is decisive, how might the arche-cinema thesis be obliged to extend itself as a consequence? In a gesture of solidarity with broadly Brechtean aesthetics, my aim in what follows is to situate sound at the heart of this ambivalence—not as the heart itself, but as what, in its collision with the image, enables us to register what beats before it.[7]

Returning, then, to the sequence in which the contrast between the abstraction of the phone directory of Manhattan and the expressivity of dreams is made, the interview with Julien Monney that occasions these remarks is followed immediately by a sequence initiated through an intervention by Jean Clottes, the head of scientific research, that begins, "Sorry. Silence, please. Please don't move. We are going to listen to the silence of the cave, and perhaps we can even hear our own heartbeats." In the wake of Cage's much commented-on adventures in the anechoic chambers at Harvard in the 1940s, this formulation struggles to contain the paradox of straining to listen to the silence of the cave—to, in effect, nothing. For Cage, the fact that his own heartbeat (and his tinnitus mistaken for an otherwise inaudible nervous system) became audible in the effort to listen to silence demonstrated that silence was less a perception than a conception, and a conception that heralded a robust future for music. For Clottes, the heartbeats of the crew emerge from and thus confirm a silence presumed to be shared with the Paleolithic artisans. As Herzog stresses repeatedly, the cave is "pristine"—that is, it sounds just as it did when the artists were at work there.

In the course of the ten shots that make up this sequence, the drama of listening to silence, of hearing (the) nothing, takes on a conspicuous form. We begin with the dialogue cited earlier, an utterance that simulates the military call for "radio silence." We see the crew, whose murmuring has been stilled, looking off-screen to the left, saying nothing. In the second shot, we see a single member of the crew turning slowly away from the camera. In this shot, the soundtrack breaks the surrounding silence by introducing noise and music. We hear dripping water from the stalactites and, faintly, we hear Ernst Reijseger's score. With apparent deliberation, Herzog produces the traditional fork between diegetic sound that is gradually de-acousmatized (to invoke Chion's term) and extra-diegetic sound, here the duo of Reijseger and Harmen Fraanje. It is certainly true that much of the sound in the film—Herzog's voice-over to be sure—has been added in postproduction, but precisely by de-acousmatizing the dripping water (we hear it before we see it) it is plain that the *illusion* (later I will consider the "phantasmatic" character of this illusion) of this fork is crucial. Why? Because it is also here that we hear the Foley sound effect of heartbeats: one-and, two-and, three-and. These enter clearly on the extra-diegetic side of the fork and fade in and out across the remaining shots of the sequence, returning dramatically in the penultimate sequence of the film (prior, that is, to the appendix). Of course, the dialogue has cued us to hear these heartbeats as "our own," meaning the crew of which Clottes is a member. This moves them across to the diegetic side of the fork, thus becoming part of the cave's broken "silence." To fix this topological paradox, Herzog concludes the sequence both by denominating the film here—"These images are memories of long forgotten dreams"—but adding immediately, "Are these their heartbeats or our own? Will we ever be able to understand the vision of such artists across the abyss of time?" The shift from sound to vision cues, appropriately, a fade-to-black that concludes the sequence.

Here the pronouns "theirs" and "ours" retrace the fork between the diegetic and extra-diegetic, adding, in an arche-cinematic gesture, the audience—indeed, the open series of all future auditors of the film—to the space of the extra-diegetical. Anahid Kassabian recently argued that, technically, if one means by "extra-diegetical" a locus radically outside the film, there is no extra-diegetical. All sound in a film is *in* the film. Or, put in terms closer to Kassabian's own, perhaps no sound is *in* film because we listen to it everywhere, even when it is "on" the soundtrack. What then becomes decisive is how the diegetic contours of particular films, give location and significance to an outside within. In *Cave of Forgotten Dreams*, this bears massively on the organological problematic of arche-cinema by posing the question not of whether Paleolithic art adumbrates animation or proto-cinema, but of the way in which cinema has continued to think and

give form to an emergent experience of movement that ties it at once structurally and ontologically to the projective force of dreaming. In Herzog's
film, which is profoundly reflective and abyssal in this regard, the diegesis
seeks to situate the moment of the arche-cinematic in the inner outside of
sound—voices, heartbeats, unheard(-of) melodies, and instruments that
resound in precisely that invaginated cavity where Chauvet and Herzog's
film converge. Put differently, all such sounds are designed to radiate from
a mnemic "outside" that is also a "before"—indeed, the very "before" of the
"arche" itself. It is as if we can overhear the machinery of tertiary retention
being moved into place, or installed, to invoke Godard's quip that specta-
tors are, in effect, cameras.

A final set of observations about the film will help frame the provocation I wish to lay before Stiegler and all those operating within the broadly
Deleuzean problematic invoked in the chapter's opening paragraph.

Of the many "interviews" that compose the film, by far the most sustained is the one with the archaeologist and curator Dominique Baffier
and her colleague Valérie Feruglio. When viewers are first introduced to
them, they are "personalizing" some of the artistic works—as if "personal
expression" were a compulsory quality for anything worthy of being designated "art"—by isolating a graphic signifier, the "signature" of a particular
cave artist with a crooked finger. The sequence proceeds to follow "him"
(height and gender are here conflated) into the recesses of the cave. But of
the subsequent thirty-five shots, some long takes using a mobile camera
(panning, tracking, tilting, and so on), perhaps the most remarkable are
those dedicated to listening to the sounds *made by* the paintings. In shot
twenty-four, Baffier stops in front of images of horses and rhinos, turns to the
camera, and says:

> Here you have an ensemble of horses, but their open mouths suggest
> the animals are whinnying, that is to say, that these images become
> audible to us. You see that the two rhinos there [she gestures] are fight-
> ing. You can see all the signs of their fury toward each other: the move-
> ment of their legs, which are thrown forward, and you can almost hear
> the sound [she makes a resounding clap to which the camera belatedly
> pans] of their horns colliding with each other in the movement of the
> fight.

Technically, of the horses visible in the shot, only one has an open mouth—
indeed, the very one shown earlier as a photographic enlargement in the
initial heartbeat sequence—and one might just have readily spelunkulated

here on the horse's *words*, on whether Paleolithic artists—also shown to shadow dance with their works as Fred Astaire did in the film *Swing Time* (1936)—saw themselves as addressed by the animals they depicted. But as the example of the rhinos suggests, the real issue here is the phenomenon of the becoming audible of the images, a problem acknowledged as such through the rhetorical "You can almost hear," followed by a resolutely audible clap. When Baffier adds that the images become audible *to us*, this scene implacably begins to repeat the problem of the heartbeats—namely, where and when *are* these equestrian utterances, sounds so clearly situated in the space the film labors to designate as "off."

It is vital to recall here that this is actually the second clap we hear echo—and I choose this word deliberately—in the cave. The first occurs almost immediately after the film crew enters and shuts itself in the "pristine" cave. As one might expect, the crew conducts a level check on the sound-recording equipment, first tapping on the windscreen covering the microphone, followed immediately by a loud "diegetic" clap. Significantly, this clap is not de-acousmatized but re-acousmatized: the shot in which it occurs is saturated with the glare of a flashlight directed into the camera, and thus our faces. As with Plato's sun, it overwhelms, and the sound source passes into the invisible, the "off." What it means here to foreground the echoed character of this sound is to note that the clap returns to the present of the sound check *from* the recesses of the cave, thereby tying together on a Moebian plane of sonic immanence the apparatus of tertiary retention (the technological preconditions of *Cave of Forgotten Dreams*) and the space of primordial retention, a space conceived by Stiegler as an incarnation, a becoming flesh, of what remains cinematic in human internal time consciousness.

Extending this, one must also stress that Baffier—like Monney and others among the scientists studying the cave—sees herself as an interpreter of the stories told by the depictions on the walls. In this, their work is very much post-Latourian. They are not technicians; they are writers—indeed, writers of science. In shot twenty-five of the sequence, Baffier, gesturing to another group of figures, says, "Here you have another *story* [my emphasis]. A story of lions. A male courting a female who is not ready for mating. She sits and growls. Look [she gestures]—you can hear the female growling. She is raising her lips, she is baring her teeth. She is not happy." This shot is followed by another in which more audible images are interpreted—notably, the sound of the very "animated" hooves that drew Azéma's attention—but shot twenty-five invites at least two specific comments. First, it seems crucial to note that here, in the person of Baffier, the film is staging the genesis of diegetic space. Each time she tells a "story," she produces an inside, a micro-world that is carved off from what is then its inner outside, the extra-diegetic. Notably, in all such cases. what surfaces is the rebus-like point at which sound and image cross. As she says, "*Look*, you can *hear* the female growling." Instead of observing that beyond simply stating that the images suggest sounds, or that Baffier is calling on the spectator, gripped by synesthesia, to hear with his or her eyes, I wish to stress that we, Baffier included, are being asked to engage not in dreaming, but in phantasizing. And, I hasten to add, that I mean this in a rather strict sense.

Specifically, I am thinking of the haunting passage in Freud's correspondence with Wilhelm Fliess in which he contrasts dream and phantasy—both crucial touchstones for a then emerging psychoanalysis—this way:

> For phantasies are psychical outworks constructed in order to bar the way to these memories [memories of primal scenes]. At the same time, phantasies serve the purpose of refining the memories, of sublimating them. They [phantasies] are built up out of things that have been heard about and *subsequently* turned to account; thus they combine things that have been experienced and things that have been heard about past events (from the history of parents and ancestors) and things seen by the subject himself. They [phantasies] are related to things heard in the same way as dreams are related to things seen. For in dreams we hear nothing, but only see.[8]

Freud, as is well known, would go on in his work to nuance this account of the strictly visual character of dreams. (Consider here the cartoon of the nurse and the crying infant that illustrates *The Interpretation of Dreams*.) But the emphasis placed here on phantasy and hearing is one that he sustains and embellishes, proposing that it is through what Jean Laplanche would later call "enigmatic signifiers"—for example, sounds of fucking that could be "misheard" as sounds of fighting—that the speaking subject, the human being, is thrust onto the oedipal stage. Thus, when I propose that Baffier is inviting us to phantasize the "growl" of the sexually harassed female lion, not only is she asking us to hear the picture, to make the ekphrastic leap, but she is also unleashing the power of phantasy within the cave of forgotten dreams, in the process suggesting that the distinctive explanatory force or pertinence of the dream is not so much forgotten as omitted, displaced. One can, of course, neutralize such a move by attributing the phantasy simply to Baffier, but in the context of Herzog's film, the sequence involving her works to place sound in and around oneiric space in a way that attaches it, however loosely, to the spatio-temporal enigma of the heartbeats that emerge from a silent cave whose silence has been compromised through the very making of the film that posits it. Put differently, the sequence involving her situates sound as the figure, the point of reference (however fraught), for a film struggling to think, to orient itself toward, the concept of an arche-cinema in and with its audience.

Let me propose that this urges us to think more carefully and systematically about the work of Iegor Reznikoff and Steven Waller, among others, scholars active in the emergent—and thus controversial—field of "archaeo-acoustics." Waller in particular has been trying not to listen to the heartbeats of caves, but to think about how Paleolithic art—specifically, the sorts of images found in the Chauvet cave—might be understood to be rebus-like "echoes" (and this is a word Waller shares with Azéma), echoes of "actual" sounds heard to be emanating from and resonating within underground grottos. This thesis is touched on in *Cave of Forgotten Dreams* when, in narrating the discovery of the cave, Herzog explains that Jean-Marie Chauvet and his collaborators were seeking out currents of air—that is, precisely the sort of airflow that produces whistling when directed over crevices and fissures with sufficient force at the right angle; in effect, what a flautist might call *embouchure*. Moreover, if one emphasizes the *gurgling* of the rainwater running into the cave rather than the ethological trope of the "waterhole," the film might also be indulging in an archaeo-acoustic gesture when it observes that "this" is why the paintings are painted around *it* (not the hole but the gurgle).[9]

Be that as it may, to take phantasy seriously here also means to avoid a certain convenient interpretive option. Specifically, since the Baffier sequence concludes by following immediately from an enigmatic stone pendant, on which one finds "the only representation of a human being in the cave [a female form ravished by a bison]," to a series of Venus figurines—those found at Wollendorf and Hohle Fels—one might justifiably assume that this evocation of sound and phantasy leads one directly to Guy Rosolato's thesis about the "sonorous envelope" of the maternal body. This is doubtless encouraged by the fact that Rosolato, without referencing Freud directly, is concerned with the phantasy of the mother's voice that resonates—at once protectively and ominously—in the sonorous envelope. This would render Chauvet a womb and its heartbeats, those of the mother pulsing in syncopation with those of the fetus, a rather clumsy and thus unconvincing equation between the pre-oedipal and the prehistoric. What this loses, even from a film such as *Cave of Forgotten Dreams*, is the sense of sound not as an *object* of phantasy, but as *structured-like-a-phantasy* by the logic of the enigmatic signifier. It is interesting to note that in the passage from Rosolato's text, where Kaja Silverman, among others, derived the trope of the "sonorous envelope," no mention is made of it. Instead, he uses two expressions: *la matrice sonore* and, even more enigmatic, *la maison bruissante*.[10] In fact, the expression "sonorous envelope" actually appears in the essay "L'enveloppe sonore du soi" (1976), by Didier Anzieu. While this may strike one as a petty philological quibble, it seems important to preserve the "matrixial" resonance of Rosolato's formulation. It gestures to, but also through, the mother to something that precedes her, and in ways not adequately captured in Bracha Ettinger's notion of the "matrixial gaze," where the problem of vision—even at its limits—again asserts itself. But more to the point, given Freud's distinction between phantasy and dream, is the suggested parallel between a "sonorous matrix" and a "rustling or noisy house," a parallel impossible to discern when the rustling house is analytically foreclosed.

This matters because the rustling house, even without further comment, evokes immediately the troubled scene of phantasmatic listening. It does so by situating sound outside the maternal body, thereby suspending the essential reduction of sound to speech or voice and opening sound back out into a less incorporated and territorialized space where it echoes originarily.[11] One might argue that, despite his persistent reference to phantasy, Rosolato resists this subordination of the phonic to the sonic. The concomitant priority that he places on the body, and the mother's body at that, is a decisive and welcome corrective to a certain phallocentric obsession with the speaking subject's wounding encounter with language and the name/no of the father, but it does not effectively counteract the stale developmental options of protection versus menace that apparently follow from reducing sound to the phantasy of the mother's voice. Put differently, many sounds matter that are not those spoken to, or near, us by others.

I conclude, then, with a final set of spelunkulations. The arche-cinema thesis holds that the cinema as an epiphylogenetic medium instances an experience of time. This experience is not that of an analogy (human time is like this), but of a structure, a structure we uniquely comprehend through our experience of the cinematic form of tertiary retention. If this thesis holds, then the different ways that phantasy and dream bear on an epiphyslogenetically mediated consciousness is of theoretical interest. One important way to measure this difference is to underscore the distinctive emphasis on sound that phantasy puts in play. The matter of how the relation between phantasy and dream succumbs to the logic of the trace becomes crucial here—that is, in what way does this distinction, precisely as it gives shape and orientation to the thinking the cinema does and is, echo a logically prior process of differentiation that neither causes nor results from the distinction, however unsteady and insecure, between dreaming and phantasy?

The temptation is strong here to invoke the brilliantly worked distinction between phantasy and "originary phantasy" in the work of Jean Laplanche and Jean-Bertrand Pontalis, and while this helps remind us that phantasy is more than a mental projection or construct, the "originary phantasy," even in the hands of Freud, who ties it to the "primal scene," all too quickly loses its potentially constitutive relation to sound. Precisely because Stiegler's own thinking about "cinematic consciousness" makes an essential reference to phonography—the retention of the experience of temporal duration—it seems crucial to hang on to the sonoric, but now as an element defining the structure of the *arkhé* in arche-cinema. The late Friedrich Kittler was also interested in phonography (the gramophone), of course, and for reasons that had to do with its perplexing yet radical indexicality (Rilke's "Primal Sound") linked it to the Lacanian concept of the Real. Despite the tensions that such an innovation might produce regarding the notion of phantasy—suggesting as it does that phantasy, whether originary or not, stands oddly against both the Imaginary and the Symbolic— this oddness may itself be generative when thinking about the thought of arche-cinema. If the Real, apart from the material specificities of the sonic trace, gives conceptual shape to the different but articulated limits of both the Imaginary and the Symbolic, then tying the Real to sound invites one to consider that sound is precisely *not* what is retained. It is, instead, what leaks out, or "whistles" between the limits of the Imaginary and the Symbolic as these frame the transcendental parameters of the speaking subject, of the human. Again, in this sense, sound *is* phantasy rather than its object. But might we not also say that, precisely like phantasy, sound is not sound, and what we use "sound" to designate (even, or especially, within sound studies) is an event or process we do not yet know how to know?

The dream, of course, is a conceptual designation of the locus where thought encounters what conditions it, both so-called day residues and primary processes but also the energy (what Marx in *Capital* called *Lebenskraft* [life power]) that spurs them. It retains the traces of these encounters, holding them in a cavity of suspended potential reactivation. By stressing, as he does, that the dreams to be found in Chauvet are forgotten, Herzog seems to be insisting that what appear there are signs of what is lost to signification and in *that* sense are Real. It seems crucial to hold on to the fact that in the film, in effect, an image document of arche-cinema, what arises as its limits, the inner outsides of the cave/film, is insistently figured in sounds—notably, echoing claps and heartbeats that return to the filmic present from a cavernous "before." The emphasis now being placed on sound in film studies is often countered by the observation—"But sound came later than the moving image"—but perhaps Herzog is challenging us to take seriously the odd counterfactual—namely, that perhaps moving images (Azéma's bison) were always already "preceded" by the sounds that echolocated them. Perhaps the sound film came logically, if not temporally, prior. But what if, as I have observed, sound is not sound? What goes missing in the difference between "it" and the image, between cinema and memory, under the blatant cover of the *"arkhē"*? Herein lies the crucial significance of the encounter between sound studies and film theory. We must, of course, stop forgetting sound but not primarily to give it its due. The aim is to forget it better—that is, to let it remind us of what resists being thought through the cinematically derived concept of arche-cinema and consider how it gestures toward resources of pharmacological vitality that have not yet seemed pertinent. If, as I have been arguing, this bears on the entire Deleuzian problematic, on the notion that theory can actually no longer be practiced noncinematically, then I hope you will recognize that the point, however interrogatively phrased, has more than mere disciplinary implications.

Notes

Epigraph: Werner Herzog, dir., *Cave of Forgotten Dreams*, documentary film, 2010.

1 Evens, *Sound Ideas*, 58.
2 Derrida, *Of Grammatology*, 56–57.
3 Stiegler, *Technics and Time*, 55–56.
4 Stiegler, *Technics and Time*, 63.
5 Azéma and Rivère, "Animation in Paleolithic Art," 318.
6 To adumbrate material I will take up shortly, the documentary *Ode to the Dawn of Man*, made as a companion piece to *Cave*, contains an extended sequence introduced with a title card that reads, "Reijseger has recently had a new cello constructed according to his specifications." Ernst Reijseger is the composer of the score of *Cave*, and although much of the sequence is given over to a lovely

performance of one of the repeated themes in the film, it begins with an exchange between Herzog and Reijseger that again animates the motif of the dream. Reijseger says, "It was a wish, a dream I had for a long time, to have, to play a cello with an extra low string, an extra low F." This is followed by a well-tempered demonstration of the five strings that segues almost immediately into the duet with Harmen Fraanje. Here Freud's steps are retraced in reverse, from wish to dream, but dream is now tied to a musical instrument that sounds repeatedly in *Cave*, linking two resonating cavities: that of the cello and that of the cave. Again, dream undergoes significant practical and theoretical pressure, adding further to what I am designating as Herzog's ambivalence toward it.

7   "Beat" here evokes pulse or rhythm, and it seems pertinent to acknowledge that, in "Listening," co-written by Roland Barthes and Roland Havas, prehistoric art, but now in the form of geometric patterns—specifically, evenly spaced and crossed lines—is tied to rhythm. They write, "Long before writing was invented, even before parietal figuration was practiced, something was produced which may fundamentally distinguish man from animal: the intentional reproduction of a rhythm: there have been found on cave walls of the Mousterian epoch certain rhythmic incisions—and everything suggests that these first rhythmic representations coincide with the appearance of the first human habitations": Barthes and Havas, "Listening," 248. Barthes and Havas link these habitations to what I later call, following Rosolato, "rustling houses" without developing the motif of "phantasy" as it relates to listening. A striking confirmation of the importance of such incisions was discovered in 2012 when the Gorham's Cave in Gibraltar was shown to contain geometric incisions, providing evidence, according to the BBC, to support the proposition that the Neanderthal peoples were not the "mere brutes" they had long been thought to be. "Brute," of course, evokes the animals Barthes and Havas believe cannot intentionally represent rhythm. The BBC concurs.

8   Freud, *The Origins of Psychoanalysis and the Letters to Fliess*, 197–98.

9   In the concluding chapter of *Percussion* I report on a "gig" (from my perspective, impromptu and unrehearsed) that occurred at the Petroglyph Provincial Park outside Peterborough, Ontario. Regarded as a sacred site by the Ojibwe peoples, *Kinomage-wapkong* (the rocks that teach) is more than simply petroglyphs, as these glyphs are set in rocks that reach deep into underground springs. The coursing of the water over these rocks produces a "gurgling" held to be the pedagogical voices of the spirits. I do not know whether this site has attracted "archaeo-acoustic" attention, but I can attest that it does attract drumming.

10 Rosolato, "The Voice between Body and Language," 81.

11 For a more detailed elaboration of this proposition regarding the "originary" character of the echo, adding only that "originaire" is not to be confused with "original," either in the sense of what inaugurates, or what innovates, I refer readers to the chapter titled "Echo," in Mowitt, *Sounds*, 21–39.

Listening to the Sirens

An "alarm" . . . would be rung for two minutes, consisting of a rising and falling sound. Once the threat had passed, a long even tone would be given to signal the "all clear." . . . The regulated "sonic" signals provided by alarms would mask and overrule other sounds, thus emphasizing the role of the state in intercepting attacks and alerting civilians.

—CAROLYN BIRDSALL, *Nazi Soundscapes*

Prelude: Sirens of Paris

It is January 9, 2015, around lunchtime. I have just left the flat I am staying in in the Marais district of Paris, near the Notre-Dame Cathedral. The two-tone sounds of police sirens appear to be everywhere; above and beyond them is the eerie sound of air-raid sirens. These sirens are tested on the first Monday of each month in Paris—they exist to warn the inhabitants of Paris of terrorist attacks and impending natural disaster. But today is a Wednesday, although the time of day is the correct one for a siren trial. But then there are the two-tone police sirens. The overarching air-raid sirens provide a blanket of sound into which the more localized police sirens provide ambiguous clues as to their placement.[1] The everyday sounds of the street remain overlaid by the multiple sounds of sirens. Yet cars and buses continue their noisy path through the crowded streets. Those of us on the street, perhaps unconsciously caught in a time loop, look skyward: is that not where danger is meant to come from? Others scan their smartphones for information while others go into cafés to listen to radios and inquire. None of us have been trained to respond to the sounds of air-raid sirens— to decipher their potential meaning and act on them. In his recent analysis of the sounds of the Iraq war, Martin J. Daughtry argued that "a sound's salience and emotional charge depends on the life histories of people who hear it, and on the comparative backdrop against which they listen to the sounds that are emplaced in a particular time and location."[2] The sounds of the "air-raid" sirens appear to be out of time and out of place in the bustle of Parisian daily life. I learn subsequently that the journalists of the satirical magazine *Charlie Hebdo* have been murdered by Islamic terrorists in another district of Paris; they are already dead by the time the sirens begin.

Air-raid sirens represent an ominous reminder of "total war" and impending death from the sky; a truncating of space between the victim and the increasingly sophisticated technologies of death available. Sirens represent the ideology of sonic protection against the threat of destruction. Sirens, in the main, are static constructions, as static as the subject populations who are to be attacked. The speed with which total war is visited on unsuspecting victims has accelerated from the 120 kilometers per hour of the zeppelin attacks on London in 1915 to the 474 kilometers per hour of the B-29 that dropped the first atomic bomb on Hiroshima to the 6.7 kilometers per minute of a contemporary intercontinental ballistic missile (ICBM).

In peacetime Paris, the concept of total war—of indiscriminate killing— had returned not with the sophisticated weaponry developed from World War I onward, but with the discrete, traditional Kalashnikov. The localized brutality of killing was met with a public/global sonic warning system, as the Parisian air was filled with the abstract sonic warnings of a country unknowingly at "war." By 2015, the sounds of air-raid sirens installed during World War II had lost their clarity of meaning. The city carried on largely as before, the one constant perhaps embedded in the historical traces gained from film and, for some, distant historical memory, that the air-raid sirens promised the hope of salvation coupled with the likelihood of destruction.[3]

The following pages visit these themes of the temporal disappearance of the sound of sirens and their persistence through a dialectic of functionality and failure embedded in their use, reception, and ideology.

Theme

The sound and delivery of air-raid sirens have remained largely unchanged until recently, when they have transformed into smartphone apps in Mexico, Israel, and elsewhere. Their presence was dominant in the cities of the world in World War II and subsequently in the Cold War world, where they acted as dummy runs for the apocalypse; to Vietnam in the 1960s and '70s and to the present day in the Middle East, Mexico, New Zealand, United States, and Japan, where they have most frequently morphed from the warning of a man-made apocalypse to one of the natural world—to warn populations of earthquakes, tsunamis, and typhoons.

Air-raid sirens represent, in the main, sonic instruments of the state that reinscribe the soundscape of a city—placed throughout the city—high up on the roofs of buildings or on lampposts so that all ideally can hear, with subject populations becoming part of a negative collectivity juggling fear, hope, and community.[4] Air-raid sirens represent the last line of a city's defense, dependent on a wide range and continually changing set of technologies and social practices, sonic and otherwise, that support their use, from the tracking of radar and satellite facilities to the eyes and ears of lookouts who, in World War II, would telephone the potential arrival of the enemy. In Britain, for example, the Air Raid Precautions Act of 1937 created a system of localized wardens and air-raid posts to facilitate rescue in the event of air attacks; a chain of radar stations placed primarily on the southern coasts of the United Kingdom, where aerial attacks were most likely to occur; and, at the outbreak of war, the construction of domestic and public air-raid shelters. Fred Taylor notes, "The radar chain was not perfect, and many of the crews operating the stations were not yet adequately trained. All the same, combined with the work of the Observer Corps . . . and a well-functioning telephone system that drew all information together and fed it into Fighter Command headquarters for processing and relaying to commanders of individual groups and sectors, the British defensive system was considerably more coordinated than the Germans believed."[5] Space was also divided up into air districts to monitor the movement of planes; as planes traveled, they triggered air-raid sirens as they entered each sector—either full alert or "preliminary alarms" to "all clear" after the planes had left each relevant sector. Embedded in this sonic narrative was an inherent indeterminacy of effect: were the receivers of siren sounds to be victims or observers? Were they targets or merely a staging post on the way to the destruction of others? This sonic indeterminacy led to feelings of both fear and nonchalance.

Air-raid sirens are also a byproduct of governments' attempts to command the air, the development of aviation itself, and the ability to develop bombs and missiles that could attack and destroy cities from London to Hanoi. Sirens are the state's response to their own dialectic of enlightenment.[6] They are a Fordist technology, the Muzak of human and, latterly, ecological destructiveness, primarily functioning and sounding the same wherever they are placed and, moreover, evoking similar responses, despite cultural differences represented by the cities and inhabitants of London, Coventry, Berlin, Dresden, Tokyo, and Hiroshima.[7] The subject positions and skills and fears engendered by citizens who thought they were to be bombed, their responses, and their descriptions remained largely similar in the many accounts of bombing during World War II and beyond.[8] While the sound and intensity of the air-raid siren itself has remained largely constant, that which it warns against has increased in power, speed, and destructiveness. Just as the speed of destruction has accelerated, so space shrank both horizontally and vertically during the twentieth century. The subject population of London in 1915 heard the drone of the zeppelin at ten thousand feet while an ICBM flies out of the hemisphere one thousand kilometers above ground before it comes crashing down at fifteen thousand miles an hour, rendering sirens redundant and populations defenseless. To understand air-raid sirens, it is necessary to situate them within a complex and often contradictory cultural, technological, and institutional matrix of the twentieth and twenty-first centuries.

Sirens of war are not, as I have noted, to be understood in isolation; they are to be understood as a response to the structural, political, and technological abolition and transformation of space that resulted in the negation of any notion of safety zones beyond the immediate and traditional notion of theater of war. Air-raid sirens have been largely absent in academic discourse. Sirens in their material manifestation have largely been discussed in relation to the sirens we hear in our streets daily—those of the police and ambulance services—or in terms of an urban aesthetic as they become incorporated into the sounds of the city, as in the music of Edgard Varèse, or in their role as signifying conflict within city populations, as in their frequent use in hip hop music.[9]

"Sirens" have also been interpreted as embracing both the seductive and destructive understanding of sound as embodied in Greek myth and, more generally, in subsequent moments in popular culture. This is in contrast to the more material warnings of destruction and danger embodied internationally in a whole range of sirens from World War II. These two strands of meaning are filtered through a range of ideologies embodying everything from Cold War nuclear warnings in cities around the world to those that represent the "feminine" as "Siren" in popular culture from *film noir* and beyond.[10]

Dominant in our understanding of sirens is their role in Greek myth through the Odyssey and beyond, whereby the Sirens represented the seductive yet fatal allure of song perceived intermittently to be embodied in some notion of the feminine. Theoretically, the Sirens of Greek myth became a central plank in a more generalized critique of Western culture in Max Horkheimer and Theodor Adorno's *Dialectic of Enlightenment*, which extended to Peter Sloterdijk's treatment of technology and space, in which he bemoans the industrialization of the siren from the mythical to the material:

> This choice of name plays with the insight that sirens can trigger archaic feelings among those that hear them, but it distorts this with wicked irony by associating the siren with a forced alarm. The most open form of listening was thus betrayed by terror, as if the subject were only close to its truth when running to save itself. At the same time, this renaming of the siren voice inappropriately coarsens it, instrumentalizing it for the most brutal mass signals. Sirens of this kind are the bells for the industrial and World War age. They do not mark the sonosphere in which a joyful message could spread. Their sound carries the consensus that everything is hopeless to all ears that can be reached.[11]

Despite the interest shown in the cultural, philosophical, and aesthetic nature of sirens both mythical and material, little attention has been paid to air-raid sirens, despite their periodic yet prominent role in the sonic practices, organization, and ideologies of the twentieth and twenty-first centuries.

Sonic Variations: From the Bell to the Air-Raid Siren

Friedrich Kittler famously attempted to reconstruct and re-create the meeting of Odysseus with the Sirens by placing real singers on what he thought would have been the rocks from which they "originally" sang. Unsurprisingly, the members of Kittler's crew failed to hear the sounds of the singing "Sirens" because of the environmental sounds that encircled them, adrift on the ocean—a limitation that extended to early physical sirens that were to warn sailors of danger in the nineteenth century.[12] Prior to sirens, bells had sometimes fulfilled the same function to sonically warn. R. Murray Schafer, for many the founder of sound studies, made the connection between the bell and the siren in the 1970s in terms of a perceived technologized sonic evolutionism.[13] Schafer noted that both technologies—the bell and the siren—"[radiate] energy in all directions uniformly" while having aims that differ yet overlap. For Schafer, "Sirens and church bells belong to the same class of sounds: they are community signals. As such they must be loud enough to emerge clearly out of the ambient noise of the community. But while the church bell sets a protective spell on the community, the siren speaks of disharmony from within."[14] Schafer situates his brief account of the bell and the siren within an analysis of the power of technology to transform the soundscape and subordinate the subject within a dominating sonic matrix of "industry, transportation and war, power over nature and power over other men."[15] Schafer, while perhaps lacking the dialectical acumen of Adorno and Horkheimer in their critique of the Enlightenment, nevertheless focuses on the power of the sonic in the transformation of cultural practices, assumptions, and formations in a way that is useful to the present discussion. The sound of the Sirens is an issue that Adorno and Horkheimer strangely underplay in their analysis of the Sirens.[16] Whereas Schafer listens primarily to the sirens in his analysis, Adorno and Horkheimer appear more interested in Odysseus and his narrative of control and mastery, with the sounds of the Sirens merely acting as a tool to their understanding of power, technology, and subjectivity.

Schafer took the siren to denote an internal disharmony representative of industrial culture. In this, he appears to be referring to sirens used by police forces that pierce the urban air with warning. In contrast to Schafer's sirens, air-raid sirens, like the church bell, attempted, albeit ideologically, to place a "protective spell" over their communities. Disharmony came not from within but from the outside.

The idea of sonic inclusivity and warning, articulated by the role of sirens for many inhabitants of cities in the twentieth century, is also central to Alain Corbin's study of the nineteenth-century French village bell. For Corbin, this inclusivity was defined largely geographically. The sounds of a pealing bell drawing in the lost ship in the fog of night or the mists of the forest create an enduring image of the inclusivity that sound might have, of sound drawing the subject in to safety. In Finistere, for example, the church bell rang out "to signal to sailors the precise location of the coastline in times of thick fog, which obscured the lighthouse."[17] Corbin's bells, however, are largely rural or pre-urban, although they remain in various parts of the world to call the faithful to prayer. In Corbin's analysis, the village bell was typically at the cultural and moral center of the villager's aural landscape. They were highly specific pieces of aural technology, modulated so that they could be heard anywhere in the village commune. The sounds of bells—each with its own distinctive and recognizable timbre—was the gate fencing in the local population, contributing to their sense of place and identity, separate from the rest. In their localized difference of timbre, they represented a cultural uniformity. Thus, the bell symbolized roots and identity in a world dominated by the slow rhythms of the seasons and the fixity of place. Corbin also charted the partial disintegration of the communal bell as French society urbanized and became increasingly secular. The bell no longer necessarily represented the romantic unified identity described much later by Schafer. Instead, it represented a more polarized, divisive aural sphere as sections of the population found the pealing of the bell intrusive and culturally irrelevant. The relatively fixed spaces of habitation of the village commune gave way to the mobile and transitory spaces of modernity articulated in the sociology of Émile Durkheim, Georg Simmel, and others.

However, in distinction to the historical narratives embedded in the work of Schafer and Corbin, the bell and the air-raid siren periodically coexisted and served similar social and sonic objectives. Both, ironically, were fixed: one in the church tower; the other atop city buildings. Both aimed to reach everybody in the locale, albeit in cities, not in village communities. Both aimed at, or signified, the creation of a "protective shell" over the subject community. Yet the movement of sonic warnings and their technological development from the church bell to the air-raid siren, from village to city, is a phenomenon of the twentieth century and represents a morally and technologically inflected development of a potentially fatal dialectic of power and protectiveness.

Siren Ideologies

> In World War Two, the moment the bombs, incendiaries, and phosphorus canisters came down, the civilians were on their own. Ideally, but certainly not always, they had been warned by the sirens and had moved into air-raid shelters.
>
> —HERMAN KNELL, *To Destroy a City*

This dialectic was signified in Adorno and Horkheimer's trajectory of progress famously defined in terms of the advances of destructiveness from the slingshot to the atom bomb. Twenty years after this formulation, Adorno commented, at the height of student unrest in Germany in the 1960s, that "barricades are ridiculous against those who administer the bomb."[18] Adorno's position was taken to represent an ethic of defeatism; the state apparatus, which administered the atomic bomb, was too powerful for the students to resist. However, "barricades" might be replaced with "sirens" to construct a parallel proposition that implicates not those who might wish to oppose state policy, but the state itself, which produced an ideology of sonic hope for its subject populations. Yet eschewing a simple either-or analysis in the vein of Schafer, a historically and technologically nuanced analysis can also demonstrate that, at times, like all good ideologies, they also serve to partially protect.

Air-raid sirens themselves represent a shifting political, cultural, ethical, and propagandist moment that differed in the early stages of World War II from the subsequent Cold War era. At the time Adorno made his comment, there was widespread mistrust of any viable defense against the hydrogen bomb, with governments already scaling back on forms of civil defense. Nevertheless, American citizens were subject to government campaigns to "duck and cover" in the event of nuclear attack. The U.S. government of the time had also trained a Ground Observer Corps to watch the sky, paradoxically, for enemy bombers—this at the time of the development of ICBMs. Sirens were sounded in the United States and elsewhere both as sonic practice and as sonic warning. As an American schoolboy recounted his typical monthly drill at school in the 1960s, "We attended school at St. Joseph, on the southwest corner of Willow and Palo Verde [in Long Beach, California], and that was the very siren that sent us scuttling beneath our wood-grain, Formica-shielded desk each month—a desk apparently specially formulated to withstand the force of an atomic bomb."[19] In the United Kingdom, there was a national warning grid controlled by local police forces, as Police Officer Simon Neilson rather quaintly recalls:

Sirens were activated from a central point to give members of the public warning to take cover. In every Police Station front office there was a small grey box on the wall with a receiver and small loudspeaker and on/off switch. When switched on it emitted a low peeping sound. The idea was that if there was an imminent threat of attack the device was turned on and if the beeping sound changed to a single humming note this meant you had a few minutes to take cover![20]

Government measures to conceal the true nature of an impending nuclear attack were manifold. The U.K. government, for example, banned the film *The War Game* from British television for twenty years due to its dystopian and realistic representation of atomic war, while paradoxically the Hollywood blockbuster film *On the Beach* (1959), which showed the aftermath of a nuclear war as destroying all human life, was shown in cinemas in both the United States and Britain.

Yet the portrayal of the results of nuclear devastation differed dramatically in these two films. *The War Game* portrayed brutally graphic scenes of devastation and government collapse in a manner that lay bare the absence of political discussion concerning atomic warfare at the time. *On the Beach,* by contrast, while somewhat downbeat as a film, never showed the close-up physical disintegration and destruction wrought by atomic bombs, instead focusing on fully intact cities devoid of humans who had been silently killed by radiation. A review published in the *New York Times* in 1959 pointed to the humanity of the film's portrayal of human extermination: "Yet the basic theme of this drama and its major concern is life, the wondrous thing that man's own vast knowledge and ultimate folly seem about to destroy. And everything done by the characters, every thought they utter and move they make indicates their fervor, tenacity and courage in the face of doom."[21] The U.K. government at this time had already estimated that there would be only a four- minute warning for the arrival of incoming ICBMs, and the results would be devastating.[22] Nevertheless, sirens continued to be sounded around the world until the end of the Cold War in 1992 and beyond.

Air-Raid Sirens and Sonic Doubt

While air-raid sirens had warned those in cities to seek shelter, in air-raid shelters, bunkers, basements, and tube stations with some success during the early parts of World War II in Europe, they became less successful as the war continued and more cities were subject to intense bombing. The scale of attacks also rendered the sounding of alarms problematic as wave after wave of bombers might bomb a city such as Hamburg for several days. "In the confusion of the evening, the air raid alarms had been set off at 9:30 p.m., followed by the all clear at 10, and then set off again at 12:33," Taylor writes. "The Hamburg police logged their 319th air raid alarm of the war at 12:51 a.m."[23] The intended clarity of the air-raid signal was rendered increasingly impossible in the continued carpet bombing of cities such as Dresden, Hamburg, and Tokyo. As the war progressed, incendiary bombs were increasingly used because pound for pound they created more devastation than normal explosives, spreading fire and destruction well beyond where they fell. This hyper-destructiveness was demonstrated in the bombing of Hamburg on July 25, 1945, when eight hundred U.S. B-17 Flying Fortresses dropped a mixture of incendiary and explosive bombs on the city, followed by British bombers some hours later. The multiple sounds of the air-raid sirens and bombs in Hamburg were replaced with the sounds of a "firestorm":

> Then the Hamburg citizens heard a shrill howling in the streets. The howling was something that had never before been recorded. The Germans named it *Feuersturm* or firestorm. Within 15 minutes of the attack, most fires were blazing unchecked. As the fires linked and grew, they needed more and more air. Temperatures reached 1,400 degrees as the fire began to suck all the air out of the city. The firestorm spread over a 4-square mile area and hit 16,000 apartment block frontages totaling 133 miles. . . . Beneath these buildings were air raid shelters, where many people died either from heat or asphyxiation.[24]

These scenes of devastation were replicated over many German and Japanese cities, with air-raid sirens frequently giving confused warnings as wave after wave of bombers flew over confusing lookouts and radar systems before the sirens themselves became silenced in the destruction. "I will never forget this raid," wrote Herman Knell. "I was in the city when it started. No alarm could be heard, because there were no more sirens. The chatter of machine guns and the howl of descending bombs told me unmistakably what was about to happen. . . . [Later] I could hear a mobile siren (mounted on a car) sound the 'all clear' in the distance."[25] Adorno frequently referred to the destruction wrought on Hiroshima by the dropping of the atomic bomb in his postwar writings. The sirens sounded when three planes, one of which was the *Enola Gay*, which carried the atomic bomb, were seen in the sky, followed by the all clear given moments before the blast that killed the inhabitants of Hiroshima in the blink of an eyelid. The sounding of the air-raid sirens would have made no difference either way. The power of the bomb rendered the air-raid siren obsolete.

Sonic Training, Routinization, and the Air-Raid Siren

> For most, the predominant experience of sirens was marked by the need to move swiftly; the hurried activity of waking and dressing (if sleeping), taking a suitcase and supplies to the cellar or running outside to a public shelter. A common experience was also that of waiting and listening in anticipation to determine whether an attack would occur. The sirens not only masked and even replaced other sounds in the urban environment, but were often accompanied by a silence due to the cessation of usual daily sounds. —CAROLYN BIRDSALL, *Nazi Soundscapes*

> Expecting the alarm was worse than the alarm itself, because at least during a raid one had something to do, bags to pack. I slept partly on my back so my right ear was completely free. Even in my sleep I always had a sense of listening. . . . One was in a constant state of anticipation, at the early warning signal my whole body was already trembling. —JÖRG FRIEDRICH, *The Fire*

Air-raid sirens demanded a training of the sensibilities. Responses to air-raid sirens were individual, collective, and institutional: subject populations learned how to listen not just to interpret the meaning of the air-raid sirens, but also for the sounds of aircraft and direction of exploding shells. City dwellers learned how to wait, experiencing time in new ways—for example, estimating the length of time it takes to run to the nearest air-raid shelter. Daily life was reorganized with the feelings of fear, expectation, and resignation incorporated into the everyday. When Anna Freud questioned young children in London during the Blitz in World War II, many said that it was the noise of the air-raid sirens that instilled fear in them, not the bombing. For adults, it was frequently both.

Fear of death from the sky predated the air-raid siren with the first bombings over London conducted by zeppelins and Gotha bombers in 1915 and 1916. Subject populations for the first time had to train themselves to listen for impending death from the air. Setting the template for subsequent descriptions throughout the century, Maggie Turner, a nurse at Great Ormond Street Hospital for children, described the experience of being bombed in 1916:

Never in my life will I forget last night. . . . I fell asleep in a few moments only to wake up to hear the most awful noise. . . . [I] felt the whole of my room shake, things falling down all over the place, screams from nurses flying down the stairs and passages, saying quickly "Nurses the Zeppelins are here!" . . . The gas and the smell of the bombs exploding was awful, one after the other—the noise and darkness was too terrible.[26]

If the raid was conducted at night, listening was paramount; in the day, it was possible to look into the distance and still respond. But increasingly in the twentieth century, as the speed of flight increased, waiting to see already made one's response too late. "Danger was recognized by sounds," writes Jörg Friedrich. "Once you could see something, it was too late to act. Shells and bombs were not visible, but they could be felt. People listened into the void to hear what was coming. When it was there, the sense of hearing was the first thing to shut down."[27] Training civilians in the art of listening for the sounds of war was treated with skepticism by the British government in World War I. This reticence among the political elite delayed the introduction of air-raid sirens at the time. The *Daily Telegraph* reported on and supported the government's position on not giving subject populations warning of impending attacks:

The authorities say, in effect: "If we raise the alarm all over the town when a Zeppelin is approaching, thousands of people will crowd into the streets, and if a bomb drops amongst them many hundreds will be killed and injured. These foolish people will not look after themselves by taking our advice to keep under cover, therefore we must protect them against themselves by not letting them know when the danger is approaching." That, in very broad terms, is the line taken by those who are responsible for the safety of the public on the occasion of these attacks from the air.[28]

The government's resistance to providing public warning systems in the event of air raids was supported by employers who thought that alarms would disrupt the work process and make it more difficult to control their workers. After further air raids on London, the mood of both government and the public changed. The *Times* reported that theaters, concert and music halls, and other places of "public assembly" would receive telephone warnings of future raids as early as possible, as would tramway authorities; rail and omnibus services would continue uninterrupted "for public safety and convenience."[29]

Yet as Carolyn Birdsall and others have noted, despite extensive air-raid drills, training, and the provision of air-raid shelters across the United Kingdom, Germany, and elsewhere, when it came to being attacked, the public response was by no means uniform. With the falling of bombs, people often lost their orientation due to fear and a sensory overload that was previously unimaginable among civilians.

Yet even in World War II, civilians frequently came to see warnings via air-raid sirens as unreliable and paid little attention to them. For cities on flight paths that took bombers elsewhere to drop their deadly cargo—but that nevertheless were subjected to sonic warning—a blasé attitude was the frequent result.

This blasé attitude increased during the Cold War as sirens became both routinized and increasingly irrelevant to subject populations who increasingly believed either that the sonic warnings were merely "drills" or that, even if a bombing was imminent, it would result in destruction anyway. The sonic shock of war increasingly became a hypothetical shock maintained by propagandist messages and activities engendered by governments. As Tracy Davis writes,

> When the Chicago White Sox baseball team won the 1959 American league pennant at a game in Cleveland, Chicago's fire commissioner authorized the ringing of bells and sounding of air raid sirens in celebration. Two thirds of Chicagoans—unsure of whether this was carnival or catastrophe—turned on their radios, the same number looked out onto the street, some discussed the situation with others, and a few phoned public agencies to find out what was going on. But among the half million households within reach of the sirens, almost none (only 2 percent) took protective action. Researchers concluded that even those who were frightened enough to want to take action did not do so because "there is no action known to them that is worth taking."[30]

Today, air-raid sirens are used largely as warnings against natural disaster or, indeed, have been decommissioned and replaced with more precise and privatized sonic technologies that warn subjects. Sirens continue to be used in Japan, Mexico, New Zealand, and parts of the United States to warn inhabitants about potential natural disasters. They remain imprecise, however, as subject to false alarm as were air-raid alarms in wartime. In Downers Grove, Chicago, tornado sirens failed to go off during a tornado that hit the town, despite the testing of the sirens each month. In Mexico City, residents complain about "alert fatigue" because the eight thousand street sirens meant to warn the residents of an impending earthquake wail at the slightest tremor. The system of sirens was installed after an earthquake in 1985 killed more than twelve thousand people in Mexico City. Earthquakes normally occur in the north of the country, giving residents two minutes of warning before a tremor. As one resident complained, "When you hear the alarm you get scared because of how loud it is. Then nothing happens, and you are left unnecessarily panicked." Another resident said she chose to ignore the sirens unless she physically felt a tremor—that is, the sense of hearing being replaced by touch.[31] Meanwhile, a loudspeaker system installed in Vietnam during the war in the 1960s and 70s to warn inhabitants of aerial attack now delivers messages from local authorities—a form of peacetime Orwellian sonic ubiquity delivered by the state.[32]

Coda: Sirens, Change, Persistence, and Ideology

> One cannot dismiss the thought that the invention of the atomic bomb, which can obliterate hundreds of thousands of people literally in one blow, belongs to the same historical context as genocide. —THEODOR ADORNO, *Critical Models*

No sirens were sounded for the European Jews of Paris, Berlin, Hamburg, and other European cities during World War II. The sirens, while sounded for the home populations, were not for them; there was to be no protection, sonic or otherwise, from the countries within which they lived. For the Jews, death would come to the strains of "Rosamunde," a popular song played to the inmates of Auschwitz and Majdanek as they were killed.[33] The myth of unified subject collectivities based on physical spaces articulated in the work of Schafer, Corbin, and others was laid bare at the very time in which states were proclaiming it.

Paradoxically, Israel today is awash with air-raid sirens that perform a dual role: one is traditional, warning its inhabitants of incoming missiles; the other is a mode of "collective commemoration" within the Israeli state. Sirens are sounded throughout Israel on three days each year: Holocaust Memorial Day, the Memorial Day for Fallen Soldiers, and Independence Day, when many Israelis pay their respects in silence as the sirens wail. Contemporary Israel appears to hark back to the sonic unity embodied in

Alain Corbin's bells of the nineteenth century, out of yet in time, with the same ideology of collective unity that fails to name the excluded within its borders. During these three days, the Israeli media focus almost exclusively on the national cultural significance of the day. As Danny Kaplan writes, "In this sense, the radio broadcast disseminates and magnifies the quality of 'selfless unisonance,' as experienced, for instance, by the audience singing the anthem during national ceremonies, and in the Israeli case is especially apparent in the piercing, awe-inspiring unisonance of the sirens. The majority who choose not to participate in the ceremonies and carry on with their daily lives nevertheless encounter the uniform memorial music wherever they go and are thus exposed to the same commemorative mode and mood nonetheless."[34]

And sirens are sounded in the traditional mode to warn of imminent attack via rudimentary missiles fired from Palestine—hence, returning to a pre-nuclear period in which the air-raid siren could still have some legitimacy as a sonic warning system. Israelis have between fifteen and ninety seconds of warning to move into their air-raid shelters, depending on where they live in relation to the Palestinian border. The government system of public sonic warning is supplemented by the development of a range of mobile apps—a privatization of the air-raid siren that exists in parallel to the official public system. One such app, Red Alert, became Israel's most popular download during the bombing campaign of 2012, with some users such as Israela Natan, 38, claiming, "It just gives [you] that extra bit of information that makes [you] feel like [you're] still in control."[35] This is similar to the response of traditional iPod users when they discuss the power of privatized music to influence their feelings of well-being.[36] These mobile apps produced conflicting responses among users that ranged from feelings of anxiety and inattention to feelings of security—the constant yet private response to sonic warnings in the twentieth and twenty-first centuries made so graphically public in the streets of Paris on January 9, 2015.

The paradox of siren warnings, both publicly and privately, was most recently experienced in northern Japan on the morning of August 29, 2017, when North Korea launched a ballistic missile over the Japanese landmass. The Japanese population was awakened both by text messages sent to users' phones and by publicly placed sirens followed by public announcement messages informing inhabitants to take safe cover. The lack of public response to this directive may be indicative of the redundant persistence of the ideology of hope embodied in the siren call for those whose history embodied the atomic destruction of Hiroshima and Nagasaki.

....

Notes

My use of the musical term "prelude" in the opening section of this chapter is in keeping with the practice of using musical metaphors for technologies and processes of death. The firebombing of Coventry that destroyed the city, killing thousands of people, was called Operation Moonlight Sonata by the German High Command, primarily because of the need for a full moon (but "sonata" nevertheless). The U.K. radar system in World War II that enabled bombers to accurately find their targets over German cities was called Oboe, primarily because the signaling device sounded like an oboe. During the Cold War in Britain, the system devised to warn the public of imminent attack was called Handel, after the baroque composer.

Epigraphs: Birdsall, *Nazi Soundscapes*, 120; Knell, *To Destroy a City*, 176; Birdsall, *Nazi Soundscapes*, 123; Friedrich, *The Fire*, 414; Adorno, *Critical Models*, 192.

1 Max Neuhaus has commented on the problems of locating the whereabouts of police sirens, writing, "It turns out these sounds have many problems, the major one being that they are almost impossible to locate. Universally people say that they cannot tell where a siren sound is coming from until it is upon them. Unable to find the sound and becoming more nervous by its approach, many drivers simply stop and block traffic until they figure out what to do. Others ignore the sound until they are directly confronted by the vehicle, sometimes with lethal results": Max Neuhaus, "Sirens," revised 1993, accessed February 14, 2016, http://www.max-neuhaus.info /soundworks/vectors/invention/sirens/Sirens.pdf.

2 Daughtry, *Listening to War*, 38.

3 Edouard Renière remembers what air raids in Brussels during World War II sounded like and how his memories of this become rekindled. He writes, "At first, it had been like some sort of annoying ritual to have to get down to the cellar, but after a while I realized this was a reaction to a very real danger of having the whole building falling on our heads. . . . It took me several years after the war to get out of the habit, when planes were overhead, of ducking and looking for a nearby shelter. Sirens are sounded for checks every first Thursday of the month at noon and even now, more than sixty years later, I still can't suppress the millisecond burst of some deep-planted feeling of fear": Edouard Renière, "A Young Boy and the '*Good*' War," revised March 2016, accessed June 16, 2016, https://wwii-netherlands-escape-lines .com/personal-narratives/a-young-boy-and-the-good-war-2.

4 See Birdsall, *Nazi Soundscapes*.

5 Taylor, *Coventry*, 52.

6 See Horkheimer and Adorno, *Dialectic of Enlightenment*.

7 Barrington Moore Jr. argued that human misery was a more uniform category than the diversity of human happiness, which appears to be confirmed in subject responses to the threat of death from the air: see Moore, *Reflection on the Causes of Human Misery*.

8 See Daughtry, *Listening to War*.

9 See Osborne, "Alarms on Record."

10 See Fleeger, *Mismatched Women*; Levy, *Sirens of the Western Shore*; Miklitsch, *Siren City*; Peraino, *Listening to the Sirens*.

11 Sloterdijk, *Spheres, Volume 1*, 500.

12 "Environmental conditions could thwart even loud sirens in the nineteenth century, so that neither foghorns nor Joseph Hersey's 'very large steam siren' nor eight huge megaphones, seventeen feet long with mouths seven feet wide, broadcasting the shrill of a steam whistle to all points of the compass could be affectively heard under foul conditions": Schwartz, *Making Noise*, 509. Sound is not a constant when filtered through environmental conditions; direction and distance confuse.

13 Schafer's analysis of sound has been interpreted as largely anti-industrial, with its focus on notions of schizophonia. He negatively interprets the transposing of sounds out of their "natural" habitats negatively, thereby consigning urban sounds to the dustbin of academic debate. The present analysis attempts a more nuanced use of Schafer.

14 Schafer, *The Soundscape*, 178.

15 Schafer, *The Soundscape*, 179.

16 Adriana Cavarero has argued that Adorno and Horkheimer are ahistorical in their analysis of Odysseus as representing the first "bourgeois" mentality: Cavarero, *For More than One Voice*. In earlier work, I have argued that, through their focus on the relationship between Odysseus and his rowers as representing the archetypal bourgeois/working-class dynamic, they underplayed the sonic dimension of Odysseus's encounter with the Sirens as representing the first act of sonic privatization. Through the blocking of the oarsmen's ears with wax, Odysseus creates an environment whereby the sound of the Sirens exists only between himself and the Sirens to the exclusion of the ship's crew. See Bull, *Sounding Out the City*.

17 Corbin, *Village Bells*, 101.

18 Adorno, *Critical Models*, 269.

19 See "News 101: When a Story Is 'News,'" *Whittier Daily News*, May 7, 2013, http://www.whittierdailynews.com/article/ZZ/20110220/NEWS/110229161.

20 International Centre for the History of Crime, Policing and Justice, Open University, "Part 4: A Policing Revolution, 1976–1992," n.d., http://www.open.ac.uk/Arts/history-from-police-archives/RB1/Pt4/pt4Hurricane87.html.

21 See Bosley Crowther, "Screen: 'On the Beach,'" *New York Times*, December 18, 1959, http://www.nytimes.com/movie/review?res=9F01E3D8103CE63BBC4052DFB4678382649EDE.

22 A ten megaton bomb was estimated to create complete devastation within a two to three square mile radius, making all housing uninhabitable for six square miles, with houses being set on fire for a fifteen-mile radius and radioactive fallout extending far beyond this area: Hennessy, *The Secret State*, 173.

23 Taylor, *Coventry*, 3.

24 Taylor, *Coventry*, 7.

25 Knell, *To Destroy a City*, 47–48.

26 Quoted in Grayzel, *At Home and under Fire*, 40.

27 Friedrich, *The Fire*, 439–40.

28 *Daily Telegraph*, February 12, 1916.

29 Grayzel, *At Home and under Fire*, 61.

30 Davis, *Stages of Emergency*, 33.

31 See Gabriela Gorbea, "Alert Fatigue? Mexico City Residents Bombarded with Earthquake Warning," October 2, 2015, https://news.vice.com/article/alert-fatigue-mexico-city-residents-bombarded-with-earthquake-warnings.

32 See Grant McCool, "Old-Style Communist Speakers Blare in Vietnam's New Era," January 19, 2007, http://www.reuters.com/article/us-apec-vietnam-speakers-idUSSP204282200611l0.

33 See Levi, *If This Is a Man/The Truce*.

34 Kaplan, "The Songs of the Siren," 325.

35 Itay Hod, "The Israeli App Red Alert Saves Lives—But It Just Might Drive You Nuts," *The Daily Beast*, July 14, 2014, https://www.thedailybeast.com/the-israeli-app-red-alert-saves-livesbut-it-just-might-drive-you-nuts.

36 See Bull, *Sound Moves*.

Entities Inertias Faint Beings

Drawing as Sounding

To draw is to make marks, and to draft is provisionality in the act of drawing, but then drawing on is not so distant from drawing down and drawing out, or the draughtsman who may draw water, drink a draught of it sitting in a draught, only illustrating the strangely slippery precision of the English language in relation to objects and actions, the firm and the soft.

Beyond linguistics, my question is whether a drawing can be a musical instrument (the defining of that heavily weighted term, "musical instrument," will have to wait a while, or perhaps forever), and what now strikes me as a rather shocking lack of personal insight is the obvious path from one line of research into another line of practice. My book *Sinister Resonance: The Mediumship of the Listener* put forward the idea that a putatively silent medium such as painting could be "heard" as a carrier of sound, and hence be regarded as a musical instrument. In a time prior to the existence of audio recording—the seventeenth century, for example—the impulse to archive intangible and transient phenomena was served through a medium developed to represent through illusion tangible objects alongside those states of flux taken

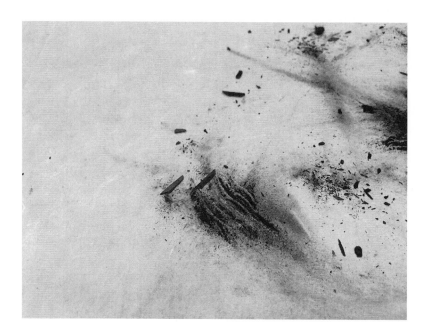

FIG 13.1 David Toop, performance drawing, charcoal, 2015.

for granted as fit subjects for an artist: movement, presence, air, depth, tactility, dimensionality, the sensorium, human feeling, psychological attributes, the gaze, and so on.

The fulcrum of my book was a series of paintings by the Dutch artist Nicolaes Maes, a pupil of Rembrandt whose early artistic career was remarkable for its success in representing the act of listening. Stretching the already expansive field of experimental organology in which the question gravitates toward not what *is* but what *is not* an instrument, I began to think of paintings as musical instruments—not all paintings, but those in which the artist showed evidence of sensitivity to listening practice or the phenomenology of sound. This was a matter of passing from one category to another, a fluidity overlapping in my mind with other crossings—for example, that permeability of the barrier between human animals and extra-human entities (often articulated by sound, as in the acquisition of animal languages by shamanic practitioners) or between animate and inanimate objects—hence, my question of whether a drawing could be a musical instrument, appended by a further question: can a soundless drawing be a sound?

During a week of solitude in August 2015, gazing at the ocean, attempting and failing to write, taking photographs with my iPhone, attempting to draw with some small success, and reading (or, at least, considering the covers) of books that included Timothy Morton's *Hyperobjects*, Tim Ingold's *Lines: A Brief History*, and Clarice Lispector's *Agua Viva*, I found myself assembling the material for a new record that came to be called *Entities Inertias Faint Beings*. Equipped only with a laptop and headphones I discovered an archive of existing material on my hard drive, all of it stoppered by a loss of faith in the purpose of releasing music to the public in the twenty-first century. My state of mind unlocked this archival material, allowing it to mingle, form into beings, come alive, a process articulated by two texts written concurrently.

One was a set of propositions:

Sound has a life; sound has a death.

Entities are the living beings given birth out of sound.

Inertias are the static or resistant points at which no entity seems to be present, for example, a silent object which is an unyielding presence.

Faint Beings are entities without credibility, a sound object denied life, lacking in properties that denote the status of objective reality, such as visibility or tactility.

The other text seemed an attempt to illuminate this process of making with sound and what it means to me in relation to the entity I call "myself," the entities that we call music and the hyperobjects of the world (none of these phenomena separated, strictly bounded, inside or outside one another):

[During the isolation period] my thoughts were sticky with beings that rose faint but unbidden, forming and unforming themselves into entities that mocked notions of substance or matter. They possessed a kind of inertia, then they were gone, yet their presence remained as a being folded in upon itself, a tremor of silence, perhaps, but somehow under the skin. In this situation it was impossible to maintain the integrity of the body, filled as it was with creatures not of itself and unable to excrete them. The body degraded every day, decomposing in its own sight, so there was some comfort in knowing that these entities were becoming the body, would live on even after death, so there would be no death, only a change of state.

FIG 13.2 Radio, Leach Pottery, St Ives, Cornwall, 2015. Photo by David Toop.

frustrated desire

This isolation period took place in St Ives, Cornwall. For reasons of personal history I was drawn to the sea, the landscape, the light and the Leach Pottery—to its dusty white museum of clay-spattered silent objects, their powerful intimations of intimacy, the hand, fluidity becoming solidity.

My acquaintance in the early 1970s with Bernard and Janet Leach came back to me, the memory of being in this place when its founders still lived and worked. This was dangerous, seductive territory, particularly the orientalism of Cornwall, which continues to draw me there. There was, for example, the friendship between Bernard Leach and Mark Tobey, who taught drawing at Dartington Hall in Devon and traveled by boat with Leach to Japan in 1934. Leach wrote about Tobey's fascination with signs and Chinese characters in Hong Kong (Leach's birthplace): "Mark's first paintings which became famous as 'white writing' were a further abstraction from this Chinese calligraphy, and when his 'white writing' became too famous he changed it to 'black writing'—black on white. We drew and we drew."

I was acutely aware of my attraction to this era and the quasi-calligraphic work of artists such as Tobey, Robert Motherwell, Franz Kline, and Henri Michaux. "Cracks, claw marks: the very beginnings appear to have been suddenly checked: arrested," wrote Michaux in *Ideograms In China*; also "any surface covered with characters turns into something crammed and seething." Crammed and seething could be descriptive of the music I had made in Cornwall. Michaux, in particular, fascinated me. He spoke about improvising music, activating surfaces for hours in an obsessive dwelling on the fluctuations of sound, and his drawings seemed both an embodiment of sounds and a mysterious writing whose meaning lay just out of reach.

Perhaps Michaux and his private experiments with musical improvisation were equivalent to my private experiments with drawing.

Pen and paper began to disappear from my life in 1987, when I bought a computer, when the acts of writing and making music began to converge within the same device. The problem persisted, however, fermenting within desire, a stubborn desire to draw whose foundation appeared to lie in physical motions of hand/body and their transference to a substrate in the form of a persistent mark. This was clearly distinct from the act of making sound, which in a given case might be described as physical motions of hand/body and their invisible transference to a substrate (a volume of air) in the form of a *fugitive* mark (vibration). More personal history was bound up in this. In my teens I drew constantly, attended art school, dropped out of art schools, took the path of musician. Gradually my skills in drawing atrophied and were forgotten, only lingering as an obsession with the materials of drawing.

Occasionally I would draw something, only to recoil with disappointment and destroy the results. There were glimmers, like the light of an eye opening once more after years of subservience to the ear. In old notebooks I find lists, methods of making sound that suggest, in their own way, inscriptions, the methodologies and materials of potential drawings. Preparing to record my *Spirit World* album of 1997, I made a list that included flashbulb, small fires, bamboo pyrophones, friction, hot metal into water, cracking ice, pouring sand, crackling neon, chemical reactions, leaves, seed pods, gas jets, blowtorches, flour, snail shells, and welding. Then in 2003, the making of a track called "Bandaged Moments" for the collaborative album with Max Eastley, *Doll Creature*, the sole indication was "broken wood." I cut bamboo from my Japanese garden, snapped and splintered it close to a microphone.

sculpture

In 2013 I began a collaboration with the artist Rie Nakajima, a conversation of practice in the broadest sense that has enabled a "soaking through" of action into non-action, intangibility into object. We began our collaborations with a performance format called Sculpture, a term originally inspired by the Singing Sculpture of Gilbert and George, the Social Sculpture concept of Joseph Beuys, the noit sculptures and one-second drawings of John Latham (Least Event as a Habit, 1970, for example, two sealed glass spheres in which there is noit, or no it).

Sculpture is a format of continuous performances in which invited participants are asked to choose beforehand a duration for their "sculpture," Sculpture being a unifying term we applied to any activity in any medium presented to an audience as performance (for example, the first Sculpture event presented an actual sculpture by Max Eastley, an air-and-water sculpture operated by Nakajima). The consistent factor in each Sculpture event was a sculpture created by myself and Rie, a situation that accelerated the development of our mutual concerns. To some degree liberated from musical or other performance modes by this framing of Sculpture, we discussed many possibilities—drawing, flowers and ikebana among them. Any hard sense of separate identities or practices quickly softened.

Methodologies and technologies were shared or overlapped in ways both informal and natural. For a performance in Athens in 2016, we began to use small LED lights in Japanese lanterns, crumpled tissue paper and baking foil. For a Sculpture performance at Fundação de Serralves, Porto, in 2016, we made a mutual drawing using graphite, a snooker ball and other indeterminate "active agents." Before this, we had made drawings at my home, working quickly and simultaneously on carbon paper, Rie marking the white paper beneath the substrate of the carbon with her battery-operated vibration motors; me writing directly on the carbon. The sound of these drawings being made was quiet, frantic drumming.

Clear precedents exist for action drawing and action painting, not that we were mindful of them at the time. Along with John Latham's one-second drawings, produced with a spray gun, there were the Japanese artists associated with the Gutai group: Atsuko Tanaka, who considered her sound installation Bell (1955) to be a painting, its activators dramatically positioned in relation to space articulated by the ephemerality and intangibility of sound; Akira Kanayama's Remote-Controlled Painting Machine (1957); Kazuo Shiraga's Ultra-Modern Sanbaso (1957), a "painting" moving through time and space and incorporating the sound of poles striking the ground. Similar tactics were shared by Yasunao Tone, associated with Group Ongaku and Fluxus. "The work is always unfinished," he wrote in 1970, "fostering the idea that it is equivalent to the everyday, to real objects and daily activities. Thus it's not at all strange that every concrete object or ordinary action suffices as a painting."

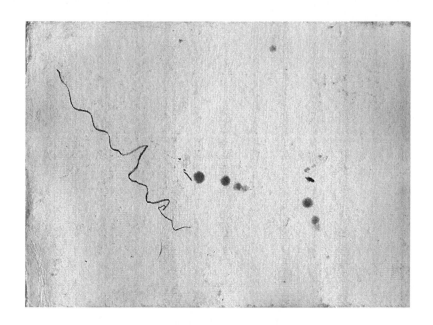

FIG 13.3 Rie Nakajima and David Toop, sculpture drawing, Porto, Portugal, 2015.

Of course, there was Jackson Pollock. According to Ming Tiampo (author of *Gutai: Decentering Modernism*), Jirō Yoshihara, the artist at the center of Gutai, wrote that Pollock's work "reveals the scream of the material itself, cries of the paint and enamel." Pollock was alert to this trans-sensory potential. Partially influenced by the Navajo sandpainting he had seen demonstrated at the Museum of Modern Art in New York in 1941, he created a series of seven paintings in 1946 called "Sounds in the Grass," canvas laid flat as if a three-dimensional field in which marks could be heard.

But this historical archive was irrelevant when it came to the making of drawings in a performance site. I asked Rie for her memory of how it came about:

"I think we talked about how we both didn't like our own drawings—it was quite similar, I remember."

"We didn't like our intentions, didn't like to see what we think through lines and compositions—maybe it's because they don't disappear as sound. (Maybe we are so stubborn too!) For me if the drawings (lines) are more ephemeral and close to the moments of appearing and disappearing, I feel more comfortable to produce."

"When I did the drawing with motors the first time, I felt sound for line, line for movement, movement for sound, all nicely collaborating. There is also the sense of duration in the drawings. It's about nothing or something else."

appearing-disappearing

This was not a question of wanting to make sound objects tangible, in the sense that they become visible (as in certain forms of sound art), or even of giving an auditory dimension to lines or marks, but of wanting to close the gap between tangible and intangible. Other, less familiar historical precedents come to light in François Jullien's book *The Great Image Has No Form, or On the Nonobject through Painting*. Describing his object ("on principle it is pointless to pursue what cannot be conceived") as the nonobject ("[that which] is too hazy-indistinct-diffuse-evanescent-con-fused to keep still and isolated"), Jullien describes a search in Chinese painting for the indistinctness of the appearing-disappearing. The somewhat philosophical answer to this problem was "inkless ink" and "brushless brush." "Let us be clear," writes Jullien, "it is not that they completely gave up the ink and brush but that they used a wash so diluted, so close to the dry-pale end of the spectrum, that it approximates the white of the paper. It is so dim that it fades away altogether. Hence the painter pictures while de-picting: in using that 'inkless ink' and that 'brushless brush', that ink grown pale and that barely-painting brush, he paints between form and without-form and renders the evanescence of the foundational."

digital manipulation

The paradoxical nature of this appearing-disappearing, something or nothing, opened out a philosophical aspect of what was in progress anyway through practice: the project of reconciling writing (words) with sound (without words). At a certain point, maybe 2005, I began to use paper as a drum amplified by small custom-made microphones and contact microphones, often drawing on the amplified paper. I also used drums for similar purposes, the skin of the drum being an equivalent substrate.

The small microphones encouraged production of many small, detailed sounds—at first dry foliage, leaves, and twigs; then crumpled cellophane

FIG 13.4 David Toop, hands in performance with crumpled cellophane, Cork, Ireland, 2010. Photo courtesy of Robin Parmar.

FIG 13.5 David Toop, horsetail, 2015.

squashed tight and allowed to expand. The two activities converged: I drew on paper (with and without ink) using black bamboo and dried stems of *Equisetum hyemale* (also known as horsetail or scouring rush), cut from my garden.

This writing, drawing, crackling and crumpling remained as creases, distressed materials (not entirely discarded) or faint marks, cumulative traces that could be construed as sound inscribed on the substrate, inaudible but possessed of the duration to which Rie Nakajima refers. Unlike the sound arising out of their stridulation and compression, their presence lingered as one element in a cluster of objects, all of them sound.

the question of the instrument

In the present case I am loath to quote from academic works for fear this will be taken as supporting evidence for a proposition that is entirely personal and speculative. Yet I was struck by a section of Julia Kelly's *Art, Ethnography and the Life of Objects: Paris, c. 1925–35*. Kelly's introduction begins with a consideration of André Breton's adjectival hybrid "magical circumstantial" and its place within what she calls "a complex of ideas and associations that [Breton] dubbed 'convulsive beauty.'" This denoted the arousal of distinct physical sensations, "marked by a temporal dynamic of the just-passed, of an ungraspable and unfixable lost moment." Circumstantial magic is, she concludes, "by nature slippery, potentially fragmentary or tangential, often fraught, but always compelling."

Within her consideration of ethnographic objects and their relationship to art, she mentions in passing the musicologist André Schaeffner's account of musical instruments held in the collection of the Paris Trocadéro (1929): "At the same time as dealing with increasingly prized objects . . . Schaeffner was also concerned with the least conservable of musical instruments: an Abyssinian 'earth drum' consisting of two holes in the ground of differing heights. This instrument could only be captured photographically, and indeed was virtually illegible in the dark photograph by Griaule published alongside the article, where only the position of the player's hands and arms gave any indication of its existence."

Having spent a lifetime collecting evidence of instruments such as this—resistant to collection, conservation or documentation—and having worked with "non-instruments" since my teenage years, I was intrigued by the appearance of the illegible earth drum, like a probe of anti-light boring its hole into an otherwise clear exposition. My question returns to the boundaries of the instrument. As a young teenager learning to play the guitar I used a solution of alum to harden my fingertips. Was the alum an extension of the guitar? Instrumentalists like myself now perform with a complex kit of what appears, under interrogation by customs officials in airports, to be an outlandish, highly suspicious collection of accessories: sticks, leaves and other foliage, stones, balloons, vibration motors, crocodile clips, battery-operated fans, toothpicks, metal rods, paper of various sizes, LED lights and so on. Are these (asking the question also of the bow of a violin or a guitarist's plectrum) instruments in their own right?

An extreme example can be found in my record collection, an LP entitled *Gabon: Musiques des Mitsogho et des Batéké*, released on the Ocora Collection Musée de l'Homme, probably in the early 1970s. The track of which I am thinking is "Voice of the Ya Mwèï (Mother of the Floods)." Mwèï is a "muddy monster" and corpse eater who maintains order with the threat of swallowing anybody who transgresses the social order. In Pierre Sallée's recordings, made in 1968, Mwèï is represented by a masked voice, described in the album's notes as "a kind of raucous tiger's roar uttered in a throaty voice by a hidden person whose pharynx has been irritated ahead of time by the consumption of a brew made of the leaves of a tiliacea." Again the question: is the inflammatory brew as much a part of the (mythological) instrument as the pharynx that roars out of sight of initiates?

magnification

Having bought large sheets of Korean paper during a trip to Seoul and yet having failed to pluck up the courage to draw on them, I began to use them in performance. In particular, at the end of a lengthy trio performance with Akio Suzuki and Aki Onda in Hong Kong in 2014, we had reached a point of silence in which the only possible transition to an ending was through instruments that made no sound. Movement was created—a draft—by slowly flapping the paper through the air, an inference of sound that could be described as amplified listening without a tangible object.

In 2015 I began drawing using a magnifying glass as an accessory (the magnifying glass once used by my mother for small print when her sight deteriorated), leaning in close to the paper and drawing with pen or pencil only in the area magnified by the lens. This attempt to circumvent failures of intention by limiting the visual field shares an intimate relation with

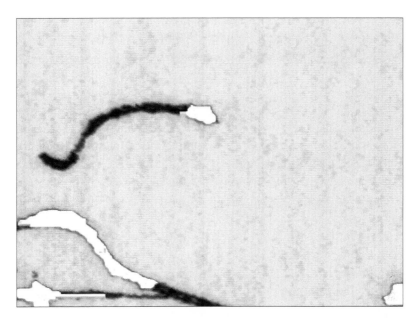

FIG 13.6 David Toop, entities, digital ink drawing, 2015.

FIG 13.7 David Toop, hammer drawing, 2015. Photo courtesy of Marie Roux.

the conditions of making sound, in which the entire durational field of the sound work, its past and future, will always be inaccessible to listeners (except, in the case of notated music, through a score).

The results were only partially satisfying, but their potential grew when I imported them into the digital domain and manipulated aspects of the images. What was the difference, I asked myself, between manipulating image files in this way and manipulating digital audio files? Both originated in physical actions; converted into packets of information they become adaptable through similar processes (filters, distortions, etc.) that in the case of the audio files leads to the creation of those grown-together entities, inertias and faint beings discussed earlier.

The next steps came quickly: drawing with a hammer and charcoal, an "instrument" whose smash was audible as a percussive marker but whose consequences—shards of unfixed charcoal—could only be photographed, not kept as an artwork. Like music, the shards were ephemeral.

Invited to perform at the launch of Daniela Cascella's book *F.M.R.L.*, I crumpled tissue paper, held it to my ear to listen to its slow, beautiful, near-inaudible unfolding, then handed pristine sheets of tissue paper to members of the audience in the hope that without verbal instructions they would follow my example, therefore creating many private concerts within the collective gathering. This was a failure. Nobody understood my intention. Yet emptied of its sounding, the crushed tissue paper birthed extraordinary forms: jellyfish, fungi, curious ancient animals. I flattened them in a scanner (Vladimir Nabokov's butterfly collecting springs to mind here), discovered entities and faint beings that reminded me of a book that was important in my formative years (ca. 1972) as an improviser: Ralph Buchsbaum's *Animals without Backbones: An Introduction to the Invertebrates*. Could there be such a thing as formless music, I wondered (bearing in mind the pejoratives aimed at improvised music, its "formless chaos")? Yet a jellyfish had a structure, albeit in flux, so elusive to the limitations of the human eye and its conceptions of life as to lie far distant from anthropocentric notions of a stable identity. These were entities, yet faint beings.

Many Private Concerts, as the tissue piece came to be called, finally achieved some success when performed at the London Contemporary Music Festival on December 11, 2015 by a group of students (sound art, fine art, and drawing) from University of the Arts London. Moving radially from a clustered group (with the unintentional air of a cult engaged in urban missionary work), each performer found at random an audience member willing to participate in this curious ritual. Each private concert

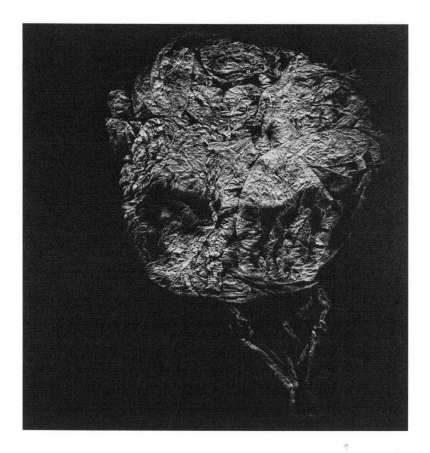

unfolded silently (and literally) as an island of knowing in a sea of indifference and incomprehension, each one connected to the others by intangible lines of shared listening behavior.

marks and signs

A calligraphic element, particularly calligraphy without meaning, combines with personal research work going back to the 1970s—secret and sacred languages, shamanic animal languages, esoteric Taoist scripts, bioacoustics and interspecies communication, the "scores" and "texts" of sound poetry. All of these strands close together in a tangle that grows more difficult

FIG 13.9 Many Private Concerts, Tomoko Hojo, performer, London Contemporary Music Festival, 2015.

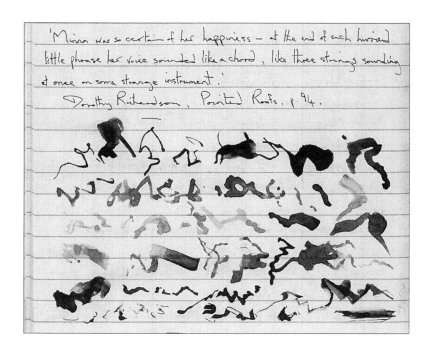

FIG 13.10 David Toop, notebook, 2015.

to unravel. Recently, my notebooks have become a mixture of calligraphic marks and decipherable writing, as if the significance of the writing can only be conveyed by the impenetrability of the marks.

cavities resonance

In 2014, I visited Nigatsu-dō temple in Nara, Japan. Nigatsu-dō is the site of the annual Omizutori ceremony (also known as Shuni-e), instituted in the year 752 and performed every year since without a lapse. I had been familiar with the sounds produced during Omizutori since the mid-1970s but was unfamiliar with details of the ceremony itself. Within the Todai-ji complex of structures that contains Nigatsu-dō there is a famous bell housed within a tower. I stood under the bell, almost inside its resonant volume, imagining its legendary long sustain, contemplating the marks, like drawing, that scoured its silent interior with age.

In 2015, I took part in a visit to a loudspeaker factory near Oslo, a trip whose purpose was to experience the so-called silence of its anechoic

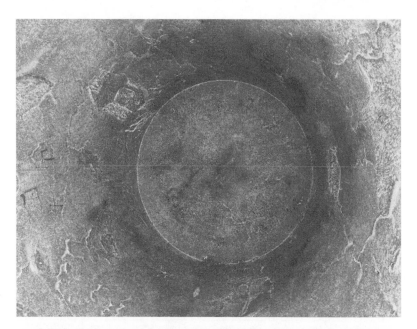

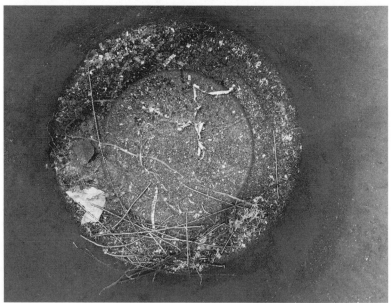

FIG 13.11 Interior of the bell at Nigatsu-dō temple, Nara, Japan, 2014. Photo by David Toop.

FIG 13.12 Waste bin, Norway, 2015. Photo by David Toop.

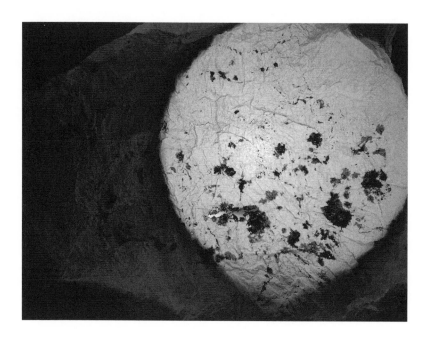

FIG 13.13 David Toop, light drawing, 2015.

chamber. During our coach trip to the factory I gave a lecture on silence, occasionally quoting Jullien's theories on the non-object and the appearing-disappearing. Obliged to speak through the coach's PA system, I found my words coming and going, sentences broken up by a faulty cable in the microphone. Wandering through the factory, I photographed inside a plastic waste bin, struck by the patterns of discarded metal shreds lying on the bottom. This was also silent drawing, another case of no it.

In *Lines*, Tim Ingold writes of the Peruvian Amazon Shipibo-Conibo shamanic healing ceremony in which designs floating before the shaman's eyes are converted into song as soon as they touch his lips. Referring to Angelika Gebhart-Sayer's original research in the 1980s, he writes, "It should be clear that Shipibo-Conibo designs form neither a script nor a score. They no more represent words or concepts than they do musical sounds. They are rather the phenomenal forms of the voice as they are made present to the listening ear. The songs of the Shipibo-Conibo, as Gebhart-Sayer herself remarks, 'can be heard in a visual way . . . and the geometric designs may be seen acoustically.' The visible lines of the designs are themselves lines of sound."

Between Christmas Day and New Year's Day, 2015, I made drawings by crumpling tissue paper spotted with black ink, unfolded them, exposed them to light. In each of these three cases, there was the illegibility of the earth drum, the most tenuous faint beings of sound growing into life.

Note

I appreciate the purpose and value of scholarly protocols—footnotes, page references, bibliography, and so on—an evidential framework that allows other scholars to consult and check sources for themselves and draw independent conclusions. Yet these protocols exist as a phantom text, an authoritative return to writing as the fount of all knowledge. In the case of texts founded in practice, resistant to verbal explication, their work is undermining. In the face of the inexplicable, they promise knowledge. In this case, the promise would be false.

Bibliography

Abromeit, John. *Horkheimer and the Foundations of the Frankfurt School.*
Cambridge: Cambridge University Press, 2011.

Adorno, Theodor W. *Aesthetic Theory*, ed. Gretel Adorno and Rolf Tiedemann, trans. Robert Hullot-Kentor. London: Athlone, 1997.

———. *Aesthetic Theory*, trans. Robert Hullot-Kentor. Minneapolis: University of Minnesota Press, 1997.

———. *Critical Models: Interventions and Catchwords*, trans. Henry W.
Pickford. New York: Columbia University Press, 2005.

———. *Dissonanzen/Einleitung in die Musiksoziologie. Gesammelte
Schriften, Band 14.* Frankfurt am Main: Suhrkamp, 1973.

———. *Essays on Music*, ed. Richard Leppert, trans. Susan H. Gillespie.
Berkeley: University of California Press, 2002.

———. *Introduction to the Sociology of Music*, trans. E. B. Ashton. New
York: Continuum, 1976.

———. *Negative Dialectics*, trans. E. B. Ashton. New York: Continuum,
2007.

———. *Negative Dialektik.* Frankfurt am Main: Suhrkamp, 1966.

———. *Philosophie der neuen Musik. Gesammelte Schriften, Band 12.* Frankfurt am Main: Suhrkamp, 1975.

———. *Philosophy of New Music*, trans. Robert Hullot-Kentor. Minneapolis: University of Minnesota Press, 2006.

Ahmed, Sara. *Queer Phenomenology: Orientations, Objects, Others.* Durham,
NC: Duke University Press, 2006.

Altman, Rick. "Moving Lips: Cinema as Ventriloquism." *Yale French Studies* 60 (1980): 67–79.

American Academy of Pediatrics, Committee on Environmental Health.
"Noise: A Hazard for the Fetus and Newborn." *Pediatrics* 100, no. 4
(1997): 724–27.

Anzieu, Didier. *The Skin-Ego*, trans. Chris Turner. New Haven, CT: Yale
University Press, 1989.

Appadurai, Arjun. *The Social Life of Things: Commodities in Cultural Perspective.* Cambridge: Cambridge University Press, 1986.

Arato, Andrew, and Eike Gebhardt, eds. *The Essential Frankfurt School Reader*. New York: Continuum, 1982.

Atlan, Henri. "Noise as a Principle of Self-Organization (1972/1979)." In *Selected Writings: On Self-Organization, Philosophy, Bioethics, and Judaism*, ed. Stefanos Garoulanos and Todd Meyers, 95–113. New York: Fordham University Press, 2011.

Attali, Jacques. *Noise: The Political Economy of Music*, trans. Brian Massumi. Minneapolis: University of Minnesota Press, 1985.

Azéma, Marc, and Florent Rivère. "Animation in Paleolithic Art: A Pre-Echo of Cinema." *Antiquity* 86 (2012): 316–24.

Bakhtin, Mikhail. *Problems of Dostoyevsky's Poetics*, ed. and trans. Caryl Emerson. Minneapolis: University of Minnesota Press, 1984.

Barthes, Roland. "The Grain of the Voice." In *Image, Music, Text*, trans. Stephen Heath, 179–89. New York: Hill and Wang, 1977.

Barthes, Roland, and Roland Havas. "Listening." In *The Responsibilities of Forms*, trans. Richard Howard, 245–60. New York: Hill and Wang, 1985.

Baudrillard, Jean. *The Perfect Crime*, trans. Chris Turner. London: Verso, 2008.

Beer, Gillian. "Introduction to *Between the Acts*." In Virginia Woolf, *Between the Acts*, ix–xxxv. London: Penguin, 1992.

Bennett, H. Stith. *On Becoming a Rock Musician*. Amherst: University of Massachusetts Press, 1980.

Bennett, Jane. "The Force of Things: Steps toward an Ecology of Matter." *Political Theory* 32, no. 3 (2004): 347–72.

———. "Thing-Power." In *Political Matter: Technoscience, Democracy, and Public Life*, ed. Bruce Braun and Sarah Whatmore, 35–62. Minneapolis: University of Minnesota Press, 2010.

———. *Vibrant Matter: A Political Ecology of Things*. Durham, NC: Duke University Press, 2010.

Bennett, Tony, and Patrick Joyce, eds. *Material Powers: Cultural Studies, History and the Material Turn*. London: Routledge, 2010.

Bentham, Jeremy. *The Panopticon Writings*, ed. Miron Božovič. London: Verso, 1995.

Bergum, Vangie. *A Child on Her Mind: The Experience of Becoming a Mother*. Westport, CT: Bergin and Garvey, 1997.

Berkeley, George. *Philosophical Writings*, ed. Desmond M. Clarke. Cambridge: Cambridge University Press, 2008.

Biancorosso, Giorgio. "Sound." In *The Routledge Companion to Film and Philosophy*, ed. Paisley Livingstone and Carl Platinga, 260–67. New York: Routledge, 2009.

Bijsterveld, Karin. *Mechanical Sound: Technology, Culture, and Public Problems of Noise in the Twentieth Century*. Cambridge, MA: MIT Press, 2008.

Birdsall, Carolyn. *Nazi Soundscapes: Sound, Technology and Urban Space in Germany, 1933–1945*. Amsterdam: Amsterdam University Press, 2012.

Blackman, Lisa. *Immaterial Bodies: Affect, Embodiment, Mediation*. London: Sage, 2012.

———. "Reinventing Psychological Matters: The Importance of the Suggestive Realm of Tarde's Ontology." *Economy and Society* 36, no. 4 (2007): 574–96.

Blackman, Lisa, and Couze Venn. "Affect." *Body and Society* 16, no. 1 (2010): 7–28.

Blesser, Barry, and Linda-Ruth Salter. *Spaces Speak, Are You Listening? Experiencing Aural Architecture*. Cambridge, MA: MIT Press, 2007.

Born, Georgina. "Music and the Materialization of Identities." *Journal of Material Culture* 16, no. 4 (2011): 376–88.

———. "Listening, Mediation, Event: Anthropological and Sociological Perspectives." *Journal of the Royal Musical Association* 135, no. 1 (2010): 79–89.

———. "Music: Ontology, Agency, and Creativity." In *Distributed Objects: Meaning and Mattering after Alfred Gell*, ed. Liana Chua and Mark Elliott, 130–54. Oxford: Berghahn, 2013.

———. "On Musical Mediation: Ontology, Technology and Creativity." *Twentieth Century Music* 2, no. 1 (2005): 7–36.

———. "On Tardean Relations: Temporality and Ethnography." In *The Social after Gabriel Tarde: Debates and Assessments*, ed. Matei Candea, 232–49. London: Routledge, 2010.

Boulez, Pierre. "At the Ends of the Fruitful Land . . ." *Die Reihe* 1 (1958): 19–29.

———. *On Music Today*, trans. Susan Bradshaw and Richard Rodney Bennett. Cambridge, MA: Harvard University Press, 1971.

Bourdieu, Pierre. *Distinction: A Social Critique of the Judgement of Taste*, trans. Richard Nice. Cambridge, MA: Harvard University Press, 1987.

———. *The Logic of Practice*, trans. Richard Nice. Stanford, CA: Stanford University Press, 1990.

Brennan, Teresa. *The Transmission of Affect*. Ithaca, NY: Cornell University Press, 2004.

Brown, Bill. "The Secret Life of Things (Virginia Woolf and the Matter of Modernism)." *Modernism/Modernity* 6, no. 2 (1999): 1–28.

———. "Thing Theory." *Critical Inquiry* 28, no. 1 (2001): 1–22.

Bruzzi, Stella. *New Documentary*. London: Routledge, 2006.

Buchsbaum, Ralph. *Animals without Backbones: An Introduction to the Invertebrates*. Chicago: University of Chicago Press, 1948.

Bull, Michael. *Sounding Out the City: Personal Stereos and the Management of Everyday Life*. Oxford: Berg, 2000.

———. *Sound Moves: iPod Culture and Urban Experience*. London: Routledge, 2007.

Bull, Michael, and Les Black, eds. *The Auditory Culture Reader*. London: Bloomsbury, 2015.

Burkhart, Patrick. *Music and Cyberliberties*. Middletown, CT: Wesleyan University Press, 2010.

Butler, Judith. *Excitable Speech: A Politics of the Performative*. London: Routledge, 1997.

Butler, Mark J. *Playing with Something That Runs: Technology, Improvisation, and Composition in DJ and Laptop Performance*. Oxford: Oxford University Press, 2014.

———. *Unlocking the Groove: Rhythm, Meter and Musical Design in Electronic Dance Music*. Bloomington: University of Indiana Press, 2006.

Carlyle, Angus, and Cathy Lane. *On Listening*. Axminster, UK: Uniformbooks, 2013.

Carpenter, William Benjamin. *Principles of Human Physiology, with Their Chief Applications to Psychology, Pathology, Therapeutics, Hygiène, and Forensic Medicine*. Philadelphia: Blanchard and Lea, 1853.

Carrithers, Michael, Matei Candea, Karen Sykes, Martin Holbraad, and Soumhya Venkatesan. "Ontology Is Just another Word for Culture." *Critique of Anthropology* 30, no. 2 (2010): 152–200.

Cascella, Daniela. *F.M.R.L: Footnotes, Mirages, Refrains and Leftovers of Writing Sound.* New Alresford, UK: Zero, 2015.

Cavarero, Adriana. *For More than One Voice: Toward a Philosophy of Vocal Expression.* Stanford, CA: Stanford University Press, 2005.

Chakravarti, Sonali. *Sing the Rage: Listening to Anger after Mass Violence.* Chicago: University of Chicago Press, 2014.

Charles, David, and Dominic Scott. "Aristotle on Well-Being and Intellectual Contemplation." *Proceedings of the Aristotelian Society, Supplementary Volumes* 73 (1999): 205–42.

Chion, Michel. *Audio-Vision*, trans. Claudia Gorbman. New York: Columbia University Press, 1994.

———. *Film, a Sound Art*, trans. Claudia Gorbman. New York: Columbia University Press, 2009.

———. *Guide des objets sonores.* Paris: Buchet/Chastel, 1983.

———. *La musique du future a-t-elle un avenir?* Paris: Institut National de l'Audiovisuel, 1977.

———. *Sound: An Acoulogical Treatise*, trans. James A. Steintrager. Durham, NC: Duke University Press, 2016.

———. *The Voice in Cinema*, trans. Claudia Gorbman. New York: Columbia University Press, 1999.

Chion, Michel, and Guy Reibel. *Les musiques électroacoustiques.* Paris: Edisud, 1976.

Chow, Rey. "After the Passage of the Beast: 'False Documentary' Aspirations, Acousmatic Complications." In *Rancière and Film*, ed. Paul Bowman, 34–52. Edinburgh: Edinburgh University Press, 2013.

———. *Entanglements, or Transmedial Thinking about Capture.* Durham, NC: Duke University Press, 2012.

———. *Not Like a Native Speaker: On Languaging as a Postcolonial Experience.* New York: Columbia University Press, 2014.

———. "Where Have All the Natives Gone?" In *Writing Diaspora: Tactics of Intervention in Contemporary Cultural Studies*, 27–54. Bloomington: Indiana University Press, 1993.

Chun, Wendy Hui Kyong. *Programmed Visions: Software and Memory.* Cambridge, MA: MIT Press, 2011.

Clarke, David I., and Eric F. Clarke, eds. *Music and Consciousness: Philosophical, Psychological, and Cultural Perspectives.* Oxford: Oxford University Press, 2011.

Conklin, Beth, and Lynn Morgan. "Babies, Bodies, and the Production of Personhood in North American and a Native Amazonian Society." *Ethos* 24 (1996): 657–94.

Connolly, William E. "The 'New Materialism' and the Fragility of Things." *Millennium: Journal of International Studies* 41, no. 3 (2013): 399–412.

Connor, Steven. *The Book of Skin.* Ithaca, NY: Cornell University Press, 2003.

———. *Dumbstruck: A Cultural History of Ventriloquism.* Oxford: Oxford University Press, 2000.

Coole, Diana H., and Samantha Frost, eds. *New Materialisms: Ontology, Agency, and Politics.* Durham, NC: Duke University Press, 2010.

Corbin, Alain. *Village Bells: Sound and Meaning in the 19th-Century French Countryside.* New York: Columbia University Press, 1998.

Coulthard, Lisa. "Dirty Sound: Haptic Noise in New Extremism." In *The Oxford Handbook of Sound and Image in Digital Media,* ed. Carol Vernallis, Amy Herzog, and John Richardson, 115–26. Oxford: Oxford University Press, 2013.

Cox, Christoph. "Sonic Thoughts." In *Realism Materialism Art,* ed. Christoph Cox, Jenny Jaskey, and Suhail Malik, 123–29. Berlin: Sternberg, 2015.

———. "Sound Art and the Sonic Unconscious." *Organised Sound* 14, no. 1 (2009): 19–26.

Crockett, Dennis. *German Post-Expressionism: The Art of the Great Disorder, 1918–1924.* University Park: Pennsylvania State University Press, 1999.

Cumming, Naomi. *The Sonic Self: Musical Subjectivity and Signification.* Bloomington: Indiana University Press, 2000.

———. "The Subjectivities of 'Erbarme Dich.'" *Music Analysis* 16, no. 1 (1997): 5–44.

Cusick, Suzanne G. "Music as Torture/Music as Weapon." *TRANS: Revista Transcultural de Música,* no. 10 (2006): 1–13.

———. "'You Are in a Place That Is out of the World . . .': Music in the Detention Camps of the 'Global War on Terror.'" *Journal of the Society for American Music* 2, no. 1 (2008): 1–26.

d'Alembert, Jean-Baptiste le Rond, and Denis Diderot. *Encyclopédie, ou Dictionnaire raisonné des sciences, des arts et des métiers,* vol. 13 (Pom-Regg). Neufchastel, France: Faulche, 1765.

Daston, Lorraine, and Peter Galison. *Objectivity.* New York: Zone Books, 2007.

Daughtry, J. Martin. *Listening to War: Sound, Music, Trauma, and Survival in Wartime Iraq.* Oxford: Oxford University Press, 2015.

Davis, Tracy C. *Stages of Emergency: Cold War Nuclear Civil Defense.* Durham, NC: Duke University Press, 2007.

Deacon, Terrence. *The Symbolic Species: The Co-evolution of Language and the Human Brain.* London: Penguin, 1997.

de la Cadena, Marisol. "Indigenous Cosmopolitics in the Andes: Conceptual Reflections beyond 'Politics'." *Cultural Anthropology* 25, no. 2 (2010): 334–70.

DeLanda, Manuel. *A New Philosophy of Society: Assemblage Theory and Social Complexity.* New York: Continuum, 2006.

Deleuze, Gilles. *Difference and Repetition,* trans. Paul Patton. New York: Columbia University Press, 1994.

———. *Foucault,* trans. Seán Hand. London: Athlone, 1988.

———. *The Logic of Sense,* trans. Mark Lester. New York: Columbia University Press, 1990.

———. *Proust and Signs,* trans. Richard Howard. Minneapolis: University of Minnesota Press, 2003.

Deleuze, Gilles, and Félix Guattari. *Kafka: Toward a Minor Literature,* trans. Dana Polan. Minneapolis: University of Minnesota Press, 1986.

———. *What Is Philosophy?*, trans. Graham Burchel and Hugh Tomlinson. London: Verso, 1994.

Demers, Joanna. *Listening through the Noise: The Aesthetics of Experimental Electronic Music.* Oxford: Oxford University Press, 2010.

———. *Steal this Music: How Intellectual Property Law Affects Musical Creativity.* Atlanta: University of Georgia Press, 2006.

Derrida, Jacques. *Edmund Husserl's* Origin of Geometry: *An Introduction,* trans. John P. Leavy, Jr. Lincoln: University of Nebraska Press, 1989.

———. *Of Grammatology,* trans. Gayatri Chakravorty Spivak. Baltimore, MD: Johns Hopkins University Press, [1976] 1998.

———. "Tympan." In *Margins of Philosophy, trans.* Alan Bass, ix–xxix. Chicago: University of Chicago Press, 1982.

———. *Voice and Phenomenon: Introduction to the Problem of the Sign in Husserl's Phenomenology,* trans. Leonard Lawlor. Evanston, IL: Northwestern University Press, 2010.

Descola, Philippe. *Beyond Nature and Culture,* trans. Janet Lloyd. Chicago: University of Chicago Press, 2013.

Didi-Huberman, Georges. "Knowing When to Cut." In *Foucault against Himself,* ed. François Caillat, trans. David Hömel, 77–109. Vancouver: Arsenal Pulp, 2014.

Dillon, Emma. *The Sense of Sound: Musical Meaning in France, 1260–1330.* Oxford: Oxford University Press, 2012.

Diski, Jenny. *On Trying to Keep Still.* London: Little Brown, 2006.

Dobrian, Christopher, and Daniel Koppelman. "The 'ᴇ' in ɴɪᴍᴇ: Musical Expression with New Computer Interfaces." *Proceedings of the 2006 International Conference on New Interfaces for Musical Expression.* Paris, 2006.

Dolan, Emily I. "Mendacious Technology." Paper presented at the American Musicological Society, November 3–5, 2016.

———. *The Orchestral Revolution: Haydn and the Technologies of Timbre.* Cambridge: Cambridge University Press, 2013.

Dolan, Emily I., and Alexander Rehding, eds. *Oxford Handbook on Timbre.* Oxford: Oxford University Press, forthcoming.

Dolar, Mladen. *A Voice and Nothing More.* Cambridge, MA: ᴍɪᴛ Press, 2006.

———. "The Burrow of Sound." *differences* 22, nos. 2–3 (2011): 112–39.

Dunan, Charles Stanislas. *Théorie psychologique de l'espace.* Paris: F. Alcan, 1895.

Eidsheim, Nina Sun. "Marian Anderson and 'Sonic Blackness' in American Opera." *American Quarterly* 63, no. 3 (September 2011): 641–71.

———. *Sensing Sound: Singing and Listening as Vibrational Practice.* Durham, NC: Duke University Press, 2015.

Erlmann, Veit. "Descartes' Resonant Subject." *differences* 22, nos. 2–3 (2011): 10–30.

———, ed. *Hearing Cultures: Essays On Sound, Listening, and Modernity.* Oxford: Berg, 2004.

———. *Reason and Resonance: A History of Modern Aurality.* New York: Zone Books, 2010.

Ernst, Wolfgang. *Sonic Time Machines: Explicit Sound, Sirenic Voices, and Implicit Sonicity.* Amsterdam: Amsterdam University Press, 2016.

Evens, Aden. *Sound Ideas.* Minneapolis: University of Minnesota Press, 2006.

Feaster, Patrick. "Phonography." In *Keywords in Sound*, ed. David Novak and Matt Saka-keeny, 139–50. Durham, NC: Duke University Press, 2015.

Feld, Steven. "Acoustemology." In *Keywords in Sound*, ed. David Novak and Matt Saka-keeny, 12–21. Durham, NC: Duke University Press, 2015.

———. "Aesthetics as Iconicity of Style, or 'Lift-Up-Over Sounding': Getting into the Kaluli Groove." *Yearbook for Traditional Music* 20, no. 1 (1988): 74–113.

———. *Sound and Sentiment: Birds, Weeping, Poetics, and Song in Kaluli Expression.* Phila-delphia: University of Pennsylvania Press, 1982.

———. "Waterfalls of Song: An Acoustemology of Place Resounding in Bosavi, Papua New Guinea." In *Senses of Place*, ed. Steven Feld and Keith H. Basso, 91–135. Santa Fe, NM: School of American Research Press, 1996.

Felman, Shoshana. "A Ghost in the House of Justice: Death and the Language of the Law." *Yale Journal of Law and the Humanities* 13, no. 1 (2001): 241–82.

Fish, Stanley. "The Law Wishes to Have a Formal Existence." In *The Stanley Fish Reader*, ed. H. Aram Veeser, 165–206. Malden, MA: Blackwell, 1999.

Fleeger, Jennifer. *Mismatched Women: The Siren's Song through the Machine.* Oxford: Oxford University Press, 2014.

Foucault, Michel. *The Birth of the Clinic: An Archaeology of Medical Perception*, trans. A. M. Sheridan Smith. New York: Pantheon Books, 1973.

———. *The Order of Things: An Archeology of the Human Sciences.* New York: Random House, 1994.

Fox, Aaron. "White Trash Alchemies of the Abject Sublime: Country as 'Bad' Music." In *Bad Music: The Music We Love to Hate*, ed. Christopher Washburne and Maiken Derno, 39–61. London: Routledge, 2004.

Freud, Sigmund. *The Origins of Psychoanalysis and the Letters to Fliess*, trans. Eric Mos-bacher and James Strachey. New York: Basic, 1981.

Friedrich, Jörg. *The Fire: The Bombing of Germany, 1940–1945.* New York: Columbia University Press, 2006.

Gaines, Jane. *Contested Culture: The Image, The Voice, and the Law.* London: British Film Institute, 1992.

Gatens, Moira, and Genevieve Lloyd. *Collective Imaginings: Spinoza, Past and Present.* London: Routledge, 2002.

Gaver, William W. "What in the World Do We Hear? An Ecological Approach to Auditory Event Perception." *Ecological Psychology* 5, no. 1 (1993): 1–29.

Goodman, Steve. *Sonic Warfare: Sound, Affect, and the Ecology of Fear.* Cambridge, MA: MIT Press, 2010.

Gopinath, Sumanth. *The Ringtone Dialectic: Economy and Cultural Form.* Cambridge, MA: MIT Press, 2013.

Grayzel, Susan R. *At Home and under Fire: Air Raids and Culture in Britain from the Great War to the Blitz.* Cambridge: Cambridge University Press, 2012.

Grimshaw, Mark, and Tom Garner. *Sonic Virtuality: Sounds as Emergent Perception.* Ox-ford: Oxford University Press, 2015.

Grusin, Richard A., ed. *The Nonhuman Turn.* Minneapolis: University of Minnesota Press, 2015.

Guattari, Félix. *Chaosmosis: An Ethico-aesthetic Paradigm*, trans. Julian Pefanis. Blooming-ton: Indiana University Press, 1995.

Guillory, John. *Cultural Capital: The Problem of Literary Canon Formation*. Chicago: University of Chicago Press, 1993.

Gura, Philip F. *C. F. Martin and His Guitars, 1796–1873*. Chapel Hill: University of North Carolina Press, 2003.

Halewood, Michael. *A. N. Whitehead and Social Theory: Tracing a Culture of Thought*. London: Anthem, 2011.

Hallward, Peter. *Out of This World: Deleuze and the Philosophy of Creation*. London: Verso, 2006.

Hamilton, Andy. *Aesthetics and Music*. London: Continuum, 2008.

Haraway, Donna Jeanne. *The Companion Species Manifesto: Dogs, People, and Significant Otherness*. Chicago: Prickly Paradigm, 2003.

———. *When Species Meet*. Minneapolis: University of Minnesota Press, 2008.

Harman, Graham. "On Vicarious Causation." *Speculations* 2 (2007): 187–221.

———. *The Quadruple Object*. New Alresford, UK: Zero, 2010.

Havens, Thomas R. H. *Radicals and Realists in the Japanese Nonverbal Arts: The Avant-Garde Rejection of Modernism*. Honolulu: University of Hawai'i Press, 2006.

Hayles, N. Katherine. *How We Became Posthuman: Virtual Bodies in* Cybernetics, *Literature and Informatics*. Chicago: University of Chicago Press, 1999.

Heinrich, Michael. *An Introduction to the Three Volumes of Karl Marx's* Capital, trans. Alexander Locascio. New York: Monthly Review Press, 2012.

Helmreich, Stefan. "An Anthropologist under Water: Immersive Soundscapes, Submarine Cyborgs, and Transductive Ethnography." *American Ethnologist* 34, no. 4 (2007): 621–41.

———. "Listening against Soundscapes." *Anthropology News* 51, no. 9 (2010): 10.

———. "Transduction." In *Keywords in Sound*, ed. David Novak and Matt Sakakeeny, 222–31. Durham, NC: Duke University Press, 2015.

Henare, Amiria, Martin Holbraad, and Sari Wastell, eds. *Thinking through Things: Theorising Artefacts Ethnographically*. London: Routledge, 2007.

Hennessy, Peter. *The Secret State: Preparing for the Worst, 1945–2010*. London: Penguin Books, 2010.

Hennion, Antoine. *La passion musicale: Une sociologie de la médiation*. Paris: Paris École des Hautes Études en Sciences Sociales, 1991.

Henriques, Julian. *Sonic Bodies: Reggae Sound Systems, Performance Techniques, and Ways of Knowing*. New York: Continuum, 2011.

———. "Sonic Dominance and the Reggae Sound System Session." In *The Auditory Culture Reader*, ed. Michael Bull and Les Back, 451–80. Oxford: Berg, 2003.

Hersey, John. *Hiroshima*. London: Penguin Books, 2001.

Hibbitts, Bernard J. "'Coming to Our Senses': Communication and Legal Expression in Performance Cultures." *Emory Law Journal* 41, no. 4 (1992): 873–95.

Hirschkind, Charles. *The Ethical Soundscape: Cassette Sermons and Islamic Counterpublics*. New York: Columbia University Press, 2006.

Holmes, Oliver Wendell. *The Essential Holmes: Selections from the Letters, Speeches, Judicial Opinions, and Other Writings*, ed. Richard A. Posner. Chicago: University of Chicago Press, 1992.

Horkheimer, Max, and Theodor Adorno. *Dialectic of Enlightenment*. London: Allen Lane, 1972.

Hubbard, Ruth. "Personal Courage Is Not Enough: Some Hazards of Childbearing in the 1980s." In *Test-Tube Women*, ed. Rita Arditti, Renate Duelli Klein, and Shelly Minden, 331–55. Boston: Pandora, 1984.

Hume, David. *Selected Essays*. Oxford: Oxford University Press, 1998.

Humphrey, Nicholas. *Seeing Red: A Study in Consciousness*. Cambridge, MA: Harvard University Press, 2009.

Husserl, Edmund. *Husserliana XIII–XV. Zur Phänomenologie der Intersubjektivität I–III. Texte aus dem Nachlass*, ed. Iso Kern. The Hague: Nijhoff, 1973.

———. *Ideas for a Pure Phenomenology and Phenomenological Philosophy: First Book*, trans. Kersten Englis. Dordrecht, Netherlands: Kluwer Academic, 1983.

———. *The Logical Investigations*, vol. 1, trans. Dermot Moran. London: Routledge, 1970.

———. *On the Phenomenology of the Consciousness of Internal Time (1893–1917)*, trans. John Barnett Brough. Dordrecht, Netherlands: Kluwer Academic, 1991.

Ihde, Don. *Listening and Voice: Phenomenologies of Sound*. Albany: SUNY Press, 2007.

Ingold, Tim. *Lines: A Brief History*. London: Routledge, 2007.

Irigaray, Luce. *I Love to You: Sketch for a Felicity within History*, trans. Alison Martin. London: Routledge, 1992.

———. *To Be Two*, trans. Monique Rhodes and Marco F. Cocito-Monoc. London: Routledge, 2001.

Jackson, Myles. *Harmonious Triads: Physicists, Musicians and Instrument-Makers in Nineteenth-Century Germany*. Cambridge, MA: MIT Press, 2006.

Jain, Sarah S. Lochlann. *Injury: the Politics of Product Design and Safety Law in the United States*. Princeton: Princeton University Press, 2006.

James, William. *Essays in Radical Empiricism*. Lincoln: University of Nebraska Press, 1996.

Jameson, Fredric. *Late Marxism: Adorno, or, The Persistence of the Dialectic*. London: Verso, 1990.

Jay, Martin. *Downcast Eyes: The Denigration of Vision in Twentieth-Century French Thought*. Berkeley: University of California Press, 1994.

Jullien, François. *The Great Image Has No Form, or On the Nonobject through Painting*, trans. Jane Marie Todd. Chicago: University of Chicago Press, 2009.

Kahn, Douglas. *Noise, Water, Meat: A History of Sound in the Arts*. Cambridge, MA: MIT Press, 1999.

Kane, Brian. "Jean-Luc Nancy and the Listening Subject." *Contemporary Music Review* 31, nos. 5–6 (2012): 439–47.

———. "Sound Studies without Auditory Culture: A Critique of the Ontological Turn." *Sound Studies* 1, no. 1 (2015): 2–21.

———. *Sound Unseen: Acousmatic Sound in Theory and Practice*. Oxford: Oxford University Press, 2014.

Kant, Immanuel. *Critique of the Power of Judgment*, trans. Paul Guyer and Eric Matthews. Cambridge: Cambridge University Press, 2000.

Kaplan, Danny. "The Songs of the Siren: Engineering National Time on Israeli Radio." *Cultural Anthropology* 24, no. 2 (2009): 313–45.

Kelly, Julia. *Art, Ethnography and the Life of Objects: Paris, c. 1925–35*. Manchester, UK: Manchester University Press, 2007.

Kittler, Friedrich A. *Gramophone, Film, Typewriter*, trans. Geoffrey Winthrop-Young and Michael Wutz. Stanford, CA: Stanford University Press, 1999.

Kohn, Eduardo. *How Forests Think: Toward an Anthropology beyond the Human*. Berkeley: University of California Press, 2013.

Knell, Herman. *To Destroy a City: Strategic Bombing and Its Human Consequences in World War II*. Cambridge: Da Capo, 2003.

Kramer, Lawrence. "From the Other to the Abject: Music as Cultural Trope." In *Classical Music and Postmodern Knowledge*, 33–66. Berkeley: University of California Press, 1995.

Kristeva, Julia. *Desire in Language*, ed. Leon S. Roudiez, trans. Thomas Gora, Alice Jardine, and Leon S. Roudiez. New York: Columbia University Press, 1980.

———. *Powers of Horror: An Essay on Abjection*, trans. Leon S. Roudiez. New York: Columbia University Press, 1982.

———. *Revolution in Poetic Language*, trans. Margaret Waller. New York: Columbia University Press, 1984.

Kursell, Julia. "Visualizing Piano Playing, 1890–1930." *Grey Room* 1, no. 43 (2011): 66–87.

LaBelle, Brandon. *Background Noise: Perspectives On Sound Art*. London: Continuum, 2006.

———. *Lexicon of the Mouth: Poetics and Politics of Voice and the Oral Imaginary*. London: Bloomsbury, 2014.

Lane, Cathy, and Angus Carlyle. *In The Field: The Art of Field Recording*. Axminster, UK: Uniformbooks, 2013.

Latour, Bruno. *Politics of Nature: How to Bring the Sciences Into Democracy*, trans. Catherine Porter. Cambridge, MA: Harvard University Press, 2004.

———. *Reassembling the Social: An Introduction to Actor-Network-Theory*. Oxford: Oxford University Press, 2005.

———. *We Have Never Been Modern*, trans. Catherine Porter. Cambridge, MA: Harvard University Press, 1993.

Lawlor, Leonard. "Translator's Introduction: The Germinal Structure of Derrida's Thought." In Jacques Derrida, *Voice and Phenomenon*, trans. Leonard Lawlor, xviii–xxiv. Evanston, IL: Northwestern University Press, 2010.

Lawrence, Amy. *Echo and Narcissus: Women's Voices in Classical Hollywood Cinema*. Berkeley: University of California Press, 1991.

Leibowitz, René. *Schoenberg and His School: The Contemporary Stage of the Language of Music*, trans. Dika Newlin. New York: Philosophical Library, 1949.

Levi, Primo. *If This Is a Man/The Truce*. London: Abacus, 1991.

Levin, Thomas Y. "For the Record: Adorno on Music in the Age of Its Mechanical Reproducibility." *October* 55 (Winter 1990): 23–47.

Levitin, Daniel J. *This Is Your Brain on Music: The Science of a Human Obsession*. New York: Dutton, 2007.

Levy, Indra A. *Sirens of the Western Shore: The Westernesque Femme Fatale, Translation, and Vernacular Style in Modern Japanese Literature*. New York: Columbia University Press, 2006.

Lispector, Clarice. *Água Viva*, trans. Stefan Tobler. New York: New Directions, 2012.

Locke, John. *An Essay Concerning Human Understanding*. London: Penguin, 1997.

López, Francisco. "Environmental Sound Matter." April 1998. http://www.manoafreeuniversity.org/projects/soundings/kompendium/pdfs/lopez_environmental.pdf.

Losonczy, Anne-Marie. "Del ombligo a la comunidad. Ritos de nacimiento en la cultura negra del litoral Pacífico Colombiano." *Revindi* 1 (1989): 49–54.

Lundgren, Ingela. "The Experience of Pregnancy: A Hermeneutical/Phenomenological Study." *The Journal of Perinatal Education* 8, no. 3 (1999): 12–20.

Lynch, Michael. "Ontography: Investigating the Production of Things, Deflating Ontology." *Social Studies of Science* 43, no. 3 (2015): 444–62.

Maitra, Ani, and Rey Chow. "What's 'In'? Disaggregating Asia through New Media Actants." In *Routledge Handbook of New Media in Asia*, ed. Larissa Hjort and Olivia Khoo, 17–27. London: Routledge, 2016.

Malina, Frank J., and Pierre Schaeffer. "A Conversation on Concrete Music and Kinetic Art." *Leonardo* 5, no. 3 (1972): 255–60.

Manderson, Desmond. *Songs without Music: Aesthetic Dimensions of Law and Justice*. Berkeley: University of California Press, 2000.

Marks, Laura U. *The Skin of the Film: Intercultural Cinema, Embodiment, and the Senses*. Durham, NC: Duke University Press, 2000.

Massumi, Brian. "Too-Blue: Colour-Patch for an Expanded Empiricism." *Cultural Studies* 14, no. 2 (2000): 177–226.

Maxwell, Richard, and Toby Miller. *Greening the Media*. Oxford: Oxford University Press, 2012.

McLeod, Kembrew, and Peter DiCola. *Creative License: The Law and Culture of Digital Sampling*. Durham, NC: Duke University Press, 2011.

Meillassoux, Quentin. *After Finitude: An Essay on the Necessity of Contingency*, trans. Ray Brassier. London: Continuum, 2008.

Meintjes, Louise. *Sound of Africa! Making Music Zulu in a South African Studio*. Durham, NC: Duke University Press, 2003.

Mellencamp, Patricia. *A Fine Romance: Five Ages of Film Feminism*. Philadelphia: Temple University Press, 1995.

Michaux, Henri. *Ideograms in China*, trans. Gustaf Sobin. New York: New Directions, 2002.

Miklitsch, Robert. *Siren City: Sound and Source Music in Classic American Noir*. New Brunswick, NJ: Rutgers University Press, 2011.

Miller, Daniel, ed. *Materiality*. Durham, NC: Duke University Press, 2005.

Mills, Mara. "Deaf Jam: From Inscription to Reproduction to Information." *Social Text* 28, no. 1 (Summer 2010): 35–58.

Moles, Abraham A. *Information Theory and Esthetic Perception*, trans. Joel E. Cohen. Urbana: University of Illinois Press, 1966.

———. *Théorie de l'information et perception esthétique*. Paris: Flammarion, 1958.

Moore, Barrington, Jr. *Reflection on the Causes of Human Misery and upon Certain Proposals to Eliminate Them*. London: Allen Lane, 1972.

Moretti, Franco. *The Bourgeois: Between History and Literature*. New York: Verso, 2014.

Morton, Timothy. *Hyperobjects: Philosophy and Ecology after the End of the World*. Minneapolis: University of Minnesota Press, 2013.

Mowitt, John. *Percussion: Drumming, Beating, Striking*. Durham, NC: Duke University Press, 2002.

———. *Sounds: The Ambient Humanities*. Berkeley: University of California Press, 2015.

Nancy, Jean-Luc. *Listening*, trans. Charlotte Mandell. New York: Fordham University Press, [2002] 2007.

Navaro-Yashin, Yael. "Affective Spaces, Melancholic Objects: Ruination and the Production of Anthropological Knowledge." *Journal of the Royal Anthropological Institute* 15, no. 1 (2009): 1–18.

———. *The Make-Believe Space: Affective Geography in a Postwar Polity*. Durham, NC: Duke University Press, 2012.

Navarro Valencia, Martha Cecilia. *Cuerpos Afrocolombianos: Prácticas y representaciones sociales en torno a la maternidad, las uniones y la salud sexual y reproductiva en la costa Pacífica Colombiana*. Quito: Editorial Universitaria Abya Yala, Universidad Politécnica Salesiana, 2012.

Nichols, Bill. *Representing Reality: Issues and Concepts in Documentary*. Bloomington: Indiana University Press, 1991.

Noë, Alva. *Action in Perception*. Cambridge, MA: MIT Press, 2004.

Novak, David. *Japanoise: Music at the Edge of Circulation*. Durham, NC: Duke University Press, 2013.

Novak, David, and Matt Sakakeeny, eds. *Keywords in Sound*. Durham, NC: Duke University Press, 2015.

O'Callaghan, Casey. *Sounds: A Philosophical Theory*. Oxford: Oxford University Press, 2007.

O'Connor, Brian. *Adorno*. London: Routledge, 2014.

Osborne, Richard. "Alarms on Record." *London Consortium Static*, no. 6 (December 2007).

Paddison, Max. *Adorno's Aesthetics of Music*. Cambridge: Cambridge University Press, 1993.

Parker, James E. K. *Acoustic Jurisprudence: Listening to the Trial of Simon Bikindi*. Oxford: Oxford University Press, 2015.

Pasnau, Robert. "What Is Sound?" *The Philosophical Quarterly* 49, no. 196 (1999): 309–24.

Peraino, Judith Ann. *Listening to the Sirens: Musical Technologies of Queer Identity from Homer to Hedwig*. Berkeley: University of California Press, 2006.

Pinch, Trevor, and Karin Bijsterveld. "New Keys to the World of Sound." In *The Oxford Handbook of Sound Studies*, ed. Trevor Pinch and Karin Bijsterveld, 3–38. Oxford: Oxford University Press, 2012.

———, eds. *The Oxford Handbook of Sound Studies*. Oxford: Oxford University Press, 2012.

Piontelli, Alessandra. *From Fetus to Child: An Observational and Psychoanalytical Study*. London: Routledge, 1992.

Pivec, Nataša. "Drags, Drugs and Dirt: Abjection and Masculinity in Marilyn Manson's Music Video '(s)AINT'." *Masculinities* 3 (2015): 105–28.

Plato. "Meno." In *Five Dialogues*, 2nd ed., trans. G. M. A. Grube, rev. John M. Cooper, 58–92. Indianapolis, IN: Hackett, 2002.

Ramshaw, Sara. *Justice as Improvisation: The Law of the Extempore*. London: Routledge, 2013.

Rancière, Jacques. *The Emancipated Spectator*, trans. Gregory Elliott. London: Verso, 2009.

———. "The Future of the Image." In *The Future of the Image*, trans. Gregory Elliott, 1–31. London: Verso, 2007.

Rangan, Pooja. "Audibilities: Voice and Listening in the Penumbra of Documentary—an Introduction," *Discourse* 39, no. 3, Special Issue on Documentary Audibilities, edited by Pooja Rangan and Genevieve Yue (Fall 2017): 279–91.

Rapp, Rayna. "Real-Time Fetus: The Role of the Sonogram in the Age of Monitored Reproduction." In *The Body Proper: Reading the Anthropology of Material Life*, ed. Margaret Lock and Judith Farquhar, 608–22. Durham, NC: Duke University Press, 2007.

Rice, Tom. *Hearing and the Hospital: Sound, Listening, Knowledge and Experience*. Canon Pyon: Sean Kingston Publishing, 2013.

Ritzer, George, and Nathan Jurgenson. "Production, Consumption, Prosumption: The Nature of Capitalism in the Age of the Digital 'Prosumer.'" *Journal of Consumer Culture* 10, no. 1 (March 1, 2010): 13–36.

Rose, Tricia. *Black Noise: Rap Music and Contemporary Culture in Black America*. Middletown, CT: Wesleyan University Press, 1994.

Rosolato, Guy. "The Voice between Body and Language." In *Voices*, trans. Christopher Phillips. Rotterdam: Witte de With, 1998.

Ruoff, Jeffrey. "Conventions of Sound in Documentary." *Cinema Journal* 32, no. 3 (1993): 24–40.

Ryan, Judylyn S. "Outing the Black Feminist Filmmaker in Julie Dash's *Illusions*." *Signs* 30, no. 1 (Autumn 2004): 1319–44.

Saint-Saëns, Camille. *Harmonie et mélodie*. Paris: Calmann Lévy, 1885.

Schaeffer, Pierre. *A la recherche d'une musique concrète* Paris: Editions du Seuil, 1952.

———. *In Search of a Concrete Music*, trans. Christine North and John Dack. Berkeley: University of California Press, 2012.

———. "Note on Time Relationships." *Gravesano Review* 17 (1960): 41–77.

———. "Son et Communication." *Cultures* 1, no. 1 (1973): 57–84.

———. "Sound and Communcation." *Cultures* 1, no. 1 (1973): 53–80.

———. *Traité des objets musicaux: Essai interdisciplines*. Paris: Seuil, 1966.

———. *Treatise on Musical Objects: An Essay across Disciplines*, trans. Christine North and John Dack. Berkeley: University of California Press, 2017.

Schafer, R. Murray. *The Soundscape: Our Sonic Environment and the Tuning of the World.* Rochester, VT: Destiny Books, 1994.

Schwartz, Hillel. *Making Noise: From Babel to the Big Bang and Beyond.* New York: Zone, 2011.

Sehgal, Melanie. "A Thousand Subjectivities: Rethinking Subjectivity with Félix Guattari and Alfred North Whitehead." Intervention Paper, Terra Critica II, Utrecht University, November 22–23, 2013. http://terracritica.net/wp-content/uploads/SehgalTC2 .pdf.

Siefert, Marsha. "Image/Music/Voice: Song Dubbing in Hollywood Musicals." *Journal of Communication* 45, no. 2 (Spring 1995): 44–64.

Serres, Michel. "The Geometry of the Incommunicable: Madness." In *Foucault and His Interlocutors*, ed. Arnold I. Davidson, 36–56. Chicago: University of Chicago Press, 1997.

———. *The Parasite*, trans. Lawrence R. Schehr. Minneapolis: University of Minnesota Press, 2007.

Sexton, Jamie. "Excavating Authenticity: Surveying the Indie-Rock Doc." In *Music and Sound in Documentary Film*, ed. Holly Rogers, 151–65. London: Routledge, 2015.

Silverman, Kaja. *The Acoustic Mirror: The Female Voice in Psychoanalysis and Cinema.* Bloomington: Indiana University Press, 1988.

Sloterdijk, Peter. *Spheres, Volume 1: Bubbles, Microspherology.* Los Angeles: Semiotext(e), 2011.

Small, Christopher. *Music, Society, Education.* London: John Calder, 1977.

Smalley, Dennis. "Spectromorphology: Explaining Sound-Shapes." *Organised Sound* 2, no. 2 (1997): 107–26.

Smith, Jeff. "Black Faces, White Voices: The Politics of Dubbing in *Carmen Jones*." *The Velvet Light Trap* 51 (Spring 2003): 29–42.

Smith, Nicholas. "Phenomenology of Pregnancy: A Cure for Philosophy?" In *Phenomenology of Pregnancy*, ed. Jonna Bornemark and Nicholas Smith, 15–49. Huddinge, Sweden: Södertörn University, 2016.

Steingo, Gavin. "Vital Signs/Life Writing." Paper presented at the symposium Biographies and the Production of Space, Stuttgart, Germany, May 19–21, 2016.

Stenner, Paul. "A. N. Whitehead and Subjectivity." *Subjectivity* 22, no. 1 (2008): 90–109.

———. "James and Whitehead: Assemblage and Systematization of a Deeply Empiricist Mosaic Philosophy." *European Journal of Pragmatism and American Philosophy* 3, no. 1 (2011): 101–30.

Sterne, Jonathan. *The Audible Past: Cultural Origins of Sound Reproduction.* Durham, NC: Duke University Press, 2003.

———. "Mediate Auscultation, the Stethoscope, and the 'Autopsy of the Living': Medicine's Acoustic Culture." *Journal of Medical Humanities* 22, no. 2 (2001): 115–36.

———. "The Software Passes the Test When the User Fails It: Constructing Digital Models of Analog Signal Processors." In *Testing Hearing*, unpublished ms., ed. Viktoria Tracyk, Alexandra Hui, and Mara Mills.

———, ed. *The Sound Studies Reader.* London: Routledge, 2012.

———. "The Theology of Sound: A Critique of Orality." *Canadian Journal of Communication* 36, no. 2 (2011): 207–25.

Sterne, Jonathan, and Mitchell Akiyama. "The Recording That Never Wanted to Be Heard and Other Stories of Sonification." In *The Oxford Handbook of Sound Studies*, ed. Trevor Pinch and Karin Bijsterveld, 544–60. Oxford: Oxford University Press, 2012.

Stiegler, Bernard. *Technics and Time, 3: Cinematic Time and the Question of Malaise*, trans. Stephen Barker. Stanford, CA: Stanford University Press, 2011.

Stoever, Jennifer Lynn. *The Sonic Color Line: Race and the Cultural Politics of Listening*. New York: New York University Press, 2016.

Strathern, Marilyn. *Partial Connections*. New York: Altamira, 2004.

Subotnik, Rose Rosengard. *Deconstructive Variations: Music and Reason in Western Society*. Minneapolis: University of Minnesota Press, 1996.

Tarde, Gabriel. *On Communication and Social Influence: Selected Papers*, ed. Terry N. Clark. Chicago: University of Chicago Press, 1969.

Taylor, Fred. *Coventry: Thursday, 14 November 1940*. London: Bloomsbury, 2015.

Tenney, James. *Meta+Hodos and Meta Meta+Hodos: A Phenomenology of 20th Century Musical Materials and an Approach to the Study of Form*. Lebanon, NH: Frog Peak Music, 1986.

Théberge, Paul. *Any Sound You Can Imagine: Making Music/Consuming Technology*. Middletown, CT: Wesleyan University Press, 1997.

Thompson, Emily. *The Soundscape of Modernity: Architectural Acoustics and the Culture of Listening in America, 1900–1933*. Cambridge, MA: MIT Press, 2004.

Thrift, Nigel J. *Non-representational Theory: Space, Politics, Affect*. London: Routledge, 2008.

Tiampo, Ming. *Gutai: Decentering Modernism*. Chicago: University of Chicago Press, 2011.

Tomlinson, Gary. "Sign, Affect, and Musicking before the Human." *Boundary 2* 43, no. 1 (2016): 143–72.

Toop, David. *Sinister Resonance: The Mediumship of the Listener*. London: Continuum, 2010.

Tournet-Lammer, Jocelyne. *Sur les traces de Pierre Schaeffer: Archives 1942–1995*. Paris: Institut National de l'Audiovisuel: Documentation Française, 2006.

Tresch, John, and Emily I. Dolan. "Toward a New Organology: Instruments of Music and Science." *Osiris* 28, no. 1 (2013): 278–98.

Ussachevsky, Vladimir. "Music in the Tape Medium." *The Juilliard Review* 6, no. 2 (1959): 8–9, 18–20.

van der Tuin, Iris, and Rick Dolphijn. *New Materialism: Interviews and Cartographies*. Ann Arbor, MI: Open Humanities Press, 2012.

Viveiros de Castro, Eduardo. *Cannibal Metaphysics for a Post-Structural Anthropology*, ed. and trans. Peter Skafish. Minneapolis, MN: Univocal, 2009.

———. *From the Enemy's Point of View: Humanity and Divinity in an Amazonian Society*, trans. Catherine V. Howard. Chicago: University of Chicago Press, 1992.

Voegelin, Salomé. *Listening to Noise and Silence: Towards a Philosophy of Sound Art*. New York: Continuum, 2010.

———. *Sonic Possible Worlds: Hearing the Continuum of Sound*. London: Bloomsbury Academic, 2014.

Vološinov, Valentin Nikolaevich. *Marxism and the Philosophy of Language*, trans. Ladislav Matejka and I. R. Titunik. Cambridge, MA: Harvard University Press, 1986.

Waksman, Steve. *Instruments of Desire: The Electric Guitar and the Shaping of Musical Experience*. Cambridge, MA: Harvard University Press, 1999.

Walker, Harry. "Baby Hammocks and Stone Bowls: Urarina Technologies of Companionship and Subjection." In *The Occult Life of Things: Native Amazonian Theories of Materiality and Personhood*, ed. Fernando Santos Granero, 81–104. Tucson: University of Arizona Press.

———. *Under a Watchful Eye: Self, Power, and Intimacy in Amazonia*. Berkeley: University of California Press, 2012.

Weintraub, Andrew. *Power Plays: Wayang Golek Puppet Theater of West Java*. Athens: Ohio University Press, 2004.

Wellmer, Gösta. "Machines to Hear for Us: Perceiving, Filtering, Storing." Panel discussion at Humboldt University, Berlin, November 27, 2015.

Whatmore, Sarah. "Materialist Returns: Practising Cultural Geography in and for a More-than-Human World." *Cultural Geographies* 13, no. 4 (2006): 600–9.

Whitehead, Alfred North. *Adventures of Ideas*. New York: Free Press, 1967.

———. *The Concept of Nature*. Cambridge: Cambridge University Press, 1995.

———. *Modes of Thought*. New York: Free Press, 1968.

———. *Process and Reality: An Essay in Cosmology*, ed. David Ray Griffin and Donald W. Sherburne. New York: Free Press, 1978.

Wilder, Thomas. "Patina and the Role of Nostalgia in the Field of Stringed Instrument Cultural Production." Master's thesis, Communication Studies, McGill University, Montreal, 2007.

Wolfe, Charles. "Historicizing the 'Voice of God': The Place of Vocal Narration in Classical Documentary." *Film History* 9, no. 2 (1997): 149–67.

Woolf, Virginia. *Between the Acts*, introd. Gillian Beer. London: Penguin, 1992.

Wright, Benjamin. "The Wilhelm Scream." In "Forum 1: Favourite Moments of Film Sound." *Offscreen* 11, no. 8 (September 2007). http://offscreen.com/view/soundforum_1.

Xenakis, Iannis. *Formalized Music: Thought and Mathematics in Composition*, trans. Christopher Butchers, G. W. Hopkins, and Mr. and Mrs. John Challifour. Stuyvesant, NY: Pendragon, 2001.

Youdelman, Jeffrey. "Narration, Invention, and History: A Documentary Dilemma." *Cinéaste* 12, no. 2 (1982): 8–15.

Young, Iris Marion. "Pregnant Embodiment: Subjectivity and Alienation." In *On Female Body Experience: "Throwing like a Girl" and Other Essays*, 46–61. Oxford: Oxford University Press, 2005.

Žižek, Slavoj, ed. *Everything You Always Wanted to Know about Lacan (But Were Afraid to Ask Hitchcock)*. London: Verso, 1992.

Contributors

GEORGINA BORN is Professor of Music and Anthropology at Oxford University. She worked previously as a musician with Henry Cow, Derek Bailey's Company, and other groups. Trained as an anthropologist at University College London, her work combines ethnographic and theoretical writings on music, sound, (new) media, and cultural production. From 2010 to 2016 Born directed the ERC-funded research program Music, Digitisation, Mediation: Towards Interdisciplinary Music Studies. She has held visiting professorships at McGill University, University of California, Berkeley, and Oslo University. She is a Fellow of the British Academy and of Academia Europaea.

MICHAEL BULL is Professor of Sound Studies at the University of Sussex. He has published widely in the field of sound, technology, and urban experience. He is currently writing a monograph on reinterpreting the sounds of World War I. He is also the cofounding editor of the journals *Senses and Society* and *Sound Studies* and is editor of the book series *The Study of Sound*, published by Bloomsbury.

MICHEL CHION, a composer, filmmaker, teacher, and wide-ranging theorist of sound, has written several influential studies on the relationship between sound and vision in film, including *Audio-Vision*, *The Voice in Cinema*, and *Film: A Sound Art*. He has also published extensively on music, poetry, and a variety of other sonic practices and aural experiences. His most recent work to be translated into English is *Sound: An*

Acoulogical Treatise, translated and with an introduction by James A. Steintrager (Duke University Press, 2016).

REY CHOW, the author most recently of *Not like a Native Speaker: On Languaging as a Postcolonial Experience,* is Anne Firor Scott Professor of Literature, Duke University, and Distinguished Visiting Professor in the School of Modern Languages and Cultures, University of Hong Kong. Her research and teaching interests include modern literary studies, film, critical theory, and global cultural studies. Chow is an elected fellow of the American Academy of Arts and Sciences and serves on the boards of more than fifty journals, book series, and research centers or platforms around the world. Her publications have appeared in more than ten languages.

JOHN DACK is currently Senior Lecturer in Music and Technology at Middlesex University. He has presented his research at conferences in Belgium, Britain, China, France, Germany, the Netherlands, Spain, Switzerland, and Turkey, and has written numerous book chapters and articles. His current research areas include history, theory, and analysis of electroacoustic music; the music and works of the Groupe de Recherches Musicales; serial thought; and "open" forms in music.

VEIT ERLMANN is an anthropologist/ethnomusicologist and the Endowed Chair of Music History at the University of Texas at Austin. He held previous appointments at the Free University Berlin, the University of Natal and the University of the Witwatersrand in South Africa, and the University of Chicago. He has won numerous awards, including a Heisenberg Fellowship and a Mercator Prize, both given by the German Research Foundation DFG. His publications include *African Stars, Nightsong, Music, Modernity and the Global Imagination,* and *Reason and Resonance: A History of Modern Aurality.* He is also a founding coeditor of the journal *Sound Studies.* His current project is an ethnography of copyright law in South Africa (to be published by Duke University Press).

BRIAN KANE is Associate Professor of Music at Yale University and the author of *Sound Unseen: Acousmatic Sound in Theory and Practice.* He works at the intersection of music studies, philosophy, and sound studies.

JAIRO MORENO teaches theory at the University of Pennsylvania. He is the author of *Music Representations, Subjects, and Objects* and *Syncopated Mo-*

dernities: Musical Latin Americanisms in the US (forthcoming). With Gavin Steingo he coedited "Econophonia: Music, Value, and Forms of Life," a special issue of *boundary 2*.

JOHN MOWITT holds the Leadership Chair in the Critical Humanities at the University of Leeds and is a former Professor in the Department of Cultural Studies and Comparative Literature at the University of Minnesota. His publications range widely over the fields of culture, politics, and theory. In 2008, he collaborated with the composer Jarrod Fowler to transfigure his book *Percussion: Drumming, Beating, Striking* from a printed to the sonic text/performance *"Percussion" as Percussion*. He is also the author of *Radio: Essays in Bad Reception* and *Sounds: The Ambient Humanities* and a senior coeditor of the journal *Cultural Critique*.

POOJA RANGAN is Assistant Professor of English in Film and Media Studies at Amherst College. She is the author of *Immediations: The Humanitarian Impulse in Documentary* (Duke University Press, 2017) and of numerous articles in journals such as *Feminist Media Histories, Film Quarterly, Camera Obscura, World Picture*, and *differences*. Rangan is the coeditor (with Genevieve Yue) of "Documentary Audibilities," a special issue of the journal *Discourse*. Her current research deals with the politics and aesthetics of accented speech and listening in nonfiction film.

GAVIN STEINGO is Assistant Professor of Music at Princeton University and the author of *Kwaito's Promise: Music and the Aesthetics of Freedom in South Africa*. He coedits (with Jairo Moreno) the book series "Critical Conjunctures in Music and Sound" for Oxford University Press.

JAMES A. STEINTRAGER is Professor of English, Comparative Literature, and European Languages and Studies at the University of California, Irvine, where he is also director of UCI Critical Theory. His most recent monograph is *The Autonomy of Pleasure: Libertines, License, and Sexual Revolution*. In addition to researching European literature and philosophy, he writes on a range of topics, including critical theory and its history, Sinophone cinema, and sound studies.

JONATHAN STERNE is James McGill Professor of Culture and Technology at McGill University. He is author of *MP3: The Meaning of a Format* (Duke University Press, 2012), *The Audible Past: Cultural Origins of Sound Repro-*

duction (Duke University Press, 2003); and numerous articles on media, technology, and the politics of culture. He is also editor of the *Sound Studies Reader* and coeditor of *The Participatory Condition in the Digital Age.* He is a coauthor (with Mara Mills) of the forthcoming, tentatively titled book *Tuning Time: Histories of Sound and Speed.* Visit his website at http://sterneworks.org.

DAVID TOOP is a composer/musician, author, and curator based in London who has worked in many fields of sound art, music, performance, and writing. He has recorded Yanomami shamanism in Amazonas, appeared on *Top of the Pops,* exhibited sound installations internationally, and collaborated with many musicians and artists. His books include *Ocean of Sound, Haunted Weather, Sinister Resonance,* and *Into the Maelstrom.* He has released twelve solo albums, including *Screen Ceremonies, Black Chamber, Sound Body,* and *Entities Inertias Faint Beings*; as a theorist and critic, he has also written for many publications. Exhibitions he has curated include "Sonic Boom" at the Hayward Gallery, London. He is Professor of Audio Culture and Improvisation at London College of Communication.

Index

air, 57, 175, 196, 223, 247, 250; as acoustic medium, 32, 40, 65, 86, 96, 171, 194; art and, 247, 250, 251, 256

air-raid shelters, 230, 236–37

air-raid sirens, 17, 228–29, 233, 234, 235; in Cold War, 230, 235–36, 240; in Israel, 230, 241–42; negation of safety zones and, 231–32; obsolescence of, 238; in Paris, 228–29, 242; sonic doubt and, 236–38; state and, 230; training of sensibilities and, 238–41; of World War II, 229, 230–31, 240, 243n3

Aleph Null (interactive visual art program), 106

allure: as morphological criterion, 42, 52n13; as attraction, 168, 181, 232

allusion, 177–181

Al Solh, Mounira, 16, 132; *Paris without a Sea*, 142–46

alterity, 124, 154, 155

Altman, Rick, 133

analysis, in Schaeffer's Program of Musical Research, 33, 48

anechoic chambers, 218, 261, 263

antenatality, 167, 172, 173, 177–79, 181n4, 181n6; listening and, 16, 168; sound and, 168, 171

anthropocentrism, 190–91, 193, 195, 197

anthropology, 89, 114, 190, 191, 192, 203n4; of listening, 79–84

anthropomorphism, 63, 190, 191, 192, 195

Anzieu, Didier, 158, 169, 224

apparatuses, 10, 115, 117, 119, 123, 221, 223, 235; cinematic, 131, 213; conceptual, 8, 85

aporia, 75, 152, 153, 177–181

archaeo-acoustics, 211, 223, 227n9

archaeology: in *Cave of Forgotten Dreams*, 216, 220; of media, 10–11

arche-cinema: Mowitt on, 17, 211–26; sound and, 216, 220, 223

arche-writing (Derrida), 16, 114, 212, 213

Aristotle, 4, 193

arkhé, 211, 225, 226

art, 3, 87, 133, 142, 220; Adorno on, 74, 80, 92n63; prehistoric, 219, 221, 223, 227n7; Toop on, 246–64. *See also* artists

articulation, 51, 52n8, 66

artifact, artifacts, 68, 82, 84, 114, 118, 175, 176

artists, 52n9, 76–77, 105, 106, 132, 142, 128n22, 247, 249–52; Foley, 5, 219; Paleolithic, 216, 218, 219, 220, 221; sound, 63, 190. *See also names of individual artists*

assemblages, 191, 195; hybrid, 187, 198; sonic, 195–96, 199

Atlan, Henri, 10

atom bomb, 235, 237–38. *See also* Hiroshima; nuclear attack

attack (aspect of sound), 40, 45–48, 54, 85

Attali, Jacques, 10

attunement, 188, 201, 202

audience, audiences, 29, 95, 143, 145, 159, 196, 219, 223, 251, 258

audio-phonatory loop (Chion), 86

audiovisuality, 5, 132

auditum, 31–32

aural, aurality, 88, 168, 171–72; visuality and, 3, 5, 17, 82

auto-affection, 113, 161

avant-garde, 59–60; musical, 53, 123

Azéma, Marc, 215–17, 221, 223, 226; "Animation in Paleolithic Art" (2012), 215–16

Baffier, Dominique, 220, 221–23

Bakhtin, Mikhail, 124–26, 129n33

balance, 38, 39, 41, 50, 52n8

Barthes, Roland, 2, 129n33, 154; "The Grain of the Voice" (1977), 121–22; "Listening" (1985), 227n7

Bayle, François, 30

beauty, 4, 31; Kant on, 3, 74. *See also* aesthetics

Beirut, 142, 143, 144

bells, 54, 55, 86, 233, 234; in Nigatsu-dō temple, 261, 262. *See also* sirens

belliphonic sounds (Daughtry), 158

Dolan, Emily, 98, 102

Dolar, Mladen, 114, 116, 134, 137, 145, 147n10

Dolto, Françoise, 171–72, 182n26

Dostoyevsky, Fyodor, 124–26, 129n33

dreams, 216, 220; Herzog and, 217–18, 226; phantasy and, 222, 225. *See also* arche-cinema

dubbing, 131, 136, 143, 255

duration, 38, 39, 41, 44, 47, 50, 52n8, 54, 63, 255

dynamic evolution, 42, 44, 46, 47, 50, 87

ears, 34, 65, 69n17, 81, 114, 125, 142, 194–95; human, 10, 11; listening, 136, 145; the tympanum and, 158–59

Eastley, Max, 250, 251

eccentric sounds, 38, 41, 43, 50

echoes, 216, 221, 227n11; in cave, 223, 226

Edison, Thomas, 115

ego, 81, 138, 158, 168

Eidsheim, Nina Sun, 136, 137, 145, 146, 147n13, 148n22

embodiment, 135, 143, 146, 195; of sound and listening, 16, 121–22; of voices, 132, 160, 263

emergence, 194, 195, 197

emission, 12, 122, 126, 145

empathy, 200, 201

empiricism, 92n63, 168, 192; radical, 198, 206n55

endosonus, 12, 194, 195

energy, acoustical 194–95

English language, 12, 246

Enola Gay, 237–38

Ensoniment (Sterne), 13

entanglement, 12, 17, 76, 79, 152, 158, 191

entendre, 91n35; Schaeffer on, 61–62

envelope, acoustic or sonorous (Anzieu), 158, 169–170, 223–224

environmental sounds, 190, 204n15, 233

epiphylogenesis (Stiegler), 213–15, 217, 224

epistemology, 1, 9, 151, 153, 157, 158, 180

epochē, 7, 9, 16, 117, 128n14. *See also* Husserl, Edmund; reduction (phenomenological)

Erlmann, Veit, 16, 282; on acoustic abject, 151–66

Ernst, Wolfgang, 10–11

Esther Jeter, in *Illusions*, 130–31, 133, 135–37, 141, 143, 146

ethnomusicology, ethnomusicologists, 28–29, 73, 151

events, 14, 62, 64, 217. *See also* sound events

exosonus, 12, 194, 195

experience: aesthetic, 2, 83, 87, 192, 198, 214; auditory, 85, 191; musical, 35, 60, 155; sonic, 17, 127n5, 189, 194, 195, 197, 199

Experimental Studio Gravesano, of Hermann Scherchen, 61

expression and expressionism, 78, 160, 164; medium vs., 162, 164

exteriority, 11, 12, 16, 87, 125, 177

externalization, 80, 81

extra-esthetic (Adorno), 83

eyes, 69n17, 81, 82, 114, 133, 141, 142, 222, 258. *See also* vision; visuality

facture, 15, 50, 52n8, 52n9; in typology of sound objects, 38, 39–41

Feld, Steven, 157–58, 204n15

Fellini, Federico: *Intervista* (1987), 215; *Satyricon* (1969), 199

feminism, 132, 133, 137, 140, 142, 199; documentary scholars and, 138–39; and fetus-mother individuation, 175, 176, 182n25

fetishism, fetishes, 15, 95, 106, 107; of sound and musical instruments, 5, 95, 97, 98, 105, 154. *See also* commodity fetishism

fetus, 223; aurality of, 167–84. *See also* antenatality

Heinrich, Michael, 96, 97, 99
Helmreich, Stefan, 171, 205–6n39
Henry, Pierre, and Schaeffer: *Orphée*
(1951), 60; *Symphonie pour un homme*
seul (1950), 29
Herzog, Werner: *Cave of Forgotten*
Dreams (2010), 211, 216–20, 223, 226,
226–27n6; *Where the Green Ants*
Dream (1984), 218
hierarchy, 3, 32, 132, 136, 142, 145, 155,
157, 213
Hiroshima, 229, 231, 237–38, 243.
See also atom bomb
historicism, historicity, 14, 53, 68, 119
Holmes, Oliver Wendell, Jr., 163
Horkheimer, Max, 77, 235; *Dialectic of*
Enlightenment (1972), 232, 233
humans, 196; sound and, 16, 187
Hume, David, 74–75
Husserl, Edmund, 9, 63, 114, 117, 122,
128nn14, 22, 171, 215; on Brentano,
167–68; Derrida on, 113, 115; *Idea of*
Phenomenology (1999), 66–67; on
infant's perspective, 177–78; phenomenology and, 1, 7, 56, 61
hydrogen bomb, 235, 245n22. *See also*
atom bomb; nuclear attack

ICBMS (intercontinental ballistic missiles),
229, 231, 235, 236
idealism, 8, 77, 86
idealization, 122; of voice, 113, 116, 137, 138,
140, 141
ideology, 75, 115, 135, 229; popular music
and, 81, 88, 89; of sirens, 235–36;
sonic, 85–90
Ihde, Don, *Listening and Voice* (2007), 13,
92n44
illusions: acousmatic, 130–46; auditory,
132, 135, 137, 141, 145; ventriloquial, 134,
135, 138, 141, 145; visual, 5, 138
Illusions (Dash, 1982), 130–33, 135, 136, 141–43
image, 2, 133, 139; Imaginary and, 34, 10,
225

immanence, 167, 196, 221
improvisation: justice as, 152; experiments
with, 250, 258
impulse (in Schaeffer's typology), 8, 30,
38, 39, 40, 41, 66
Ingold, Tim: *Lines: A Brief History* (2007),
248, 263
in-itself-ness of sound (Schaeffer), 33–34,
49
inner voice, 117; revisited, 113–16
instrumentality, 99–106
instruments, musical, 28, 29, 34, 36,
48, 63, 96, 103–4, 122, 176, 220, 223,
227nn6, 9, 255–56; Adorno on, 98,
107; bicycle horns as, 44–45; classical stringed, 25, 42, 47, 97, 226n6;
commodity fetishism and, 5, 95, 97,
98, 105, 154; design and construction of, 47, 101; magic of, 105, 106–7;
Native, 98, 100; piano, 44, 45, 46, 50;
Schaeffer and, 35, 37, 43–46, 51, 54;
as sound sources, 15, 24, 35, 39, 49,
97; spectrality of, 95, 99; visual art as,
246, 247
intensity (sonic), 47, 54, 85
intentionality, 63, 84
interiority, 12, 80, 81
International Criminal Tribunal for
Rwanda, 16, 159–61
Israel, 230, 241–42

Japan, 157, 240, 251, 261; missiles over,
242–43. *See also* Hiroshima; Nagaski
Joyce, James, 156; *Ulysses* (1922), 129n22
Jullien, François, 253, 263

Kafka, Franz, 10; "The Silence of the
Sirens" (1931), 129n22
Kahn, Douglas, 115–16
Kane, Brian, 15, 118, 203n4, 283; on
fluctuating sound object, 53–68; on
Nancy, 192–93; on Schaeffer, 8, 92n64,
128n22, 133–34; *Sound Unseen* (2014),
68, 115

metaphysics, 128n22, 129n22, 192; of presence, 113, 117; Western, 113, 115

methexis, 193, 195

Mexico, 230, 240–41

Michaux, Henri, 249–50; *Ideograms in China* (2002), 249

Mignon Dupree, in *Illusions*, 130–32, 133, 146

mimetic sound, 5

missiles, 241, 242. *See also* ICBMS

modernism, modernity, modernization, 7, 16, 17, 118, 119, 126, 156, 234; sound and, 13, 151

Moles, Abraham, 61, 68n2, 70n23

Monney, Julien, 218, 221

Moreno, Jairo, 16–17, 283; on heartbeat, 167–84

morphology: in Schaeffer's Program of Musical Research, 33, 36, 42–43, 50, 89, 92n64; vocal, 136

mouth, 9, 114, 131, 157, 220. *See also* speech; voice

Mowitt, John, 283; on arche-cinema, 17, 211–26; *Percussion* (2002), 227n9

music, 3, 10, 48, 67, 92n61, 96, 105, 131, 158, 199, 202, 156, 218, 219; abstract, experimental, or new, 6–7, 24–25, 27, 28, 29, 44; Adorno on, 15, 74, 75, 79–84, 87, 89; classical and operatic, 26, 54, 135–36, 147n13, 154, 164, 196, 200; electroacoustic, 34, 51; electronic, 53, 60, 70n21, 98, 108n13; genres of, 102, 152, 155, 189; hip hop, 102, 151, 231; language and, 43, 47, 49–50, 121; law and, 152, 160; light, 74, 83–84; logic of alterity of, 154–55; musicians and, 95, 96, 98–99, 105, 107; musicology and, 126, 136, 151, 160, 192; noise and, 18n11, 54; noninstrumental, 6–7; nonobjectiveness and, 83, 84, 89; rock, 155, 196; Schaeffer and, 23–24, 33–37, 42; scores and notational symbols of, 6, 25–26, 27, 54, 55, 58, 117; serious, 74, 80, 81, 83–84; sound and, 64, 118, 190, 198, 203nn2, 4; technol-

ogy and, 85, 96; theory of, 25, 55, 56, 61, 68n2, 73, 196; universal, 28, 29; Western, 25, 26. *See also* instruments, musical; popular music

Nakajima, Rie, 250–53, 252, 255

Nancy, Jean-Luc, 114, 116, 121, 127n3, 129n33, 193, 198, 201; *Listening* (2002), 122, 192

narration, 123–24, 125–26, 216; Bruzzi on, 140–41; "Voice of God," 137, 138–41

nativism, 114, 116, 117, 122

natural disasters, sirens and, 228, 230, 240–41

naturalism, 4, 62, 175

nature, 189; bifurcation of, 197, 198, 199, 202, 206n51, 206n55; of sound, 12–13, 191, 196

nervous system, nerves, 12, 69–70n17, 174, 218

new materialism, 151, 189

New Musicology, 154

New Objectivity, 78

Nichols, Bill, 147n20; *Representing Reality* (1990), 138

Nietzsche, Friedrich, 4, 10, 11, 62

noise (*le bruit*), 6, 10, 11, 41, 55, 58, 92n49, 152, 162, 190, 219, 233; music and, 18n11, 54

nonhumans, 189, 191, 196; sounds of, 16, 17, 185–202, 204n6, 221–22

North, Christine, 15, 33, 40

notes and notational music, 6, 25–26, 27, 54, 117; sound objects and, 55, 58

noumena, 79, 84

nuclear attack, 230, 232, 235, 236. *See also* atom bomb; Cold War; hydrogen bomb; ICBMS

objects, 9, 11, 28, 31, 34, 118, 128n14, 151, 195; phantasmatic, 117, 224; sound and, 13, 14, 15, 85, 187, 189. *See also* objectivity; *objets sonores*; sonic objects, sound objects objectivity, 12, 88; Adorno on, 76–78, 79, 80; without objects, 171–72; nonobjective, 76, 79, 90; objectification and, 137, 152; objectivism and, 78, 80, 85; objective spirit and, 76–77, 81, 89, 91n17; *Objektivität* and, 76, 77, 78, 80, 89; structure and, 8, 80, 81; varieties of, 75–79

objets sonores, 15, 23 55, 63; ambiguity of, 57–59; history of term, 57–58; Schaeffer and, 7, 14, 54. *See also* sonic objects, sound objects

O'Callaghan, Casey, 17, 194, 205n25; on sonic realism, 12, 85–86; *Sounds: A Philosophical Theory* (2007), 191–92; on sounds as events, 85–86, 191–92

Ode to the Dawn of Man (Herzog, 2011), 226–27n6

Oedipus, 116, 222, 224

On the Beach (Kramer, 1959), 236

ontology, 11, 62, 189, 197, 220; as appeal, 66–68; history and, 53, 215; of sound, 15, 63, 68, 85, 189, 203n4

organology, 15, 36, 46, 213, 218, 219, 247

origination myth and phantasy, 122, 225

otherness, 125, 136, 154, 157, 158–59

Oxford Handbook of Sound Studies (Bijsterveld and Pinch, 2012), 151

painting, 3, 142, 246–47, 253; sound and, 220–21, 223; Toop and, 17–18, 247

Paleolithic, 216 ; art and artisans of, 218, 219, 221, 223

Panopticon, 6, 92n61, 126

parasites, aural 10

Paris: sirens in, 228–29, 242; terrorist attacks in, 228–29

Paris without a Sea (Al Solh, 2007–8), 142–46

Parker, James, 161, 165; *Acoustic Jurisprudence* (2015), 160

Pasnau, Robert, 12, 86

passivity, of hearing and listening, 87, 89, 121

perception, 4, 36, 44, 47, 67, 77, 83, 86, 144, 192, 218; biases of, 133, 136, 141; human, 49, 64, 120, 168; reduced listening and, 28, 37; sound as perceptual construct and, 12, 194; of sound, 32, 34, 57, 63, 85, 194, 195; sound objects and, 23, 47, 58, 62

permanence, 44–46, 57

perspectivism, 175–77

phantasy, 117, 136, 145, 219, 225, 227n7; in *Cave of Forgotten Dreams*, 222–24; Freud and, 222–23; mother's voice and, 223, 224; phantasmagoric and, 8, 68, 92n64, 128–29n22. *See also* dreams

phenomena, 79, 198; of music, 34, 44–45, 87; sound and, 8, 31–32, 153, 194

phenomenology, 11, 59, 64, 68, 84, 93n65, 122, 168, 193, 247; of auditory experience, 192, 221; Husserl and, 1, 7, 56, 61, 66–67, 116, 128n14; reduction of, 114, 116, 117; Schaeffer and, 8, 56, 62; sound and, 13, 58, 66–67, 89, 92n44, 115; vernacular, 16–17; visual and, 1–2

philosophy, 66, 114, 122, 126, 201, 211, 213; Anglo-American, 12, 85; music and, 3–4, 73; Western, 4, 113, 115, 134; of Whitehead, 196, 206n51

phonocentrism, 160, 212

phonogène, 45, 47, 52n19

phonograph, phonography, 7, 8, 10, 37, 44, 54, 115, 119, 225; Schaeffer and, 55–56, 134

physicality, 34, 36, 38, 63; causality and, 47, 51

physiology, 69n17, 82, 194

pitch, 25, 34, 42, 47, 48, 51, 85, 102; complex mass and, 24, 41; music and, 6, 30, 37, 44; variations of, 44–45

Schaeffer, Pierre, 14, 31, 33, 57, 115, 116; on
acousmatic or reduced listening, 16,
28, 132, 145; on curtain, 117, 127n10; dialogue between Chion and, 25–27; *Étude
aux chemins de fer* (1948), 55; Husserl's
Idea of Phenomenology and, 66–67;
In Search of a Concrete Music, 55, 61;
journals and diaries of, 55, 58; Kane on,
128n22, 133–34; morphology and, 89,
92n64; on *musique concrète*, 6–7, 24,
25, 27, 34–35, 44–46, 54, 133; "Note on
Time Relationships" (1960), 59–60;
Orphée (1951, with Pierre Henry), 60;
phonogène and, 45, 47; Programme
de la Recherche Musicale, 33, 36–37,
48; Schaefferians and, 116, 117, 118; on
sonic thinking and *objets sonores*, 7–8,
9, 23–24, 32, 128n14, 133, 134; "Sound
and Communication" (1973), 58, 61;
Summary Diagram of the Theory
of Musical Objects, 42; Summary
Diagram of Typology, 37–41, *38*, 50–51,
52n8, 66; *Symphonie pour un homme
seul* (with Pierre Henry, 1950), 29, 60;
thought experiments of, 44, 45; *Traité
des objets musicaux* (1966), 23–28, 30,
31, 35, 36, 56, 61, 66, 68; universalism
of, 28, 29
Schafer, R. Murray, 7, 62, 235, 241,
244n13; on bells, 233–34; on soundscapes, 14, 190
Scherchen, Hermann: Experimental
Studio Gravesano of, 61
Schoenberg, Arnold, 74, 90n2
Schopenhauer, Arthur, 3, 62
Schubert, Franz, 200
sciences, scientists, 221; natural, 191, 197
screen, 133–38, 146. *See also* curtain of
Pythagorean sect
sculpture, 250–252
seams and seamlessness, 100, 131–32,
145
self, 154, 155, 158, 193
semiotics, 2, 67, 153, 156, 182n26

senses, 10, 81–82, 87, 121; sensorium and,
10, 247
Serres, Michel, 10, 128n17
Shiraga, Kazuo, 251
sight, 4, 85, 121, 134, 135, 256; listening and,
7, 116; sound and, 18, 121. *See also* vision
signifiance, 121–22, 154, 156
signification, 9, 54, 123, 226
signifiers, 156, 220; enigmatic, 222, 224
silence, 114, 115, 124, 129n22, 190, 246,
248; of cave, 218–19, 223; of law,
159–65; Pythagorean sect and, 69n14,
134; Toop on, 256, 259, 261, 263
Silverman, Kaja, 140, 169, 170, 224
sirens, 129n22 228, 229, 241; ideology of,
235–36; in Paris, 228–29; police, 228,
231, 233, 243n1. *See also* air-raid sirens;
bells
Sirens, legend and myth of, 129n22, 232,
233, 244n16
skin, 137, 146, 158, 163; of voice, 130–46
Sloterdijk, Peter, 176, 232
smartphones, 229; warning apps for,
230, 242
Smith, Jeff, 136, 137
society 17, 76–77, 78, 82, 142, 213–14.
See also class, social
software, 36, 100, 230, 242
son, le, 57–59, 63. *See also* French language; translation
sonic abject, 11, 154, 158, 163. *See also*
abjection
sonic aggregate, 194, 195, 196
sonic doubt, air-raid sirens and, 236–38
sonic forms, 30, 31, 90, 167
sonic ideology, 85–90
sonicity, 10–11, 28
sonic objects, 61, 117, 118–20, 126, 163.
See also objets sonores; sound objects
sonic realism, 12, 85
sonic signals, 86–87
sonic warning, 229; air-raid sirens as,
235, 240, 242; technology of, 233, 234,
240, 242, 244n12

Stravinsky, Igor, 80; Adorno on, 74, 76, 78, 90n2, 91n17

stress, 37, 52n8, 66

structure, structuralism, 2, 8, 10, 37; structuration and, 16, 117

studios, 36, 37, 45, 55, 60, 105

subject, 3, 6, 153, 192, 195, 197, 201; listening and, 12, 122, 193, 202

subjectification, 201, 202, 204n4; by nonhuman sounds, 186, 187, 193

subjectivity, 78, 80, 84, 88, 151, 161, 193, 198, 206n51; engendering of, 198, 201, 202, 203n4; entanglement of objectivity with, 12, 197; sound and, 12, 189; Whitehead and, 201, 204n4

sublime, 3, 10, 155, 159

sustainment (in Schaeffer's typology), 30

Symbolic (Lacan), 10, 153, 155–57, 225

syncopation, 81, 223–24c

synesthesia, 199, 222

synthesis, 197; in Schaeffer's Program of Musical Research and, 33, 48

"talking head" interviews, 139–40, 141, 143

Tanaka, Atsuko: Bell (1955), 251

tape, magnetic, 7, 8, 60, 61, 68, 119

Tarde, Gabriel, 201, 203n4

Taylor, Fred, 230, 237

technology, 35, 45, 90n4, 100, 101, 107, 117, 119, 120, 123, 229, 231; audio, 14, 95; of sound media and reproduction, 16, 37, 115, 119, 128n21, 187; smart beds, 188, 200, 202; of sonic warning, 230, 233, 234, 240, 244n12; as sound sources, 15, 188, 200, 202, 204n6; studies and theory of, 2, 17. See also digital technologies

telephone, 107, 119, 230, 239

temporality, 41, 63, 86, 195, 199; of sound objects, 38, 40, 60, 64, 66, 85

Tenney, James: Meta + Hodos (1964), 60–61

terrorism, terrorists, 158, 228–29, 232

text, 2, 87, 248

texture, 10, 37, 42, 50, 51, 60, 133, 139, 215

Théberge, Paul, 95, 98

theory, 1, 2, 4, 18n2, 212; Grand, 211–12, 213; of music, 25–26, 42, 55, 56, 61, 68n2; sound and, 4–6, 11, 12, 14, 124, 133, 154, 189, 191–92, 195

Thompson, Emily: The Soundscape of Modernity (2004), 14

timbre, 51, 85, 97, 122, 134, 147n13, 234; genre and, 47, 48; harmonic, 42, 46; instrumental, 49, 99

tinnitus, 192, 218

tone, 55, 134, 140; skin, 137, 146

Tone, Yasunao, 251

Toop, David, 177, 284; calligraphy, 261, 261; Doll creature, 250; on drawing as sounding, 246–64; Entities Inertias Faint Beings, 248; Gabon, 256; light drawing, 263, 264; Many Private Concerts, 258–59, 259, 260; performance drawing, 247, 256–58, 257, 259; photographs by, 248, 249, 250, 262; sculpture drawing, 252; Sinister Resonance, 17, 246–47; Spirit World, 250; on faint beings, 18, 248, 264

torture, 158, 189

transduction, 194, 205–6n39

translation, 35, 76; from French, 14, 15, 23, 33, 35, 40, 61, 70n17

trompe l'oeil, 5

trompes l'oreille, 4–6

truth, 134, 138, 139, 140, 162, 164, 232; Adorno on, 75, 78, 80; untruth and, 4, 75, 78, 81

typology, in Schaeffer's Program of Musical Research, 33, 36, 37–38, 48, 50

ultrasound, 169

United Kingdom, 230, 235–36, 238–40

United States, 162, 236; air-raid sirens in, 230, 240

universality, 113, 139, 187, 140; of music, 28, 29

Ussachevsky, Vladimir, 60

values: melody and, 44–45; of music, 37,
98, 103; of sound, 43, 46, 140
variations, 47, 50, 52n8; permanence of,
44–46; in pitch, 41, 45
veiling, veils, 132, 133, 135, 137, 147n10;
of acousmatic anonymity, 140, 145;
Pythagorean sect and, 134, 142
ventriloquism, 132; displacements of,
142–45; illusions of, 134, 135, 138, 141,
145; in *Illusions*, 131, 135; in *Paris without
a Sea*, 142, 143, 144–45
vibration, vibrations, 114, 189; acoustic,
59, 63
Vietnam, 230, 241
violence, 164, 187; sound and, 158, 159,
187, 189; terrorist attacks, 228–29; of
total war, 229–30
virtuality, 12, 35, 36, 49, 50, 51; sound
production and, 15, 34
vision, 13, 28, 84, 137, 157, 224; deception
and distortion and, 5, 132, 133, 135; hearing and, 82, 133, 146; sound and, 12, 85,
219. *See also* sight; visuality
visuality, 3, 4, 6, 67, 92n44, 137, 138, 139,
222, 219; aurality and, 5, 17, 82; impair-
ment of, 28, 199, 207n59; phenomenology and, 1–2; sound vs., 66, 131
visual art: drawings, 246, 250–51; calligraphy, 249, 259–61; paintings, 246–47,
251; sculpture, 250–52
vocalic body (Connor), 135, 141, 142; surrogate, 144
vocal sounds, 126, 136; ventriloquial basis
of, 132, 133, 145
voice, 9, 117, 120, 121, 122, 154, 164, 263;
acousmatic, 119, 139, 140, 142, 143;
Derrida on, 16, 113–14; in documentaries, 137, 138; double, 124–26, 129n33;
behind face, 130–32; gendered, 140,
141, 142, 143; human, 2, 54; idealized,
113, 116, 137, 138, 140, 141; law and, 153,
160–61; maternal, 169, 170, 223, 224; of

minorities, 136, 139, 140, 142, 146; narrative, 123–24; in *Paris without a Sea*,
142–45; as skin of, 130–46; writing and,
114, 115–16. *See also* inner voice; speech;
ventriloquism
"Voice of God" narration, 137, 138–41
voice-over narration, 16, 139, 219. *See also*
"Voice of God" narration
volume, 85, 97, 188, 189, 261
von Helmholz, Hermann, 18n19

Wagner, Richard, 4; "Ride of the
Valkyries," 164
Walker, Harry, 175–77, 178
Ward, Matt, 94, 99–100
warfare, 17, 158, 229
weaponization of sound, 158
Where the Green Ants Dream (Herzog,
1984), 218
whistling, 10, 86, 223, 225, 244
Whitehead, Alfred North, 17, 189, 199,
201–2, 204n4, 206nn51, 55; prehension
and, 196–97, 206n48
whites, 135, 136, 139, 146
women, 142, 223; African American, 130,
131, 133, 135–36, 141, 147n13
Woolf, Virginia: *Between the Acts* (1941),
186, 188
World War I, 229, 239; zeppelin attacks
in, 229, 231, 238–39
World War II, 232, 238, 241; air-raid
shelters in, 236–37; air-raid sirens in,
229, 230, 235, 240, 243n3
writing, 114, 115–16, 213. *See also* arche-
writing; text

Xenakis, Iannis, 50; *Musiques formelles*
(2001), 27–28

Yoshihara, Jiro, 252

zeppelins, 229, 231, 238–39